PHILOSOPHY OF LANGUAGE

SYNTHESE LIBRARY

VOLUME 71

FRANZ VON KUTSCHERA

PHILOSOPHY OF LANGUAGE

D. REIDEL PUBLISHING COMPANY

DORDRECHT-HOLLAND / BOSTON-U.S.A.

Library of Congress Cataloging in Publication Data

Kutschera, Franz von.
   Philosophy of language.

   (Synthese library ; v. 71)
   Translation of Sprachphilosophie.
   Originally given as lectures at the Universität München
   and the Universität Regensburg.
   Bibliography: p.
   Includes indexes.
   1. Languages—Philosophy. I. Title.
P106.K8514   401   75–12877
ISBN 90–277–0591–7

SPRACHPHILOSOPHIE

Second edition published in 1975 by Wilhelm Fink Verlag, Munich

Translated from the German by Burnham Terrell

Published by D. Reidel Publishing Company,
P.O. Box 17, Dordrecht, Holland

Sold and distributed in the U.S.A., Canada and Mexico
by D. Reidel Publishing Company, Inc.
306 Dartmouth Street, Boston,
Mass. 02116, U.S.A.

TABLE OF CONTENTS

AUTHOR'S PREFACE

This book has arisen out of lectures I gave in recent years at the Universities of Munich and Regensburg, and it is intended to serve as a textbook for courses in the Philosophy of Language.

In my lectures I was able to presuppose that the students had taken an introductory course in logic. Some knowledge of logic will also be helpful in studying this book – as it is almost everywhere else in philosophy –, especially in Section 3.2, but it is no prerequisite.

I would like to give my sincere thanks to Prof. Terrell for his excellent translation of the book, which is based on the second, revised and enlarged German edition.

Regensburg, May 1975   FRANZ VON KUTSCHERA

INTRODUCTION

Language has become one of philosophy's most important and pressing themes during this century. This preoccupation with language has its origins in the most diverse areas of philosophical inquiry. It has come from the theory of knowledge by way of a turn from the critique of reason to a critique of language; from logic as a consequence of its concern with artificial languages and the logical analysis of natural languages; and from anthropology by way of the emphasis on language as an accomplishment essential to the definition of man and through the discovery of correlations between linguistic form and man's image of the world; from ethics because of its concern with the linguistic forms of ethical statements and the demarcation of the boundary between them and descriptive sentences.

This philosophical turn in the direction of language can also be read off in quite general terms from the change in the formulation of philosophical problems. Where a question used to be raised about 'the nature of causality', for example, or 'the content of the concept of causality', nowadays we feel it more appropriate to formulate the problem as a question about the use of words, and to ask: "What is one saying when he says that an event A brings about an event B?"[1]

During the course of this development philosophical attention has sometimes concentrated so exclusively on language that it has simply been identified with linguistic analysis. This is especially true of the two main streams of *analytical philosophy*. It is true of the enterprise, beginning with Bertrand Russell and continuing from Rudolf Carnap to Nelson Goodman and Willard van Orman Quine, aimed at a logical analysis of the language of science, especially of philosophical language, in which the attempt is made to clarify and make precise the terms and propositions of that language by using the instruments of modern logic. It is still more true of the other principal direction of analytical philosophy, originating in George Edward Moore, then stamped with the distinctive mark of Ludwig Wittgenstein and developed further by the Ordinary-Language-Philosophy of the Oxford School (Gilbert Ryle, John Langshaw Austin), in which the attempt is made to clarify philosophical language by analyzing the ordinary usage of its terms.

In the Foreword to his *Begriffschrift*, Gottlob Frege says: "If it is one of philosophy's tasks to liberate the human mind from the dominion of the word, by revealing the illusions concerning conceptual relationships engendered, often almost unavoidably, by linguistic usage, by freeing our thought from the burden imposed on it by nothing but the structure of our linguistic instruments of expression, then my *Begriffschrift* (conceptual notation), further developed for these purposes, will be a useful tool for philosophers." [2]

Frege's 'if'-sentence then turns into a categorical assertion and for Russell himself the most important task for philosophy consists "in criticizing and clarifying notions which are apt to be regarded as fundamental and accepted uncritically. As instances I might mention: mind, matter, consciousness, knowledge, experience, causality, will, time." [3] And Carnap writes in the Foreword to the 2nd Edition of his book, *Der logische Aufbau der Welt*: "The new definitions [of the concepts] should fit into a systematic structure of concepts. Such a clarification of concepts, nowadays frequently called 'explication', still seems to me one of the most important tasks of philosophy." [4]

For Wittgenstein even as early as the *Tractatus*, all philosophy is language analysis [5] and in the *Philosophical Investigations* philosophy is nothing but a constant struggle against "the bewitchment of our intelligence by means of language." [6] Finally, for many adherents of Ordinary-Language-Philosophy, the turn taken by philosophy to language, the 'linguistic turn', signifies the great revolution of modern philosophy. Thus Austin says: "... it cannot be doubted that they [these methods of linguistic analysis] are producing a revolution in philosophy. If anyone wishes to call it the greatest and most salutary in its history, this is not, if you come to think of it, a large claim." [7]

In view of the large number of enterprises and directions that are grouped together under the heading of a *philosophy of language*, it can be no wonder that the title has no precise and well-defined content. We will therefore sketch briefly the themes with which this work is supposed to be concerned and the objectives that guide us in it.

Speaking quite generally to begin with, we will be investigating in what follows the *functional role* of language, and the results accomplished by it.

We will pick out three problem areas from the wealth of questions which can be put in this connection, areas that seem to us to be of a special and fundamental significance: the problem of the *grammatical articulation* and synthesis of linguistic expressions, the problem of their *meaning* and the problem of the role of *language in experience*.

After some preliminary remarks we shall be concerned in Chapter II with the question of what it is that makes up the meaning of linguistic expressions, how it is established and how communication in language functions. There then follows, in Chapter III, a discussion of the fundamental problem of grammar, how the combination in language of meaningful expressions into new units of meaning functions. Finally, in the IVth Chapter, the relationship between language and experience will be discussed, the question as to the extent in which the forms of language express particular schemata of interpretation for experience, to what extent the forms of language leave their mark on the way in which reality is experienced.

These three problem areas are also basic problems of the linguistic sciences, particularly of general linguistics as the fundamental linguistic discipline. Consequently we find a great deal of overlap between philosophical and scientific linguistic investigation. No sharp boundary can be drawn between the two. For that reason, the philosophy of language must inform itself of the results in linguistics that are relevant for its questions and must take account of them, and the opportunity arises to lend support to theses in the philosophy of language with arguments drawn from linguistics. Philosophy is not operating in a realm independent of experience, then.

The reasons that lead us to interest ourselves here in the question concerning the function and the accomplishments of language are above all the following: Language is the most elementary, the most important instrument for all of the sciences, one that we use constantly. If we assert something (describe, classify, formulate hypotheses or theories), argue, lay down rules (define, prescribe forms of measurement, etc.) we make use of language.

Since language is such an important instrument of science, a basic knowledge of this instrument is itself very useful for work in a particular science. Natural languages, which we apply for the most part even in the sciences, are not made primarily for scientific purposes and for their scientific use they must be supplemented and made precise in a great many ways. The scientist, therefore, is not only a *user* of language but also to a certain extent a *maker*. In the latter role, at least, he can not just commit himself with naive trust to the conventions of language, but he requires insights into the nature of linguistic means of expression. In this sense, the function and effect of language are one of the themes of a *propaedeutics of science.*

The question of the effect of language on the formation and organization of experience is especially of paramount interest to the *theory of knowledge.* Does speech consist only in the expression of contents of thought or perception that are independent of language, changed in no respect by the manner of their expression, or are these contents always linguistically determined, so that the forms of our language are the forms of our experience? But the problem of meaning, which, as we shall see, is closely connected with this question, also has relevance to epistemology.

These two questions, from propaedeutics and from the theory of knowledge, guide the ensuing discussions of language and determine the philosophical orientation of these investigations.

NOTES

[1] P. Alston gives this example in [67], p. 388. – The numbers in square brackets identify the author's work listed in the index according the year in which it appeared.

[2] Frege [79], p. VIf.

[3] Russell [56], p. 341

[4] Carnap [28], p. X.

[5] Wittgenstein [22], 4.0031.

[6] Wittgenstein [53], 109

[7] Austin [62], p. 3f. – For *analytical philosophy* see the presentations by Savigny [70] and Lorenz [70], Chapter I, for example. For *Ordinary-Language-Philosophy* specifically, see Savigny [69].

PRELIMINARY DISTINCTIONS

1. LANGUAGE AND LINGUISTIC UTTERANCES

Before we take up the main themes of this book – grammar, meaning and the role of language in experience – it is the intent of this chapter first to introduce some preliminary distinctions. When we refer to 'language' in what follows, this is to be understood in the sense of a general expression covering all languages or all the languages taken into account in that particular context. We understand what a *language* is by example to begin with: In the discussions that follow we are referring for the most part to *natural* languages, i.e. languages that have had a historical development, such as German, English, Greek, Japanese, etc. Within these languages we can distinguish both various stages of development and various levels, such as the *standard language*, the level that has the status of norm and ideal, and is used in literature, the schools, radio and press, etc., and *ordinary* or *everyday language*, in which the norm represented by the standard language is relaxed and sentence structure, choice of words and expression handled more freely. Besides these we can further distinguish the dialect forms of the language and finally there are still further countless special forms, which depend, for example, on their users' social status and often are differentiated only in small details.[1] All of these developmental forms, linguistic levels and variations must be specified when assertions about a natural language are made, if they are to be exact.

We make a distinction between natural languages and *artificial* languages, which play a part in logic and mathematics especially and are defined by explicit conventions. The most important examples of such artificial languages are the languages of logical symbolism.

In a broader sense of the word 'language', a sense we will not be using in what follows, one can also speak of a *gesture language*, a *signal language* (consisting of particular flag or light or sound signals) or an *animal language*, and understand a language generally speaking as a system of signs.

We have before us a linguistic utterance when X says to Y, 'Yesterday I went to the movies', when Y asks X, 'How was the film?', when X greets Y with 'Good morning', when Y makes a request of X 'Lend me your umbrella!', and so on. Such a linguistic utterance is an *act* of the speaker's, with which (as a rule) he addresses himself to a hearer. For this reason utterances are also called *speech acts* or items of *linguistic behavior*. It is also possible for a group of persons to play the part of speaker (a government makes a declaration, for example, physicians publish a Bulletin, etc.), and the hearer too is not always a single subject, but can be a more or less strictly delimited group (a lecturer speaks to his auditors as a group, a manifesto is addressed to the public, etc.).

We differentiate between the linguistic utterance as an act and the product of that act, between the act of speaking and what is spoken. The product of a linguistic utterance is also often referred to as a linguistic *utterance*. Since in the following we shall be speaking of the products of utterances above all, we will adhere to that usage. Wherever a distinction is necessary, however, we will speak of the utterance as *performance* and the utterance as *product*.

A further distinction must be drawn between *forms* of behavior and their particular realizations: between a particular waltz step (carried out by a particular person at a particular time) and the form of the waltz step, between the typical form of a curtsy and a particular curtsy, etc. In the same way, we must also distinguish between forms of linguistic behavior and their concrete individual realizations, the utterance-performances, distinguish the form of greeting 'Good morning', for example, from Y's greeting X with 'Good morning' on a particular occasion.

We also make the corresponding distinction within the realm of what is produced [by an act] and so, for example, we make a distinction between a particular occurrence of a written word and the graphical word-type to which it belongs. Thus the word-type 'and' occurs in several places on this page, i.e. there are several occurrences on this page of the word-type 'and'. We shall also use *type* and *occurrence* to express the distinction in question for utterances as performances. Type and occurrence are related as class and member: an utterance as an act or as a result or product [of an act] is always a member of a class of acts or products, which represents the utterance's type, its form.

We call the forms of utterances [linguistic] *expressions*. An expression, then, is a form of utterance, whether taken as act or as product. Wherever the distinction is important, we shall speak more exactly of expression as *performance* and expression as *product*.

Now the distinctive feature of linguistic utterances lies in the fact that by means of them we make ourselves understood to one another, communicate something, ask for something, etc., that they are, putting it generally, meaningful. Speech acts consequently have two aspects: the *phonetic* or (graphic) *aspect*, that a sequence of spoken (or written) sounds is produced, the sounds G-o-o-d-M-o-r-n-i-n-g are uttered. But at the same time an act that goes beyond the production of sounds is consummated: the act of greeting the person so addressed; that is the *semantic aspect*. Every utterance, then, has a phonetic and a semantic aspect. These two aspects are not included in two separate acts, but are two views of the same act. The phonetic aspect disregards the utterance's meaning, its communicative function, and takes account of the distinctive features of the sound pattern only. The semantic aspect abstracts from these phonetic particulars and fixes exclusive attention on the utterance's meaning. From this point of view, 'meaning' is in the first instance nothing but the function of an utterance in the communicative process.

Just as phonetic and semantic aspects are differentiated for utterances as performances, so are they for utterances as products, and this distinction carries over in an analogous manner to statements. In what follows we shall be interested in utterances and expressions as products only insofar as they are products of the phonetic act parts, i.e. as sequences of sounds or forms of sequences of sounds, or series of signs or patterns of series of signs, and this is the way in which we shall understand statements about phonetic or graphic objects. Now linguistic utterances do not have meaning in and of themselves, just by virtue of their sound patterns, for example (otherwise we could understand even foreign languages without having to learn what expressions in them mean). They only take on meaning in the context of a system of rules which say how they are applied, singly or in combination, for specific purposes in specific situations. Linguistic utterances are, then, acts governed by convention and for their effectiveness they require rules of usage that are agreed upon. In the case of natural languages, these rules are not explicitly formulated and the conventions are not formal agreements. Rules and conventions are customs and norms, rather, understood and followed intuitively; their explicit formulation and definition is the responsibility of linguistic science alone and something that is accomplished in grammars and dictionaries that codify linguistic usage.

Linguistic conventions are general rules, and so they refer not to particular utterances, but to [linguistic] expressions. For example, a convention of this sort does not say that on the morning of January 1, 1973, in Munich, under such and such particular circumstances, Hans can greet Fritz by saying 'Good Morning'. What it provides, instead, is that anyone can greet anyone else in the morning by saying 'Good Morning'. It is on the basis of this general convention, then, that a specific utterance of the expression 'Good Morning' acquires the function of a greeting. The meaning of the utterance is consequently defined by way of the meaning of the expression uttered – and by way of the *pragmatic circumstances* of the utterance (who the speaker is, to whom it is addressed, when and where the assertion is made, etc.) The meaning of an utterance like 'I saw you yesterday', in which so-called *indexical expressions* ('I', 'you', 'yesterday', 'here', etc.) occur, obviously depends very definitely on its pragmatic circumstances. It is true or false depending on who is speaking to whom and when and where he is speaking. The meaning of the expression, 'I saw you here yesterday', as an assertion-type, is consequently so thoroughly indeterminate that we can not attach any truth-value to it at all, even if the relevant factual information is available to us.

Linguistic conventions have to do with expressions, then. They primarily have to do with forms of behavior (e.g. the function of saying 'Good Morning'). But they can also be formulated as rules for expressions as products, as rules which say how phonetic or graphic signs or sequences of signs can be used. Although the question as to whether meaning pertains primarily to statements as forms of behavior or as objects is of great interest in principle – we shall go into it in Chapter II.4.5 – it is nevertheless possible, without prejudice to that question, to take over the usual manner of expression according to which the semantic conventions govern the use of expressions as objects.

A linguistic expression, as bearer of a meaning, is not a mere object, e.g. a sound sequence, but an object that is used according to definite rules. And we can not understand a language to be a set of expressions as objects but only as a set of expressions together with the rules for using them.

Furthermore, a language in the narrower sense of the word is not only a collection of individual expressions in isolation, but a system for the construction of in principle infinitely many expressions (e.g. sentences) from a finite number of basic expressions (e.g. words), so that the rules of the language include not only rules of use for individual expressions, but also rules for the combination of expressions and the use of such compound expressions, according to which their meanings are defined in terms of the meanings of their component expressions.

Ferdinand de Saussure, one of the founders of modern linguistic science, illustrated the interpretation of a system of rules by comparing a language with the game of chess.[2] Chess is a system of rules concerning how the pieces are to be set up and moved on the chess board and of rules concerning the capture of pieces, winning and losing. Just as in this case it is not just a matter of the pieces only, but of the rules governing their use, so that it would be false to say that chess is defined by the set of pieces; in the same way, a language has to do with the rules and not just the expressions in the language. And as the function of a piece can not be characterized all by itself, but only with reference to the functions of the other pieces and accordingly with the entire game, so the functions of linguistic expressions can be defined only with reference to the entire language.

We ordinarily say that the sequence of sounds /tsu:k /ʃpitsə/ and the sequence of written signs Z-u-g-s-p-i-t-z-e both represent the same word. But how is that to be understood, when the two expressions, as types as well as occurrences are entirely different?

When, following Lyons in [69], p. 56ff., we speak of different *realizations* of a word, e.g. phonetic and graphic, the following interpretation is obvious: The realizations of words in spoken language are primary, not only historically (because there was a spoken language before there was a written language), but also to the extent that we would scarcely regard a written language without phonetic interpretation as a language at all. The written realization of linguistic expressions, however, appears to us to be a *Commodum* which is of course very important in practice but expendable in principle. (For the most part, the language we use is the spoken language.)[3] To that extent we could identify the phonetic realization of the word with the word itself and say that other realizations, e.g. graphic, represent the word only to the extent that a phonetic interpretation for these realizations is stated, according to which they represent the word symbolically.

We will again follow de Saussure here,[4] however, and adopt a more abstract standpoint: it takes the various realizations of a word to be in principle equally correct – even if they do have their own peculiar advantages now and then[5] – and the word itself to be an abstract object, which we can identify with the class of its realizations. We have now seen that words are not isolated objects, but function as meaningful expressions only within the confines of the system of rules of a language. Consequently it is better to speak of various realizations of a language. A language, then, is a system of rules for the use of certain abstract objects (e.g. words) specified in the first instance only with respect to number and variety. A realization of the language arises out of this system by virtue of the identification of these abstract expressions with concrete objects (sound sequences, sequences of graphic signs, etc.). Conversely, proceeding from realizations of language, i.e. from systems $\langle A, \mathcal{R} \rangle$ where A is a set of concrete objects and $\mathcal{R}$ a set of rules for their use, one can define an equivalence relation between two systems $\langle A_1, \mathcal{R}_1 \rangle$ and $\langle A_2, \mathcal{R}_2 \rangle$ which holds between them when there is a mapping ϕ of A_1 on A_2, so that what the rules from $\mathcal{R}_1$ determine for objects a from A_1 corresponds to what the rules from $\mathcal{R}_2$ determine for the expressions ϕa from A_2. A language is then a class of such equivalent systems.[6]

This abstract interpretation of languages can also be illustrated by comparison with the game of chess: What materials the pieces are made of and how they look is not an essential feature of chess; what is important is only the number of the pieces and the differences among them. In the same way, how the expressions of a language are concretely made up, what material they consist of (sounds or graphic signs) and what form they have, is not a matter of importance for the language; what is important is only the differences between them that are relevant with respect to the rules. De Saussure also speaks in this connection of the abstract *form* of a language and the *substance* of its realizations.

It emerges from these abstract ways of looking at languages that in the following discussions we can leave the questions that relate to realizations of language out of account. In particular, we shall not concern ourselves with the theory of phonetic realizations, *phonology*.

The student of linguistic science sees his task to consist in describing language as he finds it, in understanding the actual norms of linguistic correctness, not in setting up new norms. His statements are thus intended to be *descriptive*, not *normative*.

When the linguist sets forth a German grammar and explains the meanings of German words in dictionaries, however, he is not simply describing; he is also making them more precise; explicit grammatical rules are more precise than the intuitive everyday customs, the demarcation and explication of meanings and their differences define these meanings more exactly. The work of the linguist can be linguistically creative to a certain extent, if the scientific description of the language reacts upon it and sets new linguistic norms. Standard German, for example, has certainly been influenced as a norm by German grammars and dictionaries. But this effect of feedback and normalization is rather slight: Certainly it is not a matter of fixing new meanings but of explications that make things more precise. Besides, the linguist takes account of a certain range of variation in grammatical rules for actual linguistic usage; unlike the logician, he is not aiming at a system of rules that governs every case unequivocally. Consequently, one can make the claim that the statements of linguistic science are actually descriptive.

Now how can linguistic regularities be established? The following problem arises here: The empirical material the linguist has to start with consists of the concrete utterances of those who belong to the linguistic community with which he is concerned. These linguistic utterances – language as *parole* or as *performance* – as F. de Saussure or N. Chomsky call it – or their products are not what the linguist is primarily interested in, but rather language as a system of rules, as *langue* or *competence*.[7] Now this linguistic norm must be inductively inferred from the available utterances. That can not be carried through directly, however, for there are many incorrect expressions included among the linguistic utterances, arising from a speaker's accidental or characteristic mistakes. But before one knows the rules, one can not eliminate these incorrect expressions and thus one can not use the actually available utterances directly in testing one's hypotheses about linguistic norms.

The linguist's situation, however, is fundamentally in no way worse than, for example, the physicist's. In physics, too, one can put regularities to observational test only if the results of measurement are not influenced by disturbing factors. In this case, too, however, one can only say when a disturbing factor is present if one already has knowledge of the regularities. But there is no vicious circle here. Instead, by varying the conditions of observation systematically one can discover the regularities that remain constant, as against these variations, and the domain in which they hold true.[8]

NOTES

[1] See Grebe [66], p. 25ff.

[2] See de Saussure [16], Introduction, Chap. V; Part 1, Chap. III, §4; Part 2, Chap. III. – The parallel between language and game is also fundamental to Wittgenstein's philosophy of language. See Chapter II. 4.2.

[3] Of course note should be taken of the fact that written and spoken language are, as is the case with Japanese because of historical reasons, for example, different languages, which only partially correspond, so that reproducing a written text orally often has the character of a translation. On this point see note 6 also.

[4] The statements on this point in [16] are not unambiguous, to be sure. Thus in the Introduction, Chapter VI, § 2, de Saussure defends the interpretation of the relation between phonetic and graphic realization sketched above. – On what follows see also L. Hjelmslev's expositions in [43], and Francis Bacon as well: "For the organ of tradition, it is either Speech or Writing: for Aristotle saith well, *Words are the images of cogitations, and letters are the images of words*; but yet it is not of necessity that cogitations are expressed by the medium of words. For *whatsoever is capable of sufficient differences, and those perceptible by the sense, it is in nature competent to express cogitations*. And therefore we see in the commerce of barbarous people that understand not one another's language, and in the practice of divers that are dumb and deaf, that mens' minds are expressed in gestures, though not exactly, yet to serve the turn." (Proficience and Advancement of Learning Divine and Human (1605), Bacon [57], V. III, p. 399). And almost word for word to the same point: "Hoc igitur plane statuendum est: quidquid scindi possit in differentias satis numerosas ad notationum varietatem explicandam (modo differentiae illae sensui perceptibilis sint) fieri posse vehiculum cogitationum de homine in hominem. Nam videmus nationes linguis discrepantes commercia non male per gestus exercere." (*De dignitate et augmentis scientiarum*, Liber sextus, Caput I, in Bacon [57], V. I, p. 651). Brekle also cites these passages in his introduction to Cordemoy [77], p. XXIX.

[5] See Lyons [69], p. 62f.

[6] This account involves a certain idealisation. Actually the correspondence between the different realizations is not always one to one: The same graphic expression can be phonetically ambiguous (e.g. 'read' in English – /red/or/ri:d/) and the same phonetic expression can be graphically ambiguous (e.g. /ku:/ in French – 'cou' (neck) or 'coup' (blow)). – Lyons points out in [69], p. 39ff. that to the extent in which spoken and written language differ not only in unessential particular points, but differ in their grammatical distinctions, for example, as well, they can take on the character of different languages. According to Lyons, this divergence is explained by the diverse sorts of situations and purposes in and for which we make use of spoken and written languages.

[7] On the distinction between *performance* and *competence* see Chomsky [65], p. 10, 25, 139, 187.

[8] See also Chomsky [65], p. 3f.

2. DESCRIPTIVE STATEMENTS

Linguistic utterances occur in the context of a great variety of situations and kinds of behavior and serve the most diverse ends. Language has an abundance of different functions, then. We are using language when we *ask, command, affirm, lecture, greet one another, prove, appraise, tell lies, tell jokes, make pleas* or *pray*. Depending on the way in which language is being used, on the type of discourse, as we choose to put it, the mode in which linguistic expressions are meaningful will change, too, for 'to be meaningful' means nothing other than 'to have a specific function in a context of linguistic usage'.

Within the science of linguistics it is not possible for us to give any of these types of discourse or any mode of meaning an absolute status and make it an exclusive object of consideration, if we do not wish to impose very sharp limitations on the range of investigation from the very beginning. But since our primary interest here, from the aspect of a propaedeutics for science, is in the scientific type of discourse, in the way in which language is used preeminently in the sciences, we shall be occupied throughout long stretches of what follows with this type of discourse and we shall not go into other types in greater detail except in Chapter II.4.5.

What is important for the scientific use of language is in the first place linguistic utterances of the type of declarative or assertive sentences. Sentences of this type are used to make reports, to give information, to describe something, to establish that something is the case. With such sentences, we assert that the facts about something are thus and so. They speak about something and they have, therefore, as we say, a *descriptive content* or a *descriptive meaning*.

The following analysis will thus concentrate very heavily on declarative sentences. The more detailed studies in scientific linguistics are available for them, while the analysis of questions, commands, etc., has received the necessary attention only very recently. A certain (ex post facto) legitimization of this focus of our interest will emerge in Chapter II.4.5.

In order to explain the distinctive character of declarative discourse and descriptive meaning somewhat more precisely still, and to emphasize from the outset that it is only one among a great many other ways in which

language is used, we will make a brief reference to a distinction drawn by
K. Bühler. Within the confines of these preliminary remarks, this reference
has a provisional character only; we shall return to it for more exact
consideration in Chapter II.4.5.

K. Bühler differentiates three components in connection with every
utterance: *speaker, referent* (what the utterance refers to) and *hearer*. He
coordinates a component of the utterance's meaning to each of these
components: to the speaker, the *expressive* component or *Kundgabe*, to
the referent the *descriptive* component, and to the hearer the *evocative*
component or *Appell*. By *Kundgabe* is meant what the speaker expresses of
his own feelings, sensations, inclinations, of attitudes or goals in his utter-
rance. Thus, for example, his disgust when he says 'Pfui', his approval in
'Bravo', his intent in the sentence, 'I am going to Rome tomorrow'.
Kundgabe often involves the use of particular emotive or value-toned
words, as in the use of 'nigger' instead of 'Negro' or of 'helper' instead of
'assistant'. *Kundgabe* does not mean, however, what conclusions can be
drawn about the speaker on the basis of his utterance – as, say, his excite-
ment can be inferred from his rapid, incoherent speech. *Kundgabe* is consequently not what the utterance is a symptom or sign of, nor is it what the
speaker explicitly says about himself in his utterance, his feelings, goals,
etc., as in 'I (personally) find that marvelous' or 'I am planning on taking
a student tour to Africa'.

The *Appell* is supposed to be those components of an utterance's meaning by virtue of which it aims at a reaction of the hearer's, seeks to call it
forth. This *Appell* becomes particularly clear in commands, which call
upon the hearer to do something, and in questions, which call upon him
for an answer. But an *Appell* lies also in the evocative meaning of value-
statements such as 'That is good' in the sense of calling on the hearer to
act accordingly or 'That is bad' in the sense of calling on him to refrain.[1]
And it may be a matter of the suggestive meaning of such statements as
'Isnt' that dreadful!' or 'It is quite obvious that he did that only to advance
himself'. *Appell*, however, does not consist in the actual or intended
effect of an expression on the hearer.[2]

These components of meaning enter into the various types of discourse
with varying strength. We will not, however, advance the opinion that the
various types of discourse can be adequately characterized solely in terms
of the relative strength with which these three components of meaning

occur. That would be much too simple a picture of the functions of language. Generally speaking, one will be able to characterize the various types of discourse only by way of their functions in the total context of action in which they are used. The modes of meaning will also be just as diverse as these pragmatic contexts of language use. We shall go into this more closely in Chapter II. Here it is sufficient that we can define descriptive meaning more exactly by way of a contrast with evocative and expressive meaning.

Even in the sentences that are characterized as declarative sentences in grammar (and contrasted with interrogative and imperative sentences), expressive and evocative components have a role. In the sentence, 'That was an extraordinarily good performance', the expressive component is dominant. The speaker's evaluation of the performance is very much in the foreground, while nothing is said about the performance's objective characteristics, if no factual criteria of evaluation have been involved. The sentence, 'Presumably Fritz is sick', includes, by virtue of the word 'presumably', an expressive component which expresses the speaker's attitude toward the sentence's validity. And the sentence 'You can't do that!' contains a strong evocative component along with its expressive component.

The descriptive component, on the other hand, is dominant in declarative sentences as used in the sciences. The expressive component resides only in the assertive character of these sentences and the evocative component is almost entirely withdrawn.

We can cite as one last definition of descriptive statements that only such statements are true or false, for they are the only ones to maintain that something is the case and can thus be confronted with facts. To be sure, the truth value of a declarative sentence, i.e. its truth or falsity, can depend on the context of its utterance, if it includes index expressions the reference of which is defined only in terms of the context of their utterance and therefore can refer to different persons, things, places and points in different contexts. Only when these index expressions are replaced by expressions with meanings that do not depend on context will the statement as such, independently of the circumstances of its utterance, be true or false.

NOTES

[1] The emotive and evocative components in ethical statements and value statements

have been elaborated by Stevenson in [44], e.g. His emotive theory of these statements is based precisely on the denial of a descriptive content to them.

[2] K. Bühler in [34], p. 28ff. distinguishes *expression* [*Kundgabe*] (more in the sense of a sign of the speaker's feelings, than in the sense of anything informational), *representation* [*Darstellung*] and *Appell*. Accordingly he speaks of linguistic expressions as *symptoms*, *symbols* and *signals*.

3. The use and mention of signs

The distinctive characteristic of signs, that of meaning something, requires, especially when we are speaking about language, a precise distinction between sign and significatum, between the linguistic expression as a sequence of sounds or written signs and its meaning. Simple as it is to distinguish the name 'Felix' from the man, Felix, it designates; the adjective 'red' from the property of being red; or the sentence 'Felix has red hair' from the fact that Felix has red hair[1], experience shows that a precise distinction comes very hard when expressions are being spoken of.

When I say, 'Felix has red hair', I am using the word 'Felix' to say something about Felix, the man. That sentence says nothing about the word 'Felix'. But when I speak of the sentence and say, for example, that the word 'Felix' occurs in it, I am not using the word 'Felix'. Instead, I am *mentioning* it, *referring to* it. Likewise, in the sentence 'Munich has more than a million inhabitants' I am using the word 'Munich' to say something about the city of Munich; while in the sentence ''Munich' has two syllables' I am using the word 'Munich' to say something about the word.[2]

A clear graphic distinction between the use and the mention of a word is indicated. The usual convention is to place expressions that are being mentioned, not used, within quotation marks, as we have already done above. The expression together with these quotation marks then constitutes a new expression, which we use in order to speak of the original expression. According to this convention, then, an expression never stands for itself: 'Felix' never stands for 'Felix', only for Felix. What stands for 'Felix', on the other hand, is ''Felix'' and once again, '''Felix''' for ''Felix'', and so on. Consequently we have to write ''Munich' has two syllables' instead of 'Munich has two syllables'. The expression 'Munich' does not occur in this sentence, then (we are not speaking of Munich); it is rather the expression ''Munich'' that occurs, since we are speaking of 'Munich'.[3]

Related to the distinction between use and mention, there is also the distinction between the language spoken of, as the *object* language, and the language being used to speak of it, as the *metalanguage*. So when we are speaking, in German, about English grammar, English is the object language and German the metalanguage. This distinction always refers to a relation involving the application of one language to another; one can also speak in English about the German language, in which case English is the metalanguage and German the object language. Further, object and metalanguage can coincide, as in speaking in German about German grammar. For systematic reasons, however, it is always to be recommended that we distinguish between object and metalanguage, and so separate even in the latter case the metalinguistic use of German from its consideration as object language. This is all the more important in that neglect of this distinction can lead to the so-called semantic antinomies.[4]

To conclude these preliminary remarks, let us mention the important distinction between *syntax, semantics* and *pragmatics,* first fixed as to terminology by Charles Morris in [46]. It is oriented toward the distinction between the linguistic expression, its meaning and the context in which it is used and it has to do with scientific studies about language. If an inquiry is concerned only with linguistic expressions, their spoken or written form, in abstraction from their meaning or context of use, it is identified as *syntactic.* If the meaning of the expression is also being considered, one speaks of a *semantic* inquiry and, finally, if the practical context of its use is taken into account, one speaks of a *pragmatic* inquiry.[5]

Where the term 'semantics' is used in this sense, the ancient Stoic designation 'semiotic' is often used for a theory that embraces all of these aspects of linguistic expressions, or more broadly still: for a general theory of signs.[6]

NOTES

[1] These examples are not intended to anticipate any theory of meaning, along the lines, say, of generally presupposing that predicates refer to properties. The examples are only supposed to illustrate the distinctions that are necessary in any study of languages.
[2] The terminology 'use' – 'mention' was introduced by Quine; see Quine [51b], 4. – The distinction itself is quite old and was given extensive treatment in the scholastic theory of supposition, for example.
[3] The usual procedure in literary quotation, which is also adopted in the text, is to use a mixture of single and double quotes. These may be understood as merely typographical variants of the same quotation device.
[4] See Tarski [35] and [44], as well as the presentation in Kutschera [64].
[5] According to some of the theories of meaning reported in Chapter 3, the meaning of a linguistic expression is actually nothing other than its use, so that semantics can not meaningfully be separated from pragmatics.
[6] The label 'semiotic' is used in this sense by Locke, Peirce and Morris, for example.

CHAPTER II

THEORIES OF MEANING

1. REALISTIC SEMANTIC THEORIES

In this chapter we will turn our attention to this work's first main theme, the question of the meaning of linguistic expressions. This question directs itself in the first instance to all of the ways in which language is used, to all types of discourse, such as assertions, questions, commands, etc. The principal interest of the philosophy of language, particularly under its aspect of scientific propaedeutics, is concentrated, however, as has already been said in I.2, on declarative discourse as the most important way in which language is used in science. In this sense, we intend to concentrate our attention in what follows preeminently on the investigation of problems of meaning connected with descriptive discourse.

When we speak of 'sentences', what is meant by that is for the most part descriptive sentences, and what we understand by 'meaning' is for the most part descriptive meaning in the sense of I.2.[1]

Since we intend to go into composition of meaning separately in Chapter III, we shall be less concerned in this chapter with the question as to how the meaning of compound expressions arises from the meaning of their parts than with the question of how the meanings of simple words or of simple linguistic structures can be characterized.

Now there are distinctly different theories about linguistic expressions in connection with descriptive discourse. In the following, we will present and discuss some especially important types of such theories.[2]

The first and the oldest group of theories of meaning that we will consider in this chapter is constituted by the *copy* theories or *realistic* semantic theories. The explanation of the latter designation is that these theories presuppose a realism of concepts, as will become clear in what follows. They interpret meaning as a conventional relationship between signs and concrete or conceptual entities, which exist independently of the linguistic signs. On this interpretation the meaning of a linguistic expression does not depend on its use in concrete situations, but the use is determined by

the meaning, so that a sharp separation between semantics and pragmatics is possible.

1.1. *Naturalism and Conventionalism in Realistic Semantics*

The oldest treatise on language that has survived to our times is Plato's
'Cratylus' (ca. 388 B.C.). Plato concerns himself in it with a problem
posed at the beginning of any inquiry into linguistic meaning: By virtue
of what is it that an expression receives its meaning? Does it have this
meaning by nature or is it assigned to it by convention?

There are two opposed positions with respect to this question, which
have been designated in the history of semantics as (semantic) *naturalism*
and *conventionalism*.

Naturalism in the sense that one can infer the meaning of a word just
from its sound alone has never been seriously put forward and it would
be obviously absurd. For if that were the case we would not have to learn
foreign languages with much effort, but we would understand them immediately. And the occurrence of homonyms, i.e. words with the same sound
and different meanings would be impossible to understand.[3]

Naturalism, as Plato describes it in the Cratylus, maintains only that
there is a natural affinity between the sound of a word and its meaning.
One possibility for such an affinity lies in the formation of words by way
of phonetic imitation of sounds in order to designate those sounds and
thereby indirectly to designate animals, objects or events for which those
sounds are typical, as in so-called *onomatopoeia*. Examples of onomatopoetic words are 'cuckoo', 'whisper', 'baa'.[4] But such words are rare and
only the very fewest of the things we talk about are characterizable by
typical sounds. In his presentation of naturalism in the Cratylus, consequently, Plato emphasizes the fact that the naturalistic thesis – words
characterize what they refer to by their sound – is not to be understood in
the sense that they imitate sounds, but in the sense that they present the
essence of the things.[5]

According to the naturalistic point of view, this presentation is based
upon an affinity sounds and sequences of sounds have with attributes,
events, actions, etc. Thus, for example *r* as a sound produced by vibration
is supposed to suggest movement, the occlusives *d*, *t*, *b*, *p* to suggest the
enduring, the binding, etc.[6] By virtue of such affinities some words have
their meanings directly attached to them. Then other words are formed

from them, words which also have a natural meaning on the basis of their composition and etymological derivation.[7] Finally there are metaphors, i.e. transferences of words to things which manifest certain relationships to the objects originally designated by the word ('bottleneck', 'elbow-pipe', etc.) as well as a great many variations on the derived words, which can obscure their origins.

Now Plato himself lays stress on the fact that the affinity between sounds and attributes is very thin[8] and even he looks on his etymological analysis with skepticism.[9] For this reason he considerably weakens the naturalism he had advanced by emphasizing the fact that conventions also play a part in determining the meanings of words.[10] The criticism directed against naturalism to the effect that it is unable to explain the occurrence of synonyms, i.e. of expressions with the same meaning but different sounds, nor the differences of one natural language from another, Plato refutes by noting that just as there are different pictures of the same object, all of which exhibit some relation, even if different ones, to it, so there can also be different phonetic presentations of one and the same fact.[11]

If Plato adhered to the essential features of the naturalistic position in the *Cratylus*, despite the difficulties he recognized in it, it was on the basis of the following argument:[12] There are true and false sentences. Thus the sentence 'Cats meow' is true and the sentence 'Dogs meow' is false. Now if it were a matter of mere convention whether cats were designated as 'cats' one could just as well call them 'dogs' and say 'Dogs meow' instead of 'Cats meow'. But these sentences have different truth values and consequently we can not simply say 'dogs' instead of 'cats', but cats must be called 'cats'; i.e. for all things there are designations that are just as objectively correct and false as the sentences formed with them are objectively true and false.

But this argument is untenable because a sentence is not true or false on the basis of its sound pattern alone, but only on the basis of a semantic interpretation of that sound-pattern.[13] I.e., the sentence 'Dogs meow' is not false as such, but only on the usual interpretation of the words 'dog' and 'meow'. If one interprets the word 'dog' as one normally interprets the word 'cat', this sentence becomes true.

Along with this argument the most important rationale for a non-conventionalistic interpretation of meanings collapses, however, and conventionalism then becomes the most plausible position.[14] This does not require us to assume that linguistic signs were originally chosen quite arbitrarily – in particular, for example, there may be affinities between the sounds and expressive components of statements[15] – but for languages as we have them before us now a natural affinity between sound-structure and meaning is certainly no longer demonstrable except in a few special cases, as for example onomatopoetic formations. Therefore, we can proceed on the practical assumption that the relation between sign and significatum is arbitrary and depends on conventions.

Now this semantic conventionalism must, however, be restricted in several respects. Thus Plato emphasizes in the *Cratylus* that linguistic conventions are not explicit and formal agreements (συνθήκη), but customs (ἔθος) of linguistic usage handed down by tradition,[16] and that linguistic meanings can not be fixed by everyone to suit himself.[17] Language can fulfill its function of intelligible communication only if all who participate use the words in the same way (i.e. in the same sense) and if the norms of usage (νόμος) remain practically constant.[18]

While the previous statements on the controversy between naturalism and conventionalism hold true for all theories of meaning, for a realistic theory of meaning as Plato presents it,[19] there arise still further restrictions on conventionalism, not required by other theories of meaning, or not required in the same degree.[20] According to Plato things in themselves exhibit certain objective attributes, relations and differences. It is now the task of language to give appropriate expression to these attributes. If, for example, a language is unable to express an objectively given difference and has the same word for gold and iron, say, then it is not adequate.[21]

This requirement of Plato's, that an adequate language must be able to represent all real entities, one which essentially concerns the language's range of expression, is to be supplemented on one important point:

Language is definitely not just a set of isolated names for designating entities (things, attributes and the like), but a system in which out of a finite number of linguistic basic elements (e.g. words) we are able to construct infinitely many sentences. These sentences have a certain grammatical structure and this structure must correspond to their structure of meaning and consequently, on the realistic interpretation, to the ontological structure of the states of affairs of which they speak. That is to say, one can not construct a language by arbitrarily introducing some signs for entities; these signs must form a system, in which they can be grammatically combined in such a way that they reflect the ontological relationships in which the entities designated stand. For example, if one wants to express the fact that a thing α stands in the relation ρ to a thing β, one needs not only linguistic signs for α, β, ρ (e.g., a, b, R), but also a syntactical relation between these signs with which the relation between α, β and ρ can be represented (e.g. as $R(a, b)$). Grammar must therefore be constructed in accord with ontology. Not all the systems of signs you might choose come into question as languages, but only those that have a grammar which permits the expression of ontological differences and relationships.

Plato also compares language with a set of tools (ὄργανον), which must be of such a kind that we are able to work on the things linguistically with them, tools which must therefore be constructed properly for describing, differentiating, comparing, etc., things. Just as one can not work on any material you please with any tool you please, but only with such tools as are suitable to the material and the work to be done on the occasion, one can not describe, distinguish, etc., with any linguistic expressions you please, but only with a linguistic *organon* that is properly constructed. And conventionalism finds its limit in this requirement, that the linguistic tools be true to their tasks.[22]

From these considerations the following interpretation of realistic semantics emerges: language as an abstract system of signs in the sense of I.1 must correspond to the ontology of the range of objects to which the language refers. In particular, the ontological structures must be presentable in terms of grammatical structures and every grammatical structure must correspond unambiguously to a definite ontological structure. In the ideal case language and ontology would be isomorphic structures.

Language as an abstract system of signs is thus determined by the range of meaning it is supposed to represent. Here conventions have no place. The only conventional aspects are the various realizations of language that are used.

Later on, Leibniz speaks to the same effect in his *Dialogue*:

Even if the marks are arbitrary, there is something about their use and combination that is not arbitrary – a correspondence between marks and things and the relations between different marks that mean the same thing. This relation or this reference is the basis of truth.[23]

But taking all that into account, for a realistic semantics these limits of conventionalism consist only in requiring that the conventions serve the purpose of linguistic constructions, that of representing adequately antecedently given ontological structures and distinctions, that they be suited to their intended purpose from the realistic standpoint. But being suited to an intended purpose is obviously a general requirement for conventionalism as well.

1.2. *Basic Ideas of Realistic Semantics*

What we will do now is first of all to present the basic ideas of the conventionalist copy-theory and then discuss some important theories of this type that have been proposed in the modern literature.

Realistic semantics takes on its simplest form when it is said that linguistic expressions have only *one* semantic function, which consists in the fact that (on the basis of convention) they *designate* certain entities.

Thus the meaning of a *proper name* consists in its designating an object: I introduce a young man and say: 'This is Frederick Schulze'; I point to a town and say 'That is Frieding'; I point to a mountain and say 'That is the Jungfrau'; I point to a constellation and say 'That is Orion'. On each occasion, then, I indicate an object and stipulate that a certain expression is supposed to function as the name of this object. That constitutes the entire semantic function of this expression.

One proceeds in a similar way with *predicates*, saying, for example: The predicate 'red' stands for the quality you can observe on this object and this object, but not on this one and that one; the predicate 'larger than' stands for the relation that holds between the members of this pair and that pair of objects, but not between the members of such and such other pairs. Predicates thus designate qualities and relations or, more generally, *attributes*.

Finally, for sentences with the simple structure subject-predicate-object(s), symbolically $F(a_1, \ldots, a_n)$, it is stipulated that they designate the state of affairs that the attribute designated by F belongs to the n-tuple designated by $a_1, \ldots, a_n$. The sentence 'The Jungfrau is a mountain' thus designates the state of affairs that the Jungfrau is a mountain; the sentence 'Munich lies between Garmisch and Nuremberg' designates the state of affairs that Munich lies between Garmisch and Nuremberg, and so on. What simple sentences designate is thus defined as a function of what the proper names and predicates that occur in them designate together with the way in which the sentence is constructed out of those terms. What determines the meaning of a sentence is the meanings of the words that occur in it and their position in the sentence – 'Fritz strikes Hans' means something different from 'Hans strikes Fritz', even though the same words occur in both sentences, so that order also plays an important role. Furthermore, a sentence is called *true* if and only if the state of affairs it designates is a fact. The sentence 'The Jungfrau is more than 6000 feet high' is true if and only if the Jungfrau is more than 6000 feet high.[24]

The meaning of complex sentences is then determined in a similar fashion, with the aid of the semantic rules for grammatical combinations and with reference to the meaning of the simple linguistic expressions. This will be presented in III.2.1.

By virtue of stipulation, which is the gist of this theory, linguistic expressions are conventionally attached to certain entities (objects, attributes, facts). This relationship is called the *name-relation* and the semantic function of the expressions consists in this relationship entirely. According to this theory, that is all there is to the meaning of linguistic expressions.

If we have previously spoken of attributes (qualities and relations) and states of affairs, this requires some further elucidation. These terms are often used in such a way that they are supposed to designate something real, so that attributes and facts are something actually present in the world. Attributes and states of affairs are then contrasted with *concepts* and *propositions*, these latter as something in thought only, as in conceptualism, or as entities that constitute a realm of reality of their own, as in Platonism. While 'red', for example, is a quality found in the world, and consequently an attribute, 'prime number' would be a concept; and while 'This rose is red' is a fact which is actually encountered in the world, '17 is a prime number' would be a proposition, which does not occur in the world.

But this distinction between attributes and concepts on the one side and states of affairs and propositions on the other would first have to be made more precise: what 'real' or 'actual' means has not been generally established. Indeed, the word "real" has quite different meanings in different contexts, as the examples, 'a real (i.e. true) friend', 'a real (i.e. not an imaginary) illness', 'a real (i.e. effective) help', demonstrate.

Take the case of clearly defined predicates. Shall we say that all of the predicates that can logically be constructed out of them also denote attributes, as they do ('non-red' along with 'red', 'square circle' along with 'circle' and 'square')? If yes, how is it that all logically possible conceptual structures are also actually realized? If no, then there are sentences formed with the aid of logical connectives out of sentences that denote the real which do not themselves denote anything real, i.e. there are sentences that change their meaning in certain contexts.

The following definitions for attributes and states of affairs would come easily to mind: We could (1) interpret attributes (such as 'red', 'unicorn' but not 'prime number') as concepts that are defined only for empirical objects (concrete things or animals, plants, human beings); or (2) as concepts under which an empirical object falls ('red' but not 'unicorn'). And one could interpret states of affairs (3) as propositions that refer to empirical objects (such as 'Munich has less than a million inhabitants' but not '3 is a prime number') or (4) as propositions which are true, i.e. which say what is actually the case (such as 'Munich has more than a million inhabitants' but not 'Munich has less than a million inhabitants'). However, according to definitions (2) and (4) the meaning of a predicate or a sentence would depend on empirical circumstances: If marmots were to become extinct, the word 'marmot' would change its meaning and the sentence 'Munich has less than a million inhabitants' would have changed its meaning since 1950.[25] On definitions (1) and (3), however, the term 'empirical' remains vague and, besides, the distinction between 'empirical' – 'nonempirical' is scarcely any more important for semantics than the distinction between 'animate' – 'inanimate'.

In what follows we will make no such distinction, therefore, and use the terms 'attribute' and 'concept' or 'state of affair' and 'proposition' as synonyms. We will also not go into questions concerning the nature and ontological status of concepts and propositions right away. These questions will be cleared up in the course of further discussion.

Another version of realistic semantics arises if the conceptual entities – possibly because their ontological status looks all too obscure – are identified with mental contents, for the most part called 'ideas', and in line with this, linguistic expressions are said to denote ideas. On that view, the word 'this rose' would not directly denote this rose. Instead, it would immediately refer to an idea of the rose and only by way of the relation between the rose and the idea of it have any reference to the rose itself. And the word 'red' would not denote the attribute 'red', but a "general idea" of 'red'. But the general nature of such ideas remains completely in the dark – still more obscure, if possible, than that of concepts. Besides, as a mental state an idea is in each case a state (or content of experience) of a subject: two ideas belonging to different persons are different even though they refer to the same thing: X can not have one of Y's ideas and *vice versa*. But that would imply that the sentence 'This rose is red' would mean quite different things for the speaker and the hearer. Besides that surely we use the sentence 'This rose is red' to speak not of our idea or of other people's ideas of the rose but of the rose itself.[26]

After this brief excursion on attributes, concepts and ideas, back to the simple form of realistic semantics!

This simple form of the copy-theory runs into some difficulties. There is already a certain difficulty in the fact that we cannot point to attributes and facts, as abstracta, in the same way as we can to concrete objects in establishing the name-relation.[27] If we want to say which attribute 'red' designates, we can not produce this attribute itself, not point to it as to a mountain, a village, a constellation; we can only point out some instances and counter-instances of the attribute: some red and some non-red things. But it is clear that a finite number of examples and counter-examples will not be sufficient to distinguish an attribute unambiguously. And so one runs into the problem: Why does the learning of predicates by examples work and to what extent does it work? But we will discuss this question more exactly only somewhat later on.[28] Right here we will simply be satisfied with the fact that, as experience shows us, it does work very well.

Furthermore, from a nominalistic standpoint, one could object that there are only concrete objects, and no abstracta such as attributes, and that consequently predicates could not be names because there is nothing they could denote.[29]

According to the nominalistic interpretation, predicates, in contrast to proper names and sentences, do not have meaning in and of themselves, but are *synsemantic* or *syncategorematic* expressions, i.e. expressions that have meaning only in the sentence context. The word 'rose' means nothing alone, then, but only sentences such as 'This rose is red', 'Fritz has a red shirt', etc., have meaning. The traditional formulation of this point of view is *universale est vox*, that is, the objects that fall under a predicate F have nothing in common except that they are called F. Red objects, then, do not have a common color or quality – what they have in common is nothing but being called 'red'. But this interpretation leads on its part to the following fundamental difficulty: If 'red' does not have any meaning in and of itself, then the meaning of the sentences 'a is red', 'b is red', etc., is not determined by the meaning of the terms 'a', 'b' and 'red'. Rather, the meaning of all of these sentences is to be determined separately in each case, i.e. all of them are to be regarded as distinct sentence constants. But then it is no longer possible to communicate new facts with sentences of the form 'c is red', i.e. to make an assertion about the color of a new object c, to which the predicate had not previously been applied, because the meaning of 'c is red' must first be defined. A language in which no new facts can be communicated is of no use, however, and therefore we shall not be able to avoid assigning meanings to predicates also.

Since a nominalist does not admit propositions either, one can not define the semantic function of predicates on the basis of propositions. The meaning function of sentences is supposed to consist simply in the fact that they are true or false. The stipulation that certain sentences 'a is an F', 'b is an F', ... are supposed to be true and other sentences 'c is an F', ... false, says nothing about F – 'F' is defined simply as a predicate that applies to a, b, ..., but not to c, d, ... – and consequently the sentences 'a is an F', ... etc., do not say anything about the objects a, b, c, d... either.

[Nominalism offers no reasonable starting point for a theory of meaning, then] We can therefore set it aside in what follows. The ontological objections against assuming abstract entities such as concepts and propositions will be solved in later discussions in a different way.

By way of contrast, the following objection to the simple form of realistic semantics is of fundamental significance: We usually understand by the meaning of a linguistic expression something based on the understanding of language alone, and independent of empirical data. In order to know what an expression means, I have to master the language to which it belongs; in doubtful cases I have to consult dictionaries and grammars, but not any knowledge of facts. Therefore the question of the synonymy, the identity of meaning of two proper names must be capable of being decided on the basis of knowledge of language alone. But if we identify the meaning of a proper name with the object it denotes, then the question, for example, of whether the expressions 'morning star' and 'evening star' are synonymous becomes an empirical question: the synonymy of these two expressions can only be determined by astronomical observations.[30]

Furthermore, the sentences 'The morning star is identical with the morning star' and 'The morning star is identical with the evening star' have different meanings as we usually understand them. The first is a logical tautology, the second an empirical statement. Now since the meaning of a sentence can depend on nothing other than the meanings of the words that occur in it and their position in the sentence, and since the two sentences differ only in the words 'morning star' and 'evening star', the meaning of these two words must be different even though they name the same object. And so we can not identify the meaning of a proper name with the object it names.

There are also meaningful proper names that denote no (real) object, as for example, 'Odysseus', 'the smallest real number greater than 0', 'the present king of France'. These names are not completely meaningless, however, as are expressions like 'Ripht', 'Kaluphem' etc., but they are different from names like 'morning star', 'the smallest natural number greater than 0', 'the King of France in 1182' only by virtue of the fact that, because of the constitution of the world or the real number axioms, there is nothing they name. Thus Quine says that "A singular term need not name to be significant."[31] And in [53], 40 Wittgenstein pointed out that a proper name does not lose its meaning by virtue of the fact that the object it names ceases to exist. The name 'Socrates' is also meaningful today, when there is no longer any Socrates. Nor can we say that the meaning of the word 'Zugspitze' is 3000 meters high. It follows from this, too, that the meaning of a proper name can not be identified with the thing it names. We must, then, distinguish the *meaning* of a proper name from its *reference*, i.e. from the object it names – if there is one.[32] And we must distinguish between proper names that are meaningless and so have no reference either (like 'Kaluphem', 'Ripht'), proper names that have meaning but no reference (like 'the present King of France') and proper names that have both meaning and reference (like 'morning star', 'the smallest natural number greater than 0'). In order to emphasize terminologically the difference in the relations of the proper name to its meaning and to its reference, it is often said that a proper name *expresses* its meaning and *designates* or *names* the object for which it is a name. In German *Bedeu-tung* (meaning) is distinguished from *Bezug* (reference).[33]

What, now, does constitute the meaning of a proper name if it is not to be identified with its reference? We will defer answering this question and return once again to the meaning of predicates and sentences.

For a *predicate* we can continue to identify its meaning with the concept it stands for. There are no two predicates that stand for the same concept of which we would claim that they are different in meaning (in the usual sense). And there is no meaningful predicate of which we could not say that it stands for a concept.[34] Concepts, as we saw above, are not present in the world like objects: it is not an empirical but a logical question whether a specified concept exists. So concepts are meanings of predicates and we say now, following the terminological distinction between 'name' or 'designate' and 'express', that predicates *express* (not *designate* or *name*) concepts.[35]

Predicates lack direct reference and it is not necessary to construct such a reference. For reasons of symmetry, however, we can say that a predicate refers to (designates) the class of things that fall under the concept the predicate expresses. What this class looks like, i.e. what elements it includes, is then once more an empirical question and it is also an empirical question whether two predicates refer to the same class, whether for example the predicates 'animal with kidneys' and 'animal with a heart' have the same reference. This construction of a reference for predicates will prove to be very useful in what follows.

We can also, in the case of a sentence, identify its meaning with the proposition it stands for. Again, there are no two sentences which stand for the same proposition and which we would claim to be different in meaning (in the usual sense), and there is no meaningful sentence of which we could not say that it stands for a proposition.[36] Propositions are no more empirically given things than concepts are: it is not an empirical question whether a proposition exists or not or whether two propositions are identical. So we say that a sentence *expresses* (not *designates*) a proposition.

There is also a natural way in which one can assign a reference to prop-ositions: their *truth-value*. Whether a sentence is true or false is a question of fact, which generally speaking cannot be answered if we know only the sentence's meaning. We know what the sentence 'It is now raining in New York' means; but in order to determine whether it is true, one must make empirical observations. But since 'true' and 'false' are predicates, we do not say – as Frege does – that a sentence *designates* its truth value, that it is a *name* for it.

Since a simple (atomic) sentence is constructed out of proper names and a predicate, its meaning depends entirely on the meanings of the words that occur in it (the proper names and the predicate) and the way in which these words are connected together in the sentence. The reference of a sentence will also depend on the reference of the proper names that occur in it: the truth-value of the sentence 'Fritz is blond' depends on which individual is designated by the name 'Fritz'. And if a proper name that designates no object occurs in a sentence, such as 'Odysseus' or 'the present King of France', then reference can also be denied of it.[37]

Whether a sentence has a reference, then, is also an empirical question. Now if one were not to assign any reference to predicates, then the reference of a sentence would not only depend on the words that occur in it and their connection, but on their meanings as well. But if we assign a reference to predicates in the way described, then the reference of the sentence can be interpreted as a function of the references of words occurring in it and their connection in the sentence.[38]

Now proper names and sentences can also be constructed from a predicate F without the use of proper names. Examples such as the expressions '$\lambda x F(x)$' ('the class of objects with the property F'), '$\imath x F(x)$' ('the thing that has the property F'), '$\Lambda x F(x)$' ('All things have the property F'), '$V x F(x)$' ('Some things have the property F') show that this is so. The reference of these expressions depends on the range of objects being spoken of in the specific context and on the meaning of the predicate. The truth-value of 'All numbers are divisible by two' depends on whether I am considering only even numbers, or any natural number you please, and the truth-value of the sentence 'There is a square root of -1' depends on whether I am considering real or complex numbers. The reference to a domain of objects in the quantifiers (over which the variables within these quantifiers range) thus determines the reference of the sentence in these cases.

Now let us return to the meaning of proper names! In the first place there is the group of proper names that take the form of a *definite description*, such as 'the author of *Kabale und Liebe*', 'the present President of the United States', 'the first place you come to when you go south on B2 from Murnau', etc. They are constructed with a predicate F and we write them symbolically in the form $\imath xF(x)$. If the description is supposed to be successful, i.e. to designate a well-defined object, then exactly one object must fall under the predicate.[39] Whether the description is a name and, if it is, for what object is a question of fact and it is equally a question of fact whether two descriptions such as 'the morning star' and 'the evening star' refer to the same object. If there is no object that falls under F, then $\imath xF(x)$ is not a name (as, for example, 'the present King of France', 'the smallest real number greater than 0'). Likewise, in the case in which several objects fall under F, one will also say that $\imath xF(x)$ is not a name (does not denote anything), as for example 'Heidegger's book', 'the son of Jacob'. In these cases, then, definite descriptions have no reference.

We can now determine the meaning of a definite description by way of the meaning of the descriptive predicate. So for this case we can reduce the question of the meaning of proper names to the question of the meaning of predicates. The like also holds for other proper names constructed from predicates, as for example the class-names '$\lambda xF(x)$' ('the class of things that have the property F'), or for function-expressions '$f(a)$' ('the value of the function f for argument a') since functions can be interpreted as many-one relations.[40] In these cases, too, we can define the meaning of these names in terms of the meaning of the predicates from which they are constructed. The meaning of these proper names, then, is the way in which the objects they designate – if there are such – are conceptually defined by the names.

How does it stand with the remaining proper names now, those that do not have the form of a definite description, a class term or a function term? We will call them *ostensive* proper names. 'Socrates', 'Munich', 'the Zugspitze', for example, are proper names of this sort. We can say of these proper names that their primary semantic function consists in their reference. There are, however, meaningful proper names with no reference, such as 'Odysseus', so that we can not disregard meaning entirely in connection with these names. What one could now say is that ostensive proper names are more or less exactly defined in their meaning by a more or less sharply delimited set of assertions in which they occur and which have a quasi-analytic character. On this view, the meaning of 'Aristotle', for example, would be defined by assertions such as 'Aristotle was a pupil of Plato's', 'Aristotle was the teacher of Alexander the Great', 'Aristotle wrote the *Organon*', etc., thus by assertions which for us are always bound up with the name 'Aristotle'. There are such assertions even for a name introduced by indicating the object for which it stands, for an object is never given to us as a bare individual but always under certain conceptual specifications. It is clear, however, that – apart from special cases, like the introduction of a proper name in a system of implicit definitions (such as the term '0' in the Peano axioms, for example) or names for fictitious persons of whom assertions are made in a story ('Odysseus' as this name is used in the *Iliad* and the *Odyssey*) – for ostensive names no group of such identifying descriptive assertions with strictly fixed boundaries can be given. Different people connect quite different identifying assertions with the same name and even the single individual can not give a sharp boundary between assertions which serve as identificatory for him and other assertions.[41] One can not regard all of the assertions that hold true of a proper name as identificatory for it in the sense of an implicit definition either, for otherwise all of these assertions would be analytic.

Even if one defines the meaning of ostensive proper names as the meaning of the predicate that arises from the conjunction of the identificatory assertions by replacing the proper name in question by a variable, it is clear that it follows from this that the meaning of such proper names is generally very indefinite.[42] This indefiniteness of meaning is pointed out in many accounts of semantics where meaning is not interpreted in quite another sense and identified, for example, with reference.[43] The meaning of ostensive names may, however, also be defined so that it is determined solely by their reference. This interpretation as *standard names* is discussed in Chapter II.1.5.

1.3. *Wittgenstein's Picture Theory of Language in the Tractatus*[44]

We shall now present and discuss some realistic semantic theories. In doing so, however, we will not make any great, wide-ranging excursion into history, but limit ourselves to a few particularly important modern theories. This section is intended to deal with the basic features of Wittgenstein's semantics in the *Tractatus* ([22]). We shall not take account of the many complex details, which are not necessary for the theory, nor of the other themes the *Tractatus* deals with. What we are about in the following is not an interpretation of the entire *Tractatus* but only its basic semantic ideas. For the interpretation of the difficult text we are making use of the detailed and thorough work by E. Stenius [60].[45]

Wittgenstein starts from ontological presuppositions, entirely in the realistic manner.[46] According to his presuppositions, entities are to be categorically subdivided into *states of affairs, objects* and *attributes. Facts* are existing (realized) states of affairs ([22], 2). The world is presented as the fact that such and such states of affairs, such and such relationships among things exist ([22], 2.01). States of affairs can be simple or complex. A complex state of affairs can be analyzed into simpler states of affairs. According to Wittgenstein the world is a complex fact which can be analyzed *without ambiguity* (herein lies the *absolutism* of the *Tractatus*) into atomic facts of the *utmost simplicity* (in the postulation of such ultimately simple facts lies the *atomism* of the *Tractatus*). Wittgenstein calls the (simplest) objects and attributes that are present in these atomic facts the *things*, which together constitute the *substance* of the world ([22], 2.021). How these atomic states of affairs and things are supposed to look remains unclear. In any case, it becomes apparent from Wittgenstein's further remarks that things can not be identified with the concrete objects and their attributes that we usually have in front of us, whether in everyday life or in the sciences. Their existence is merely postulated; they are not described more precisely or exemplified.

Now according to Wittgenstein an atomic sentence is a picture of an atomic fact ([22], 3 and 4), while complex sentences can be interpreted as pictures of facts only indirectly, namely insofar as they can be transformed into compounds of atomic sentences which can be represented as pictures of factual complexes. Since these transformation rules are not given more exactly, however, and the treatment of complex sentences does not have to do with the basic semantic ideas in the *Tractatus*, we will restrict ourselves here to the semantic function of atomic sentences.

Obviously, by the claim that sentences are pictures of facts it can not be intended that a sentence is a picture in the naturalistic sense, as a photograph or a portrait is a picture of a person. For sentences have no superficial similarity with facts. To define his picture concept Wittgenstein proceeds rather from the concept of isomorphic mapping. One says that there is an *isomorphy* between a structure $A = \langle A, R^1_{n_1} \dots, R^m_{n_m} \rangle$, composed of a (non-empty) set of objects A and m n_i-place attributes $R^i_{n_i} (i = 1, \dots, m)$, and a structure $B = \langle B, S^1_{n_1}, \dots, S^m_{n_m} \rangle$ of the same type, composed of a (non-empty) set B and m n_i-place attributes $S^i_{n_i}$, if there is a one-to-one mapping ϕ of A on B, so that the following holds:

(I) $R^i_{n_i}(a_1,\ldots,a_{n_i}) \equiv S^i_{n_i}(\phi(a_1),\ldots,\phi(a_{n_i}))$ for all i and all n_i-tuples $a_1,\ldots,a_{n_i}$ from A. ϕ is then called an *isomorphy-correlator*.

For example, if $A = \langle\{a, b, c\}, R^1_1, R^2_2\rangle$ and $B = \langle\{d, e, f\}, S^1_1, S^2_2\rangle$ and if it is the case that $R^1_1 a$, $\neg R^1_1 b$, $R^1_1 c$, $R^2_2 ab, R^2_2 cb$ and $\neg R^2_2 xy$ for all other pairs x, y from $\{a, b, c\}$, and also that $S^1_1 e$, $S^1_1 f$, $\neg S^1_1 d, S^2_2 ed$, $S^2_2 fd$ and $\neg S^2_2 xy$ for all the remaining pairs x, y from $\{d, e, f\}$, then the mapping ϕ, defined by $\phi(a) = e$, $\phi(b) = d$, $\phi(c) = f$, is an isomorphic mapping of A on B.

Both structures can be illustrated graphically by the following figures, in which $R^1_1 a$ is represented by ⓐ and $R^2_2 ab$ by $a \rightarrow b$, $S^1_1 a$ by 🄰 and $S^2_2 ab$ by $a \Rightarrow b$.

A simple example may make this picture concept clear. Five tokens of two colors, viz. green or red and blue or yellow, and with different sizes can represent the relationships in a family of five persons, if a token is assigned to each person according to the rules that larger tokens correspond to older persons, red tokens to the men in the family, green to the women, blue to parents and yellow to children.

Now in order for Wittgenstein's idea of the sentence as a picture to be carried out, he interprets the sentence not as an object but as a fact: The proper names in the sentence – e.g. 'a' and 'b' in 'aSb' – are objects to which objects a and b in the fact to be pictorially represented are assigned, by virtue of a rule of interpretation (an isomorphic mapping of the (atomic) objects in the world onto the proper names). The predicate sign 'S' is to be distinguished from the syntactic S-relation, in which the objects 'a' and 'b' stand in the sentence 'aSb', namely from the relation of standing to the left or to the right of the sign 'S'. It is this S-relation, not the sign 'S', which corresponds to a (here two-place) attribute S in the fact to be pictured.[47]

According to Wittgenstein, then, it is not the predicates as objects, i.e. as expressions, that are names of attributes, but the syntactic relations. And the pictures (names) of facts are not sentences in the usual sense (as objects, sound sequences) but syntactic facts. So names, according to Wittgenstein, are always of the same ontological category as what they stand for.

In order for a sentence to be a picture of a fact, on Wittgenstein's theory, it is sufficient that the sentence and the fact are of the same structural type, i.e. that the same number of objects, or proper names, occur in them and the same number of attributes with a like number of places and that a rule of interpretation ϕ is available. He does not require that the isomorphy conditions (I) are fulfilled, for example that aSb holds when the sentence reads 'aSb', but bSa, for example, can also be the case. A sentence is a *correct* picture of a fact, i.e. true, if and only if the isomorphy conditions are fulfilled.[48]

The sentence represents its sense as a fact, i.e. it represents 'how things are, if it is true' ([22], 4.022). "To understand a sentence is to know what is the case when it is true" ([22], 4.024). "The meanings of the simple signs must be explained for us to understand them. But we use sentences to explain and make ourselves understood" ([22], 4.026).

In Wittgenstein's system, then, the rule of interpretation ϕ corresponds to the name-relation for proper names. Combined with it there must be a coordination of syntactic relations and attributes.[49] On the basis of these two correlations the sentence as a specific relation between names then represents a fact as a relation between things, just as the model using tokens, in the example above, represents which family relationships are before us.

In view of all this, the semantics of the Tractatus essentially differs from the basic form of realistic semantics delineated in II.1. in that predicates and sentences are not interpreted as objects, but as relations and facts. Consequently, the semantic function of language does not consist simply in naming or expressing, but also in a correspondence of the categorical structure of the expressions to the categorical structure of reality. The predicative nature of attributes is communicated by the predicative nature of the syntactic predicate relationships and the inner structure of the fact is communicated by the inner structure of sentences as syntactic facts.[50]

If Wittgenstein goes beyond the realistic account in this point, as we have seen above[51], there is in his system, on the other hand, no distinction between meaning and reference. For him proper names mean objects, predicates, classes. That may be connected with the fact that in making his observations he has in mind an ideal language that is regarded as being purely extensional as the artificial languages of modern logic, which likewise have expressions for which only a reference is stipulated, but not a meaning. For a general semantics, however, the distinction between reference and meaning is of fundamental importance. Wittgenstein first reinstated this distinction in [53].

Many more critical remarks can still be made concerning Wittgenstein's semantics, particularly in connection with his absolutism, his atomism and his theory of the semantic function of compound sentences. Since we have not presented these theories here and since the basic semantic ideas of the *Tractatus* are independent of absolutism and atomism, we will not go into them any further here. What is important in our context is only that Wittgenstein's semantics in the *Tractatus* is a good example of the simple form of realistic semantics, since it develops the ontological presuppositions and the correlation theses of this semantics in a completely explicit manner.

1.4. *Frege's Semantics*

Frege formulated his ideas on semantics, which had the greatest influence on the development of modern theories of meaning, primarily in [92] and in the fragment 'Ausführungen über Sinn und Bedeutung' (ca. 1895).[52] He proceeds from the idea that proper names mean objects. Starting from here, however, as we have already shown in terms of a Fregean example in II.1.2, one falls into the difficulty that the meaning of a sentence can be changed by replacing a proper name by a proper name with the same meaning. Frege concluded from this that proper names have two semantic functions: in the Fregean terminology they *mean* (*bedeuten*) an object and *express* (*drücken aus*) a *sense* (*Sinn*). Frege thus distinguishes between the *sense* and the *meaning* (*Bedeutung*) of proper names: every proper name that is meaningful at all (in our earlier sense, that it stands for something, and is not, like the expressions 'Kaluphem' or 'Ripht', for example, a mere series of letters without a semantic function) has a sense. Proper names with the same sense also have the same meaning in Frege's terminology, but proper names that have the same meaning in Frege's terminology do not always have the same sense.

It is an unfavorable feature of Frege's terminology that he designates the reference as 'meaning', for meaning as usually understood is something given as immanent within language, the existence and character of which does not depend upon extralinguistic facts. For this reason we have not adopted the Fregean terminology. If one makes use of the Fregean expression 'meaning', then, one must always keep it in mind that this word as used by Frege is not used in its normal way. That will avoid the appearance of inadequacy that some of Frege's statements have. In order to draw a clear distinction between 'meaning' in our sense, described in II.1.2, and 'meaning' in the Fregean sense, in the following we will identify it, and related terms, by attaching the subscript 'F'.

Now if one assumes along with Frege that the assertive content of a sentence depends on the sense of the proper names that occur in it, then the different content of the sentences 'The morning star is identical with the morning star' and 'the morning star is identical with the evening star' can be explicated by way of a difference in sense between the two (identical in meaning$_F$) proper names 'morning star' and 'evening star'.

Now what, according to Frege, constitutes the sense of a proper name? He interprets the sense of a proper name as the way in which the designated object is given by means of the name. Thus by way of the proper name 'morning star' the planet Venus is given as the star that shines brightest in the morning, by way of the name 'evening star' as the star that shines brightest in the evening. And the point S in the figure below is characterized in different ways as 'the intersection of the medians on a and b' and as 'the intersection of the medians on b and c'.

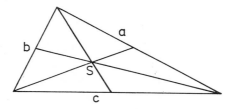

For Frege does every proper name have a determinate sense? We have seen that this is questionable for ostensive proper names like 'Aristotle'. Frege, too, concedes that not all proper names have a determinate sense, nevertheless he wants to exclude such cases for precise scientific languages.[53] Frege also acknowledges proper names that have a sense but are without meanings$_F$, such as 'Odysseus', 'Pegasus', 'the smallest real number greater than 1.' Proper names of this sort are to be excluded from assertive discourse, however, especially in scientific contexts, because sentences that include such proper names are neither true nor false.

The sense of a proper name for Frege is a conceptual, platonistic entity, i.e. something intersubjective, objective and to be strictly distinguished from the subjective ideas and associations which a given individual idiosyncratically attaches to a proper name. For him the sense of a proper name is something that various people attach to this proper name in the same way.[54] Frege gives no criterion for identity of sense for proper names. But, as the following shows, one will have to interpret the concept of sense very narrowly, so that, apart from trivial cases of identity of sense such as arise from explicit definition, for example, different proper names as a rule also have different sense. Although Frege never uses identifying descriptive concepts to define the sense of a proper name in the form of a description, such an interpretation, as we have seen in II.1.2, would nevertheless be very compatible with Frege's assertions.

Frege now ascribes to predicates and sentences as well a double semantic function in analogy with proper names. Sentences too have sense and meaning$_F$. Frege assumes that the meaning$_F$ of a sentence depends only on the meaning$_F$ of the proper names that occur in it, not on their sense. This implies that the sentence content, the proposition, can not be the meaning$_F$ of the sentence, as the above examples show. So Frege holds that the proposition or the *thought* (*Gedanke*), as he says, is the sense of a sentence. Now if one takes account of the fact that what Frege understands by 'meaning' is the reference, there is nothing artificial about Frege's regarding the truth-value of a sentence as its meaning$_F$, so that there emerges here an exact analogy with the meaning$_F$ of proper names.[55] Corresponding to his acceptance of meaningless$_F$ proper names Frege also admits sentences that have sense well enough, but are not meaningful$_F$, i.e. are neither true nor false. This is true in particular of sentences like 'Odysseus landed in Ithaca' which contain meaningless$_F$ proper names. But as we have said, such sentences are to be excluded in scientific contexts. Nevertheless, every sentence whatsoever with a semantic character has a sense.[56]

Frege's account of the sense and meaning of sentences and the general principle of substitution, that in all sentences expressions with the same meaning$_F$ can be exchanged for each other without altering the truth-values of the sentences (because the meaning$_F$ of a sentence depends on the meaning$_F$ of the expressions that occur in them, not on their sense) can only be sustained if it is assumed that the expressions do not have their usual meaning$_F$ in all contexts. For there are contexts in which the exchange of expressions with the same meaning$_F$ alters not only the sense, but also the truth-value, the meaning$_F$ of a sentence. Along with Frege, Russell in [05] and Quine in [64b] have given examples of such cases. Frege brings in the example: 'A lied in saying that he had seen B'.[57] If this sentence is true then 'A saw B' is false. Now let 'A saw C' also be false; despite that, 'A lied in saying that he had seen C' may be false. Russell offers the example of the true sentence: 'George IV wished to know whether Scott was the author of Waverly'. From it, by replacing the proper name 'the author of Waverly' with the proper name 'Scott', which has the same meaning$_F$, there arises the false sentence: 'George IV wished to know whether Scott was Scott'. Quine, finally, introduced the example of the true sentence: 'It is a truth of mathematics that $9=9$', from which by replacing the proper name '9' with the proper name 'the number of planets', which has the same meaning$_F$, there arises the false sentence 'It is a truth of mathematics that the number of planets $=9$'. Frege now assumes that in all contexts in which such an exchange of expressions which have the same meaning$_F$ is not possible *salva veritate* – he calls them *indirect* or *oblique* contexts – the meaning$_F$ of an expression is its sense. This assumption is natural enough, since in indirect discourse, such as 'Fritz said that he had read the book', for example, we are speaking only about the content of a statement of Fritz's without making that statement ourselves. Thus we are not speaking, as in the sentence 'Fritz has read the book' about the book and Fritz's reading of it, but about the sense of an assertion which is an assertion about the book only as a direct statement.

Frege shows in [92] in a detailed analysis of various types of subordinate clauses – indirect contexts are mostly subordinate clauses – that this account can be carried through.

Frege said nothing about the sense and the meaning$_F$ of predicates in [92]. Some intimations about them are to be found, however, in the fragment cited above *Über Sinn und Bedeutung*. In it Frege introduces as the sense of a predicate the concept it expresses, and as its meaning something that could be called an *extensional concept*. Extensional concepts are supposed to be predicative, i.e. they are not objects (and so, particularly, they are not classes). Furthermore, they are supposed to be identical when they apply to the same objects, i.e. when they determine the same classes. According to this stipulation, the meaning$_F$ of a sentence then depends only on the meaning$_F$ of the predicates that occur in it, but not on their sense. In this case Frege's construction is somewhat artificial. The only reason for not introducing classes as predicate meanings$_F$ is that they have no predicative character and so their application to objects does not produce any truth-values as objects.

A paradox has been stated in connection with concepts similar to the paradox of identity illustrated by the sentence pair 'The morning star is identical with the evening star' – 'The morning star is identical with the morning star'. It originates with G. E. Moore and is called the *paradox of analysis*.[58] According to it, sentence (a) 'The concept "brother" is identical with the concept "male sibling"', has a different sense from sentence (b) 'The concept "brother" is identical with the concept "brother"', because the sense of the former is not trivial and is relevant in connection with the analysis of concepts. But if these sentences are different in sense, then the expressions 'the concept "brother"' and 'the concept "male sibling"' must be different in sense and therefore the two concepts must be different. Analysis of concepts, so it seems, must be either trivial, like (b), when the concept analyzed is identical with the concept given as analyzing it, or false, like (a), when these concepts are different.

In [46] A. Church has recommended resolving this paradox analogously with the Fregean paradox of identity of objects, by interpreting the expressions 'the concept "brother"' and 'the concept "male sibling"' as identical in meaning$_F$ but different in sense. But what is the sense of a concept name supposed to be in contrast with its meaning$_F$ in this case? Frege's distinction with regard to this point can not be used here, since as analyses of concepts (a) and (b) do not concern classes as ranges of the concepts (or extensional concepts as Frege understands them), but the concepts themselves. Otherwise we would have before us not any analysis of a concept but an empirical claim. The sense element, the meaning, lies precisely in the conceptual, and what – in Frege's way of speaking – is supposed to be the *way* in which a concept is given by a name? Concepts are not defined by (other) concepts nor identified like objects, but are the instrument of definition.

Statement (a) will be more correctly formulated in this way: (c) 'The predicate "brother" is identical in meaning (synonymous) with the predicate "male sibling"'. Then the paradox does not arise, for the terms '"brother"' and '"male sibling"', as they occur in (c), are not only differ-

ent in sense, but also different in meaning$_F$ – they do in fact designate
different expressions – and so the substitution of identical items is out of
the question from the very beginning. Formulation (c) is also more adequate than (a) because so-called analyses of concepts do not have to do
with establishing the identity of concepts but with assertions about the
meanings of predicates.

If one wishes to speak of concepts, however, then either the concepts
'brother' and 'male sibling' are identical – in that case this identity is not
an empirical or a linguistic, but a logical fact and just as trivial as the
identity of 'brother' and 'brother', or they are not identical and then
statement (a) is false. That (a) has a non-trivial look to it is probably
attributable to nothing but the fact that we understand it in the sense of
(c).[59]

Frege's semantics has been criticized from many sides. The only sort
of criticism we will go into here is that which stands on the ground of a
realistic semantics itself, for we shall concern ourselves extensively later
on with the more radical criticism of the realistic account as such. Looked
on from the standpoint of the semantic scheme given in II.1.2, one could
especially object to the Fregean construction of predicate meanings$_F$, but
still, taken as a whole, the differences are not very troubling.

Carnap has offered a more fundamental criticism of Frege's semantics
in [56]. Above all, Carnap makes the following objections to Frege's
account:

(1) According to Frege, the same expressions can have different mean-
ings$_F$ in different contexts. – That is correct, but not a decisive objection,
especially when one reflects that the meaning$_F$ is in fact the reference and
that naturally in indirect contexts the usual reference of an expression is
replaced by its sense.

(2) According to Carnap it can even come about that one and the same
occurrence of an expression has different meanings$_F$, namely its usual
meaning$_F$ and its usual sense, for instance, in the example Frege gave in
[92], 'Bebel has the illusion that...'. In this case 'has the illusion that...'
stands for 'believes that..., and not...'. In the latter expression '...'
stands at one time in an indirect context and at another time in a direct,
and so in its abbreviated form 'has the illusion that...' '...' must have both
its usual meaning$_F$ and its usual sense at one and the same time. – But it is
sufficient for a correct response to all questions of substitution and syn-

onymity concerning this sentence to assume that '...' stands in an indirect context here and means$_F$ its usual sense.

(3) A name can be introduced for every entity, including sense-contents. But what is the sense of such names of senses, the sense of names for the latter sense contents and so on? An infinite hierarchy of sense contents would have to be assumed. – A. Church has attempted to give such a hierarchy of sense contents and so make the ontology of the Fregean semantics more precise.[60] But this system is of only formal interest and of little relevance to semantics, for the sense contents of higher levels are not precisely characterized and described in intuitive terms. On the other hand, however, it is not at all necessary to introduce names for sense contents and then ascribe to them a sense. Names for sense contents are needed in Frege's system no more than they are in Carnap's. In order to speak of sense contents, not new names, but indirect contexts are used.

To be sure, Carnap says that sense contents of higher order would actually be needed in a variety of oblique contexts, as for example 'It is not necessary that Hans believes that it is possible that p'. But here too it is sufficient for all pertinent semantic considerations to assume that p simply stands in indirect context and means$_F$ its usual sense.

Actually Frege's semantic account is not so entirely different from Carnap's method of extensions and intensions in [56], which we will consider in the next section. While Frege holds to the general substitution principle and therefore has to change the meaning$_F$ of expressions in indirect contexts, Carnap restricts the substitution principle and can therefore require that expressions have the same meaning$_F$ in all contexts.

Finally, Quine too has criticized Frege's (as he has Church's) notion that expressions in indirect contexts mean$_F$ their usual sense. According to him this account is insufficient: For example if p is a factually true sentence, then it is true that $f = \iota g(p \wedge g = f)$, i.e. the concept f is identical with that concept g of which this holds: p, and g is identical with f. The predicates '$f(x)$' and '$\iota g(p \wedge g = f)(x)$' have the same meaning, but despite that it is not true that along with '$N(f(a))$' ('$f(a)$ is logically necessary'), '$N(\iota g(p \wedge g = f)(a))$' is also true, for from the latter sentence there follows the false proposition '$N(p)$'. There are cases then, in which the exchange of expressions with the same sense can change even the meaning of the context.[61] The way out of the difficulty by saying that the expressions 'f' and '$\iota g(p \wedge g = f)$' have the same meaning$_F$, to be sure, but differ in sense, is not available here, for it is not these expressions (as proper names for concepts) that are exchanged in the context in question but the predicates '$f(x)$' and '$\imath g(p \wedge g = f)(x)$', which stand for the same concepts and so are alike in sense. A possible difference in the sense of the concept names is thus irrelevant to the problem.

This objection of Quine's again raises the question we have already discussed above, whether there are predicates that differ in meaning but which stand for the same concept. We have answered this question in the negative. And Quine's criticism is no reason to give this position up now. The expression '$\imath g(p \wedge g = f)(x)$' does not make sense in this form, for in it a proper name ('$\imath g(p \wedge g = f)$') is placed in the position of a predicate sign in front of the argument '(x)'. The correct way of writing it must read: '$x \in \imath g(p \wedge g = f)$' ('the object x falls under the concept $\imath g(p \wedge g = f)$') – but in that case the proper name $\imath g(p \wedge g = f)$' occurs in '$N(a \in \imath g(p \wedge g = f))$' for which one can assume that it has a different sense from 'f', so that now a difficulty for the Fregean semantics no longer arises. Alternatively, one must replace the proper name by a predicate, namely by the expression $p \wedge f(x)$ (It is surely supposed to be true that $\wedge x(\imath g(p \wedge g = f)(x) \equiv p \wedge f(x))$) – but in that case it is obvious that the concepts $f(x)$ and $p \wedge f(x)$ are not identical and so the predicates '$f(x)$' and '$p \wedge f(x)$' do not have the same sense, so that the difficulty is once again avoided.

In the case of Frege himself a formula like $\imath g(p \wedge g = f)$ is also completely impossible because identity is defined only for objects and only objects can be identified by description, not predicates which according to their basic definition are always predicatively applied.

1.5. Carnap's Method of Extensions and Intensions

To develop his basic semantic ideas in [56], Carnap proceeds from the distinction between *intension* and *extension*. This distinction is especially natural for *predicates*: We construe the intension of a predicate as its meaning, thus for example a one-place concept as the intension of a one-place predicate[62]; we construe its extension, on the other hand, as the class of objects that fall under the concept. Thus on this view, for example, the extension of a two-place predicate is a class of ordered pairs that stand in the relation the predicate signifies. Two *n*-place predicates have exactly the same extension, therefore, if they apply to the same *n*-tuples of objects. While the question of the identity of intension of predicates is a linguistic question, the question of the identity of their extensions is (for empirical predicates) an empirical question. Predicates with the same intension always have the same extension, but the converse does not hold, as is shown by the example of the predicates 'creature with a heart' and 'creature with a kidney', if we may assume that precisely those creatures that have a kidney also have a heart.

The distinction intension – extension is now carried over by Carnap to sentences and proper names as well. The proposition is regarded as the intension of a *sentence*, its truth-value as its extension. What is specified as the intension of a *name* is the *individual concept* – this term remains without any more exact explication, but perhaps we can regard the individual concept as an identifying concept, however chosen. The object it designates is specified as the extension of a name. It is plain that this distinction corresponds to the Fregean distinction between sense and meaning$_F$. There are two differences between Carnap and Frege, however:

(1) In the first place, Carnap misses in Frege a more precise criterion for identity of sense and he himself offers two explications of the concept. The first concept is that of *identity of intension*. In this connection intension is understood in an essentially broader way than Frege's sense. Namely, it is the case for Carnap that two *predicates* have the same intension when it is logically provable that they apply to precisely the same arguments, that two *names* have the same intension when the identity of the objects they designate is logically provable and that two *sentences* have the same intension when their equivalence is logically provable. For the sake of brevity, we will, like Carnap, speak of the *logical equivalence* (in short, *L*-equivalence) of expressions in all three of these cases. Carnap thus defines identity of intension by way of *L*-equivalence.[63]

A sharper concept of identity of sense than that of identity of intension is that of *intensional isomorphism*, which we will discuss below.

(2) In order not to have to admit as Frege does that the same expressions have different meanings (or intensions and extensions) in different contexts, Carnap furthermore abandons the general principle of substitution, according to which substitution of expressions with the same meaning in any context you please is possible *salva veritate*. Instead Carnap defines extensional and intensional contexts as follows:

He calls an occurrence of an expression in a sentence *extensional* (*inten-*

sional) (or says that this expression stands in an extensional (intensional) *context*) if substituting for it an occurrence of any other arbitrarily chosen expression with the same extension (intension) does not change the extension (intension) of the sentence (and if it is not extensional).[64] So far as its content is concerned, this procedure comes out the same as Frege's: There are contexts in which reference is made essentially to the sense of linguistic expressions (in which what is being spoken of is not their meaning$_F$ but their sense), and so in these contexts expressions with the same meaning$_F$ can not be exchanged *salva veritate*.

The substitutability of expressions with the same extension *salva veritate* is restricted to extensional contexts, then, and the substitutability of expressions with the same intension *salva intensione* is restricted to intensional contexts.

Now there are, however, also *non-intensional* contexts, i.e. contexts in which the unregulated substitution of intensional expressions can alter the context's intension, indeed not only the intension but the truth-value as well. For example, belief sentences like 'Hans believes that p' are of this kind. This sentence can be true and a sentence 'Hans believes that q' can be false, although p and q are L-equivalent.

No matter in which particular way one may interpret belief sentences[65], whether in the sense of 'Hans has the disposition to affirm the sentence 'p' (or a synonymous sentence)' or in the sense of believing a proposition – in any case of a rational and adequate interpretation of the concept of belief it can be shown that belief contexts are not intensional. One must have a narrower concept of sense than that of intension in order to find a criterion of substitution in these cases.

Carnap introduces the concept of *intensional isomorphism* for that purpose[66] in the following way: two sentences are intensionally isomorphic precisely when they are built in the same way (with the same logical operators in the same order) out of descriptive constants of the same type that have the same intensions. For example, the two sentences '$F(a) \wedge \wedge \neg G(b)$' and '$H(c) \wedge \neg I(e)$' are intensionally isomorphic if the sentences '$\wedge x(F(x) \equiv H(x))$', '$\wedge x(G(x) \equiv I(x))$', '$a = c$' and '$e = b$' are logically true. On the other hand it does not hold true that sentences that are produced from each other by logical transformations are intensionally isomorphic or that, for example, the two sentences $F(a, b)$ and $F(b, a)$ are intensionally isomorphic, even if the sentence $\wedge xy(F(x, y) \equiv F(y, x))$ is logically true.[68]

Carnap applies this concept of intensional isomorphism for an analysis of belief sentences and the paradox of analysis.[69] We do not wish to go into it any more deeply here, however, and will only remark that as an explication of the concept of identity of sense according to Frege the concept of intensional isomorphism is on the one hand too narrow – we saw above that Frege regards the sentences $A \wedge B$ and $B \wedge A$, for example, which are not intensionally isomorphic, as having the same sense; and on the other hand, it depends on the choice of basic constants whether this concept is not too broad for the criterion of substitution in belief sentences. For if $F(x)$ and $G(x)$ are two concepts in number theory, for which $\wedge x(F(x) \equiv G(x))$ holds true as a non-trivial mathematical principle, then the sentences $F(a)$ and $G(a)$ would be intensionally isomorphic: it could be, however, that Hans believes that $F(a)$ but not that $G(a)$ is true.[70] With an adroit choice of basic constants, however, one will always be able to bring it about that the concept of intensional isomorphism is not in any case too broad.

✳ Carnap's most striking contribution to realistic semantics in [56] lies in his formulation of criteria for identity of intensions which show how intensions may be defined.

According to Carnap two expressions, e.g. two sentences A and B have the same intensions if they are L-equivalent, i.e. if the sentence $A \equiv B$ (A iff B) is logically true. $A \equiv B$ is logically true, if it is true in all interpretations of the individual and predicate constants occurring in A and B. This can also be expressed by saying: $A \equiv B$ is logically true, if it is true in all logically possible worlds. Then its truth value is independent of contingent facts. This means: A and B have the same intensions, if they have the same extensions, the same truth-value, in all possible worlds. And this may be generalized: Two expressions have the same intensions, if they have the same extensions in all possible worlds. But this means that we can determine the intension of an expression A as that function which assigns to A in every possible world the extension A has in that world.

If we know the meaning of A, and therefore its intension – synonymous expressions always have the same intensions – we can determine the extension of A in a world i in principle (i.e. if we are provided with the necessary factual information on i): the object which a proper name A designates in i, the class of objects having the property expressed by a predicate

A, and the truth-value of a sentence A. We can, therefore, coordinate to A a function, assigning the extension of A in i to i for all possible worlds i.

The inversion of this principle, that this function also uniquely determines the intension of A, defines the notion of intension in contradistinction to that of meaning. As S. Kripke, R. Montague and others have pointed out, this Carnapian idea for the definition of intensions may also be generalized into a definition of meanings. As we have seen, the intensional identity of two expressions A and B does not imply their synonymity. Only if A and B may be substituted *salva veritate* for each other in all contexts, can we say that they are synonymous. Belief-sentences, for instance, show, however, that such a general substitutivity does not hold for intensionally identical expressions. But we can narrow the concept of intension into a concept of meaning by admitting not only logically possible worlds but also logically impossible ones. Not every logical inconsistency is obvious; so there may be worlds that some person considers possible although they are inconsistent. If a function f assigns extensions of A also to those worlds that are possible only in a weaker sense, then we may define the meaning of A by f. A and B are then synonymous if they have the same extensions in all weakly possible worlds.

We shall not elaborate this point. It was only mentioned to show how meanings may be brought into intensional semantics.

The effect of Carnap's definition of intensions may be illustrated by the problem of ostensive proper names that was pointed out in Chapter II.1.2. We can now determine the sense of a proper name A, its individual concept, as that function g, which assigns each world i the object designated by A in it. If A has the form of a definite description $\imath x F(x)$ its extension $g(i)$ in i depends on the extension of the defining predicate F in i, i.e. on the function f which determines the extension of F in every world. From f we obtain g by postulating that $g(i)$ be that object a such that $g(i)$ is the unit class of a in case such an object exists; otherwise $g(i)$ is to be an arbitrary object b (the same for all i). (If F does not fulfill the normal condition for a description that it applies to only one object then it is usual to interpret $\imath x F(x)$ as a name for such an object b.) The intension g of $\imath x F(x)$ is therefore determined by the intension f of F, as we maintained in II.1.2. The reference of $\imath x F(x)$ will generally be different in different worlds. For ostensive proper names, however, it seems adequate to interpret them as *standard names*, i.e. to assign them the same reference in all worlds. For with such names we designate objects as individuals, independently of their contingent properties. There is no reason, then, to designate Chicago by 'Munich' in another world. This procedure implies that the function f which represents the intension of an ostensive proper name A has the same value in all worlds; the reference of A, therefore, also determines the intension of A. That is the reason to say that such names are semantically completely characterized by their reference and have no meaning over and independent from that. For a detailed discussion of these questions see Kripke [72].

1.6. *The Concept of Truth in Realistic Semantics*

We will not go into the criticism of the fundamental principles of realistic semantics until the sections following. In concluding the presentation of this semantics, however, reference should be made to one further point that has on occasion been the basis of an unjust criticism of semantic realism. The criticism in question has to do with its concept of truth.[71]

In semantics nowadays the predicate 'true' is applied for the most part to sentences, not to propositions.[72] In ordinary usage, on the contrary, 'true' is certainly more frequently applied to propositions. Thus for example, we say 'It is true that Kuno is 40 years old' rather than '"Kuno is 40 years old" is true'. But since one can move from a concept of truth for propositions to a concept of truth for sentences and vice versa – the following principle does hold: A sentence is true if and only if the proposition is true that it expresses – this distinction does not play any important role.

The *correspondence theory* describes the concept of truth in realistic semantics. This concept has been formulated for modern logic by Alfred Tarski in [35], by the following truth convention: (K) A sentence '....' is true if and only if.... On this account, then, the sentence 'It was raining in New York at 10:15 local time on February 4, 1960' is true if and only if it was raining in New York at 10:15 local time on February 4, 1960.

This concept of truth is derived from Plato and Aristotle and in the philosophical tradition it was usually formulated in the following way, or something similar: 'A sentence is true if and only if the proposition it expresses agrees with reality'. The abbreviated formula reads: *veritas est adequatio intellectus ad rem*. This formulation is supposed to give an

answer to the question of the content of the concept of truth. In contrast
to the meaning relationship, one cannot stipulate the concept of truth in
a purely conventional way: If the meanings of the terms of a sentence are
fixed, then the question of its truth is a question of fact, not any matter of
stipulation.

The traditional definition of truth has been legitimately criticized. For
what does 'agreement' mean in this case? When does an abstract, conceptual structure like a proposition agree with concrete reality, or a sentence like 'Emil is happy', as a sequence of written signs, with Emil's
happiness? To explain the concept of truth by the concept of agreement is
to explain one obscure concept by another one that is still more obscure.[73]

On the basis of this difficulty and other inadequacies in the correspondence concept,[74] not always understood quite correctly, to be sure, attempts have been made to replace this concept with others. For example,
Franz Brentano wishes to replace the correspondence concept with a
concept of evidence, by stipulating:

A judgment (sentence) is true if it is made with evidence or if anyone
who made an evident judgment about the same object would accept that
judgment.[75]

But apart from the fact that the truth-conditions for the subjunctive
conditional occurring (necessarily) in the second part of the definition are
not determined,[76] there is still no absolute evidence from which the truth
of a sentence would follow with rigor. And so Brentano's definition gives
an answer rather to the question of when we are justified in making a truth
claim – namely when we have good reasons, i.e. 'evidence' – than to the
question of truth.

Further, an attempt has been made to replace the correspondence
theory with a *coherence theory* of truth, according to which the truth of
sentences is not defined in terms of their agreement with reality, but in
terms of their (logical) compatibility with each other. But what that
amounts to is the acceptance after the manner of the *convention theory* of a
contradiction-free set of sentences as true by convention and then
defining the truth of other sentences in terms of their compatibility with
the sentences already accepted as true. Such a theory was formerly advanced by Carnap and the Vienna Circle, for example.[77] But we do not
call a sentence true because we accept it by convention, but we accept it
because, on the basis of observation, for example, we hold it to be true.

The convention theory is thus hard to reconcile with the empirical procedure of the sciences.

Another objection to the correspondence theory, which also concerns formula (K), has been advanced by P. F. Strawson in [49] and [50]. According to Strawson the predicate 'true' is not a descriptive predicate, but serves an expressive purpose in ordinary discourse, namely the confirmation of one's own or someone else's statements, as in 'What I said is true' or 'What Fritz said is true', for example. In such sentences I am not talking about sentences but confirming them. In its descriptive use, on the other hand, the sentence 'The sentence A is true' says nothing more than the sentence A itself, i.e. adding the word 'true' says nothing, the assertive power of the sentence lies not in the addition of the word 'true', but, as Frege says, in the form of the sentence itself.

Even if there are other non-descriptive uses of the word 'true' besides its descriptive use, it does also have an important descriptive function, so that by no means do we lack an explanandum for convention (K) in ordinary language, as Strawson says. For we divide sentences into true and false and we say, for example, 'If A and B are true, then $A \wedge B$ is also true', 'All logical consequences of true sentences are true' and so on. In the semantic characterization of sentences the word 'true' actually plays an important role, then, and in this role the word is purely descriptive.[78]

The difficulties in the traditional formulation of the correspondence theory that have been cited are best evaded by asking about the meaning, or the use of the predicate 'true' instead of about the nature of truth – as if truth were a pre-existing concept we could describe by virtue of a platonistic talent for observation. For just as the question of the essence of redness leads to difficulties, although we are familiar with the sense of the word 'red' and know how to use it correctly, the question of the essence of truth is only a misleading formulation of the question of the use of the predicate 'true'. If we ask about use, we can say along the lines of the correspondence theory: A sentence 'A' is called true if and only if reality is just as the proposition represents it. But reality is just as the proposition A represents it if and only if A. That is, we can say 'A sentence 'A' is true if and only if A'. The use of the word 'true' is so specified and this convention is simply what remains of the correspondence theory of truth as it was formulated by Tarski.[79]

The semantic realist may now feel his real intentions betrayed by these reductions, as he wanted to understand truth as a relation between sentences and reality. But this relation is not some third thing that ties reality and the sentence together, rather declarative sentences are used to make true statements about reality. The reference to reality in question lies in the sentences themselves, then. To that extent the sentence '*A* is true' says no more than the sentence *A* itself, and the concept of truth is reduced to convention (K), to characterizing the truth of *A* by *A* itself. There is no general, independent meaning of the predicate 'true'. What it means that *A* is true can only be explained in terms of *A* or in terms of conditions equivalent to *A* that vary from one sentence to another. Likewise there is no general criterion of truth, but the testing of sentences looks quite different from case to case. In order to determine whether it is raining, one must look out the window, to determine whether a material contains iron, one must make a chemical analysis, and in order to determine whether there is an infinite number of prime numbers, one must carry out a proof. The criteria of truth for sentence *A* are nothing but the criteria for the use of *A*.[80]

Therefore the general problem of truth that may originally have been intended does not even exist.

The situation is similar with the relation of concept and object. That a concept applies to an object does not consist in the fact that a relation holds between the two, such that the one satisfies the other, a relation that could be defined generally in and of itself. On the contrary, the concept is itself predicative, the concept itself applies to an object or does not apply. Therefore the question of the nature of the satisfaction relation also reduces to the convention: Object *a* satisfies concept *F* if and only if $F(a)$.[81]

NOTES

[1] The boundary between descriptive meaning and other modes of meaning will be stated more precisely in II.4.5.

[2] Along with many other theories of meaning that could not arouse any general interest, we shall not take up in what follows the so-called *verification theory*, which is expressed in Moritz Schlick's formula: "The meaning of a proposition is the method of its verification" ([36], p. 148), although it has played a certain part in discussions falling within the philosophy of language. The reason is that this theory belongs in the context of a discussion of empirical criteria of meaning, and that belongs to the methodology of the empirical sciences. See Kutschera [72], 3.4.

[3] See also the presentation of naturalism in Lyons [69], p. 4ff.

[4] See also Grebe [66], p. 419ff.

[5] Cratylus 423b–e. (Citations follow the edition by H. Stephanus, Paris 1578.)

[6] 426c–427b.

[7] See 422d–e. – In 393b–421c Plato gives a series of etymological analyses that are almost without exception fully untenable.

[8] See 435c.

[9] See e.g. 399a.

[10] 435a–b.

[11] 432d. Thus the German 'kikeriki', the English 'cock-a-doodle-doo', and the French 'coquerico' are different onomatopoetic formations with the same representational content. See Grebe [66], p. 419.

[12] See 385b–d.

[13] For this reason the predicate 'true' is often applied not to sentences but to the meanings of sentences, propositions, as the Stoics did, for example.

[14] The formulation of conventionalism in the *Cratylus* is given by Hermogenes in 384c–d: "... I can not convince myself that there is any principle of correctness in names other than convention and agreement. Any name which you give, in my opinion, is the right one, and if you change that and give another, the new name is as correct as the old – we frequently change the names of our slaves, and the newly imposed name is as good as the old. For there is no name given to anything by nature (φύσει); all is convention (νόμος) and habit (ἔθος) of the users." [Benjamin Jowett's translation.]

[15] Indeed it is generally the case that not all non-linguistic signs are equally suited for all purposes. Thus the sign '→', because it suggests a direction, is better suited to serve as a signpost than the sign '0' is, etc.

[16] See 435a–b.

[17] 390d–e.

[18] See 388d.

[19] See 368d–e.

[20] See Chapter II.4 and Chapter 4.

[21] Since the philosopher (διαλεκτικός) is the one who correctly comprehends the ✓ essence of things, it is also his task to lay down the correct linguistic norms, i.e. he must function as linguistic lawgiver (νομοθέτης, ὀνοματουργός) (390c–d).

[22] Thus this comparison of words with tools (ὄργανον ἄρα τί ἐστι καὶ ὄνομα 388a), which later became fundamental in Wittgenstein's philosophy of language, appears as early as the *Cratylus*.

[23] *Dialogus*, in: *Die philosophischen Schriften von G. W. Leibniz*, edited by C. J. Gerhardt, VII, Berlin 1890, p. 192. The passage cited reads: "Nam etsi characteres sint arbitrarii, eorum tamen usus et connexio habet quiddam quod non est arbitrarium, scilicet proportionem quandam inter characteres et res, et diversorum characterum easdem res exprimentium relationes inter se. Et haec proportio sive relatio est fundamentum veritatis."

[24] On realistic semantics' concept of truth see also Chapter II.1.6.

[25] The meaning of this sentence depends on the time at which it is uttered. But according to (4) – and this is our argument – it would not depend only on that.

[26] G. Frege and E. Husserl especially reacted strongly against psychologism in semantics (and in logic), as it dominated the last half of the 19th century. See Frege [18], Part I, and Husserl [00], as well as the correspondence between Frege and Husserl.

[27] Naturally that is also true of proper names for abstract objects such as numbers, classes and the like.

[28] See Chapter II.4.4.

[29] On the problem of universals see Stegmüller [56], for example.

[30] The example comes from Frege, see [92].

[31] Quine [48], p. 9.

[32] The distinction between meaning and reference is just as old as semantics itself. According to Aristotle (*De interpretatione*) linguistic expressions mean (in a conventional manner) ideas or concepts and not just objects.

And Sextus Empiricus says in *Adversus mathematicos* VIII, 11 : "The adherents to the Stoa say that the following three things belong together: What is meant, what is supposed to mean, and the thing. That which has the function of meaning is supposed to be the sound (in language) itself, e.g. 'Dion'. What is meant is the proposition, made intelligible through the words and which we comprehend because it is in our mind, but which the barbarians do not understand even though they do hear the spoken sound. The thing itself is what exists outside (of our consciousness), e.g. Dion himself. Among the items named here, there are supposed to be two of a corporeal nature, namely the sound and the thing, and one of an incorporeal, namely what is meant, the *lekton*, which also possesses the property of truth or falsity."

[33] In the German edition, the reference is to the way in which the distinction is drawn in English, and Quine [64c] is cited.

[34] This view is not shared by a large number of authors, such as e.g. A. Church [51a] and W. V. Quine [64b]. We shall come back to this point in the context of Chapter II.1.4.

[35] Frege made this terminological distinction in [92].

[36] What was said in note 34 is correspondingly true here.

[37] How one chooses to proceed here is also a matter of expediency. – In logical atomism (see e.g. Russell [18]), in order to assure a reference for all proper names and a truth-value to all sentences, an ideal language was postulated in which proper names stand only for unanalyzable atomic objects. See also Chapter III.2.1.6.

[38] That holds true only for so-called *direct* or *extensional* contexts. Generally speaking, the statement is true only if supplementary assumptions as to the reference of words in oblique contexts are made, as Frege did. See Chapter II.1.4.

[39] On the theory of definite descriptions see e.g. Carnap [56], §§ 7, 8, Linsky [67], Searle [58] as well as Kutschera [71], 13.2.

[40] See e.g. Kutschera [67], 5.3.

[41] See also what Wittgenstein says in [53], 79.

[42] Quine, taking this line in [48], recommended that all proper names be replaced by definite descriptions. This procedure – if agreement as to the descriptive predicates could be reached in translating proper names into definite descriptions – would be logically correct. But it is another question whether ostensive proper names are not practically indispensable nevertheless. For proper names give sentences a direct and simple reference, while the reference of sentences without proper names is significantly more complex. That comes out in the fact, for example, that a sentence like 'Hans is blond' can be decided by direct observation, by checking only one object, whereas the sentence 'There is one and only one thing with such and such a nature and that thing is blond' would require examination of the whole universe in order to determine its truth-value, and as a combined universal and particular proposition would not be definitively decidable. Furthermore, it is extraordinarily difficult to cite identificatory predicates that do not contain ostensive proper names (e.g. names of spatial and temporal locations) themselves. – Ayer takes this line in [63], p. 150.

[43] G. Ryle in [66] calls attention to the fact that ostensive proper names are not entered

in dictionaries, in which meanings of words are given, and that there are no translations for such names. That too shows: their primary function lies in their reference, not in their meaning. One does not ask 'What does "Salvador Dali" mean?', but 'Who is Salvador Dali?' On the meaning of proper names see also Strawson [50a] and Searle [58].

44 Wittgenstein [22].

45 See also the clear and brief presentation in Stegmüller [65], pp. 525–561, which follows Stenius.

46 There is no lack, among the many interpretations of the *Tractatus*, of such as interpret the semantics of the work, despite the large number of Wittgenstein's unambiguously realistic formulations (which are then dismissed as 'metaphorical' or 'non-essential'), as non-realistic. See e.g. Schwyzer [62], Shwayder [60] and [63], and Lorenz [70], Chapter I, 3. So far, however, these interpretations have not been supported by sufficiently convincing arguments.

47 In his remarks Wittgenstein always presupposes an ideal language along the lines of the symbolic language of modern logic; correspondingly simple assignments cannot be given for ordinary languages.

48 Instead of this Wittgenstein could also have said: A sentence is a picture of a state of affairs [Sachverhalt] if the isomorphy condition is satisfied, and it is true if the state of affairs of which it is a picture is a fact. It may be that Wittgenstein did not take this course because he wanted to admit only pictures of 'existing' entities (facts, not states of affairs), and only facts as pictures of facts. – Wittgenstein also speaks of a sentence *presenting* a state of affairs but *picturing* a fact.

49 For structures this coordination is expressed in the fact that they are taken to be ordered *n*-tuples, in which the *i*th relation in the first structure corresponds to the *i*th relation in the second.

50 From the differentiation between the function of language as *representing* and as *communicating* or *showing*, which is based upon naming, Wittgenstein derives some quite drastic consequences for epistemology. We shall come back to them in Chapter IV.4. This epistemological thematic is the central concern of the *Tractatus*; the semantic theory on the other hand serves only to provide a foundation for the epistemological theses. Thus Wittgenstein writes to Bertrand Russell on August 19, 1919: "Now I'm afraid you haven't really got hold of my main contention to which the whole business of logical propositions is only corollary. The main point is the theory of what can be expressed by propositions, i.e. by language (and, which comes to the same thing, what can be *thought*) and what cannot be expressed by propositions, but only shown: which I believe is the cardinal problem of philosophy." (Cited in Griffin [64], p. 18.)

51 In this point Wittgenstein is perhaps already preparing his later notion, which we shall go into in II.4.5, that sentences and predicates are meaningful not as objects, but as speech acts.

52 Reprinted in Frege [69]. – On what follows see also Ch. Thiel's presentation in [65].

53 See Frege [92], p. 27, Note 2.

54 See Frege [92], p. 29ff.

55 Frege knew only the categorial distinction, concept (or more generally: function) and object. For him propositions (thoughts) are objects. But now the property of being true is not a genuine property, for the sentences 'It is raining' and ' "It is raining" is true' have the same content. The declarative character of sentences does not lie in the addition of 'is true', but in the form of declarative sentences (see Frege [92], p. 34). So

all that remains is to regard truth values as objects. – What lies behind this rather inadequate solution is just Frege's antecedent decision to interpret concepts as functions with the values 'true' and 'false', which is possible only if truth values are regarded as objects. This artificial simplification permits him to unify his symbolism in an important respect even if it does not contribute to its perspicuity.

56 See Frege [92], p. 32f.

57 Frege [92], p. 37.

58 See Schilpp [42], p. 660–667

59 For discussion of Moore's paradox, see also Carnap [56], p. 63, and Langford [42].

60 See Church [43a], [43b], [51a], [51b].

61 See Quine [64b].

62 Carnap is more inclined to the locution which has it that the intension of a predicate is an attribute, see [56], p. 21, but this way of putting it surely has to do above all with the drawing of a line between concepts and ideas in Frege's sense, i.e. subjective mental data.

63 Frege formulates a corresponding criterion for predicates of which the substitution instances are not (not all, or all not – that remains open) logically determined in the fragment cited, '*Ausführungen über Sinn und Bedeutung*'. Such predicates are supposed to have precisely the same meaning if and only if they have identity of intension in Carnap's sense. In [18], Part III (pp. 39, 44, 48) Frege gives many L-equivalent propositions an identical meaning, e.g. the propositions $A \wedge B$ and $B \wedge A$, A and $\neg \neg A$, $A \supset B$ and $\neg B \supset \neg A$, and so on. But it is very much in question whether this criterion is not too broad for Frege's purposes (validity of the general substitution principle): For belief sentences a more narrowly defined identity of meaning for predicates and sentences perhaps has to be adopted. – In his article *Satz und Tatsache*, reprinted in Patzig [70], G. Patzig discusses whether facts can be conceived of as Carnapian intensions of true sentences.

64 The case of non-extensional contexts, which on substitution of expressions with the same intension do change their intension but not their extension, is not expressly characterized. The following survey may clarify the terminology.

(1) If substitution of expressions with the same extension leads to contexts with the same extension, then we have an *extensional* occurrence.

(2) If substitution of expressions with the same extension does not lead to contexts with the same extension, then their occurrence is non-extensional.

These non-extensional contexts subdivide as follows:

(2a)   If L-equivalent substitution leads to L-equivalent contexts, then that is an *intensional* occurrence

(2b)   If an L-equivalent substitution does not lead to L-equivalent contexts, then it is a *non-intensional* occurrence.

These non-intensional occurrences can be further subdivided – as noted, Carnap does not do this –

(2ba)   An L-equivalent substitution leads to contexts with the same extension.

(2bb)   An L-equivalent substitution leads to contexts that do not have the same extension.

We can illustrate this with the following figure:

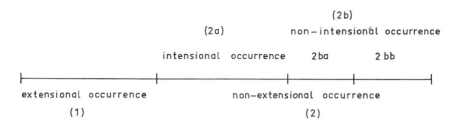

[65] See Carnap in [56], pp. 53–55.

[66] See Carnap [56], p. 56ff.

[67] This definition presupposes an artificial language constructed according to strict formation rules.

[68] Cp. C. I. Lewis's similar concept of synonymity in [43], discussed in Carnap [56], p. 60ff.

[69] See Carnap [56], 15, especially p. 61f. Church's critique of these analyses is to be found in [50], [54], Carnap's reply to them in [56], p. 230ff.

[70] See Mates [50], Scheffler [55], Putnam [54], Pap [55] and [57], Church [54], Davidson [63], Linsky [49].

[71] On what follows see Stegmüller [57], Chapter XII also.

[72] At any rate, in the case of states of affairs (*Sachverhalten*) we do not speak of 'true' and 'false', but of 'subsistent' and 'non-subsistent' states of affairs.

[73] This difficulty is also illustrated by a notation in Wittgenstein's journal for Oct. 27, 1914: "The difficulty faced by my theory of logical picturing was that of finding a connection between the marks on the paper and a state of affairs out there in the world. I always said truth is a relationship between the sentence (*Satz*) and the state of affairs (*Sachverhalt*), but was never able to make out such a relationship." ([61], p. 19f.)

[74] Franz Brentano criticizes it, contending that:

(a) mathematical or logical propositions (*Sätze*), that do not say anything about real, but only about ideal structures, would not be true according to this definition (but that holds only if one is not a Platonist and takes the concept 'reality' too narrowly in the sense of 'physical reality'),

(b) true sentences to the effect that a certain object *a* does not exist could agree only with non-existent things, and consequently there could be no talk of agreeing or corresponding with reality in this case (but propositions are not supposed to correspond to things, but rather to states of affairs, and it is a real state of affairs that there is no *a*),

(c) on this definition, establishing the truth of a proposition would lead to an infinite regress, since in order to establish that a proposition *A* is in accord with a state of affairs *B*, one would have to have already formulated a true judgment about *B* (but the correspondence theory is supposed to characterize the concept of truth, not to provide a criterion of the truth of propositions).

[75] See Brentano [30].

[76] Cf. however D. Lewis [73].

[77] See Carnap [32], Hempel [34] and Neurath [32]. – We will come back again to the role of conventions in defining true sentences in another context in Chapter II.4.4.

[78] Stegmüller also expresses himself along these lines in [57], p. 225ff.

[79] In the formulation of the truth convention as ' "*A*" is true if and only if *A*', '*A*' is to

be read as a quasi-quotation, i.e. much in the same sense as 'the mention of *A*'. (See Kutschera [67], I.3.1.1.)

[80] Kant, too, emphasizes that there is no general criterion of truth in the *Critique of Pure Reason*, B 83, where he says:

"If truth consists in the agreement of knowledge with its object, that object must thereby be distinguished from other objects; for knowledge is false, if it does not agree with the object to which it is related, even although it contains something which may be valid of other objects. Now a general criterion of truth must be such as would be valid in each and every instance of knowledge, however their objects may vary. It is obvious however that such a criterion [being general] cannot take account of the [varying] content of knowledge (relation to its [specific] object). But since truth concerns just this very content, it is quite impossible, and indeed absurd, to ask for a general test of the truth of such content. A sufficient and at the same time general criterion of truth cannot possibly be given. Since we have already entitled the content of knowledge its matter, we must be prepared to recognize that of the truth of knowledge, so far as its matter is concerned, no general criterion can be demanded. Such a criterion would by its very nature be self-contradictory." [Norman Kemp Smith's translation.]

[81] The satisfaction relation was introduced by Tarski in [35]. On the predicative nature of concepts see also Frege [92b].

2. BEHAVIORISTIC THEORIES OF MEANING

We discussed the realistic semiotic first above because historically it represents the oldest type of theory of meaning and is at the same time the reference point from which all other theories set out. They have all been built up from a criticism of the realistic account, which at first glance seems so natural and convincing.

There are two points in particular in which all of the semiotic theories discussed in what follows basically differ from realism. Realistic semantics starts out, as we have seen above, from the idea that the meaning of linguistic expressions consists in a representational relationship to things, established by convention and capable of being considered in abstraction both from the expression's relation to speaker and hearer and its use on particular concrete occasions. This isolation of language from its context of use and this rendering absolute of its representational function is cut to fit the descriptive meaning of declarative discourse above all, which is the almost exclusive subject of inquiry in realistic semantics.

The semiotic theories referred to in the following – if one wanted to have a single general name for these very diversified theories, one could contrast them to realistic theories as *pragmatic* theories, with reference to the philosophical direction of pragmatism, which was founded by Charles Peirce, William James and John Dewey and was understood by Peirce to be a semiotic theory to begin with[1] – start out, as against realism, from the following two ideas:

(1) Speech is a form of human behavior that has its place in the general course of human life. Therefore its function is always to be analyzed with this context as a background. The realistic account, according to which the semantic function, the meaning, of a linguistic expression can be defined independently of the context of its use, is therefore false. Language is used in the course of various activities, for various purposes, in various situations. Therefore one can not ascribe to language just *one* semantic function, but there are as many semantic functions as there are contexts of activity in which language is used. Semantics can consequently not be pursued independently of pragmatics. As against the realistic account, which is directed from the beginning at declarative discourse alone, pragmatic semiotic thus reveals anew the variety of types of discourse and wishes to undertake a more comprehensive analysis of lin-

guistic behavior, one which brings in the particulars of the context of utterance.

(2) Abstract entities, such as concepts and propositions and the meanings of linguistic expressions in the realistic account generally, are no more available to scientific, intersubjective, empirical observation than ideas and intentions in the mind, which represent meanings in psychological semiotic theories. The only thing available to such observation and hence the only thing a scientific study of language has to go on is language use. Meaning has to be determined by it. On this view, whenever two expressions systematically differ in their use, one will also have to make out a difference in meaning between them, just as conversely differences in meaning can only be made out where there are differences in use. There is, then, a one-to-one relationship between meaning and language use and it requires but a small stroke of Occam's razor to give up the assumption of abstract meanings as entities entirely and to identify the meaning of a linguistic expression with its use. Pointing in this direction, Peirce, the founder of pragmatism, had already said "... there is no distinction of meaning so fine as to consist in anyting but a possible difference of practice." [2]

Behavioristic theories of language constitute an initial group within what we have called pragmatic theories of meaning. In them the identification of language use and meaning and the methodological viewpoint that language theory has to start from intersubjectively observable linguistic phenomena is fulfilled in a very radical way. The phenomenon of speech is understood as overt conduct in the behavioristic sense, and language use as linguistic behavior, which is then described in terms of the classical behavioral concepts, stimulus, response, etc.

In the following we shall present behaviorism in terms of the ideas of two of its principal advocates, Charles Morris and Burrhus F. Skinner.

2.1. *Charles Morris*

We will first go into semiotic as Charles Morris developed it in his book, *Signs, Language and Behavior* (1946). Morris bases his theory on a behavioristic conceptual apparatus in which behavior is described in the stimulus-response scheme.

(a) *Signs*. Morris starts out from a general concept of sign, which is not restricted to linguistic signs, but according to which the sound of a bell that regularly precedes a dog's feeding is for the dog a sign of food. He refers to older behavioristic definitions according to which a sign for *a* is a substitute stimulus that evokes the same reaction *a* would evoke if *a* were present. The sound of the bell is a standard example of such a substitute stimulus for the food, which evokes the same response as food itself does (Pavlovian response).

This definition, however, is not usable, since linguistic expressions or signs do not have to evoke immediate reactions. (A sign that an Alpine pass I do not wish to travel over is closed does not interest me and so evokes no response in me, but if I do want to travel by it, the response, instead of being immediate, does not come into play until the next cross-roads, where I can turn off in the direction of another pass.) Furthermore, a word like "boss" does not evoke the same response as the boss himself in the flesh, but may evoke quite different responses (one might curse him out, something one would refrain from doing in his presence).

In view of these flaws in the definition, Morris developed a more complicated account along the lines of a definition which reads somewhat as follows:

(I)   If Z is a preparatory stimulus which produces in an organism a disposition to respond under certain circumstances with a (goal-directed) form of behavior of type T and if a is a stimulus object that evokes (goal-directed) behavior of type T, then Z is a *sign* for a.[3]

A *preparatory stimulus* in this connection is a stimulus that affects responses to other later stimuli.

Despite these modifications (preparatory stimulus, which does not have to be sufficient to release a response all by itself, evocation of dispositions to respond instead of responses, similarity instead of identity between the responses to the sign and what it signifies, and response not to the sign itself but the inclusion of further stimuli from the environment) and qualifications (Morris understands condition (I) to be only a sufficient, not a necessary condition for signs[4]) of the original definition this account is not yet sufficient. For in the first place, this stipulation does not cover a broad spectrum of linguistic signs (for example, reports of past events, such as 'Thutmosis I died in 1510 B.C.', generally do not evoke any disposition to respond and sentences the hearer does not hold to be true do not evoke any disposition to respond either[5]). Furthermore (I) is also too broad, as a sufficient condition, (a drug that increases excitability and so produces a disposition to respond violently to a derogatory remark ('certain conditions') – a similar response, then, as might otherwise be provoked by a physical assault – we will scarcely want to claim is a sign of a physical assault). And finally the definition's conditions are formulated very vaguely. (How is the talk of similarity of responses to be understood, for example? What are the 'certain conditions'? There is also no reference to the subjects in whom responses or dispositions are evoked: Is it all human beings or some of them or most of them?[6])

Furthermore, 'definition' (I) takes no account of the fact that linguistic signs at least have meaning in a conventional way, i.e. they do not evoke certain dispositions by virtue of their syntactic nature alone, but by virtue of their use as established by means of conventions. Signs have to be understood in order to produce a behavioral disposition. If someone does not understand a linguistic sign, it will not evoke any disposition in him. I.e., only those persons who do understand the sign in question can be admitted as organisms in which a disposition is evoked according to (I). A sign does not count as such without qualification but only for certain persons. The concept of understanding, however, is not a behavioristic concept.

Besides that, it should be noted that under the same circumstances different hearers can respond quite differently to the same linguistic signs. Thus for example, X_1 is very happy at the news that Mrs. N. N. is dead (he owed her money), X_2 is sad (she owed him money), the news does not affect X_3 at all, since he did not know Mrs. N. N. If need be – although it would be very artificial – these differences can be blamed ('certain conditions') on existing dispositions in X_1, X_2, and X_3, but Morris' account makes no provision for that, since he understands 'certain conditions' in the sense of environmental conditions.

The example of Morris' attempt at a definition already shows how extraordinarily difficult it will be to define the concept of sign behavioristically, since we have to do with a very general, abstract concept that does not relate to any homogeneous type of responses or dispositions to respond.

Going on from this concept of sign Morris then defines the *interpretant* of a sign as the behavioral disposition the sign evokes in the hearer, its *referent* (*denotatum*) as an object toward which the action the sign disposes the hearer to perform is directed, its *meaning* (*significatum*) as the conditions of which it is true that everything which fulfils them is a referent of the sign. In the example of the bell as signal of the dog's food, the sound of the bell is the sign, the dog's disposition to look for food in a particular place the interpretant, the food the referent and the possibility of being eaten in a certain place the meaning of the sign.[7]

Linguistic signs are then defined as signs that come into play in the context of social behavior and have the same meaning for speaker and hearer,[8] and are limited as to the possibilities of their being combined by syntactic rules of language, for example. A language is then a set of such linguistic signs.[9]

That a linguistic sign has the same meaning for X and Y presupposes that it evokes the same dispositions to goal-directed actions in X and Y, for same meaning presupposes same referent (the same class of reference objects) and same referent once again presupposes dispositions to actions directed toward the same objects. But if X says to Y, 'There is a hornet on your head', there can be no talk of like dispositions, i.e. the condition is much too narrow for linguistic expressions. Furthermore, single words like 'red' or 'Zugspitze' would not be linguistic signs on this view, because – outside the context of a sentence – they do not evoke any definite behavioral dispositions to respond in and of themselves. Sentences on the other hand do not evoke behavioral dispositions similar to those evoked by stimulus objects, but at most like those evoked by stimulus situations.

(b) *Types of Expression.* Morris next attempts to define behavioristically certain basic types of expressions, namely *identifying* expressions such as 'here', 'in this or that place', 'at this or that time', for example, *descriptive*, such as 'blue', 'warm', 'hard', *evaluative* (*appraisive*) such as 'good', 'bad', and *prescriptive* expressions such as 'should'. His project is already subject to the objection that words are not used either descriptively or evaluatively, etc., but can have different characters in different contexts and can be both descriptive and evaluative in the same context. Now this classification is supposed to be carried out behavioristically on the basis of the way in which these expressions signify, i.e. what sorts of disposition they evoke in the hearer. If the disposition evoked is inclined to concentrate responses on certain space-time locations, then we have an *identificator* before us, if it is inclined to direct behavior toward things with certain characteristics, then we have a *descriptor*, if the disposition is directed toward preferring certain objects, we have an *evaluator* (*appraisor*), and if the disposition is directed toward preferring certain forms of behavior, we have a *prescriptor*.[10]

Now these definitions are obviously much too primitive, for the expression 'on November 4, 1940' evokes no disposition to direct responses to November 4, 1940, in me – how would I even do that?! And if a lowbrow philistine says, 'This picture is beautiful' – I don't prefer it to another on that account. And likewise a beggar's appeal, 'Lend me a hundred dollars, please', does not yet bring it about that I carry out that action or even have a disposition to do so.

(c) *Types of Discourse.* Morris also attempted to describe the differences among the various types of discourse in terms of his behavioristic concepts and to give a classification of types of discourse. He chooses his arrangement of classes according to *modes of signifying*, i.e. according to the main type of expression in the statement and according to its purpose (from the speaker's point of view) and arrives at Table II.[11]

In this scheme, *formators* are formal expressions such as logical operators, punctuation marks, etc., for example,[12] and systematic use is a use for the systematization of a body of knowledge or a set of statements. Morris says: The systematic use of signs is a use with the intention of systematizing the behavior evoked by other signs.[13] Since these two concepts both remain very vague, we will pay no attention to the last column on the table. The types of discourse entered in the individual compart-

TABLE II

Mode of Signifying	Informative	Evaluative	Evocative (incitive)	Systematic
Designative (predominantly descriptors)	Scientific Language	Story-telling (fictive)	Juridical	Cosmological
Evaluative (Evaluators)	Mystical	Poetic	Moral	Critical
Prescriptive (Prescriptors)	Technological	Political	Religious	Propagandistic
Formative (Formators)	Logico-mathematical	Rhetorical	Grammatical	Metaphysical

ments are not supposed to be defined by this classification, but merely constitute illustrations of the classification types. This looks somewhat as follows:

A *story* (*fiction*) is written in descriptive language, but it does not serve the purpose of informing about facts, but of evaluation, as in a novel of social protest, for example.

A *poem* is written in evaluative language and serves valuational purposes as in Schiller's 'Ode to Joy', for example.

In *myth* a story is told in valuational language for the purpose of information, as in the tale of Buddha having been a hare in an earlier incarnation, who offered himself to a starving monk as food and before he leaped into the fire shook himself so that no insect in his fur would be killed.[14]

It is obvious that the characterization of concrete types of discourse by way of this classification is much too rough. The classification can only be understood as an indication of how types of discourse could be defined from the behavioristic point of view.

In estimating the value of Morris' book, one must take note that Morris himself was very well aware that what he had provided was more a program than a scientific theory. He writes: "Our account bristles with problems, it sketches a program more than it records an achievement."[15] So far as we have not already done so above, here too we will make no criticism of the details – for the details can be modified – nor will we make any criticism of the fact that Morris has used concepts in his analysis that do not belong to the behavioristic vocabulary, such as 'valuational', 'purpose', 'command', etc.[16] Instead we will go into nothing but the fundamental features.

If Morris' definitions were supposed to lay down the foundations of his semiotic and to show that the basic semantic concepts can be satisfactorily defined on a behavioristic basis,[17] then this plan can not be described as successful. The definitions can rather serve as illustrations of the extent of the chasm that yawns between program and execution in that theory. As in the case of the behavioristic definitions of psychological concepts we are left at the beginning with general declarations of intention. Precisely by their total failure to satisfy, the definitions give an impression of the dreadful difficulties any execution of this program encounters. Certainly a sign is for the hearer a stimulus – the sound or the mark is an acoustic or optical stimulus – otherwise the sign would not be perceived. And certainly the understanding of signs can be described as a behavioral disposition, if it be only a disposition to give a suitable answer to the corresponding question. But the nature, the manner of the connection between stimulus and disposition is so complex – and the dispositions take so many different forms – that a description of the semantic function of linguistic expressions in terms of these concepts is, at least at this time, an extremely – one might almost say a hopelessly – complicated enterprise. We lack any terms in which to characterize semantic categories (proper name, predicate, sentence), to analyze phenomena such as indirect discourse, etc. To that extent is the behavioristic conceptual apparatus wholly incapable of being used to analyze concrete, even simple and fundamental linguistic facts.

√ Further, it is certainly possible to study speech as concrete behavior, to ask: How does a hearer react to being stimulated by certain speech sounds, how does he put them to use, and so on. And it is entirely possible that these investigations will bring interesting results to light. But the question is whether such investigations are relevant to the problems in the philosophy of language that concern us here.

Let us take an example: The mathematician also uses signs and one can inquire about his behaviour in using these signs, can study which mathematical signs he responds with upon which stimuli, and so on. But all of that is wholly irrelevant to mathematics itself. For arithmetic, the assertion that one often responds to the sign '$2+2$' with the sign '4' or the like is totally insignificant. The mathematician is not interested in the behavior of mathematicians but in mathematical concepts and operations. Behavioristic analyses provide no information about them, however. The behavioristic approach to language resembles the attempt to understand mathematics by observing the behavior of mathematicians.

Furthermore, the behavioristic theory of language is also mistaken because it attempts to grasp the phenomenon of language as a naturalistic phenomenon. When a behaviorist speaks of language neither he himself nor his audience understands it as a natural process of the sort he describes: as responses to stimuli or as the production of substitute stimuli. Understood in this way, his utterances remain totally irrelevant scientifically speaking, as much so as his yawning or clearing his throat or his imposing mannerisms.[18] In fact, the behaviorist's speech is of quite a different sort from the language he is speaking of; but it remains beyond the horizon of his inquiries. In terms of the philosophy of language, however, the question as to how the language behavior of others can be described scientifically is not relevant. The relevant question is: What are we doing when we are talking about something, when we make statements with the claim that they are true, for example?[19]

2.2. *B. F. Skinner*

In order to round out the picture of behavioristic semantics, we will briefly comment on B. F. Skinner's book *Verbal Behavior* [57], which plays an important role in recent discussions of the philosophy of language. Skinner, who has worked predominantly in the area of research in animal behavior, attempts in this book to apply the conceptual apparatus of experimental behavioral research to the phenomenon of language. He believes that recent progress in the area of behavioral research makes the prospects for such attempt appear to be very good.[20]

Skinner's work has been extensively discussed by N. Chomsky in [59b] and we shall refer to his excellent critique often in what follows.[21]

Skinner starts from the model of simple behavior experiments. One experiment has already been considered above, that a dog learns to look for food in a certain place (response) when he hears the sound of a bell (stimulus). What we have to do with in this case are *conditioned responses* evoked by a specific stimulus, and Morris has responses of this type in mind when he wishes to analyze linguistic activity behavioristically. An experiment of another type consists in placing a rat in a cage in which there is a lever the rat can work. Now if a pellet of food falls into the cage when the lever is pressed, the rat learns to get food by working the lever when it is hungry. In this case it is not a matter of behavior evoked by a stimulus, but of *instrumental* behavior, and Skinner as opposed to Morris interprets language behavior as instrumental behavior of this sort. One can go on to put a light in the cage as well and arrange things so that a pellet falls into the cage only if the light is on. Then the rat learns to press the lever only in case the light is on.

With experimental designs of such a simple kind the rat's behavior can be controlled by experimentally specifiable parameters and so can be described as a function of those parameters. Skinner's intention is to analyze language behavior in a similar way as a function of observable parameters. Now since language behavior is not behavior that is controlled through simple experimental conditions, however, the question arises as to what behavioral parameters to take into account in this area, what counts as stimulus and what as responsive or instrumental behavior.

In general, a *stimulus* is supposed to be a physical object or event that regularly produces certain responses. *A response*, on the other hand, is an item of behavior that regularly follows upon certain stimuli.

Right here we encounter the first fundamental difficulty for the behavioristic conceptual apparatus. If we define stimulus and response independently of each other, and so admit as stimuli everything that can release responses – thus practically all of the objects and events the organism can perceive – and as response every form of behavior, then it is not possible in general, on the basis of the experimental results, to give any functional analysis of behavior within the stimulus-response scheme, in which behavior is determined as a function of external conditions according to laws. The connection between the behavior and the external conditions is in general much too complex and so far it has evaded adequate description. On the other hand, if we define stimulus and response, as above, by way of their law-governed connection, then if we explain responses in terms of stimuli, we are in effect explaining responses by themselves, for a stimulus is only a stimulus if the response follows it. To put it another way: A specific, non-trivial definition of stimulus and response can be given only for the simplest cases, in which a lawful connection between stimulus and response phenomenon has already been demonstrated or is suspected. Thus for example, in the simple experimental set-up described turning on the light can be defined as stimulus and pressing the lever as response. But that holds only for this experiment; in general not every case of turning on a light is a stimulus and not every case of pressing a lever a response.

Along with the basic concepts of stimulus and response, Skinner also uses other behavioral concepts in his book, in particular so-called *operants*. These are forms of behavior for which no stimulus directly releasing them can be observed. An example of an operant is pressing the lever when the light is not on. If pressing the lever results in food being delivered, the operant is thereby *re-inforced*. The *strength* of an operant can be defined in terms of the number of actions (lever-pressings) during the period of *extinction*, i.e. from the last re-inforcement to the time action stops. If pressing the lever when the light in the cage lights up always produces food, and the rat thus learns to press the lever when the light is on, lighting the light then serves as a *secondary re-inforcement* of the operant, pressing the lever.

Skinner now wishes to apply these and similar behavioral concepts to language behavior. Once again the difficulty arises that these concepts are defined only for simple experimental set-ups. What the strength of an operant is in general, for example, remains completely open. If one wishes to describe speech-activities, say, as operants, what then is the strength of these operants? What is the period of extinction in this case? Skinner generalizes the use of these terms without any more detailed explanation. The terms still have a scientific ring to them, to be sure, but they are no longer precise and well-defined scientific terms. For Chomsky has shown in [59b] that on the basis of the narrow, well-defined use of these terms derived from behavioral research Skinner's analyses seize on almost no relevant aspect of linguistic behavior, but that upon a metaphorically generalized use they are unclear and their use signifies no scientific progress in any case.[22]

Going beyond that, many analyses and definitions on Skinner's part are simply inadequate. When, to take a Skinnerian example, a sonata is played and a listener says 'Mozart', the music is supposed to be the stimulus and the word 'Mozart' the linguistic response aroused by this stimulus. The listener might equally well say 'awful', 'beautiful', 'My grandmother always liked to hear that', and so on. In order to explain a specific response Skinner has to assume a specific stimulus, which is different in all the cases of responses cited. But what objective stimulus corresponds to the last answer? It is obvious that subjective factors define the stimulus in this case, i.e. stimuli lose their external, physical character. Besides, we can only identify the stimulus by way of the response, and so we can not explain or predict responses on the basis of stimuli. With that this analysis becomes worthless.

Further, according to Skinner a proper name, for example, is a response to a specific person or a specific thing,[23] but proper names are also used in the absence of the object they denote, indeed even when the speaker has never seen that object. Where then is the stimulus in this case? And if it is said that for the speaker the referent of an expression (which Skinner identifies with its meaning) is nothing but the probability that the speaker will utter the name in the presence of the relevant object,[24] that too is inadequate. The probability that a German will use the word 'Munich' while he is in Munich is rather less than when he is in America, for example.

Going on beyond general behavioral terms, Skinner also uses special terms for linguistic behavior. According to him[25] 'language behavior' is behavior that is re-inforced through the intervention of other people. But this definition is obviously much too broad, since otherwise even training an ape, for example, would be language behavior.[26] Besides that, the definition is also much too vague for anything to get started with it.

Going on beyond this, there are still further specific forms of linguistic behavior to be found in Skinner, such as 'mands', 'tacts',[27] 'echoic' and 'autoclitic operants' and the like, none of which are well-defined and which are used again and again – so far as one can determine – in ways that deviate from their definitions. Chomsky is right, then, in saying that Skinner's procedure is "just a kind of play-acting at science".[28] All that is presented is a bombastic pseudo-scientific terminology which offers nothing for any relevant distinctions, descriptions or explanations.

Finally, K. S. Lashley has emphasized in [51] that the behavioristic accounts of linguistic theory in no way do justice to grammatical phenomena. Sentences are not sequences of words with which some stimuli happen to be coordinated. So far, however, we lack any usable account that interprets grammatical structures behavioristically.[29] In the final analysis, then, not a single relevant linguistic distinction can be adequately expressed in terms of behavioristic concepts. And so in what follows we can neglect the behaviorists' attempts at philosophy of language with a good conscience.

NOTES

[1] 'Pragmatism', too, is an over-all title for very different sorts of philosophical enterprises, so that we are not running too great a risk that our designation of semiotic theories as 'pragmatic' will cause their authors to be regarded as pragmatists in some special sense.
[2] Ch. S. Peirce, Collected Papers V, ed. Ch. Hartshorne and P. Weiss, Cambridge, Mass. 1965, p. 257.
[3] See Morris [46], p. 10.
[4] See Morris [46], p. 12.
[5] On this point see Stenius [67], p. 261 also.
[6] The 'definition' (I) has the following form: '$R(Z) \wedge D(Z, X, T, B) \wedge O(Y) \wedge \wedge B(Y, T, X) \supset S(Z, Y)$', where '$R(Z)$' stands for '$Z$ is a preparatory stimulus', '$D(Z, X, T, B)$' for 'Z produces in X a disposition to behave along the lines of T under

condition B', '$O(Y)$' for 'Y is a stimulus object', '$B(Y, T, X)$' for 'Y produces behavior of type T in X', and '$S(Z, Y)$' for 'Z is a sign for Y'. Either that is to be understood in such a way that there are still quantifiers to take their places in the antecedent (otherwise free variables occur in the 'definiens' that do not occur in the 'definiendum') – but in that case the question is open as to where to put the quantifiers: different groupings of quantifiers lead to quite different stipulations – or these variables are actually supposed to be free – then one can also write (I) as '$R(Z) \wedge \vee TBX (D(Z, X, T, B) \wedge O(Y) \wedge \wedge B(Y, T, X)) \supset S (Z, Y)$' thus arriving at the absurd conclusion that any preparatory stimulus Z is a sign for any stimulus object Y that evokes a goal-directed behavior pattern T, for there is for every Y a T and a B – namely the condition that Y itself is present – such that $D(Z, X, T, B) \wedge O(Y) \wedge B(Y, T, X)$ is true. Presumably it should read: There is a T and a B (dependent on Y and T) such that for all X.... We base what follows on this interpretation.

[7] See Morris [46], p. 17.

[8] Morris calls such signs *consigns*, see Morris [46], p. 33.

[9] See Morris [46], p. 36.

[10] See Morris [46], p. 66.

[11] See Morris [46], p. 125.

[12] See Morris [46], p. 87.

[13] See Morris [46], p. 104.

[14] Morris gives this example in [46], p. 134f.

[15] Morris [46], p. 246.

[16] It is quite dubious and in any case an entirely unproved thesis, up to the present, that there will be any success in translating these terms into behavioral terms.

[17] See Morris [46], p. 60.

[18] See Russell [40], p. 4 also.

[19] In the philosophy of language we are not interested in describing linguistic behavior as a natural process but in understanding the meaning and purpose of speech acts as actions. This makes for a vast difference in the conceptual apparatus involved.

[20] Skinner writes ([57], p. 3): "It would be foolish to underestimate the difficulty of the subject matter, but recent advances in the analysis of behavior permit us to approach it with a certain optimism. New experimental techniques and fresh formulations have revealed a new level of order and precision. The basic processes and relations which give verbal behavior its special characteristics are now fairly well understood. Much of the experimental work responsible for this advance has been carried out on other species, but the results have proved to be surprisingly free of species restrictions. Recent works have shown that the methods can be extended to human behavior without serious modification." Other behavioral researchers do not share this optimism. N. Tinbergen, for example, says: "We may now draw the conclusion, that the causation of behavior is immensely more complex than was assumed in the generalizations of the past.... Second, it will be obvious that the facts at our disposal are very fragmentary indeed." ([51], p. 74, quoted in Chomsky [59b]).

[21] For criticism of Skinner see also Hörmann [67], p. 214ff.

[22] See Chomsky [59b], p. 31.

[23] See Skinner [57], p. 113.

[24] See Skinner [57], p. 115.

[25] See Skinner [57], p. 2.

[26] See Skinner [57], p. 108, note 11, on this point. ('The animal and the experimenter comprise a small but genuine verbal community'.)

[27] Skinner gives this definition: "A 'mand', then, may be defined as a verbal operant in which response is reinforced by a characteristic consequence and is therefore under the functional control of relevant conditions of deprivation or aversive stimulations" ([57], p. 35f.). And: "A tact may be defined as a verbal operant in which a response of given form is evoked (or at least strengthened) by a particular object or event or property of an object or event." ([57], p. 81f.). Mands are thus supposed to be something like imperative (evocative) expressions, tacts something like descriptive expressions, but it is not possible to extract that from the 'definitions'. They are so vague that one can not assess them as anything but helpless appeals to the reader's good will.

[28] Chomsky [59b], p. 39.

[29] Chapters 12 and 13 in Skinner [57] also illustrate the total inadequacy of the behavioristic conceptual apparatus for characterizing grammatical structures.

3. Quine's philosophy of language

Quine's most important ideas on semiotic are contained in his books, *From a Logical Point of View* [64a], *The Ways of Paradox* [66], and *Ontological Relativity* [69a].[1]

Quine's pragmatic approach is already distinct in the introduction to his principal work in the philosophy of language [60], when he writes: "Language is a social art. In acquiring it we have to depend entirely on intersubjectively available cues as to what to say and when. Hence there is no justification for collating linguistic meanings, unless in terms of men's dispositions to respond overtly to socially observable situations."[2] These statements even bring Quine into the neighborhood of linguistic behaviorism. It may not be ignored, however, that Quine contrasts favorably with the proponents of behaviorism we discussed in II.2. His ideas are essentially more detailed, more precise and better founded. That becomes possible because he perceptibly goes beyond the, as we saw, much too narrow compass of behavioristic analysis of language. Actually the behavioristic approach expressed in the above quotation remains with Quine only a program which is never put into practice. Quine almost never attempts to present semiotic distinctions in terms of purely behavioristic concepts. Indeed, the 'hence' in the above quotation is a *non sequitur*, for the acceptance of non-behavioristically defined meanings is justified if the function of language and linguistic behavior can be better understood and analyzed with them.

Referring to Quine's formulation, N. Chomsky in [68] has shown in particular that linguistic response dispositions are very different from individual to individual (they depend on mood, information, education, capacity for perception, etc.), so that they are not eligible as (intersubjective) meanings. On account of the wealth of possible ways of formulating something in language, furthermore, the probabilities of a specific linguistic response that define such dispositions lie close to 0 for all expressions.[3] We can therefore leave Quine's behavioristic-programmatic statements out of account.

In the following we will select from what Quine has said about the philosophy of language three topics that have special systematic interest.[4]

3.1. *Quine's Elimination of Meanings*

Quine differentiates two theories in semiotic: a *theory of reference* of lin-

guistic expressions and a theory of meaning.[5] Now while according to
Quine the theory of reference, thanks to the work of Tarski,[6] is an essentially sound scientific discipline, the theory of meaning suffers from the
fact that its basic concepts are unclear and its basic assumptions doubtful.
Without yet presupposing the pragmatic identification of meaning and
use, Quine wishes to show first of all that assuming meanings along the
lines of realistic semantics is not justified.

In discussing this thesis, we will restrict ourselves to the realistic
meanings of sentences, propositions, since the arguments for concepts
sound much the same.

The starting point of Quine's claim is that (1) it is superfluous to accept
propositions, that (2) besides, an unobjectionable definition of propositions is not possible and that (3) the acceptance of propositions would
imply making meanings something absolute, for which there is no empirical basis.

We will now go into these three claims in greater detail:

(1) According to Quine the argument most commonly offered in favor of
assuming sentence meanings reads somewhat as follows: We distinguish
between meaningful and meaningless sentences, and so the predicate
'meaningful' obviously has a well-defined content. But a sentence can be
meaningful only if there is something it means, for 'to mean' is a transitive
verb. If someone claims that a sentence A is meaningful he must be able
to say what A means. If there were no meanings of sentences, then there
would be no meaningful sentences either.[7]

Quine argues against this that we in no way have to interpret the predicate 'x is meaningful' – symbolically $S(x)$ – in the sense of $\bigvee yB(x,y)$ where
$B(x,y)$ stands for 'x means y'. Instead, we can regard this predicate as a
basic predicate. Indeed there are many linguistic expressions whose
grammatical usage does not correspond to their logico-semantic function.[8] Besides that, we do not answer the question of the meaning of a
sentence by indicating a proposition, but by giving a synonymous sentence
(which is formulated in another language or in simpler or more precise
phrasing, etc.) And so we do not need to assume any meanings of sentences; it is sufficient to make use of the two concepts 'meaningful' and
'synonymous' – in symbols $G(x,y)$.[9]

The significance of Quine's proposal lies in the fact that in this case the realm of dubious propositions is eliminated. The range of application of the two basic predicates $S(x)$ and $G(x, y)$ is the set of sentences, thus concrete linguistic expressions, while the range of y in $B(x, y)$ was the totality of all propositions.

While $S(x)$ and $G(x, y)$ can be defined in terms of $B(x, y)$ ($S(x) := \bigvee y B(x, y)$ and $G(x, y) := \bigvee z(B(x, z) \wedge B(y, z))$, on account of the difference in the ranges over which they are defined, $B(x, y)$ cannot be defined in terms of $S(x)$ and $G(x, y)$. Classes of synonymous sentences are co-ordinated with the meanings of sentences in the realistic sense, however, and therefore it is now possible to regard or represent the meanings of sentences as classes of this sort and to define a relation $B^*(x, y)$ corresponding to $B(x, y)$ by way of $B^*(x, y) := y = \lambda z G(x, z)$.

On this reconstruction of the meanings of sentences, they no longer appear to be independent of language, as on the realistic interpretation, but appear definable only with the aid of linguistic expressions, as on the pragmatic interpretation.

To be sure, the problem of the meaning of sentences is not eliminated without anything left over, for the question remains as to how the relation of synonymity, which we usually understand as identity of meaning, is to be defined as a basic relation intuitively without recourse to meanings. But on the pragmatic interpretation this question can be answered by saying that sentences are synonymous if they are used in the same way (for the same purposes, in the same situations), and are thus exchangeable for each other in all contexts. Of course that is only a preliminary answer, since the concept of the use of linguistic expressions still requires much clarification itself, but we will not go into that until Chapter II.4.3.

Indirect contexts, such as 'X says (wishes, claims, knows, believes, desires, etc.) that...' and 'X asks (doubts, inquires, etc.) whether...' constitute a further argument for accepting propositions. These contexts are interpreted in realistic semantics, as we saw, in such a way that what we have before us in these cases is a relation between a person and a proposition, for obviously nothing is said about sentences, about utterances of X in them. If X says that it is raining, it does not follow therefrom that X says 'It is raining'. He can also say, for example, 'Es regnet.'

But these contexts can also be interpreted in such a way that they do make an assertion about a sentence which is invariant in truth-value (as in content) upon the replacement of this sentence by any other synonymous sentence.[10] In order to make this explicit and clear, in the sentence 'Fritz says that he was in Munich' the predicate 'saying that...' can be replaced by a predicate 'saying*'..., which is then explicated as follows: a says* 'A' if and only if x says that A.[11] Then it is true of 'saying*', as opposed to 'saying', that: A is synonymous with $B \supset (x$ says* $A \supset x$ says* B).[12] On this interpretation the occurrence of such intensional contexts does not force us to accept propositions – at least not propositions which can not be defined as classes of synonymous sentences.

In a similar vein, Quine has proposed reconstructions of such contexts according to which they are not assertions about sentences.[13] He starts with the attempt to replace the sentence (1) 'Galileo said that the earth moved' with the sentence (2) 'Galileo said, "The earth moves"'. That is obviously inadequate, since Galileo did not speak English, so that (1) is true and (2) false. Therefore Quine reconstructs (1) by means of sentence (3) 'Galileo said in Italian, "The earth moves"'. The predicate 'saying in Italian' is on this account a new basic predicate, which can be explicated as follows: 'x says y in Italian' means the same as 'x utters an Italian sentence which is synonymous with y'.

The like direction is taken by a proposal of Scheffler's in [54], which translates (1) as (4) 'Galileo made a "The earth moves" – utterance'. Here the expression '"The earth moves" – utterance' can be defined as the designation of an utterance synonymous with the sentence 'The earth moves'.

It is crucial to both proposals that 'synonymous' be regarded as a well-defined predicate which is not clarified in terms of 'meaning the same proposition'.[14]

The reconstruction of wish and belief sentences in Quine is less convincing, however, since in these cases statements about wishes, etc., do not come into play. Consequently, the general proposal offered above for the understanding of such contexts taken altogether appears to be the most acceptable one. Even it is of only limited interest, however, since Quine's rejection of propositions, as we shall yet see, proves to be unfounded.

(2) We now come to Quine's second and stronger thesis, that an unobjectionable definition of propositions is impossible.

A minimal requirement for a definition of propositions is that it must include a criterion for the identity of propositions. That is, a criterion for the identity of sentence meanings, i.e. for the synonymity of sentences must be given. Now Quine maintains that a sufficiently sharp classificatory concept of synonymity, according to which two propositions are either synonymous or not, can not be given.

Quine's claim is directed not only against the realistic assumption of autonomous propositions independent of language, but also against the usefulness of the pragmatic reconstruction of sentence meanings as classes of synonymous sentences, and against the scientific use of any talk of sentence meanings and synonymy whatever.

To begin with, according to Quine the everyday pre-scientific concept of synonymity can not be used as a scientific concept, for it is very imprecise and a decision as to the synonymity of two sentences can be justified only in very simple cases. Furthermore, this concept is more a comparative than a classificatory concept, i.e. the synonymity we mean in ordinary discourse is more a matter of more-or-less than of either-or. As a rule there is only a greater or a lesser similarity of meaning between two sentences, not any strict identity of meaning.[15]

And finally synonymity in the pre-scientific sense always holds only for specified contexts and under specified conditions, never without qualification. The pre-scientific concept, especially as a comparative concept, is not suited, then, for the definition of propositions, for propositions are either identical or they are not – they are not more or less identical.[16] Indeed, as a comparative concept the pre-scientific concept is not even capable of being used as the basis for introducing a classificatory scientific concept by way of an explication to make it more precise. So the scientific concept would have to be given an entirely new definition.

But Quine has already emphasized in [51] that there is no general definition of 'synonymous'. For example, if '$G(A, B)$' were to be defined by '$A \equiv B$ is analytically true', that would be circular. For analytic sentences are defined precisely as just those sentences which are logically true or can be derived from logically true sentences by substituting for some expressions others that are synonymous.[17]

But if '$G(A, B)$' is defined by 'A and B are definitionally equivalent',[18] that is noo narrow, for natural languages in any case, which lack explicit definitional stipulations,[19] but which do contain synonymous sentences, such as 'Fritz is a bachelor' and 'Fritz is an unmarried man'.

Finally, if reference were made in the definition of synonymity to criteria of substitution, one would once again be involved in a circle. For if '$G(A, B)$' is defined as 'A can be substituted for B in all contexts (sentences) without any change in their *meaning*', one would have to know beforehand what the meaning of a sentence is, or when two sentences are synonymous. But that is precisely what is supposed to be defined. But if '$G(A, B)$' is defined as 'A can be replaced by B in all contexts *salva veritate*', then there are among these contexts either contexts that are also intensional like 'A is analytically equivalent to B' – and then one is no wiser than before[20] – or the contexts are restricted to extensional sentences – and then the criterion is too broad and would have to be sharpened by the requirement of *salva analyticitate* instead of *salva veritate*.

Now naturally one could regard 'analytic' as a basic concept, i.e. forego a definition of this concept and define 'synonymous' with its help. For Quine, however, the concept of analytic sentence is problematic through and through, as we shall see, and so that procedure is excluded for him.

The arguments advanced by Quine against accepting a precise definition of synonymity, especially one precise enough for defining propositions, are not sound, however. In the first place, a classificatory concept of synonymity can be defined even with a comparative concept 'x and y are equally or less similar in meaning than u and v': x and y are *synonymous*: = x and x are less or equally similar in meaning than x and y. Lexicons, dictionaries, and the criteria we use in determining the correctness of a translation also bear witness against the claim that the pre-scientific concept of synonymity is so imprecise as to be completely useless for the analysis of meanings. And even if synonymity should exist only for specific contexts and consequently the meaning of a sentence would always have to be established only for specific contexts, that would be no serious hindrance to defining propositions on the basis of the everyday concept of synonymity by way of abstraction, since Quine himself remarks that every linguistic expression has a definite meaning only in definite contexts.[21]

On the basis of Quine's arguments, then, there is no justification for supposing that the pre-scientific concept of synonymity does not constitute a foundation for a scientific explication of this concept, as linguistics does indeed undertake to do. Naturally the concept, like all empirical concepts, has a certain horizon of vagueness and is not defined with absolute precision; it may even require, more than many other empirical concepts, supplementary delimitations, but it is not plain why such delimitations should not be possible and why the concept should not function well in practice. We do not forego talking of biological species or of the juristic properties of the facts of a case because it may be impossible to define them with ultimate clarity in all cases.

The following objection is more decisive: As we saw in Chapter II.1.5. Carnap has shown in [56] a way for the definition of intensions and meanings by extensional concepts. This approach has been developed in recent years, especially by Richard Montague into an intensional semantics, which works with the extensional concepts such as 'function' and 'class' acknowledged even by Quine. Within its bounds the concept of proposition can be exactly defined, as well as the concepts of the intensions of predicates and proper names. Quine's critique of the theory of meanings has been largely overtaken by this development.[22]

(3) Quine's third argument against accepting propositions goes:

If we assume that propositions are determinate entities, then identity must be defined for them as well. If a definition is then given along the lines of realistic semantics: 'Two sentences are synonymous if and only if their meanings are identical', then what we have is a sharp classificatory concept of synonymity which holds not only for sentences in one language but can be applied to sentences in different languages. But according to Quine there can be no such absolute concept of synonymity because of the thesis of indeterminacy of translation.

Since we will bring forth arguments against this thesis below, we will not go into Quine's argument in any greater detail here.

Quine makes the same criticisms of accepting concepts as meanings of predicates as he makes against accepting propositions. His arguments run quite parallel to those discussed above, however, and therefore we will not go into them more closely here.

3.2. Quine's Arguments Against Analytic Judgments

A distinction is usually drawn in philosophy between *truths of reason* and *truths of fact*, between *analytic* sentences, whose truth results from the meanings of the terms that occur in them alone, and *synthetic* sentences, for which that is not the case.[23] In his essay, 'Two Dogmas of Empiricism',

Quine attacked this distinction and he has further expanded on his arguments in later publications.

Quine gives essentially two reasons for his thesis that there are no sharp boundaries between analytic and synthetic sentences:

The *first* argument runs as follows: The concept 'analytic' is an artificial concept of science which has to be defined. The usual definition is: A sentence is analytic if and only if it can be derived by the replacement of terms in a logically determinate sentence (i.e. a sentence which is true or false on purely logical grounds) by other synonymous terms. But according to Quine, this definition can not be used, since, as was discussed above, a concept of synonymity sufficiently precise for the definiens is not available.

Our response to that has been that the ordinary concept of synonymity is actually not as imprecise as Quine makes it out to be and that it can be defined exactly within intensional semantics. But since we have already urged that the definition of analytic sentences, as Quine gives it, is too narrow, even with a sufficiently precise definition of synonymity, one would not obtain any satisfactory definition of analytic sentences.

Second, according to Quine's behavioristic program, the term 'analytic' is to be defined so that we can tell by observing the linguistic behavior in a population P whether a sentence is used in P as an analytic sentence or not. It is problematic, however, if there are any sentences at all which are used in a clearly analytic way.

The difference between analytic and synthetic sentences is by no means as clear and unambiguous as it is often represented to be. One already gets into trouble when one wishes to cite analytic sentences that are not logically determined. The following examples are found:

(1)   All bachelors are unmarried.
(2)   All bodies are extended.
(3)   What is green is not (all) red.

But with a little imagination for all of these sentences empirical conditions can be found under which one would possibly regard them as false, so that the analytic character of these sentences is doubtful. If, for example because of some blunder in the legislative process, every man were declared married? And if on the basis of physical theory it should prove to be meaningless to apply the concept of spatial extension to elementary particles (as bodies)? Or if all men were to become color blind and so could no longer distinguish between red and green? Would one still regard sentences (1) to (3) as true in these cases?

Naturally, one could always say that sentences (1) to (3) hold afterwards as they did before, for there would just no longer be any bachelors, according to physical theory elementary particles would not be bodies, and after as before no objects would be red and green at the same time, but we would just have lost the capacity for distinguishing between red and green.

But we could also say that the sentences would then be false: A bachelor would still be a man not living in matrimony; every object that may be localized would still be a body; and 'red' and 'green' would designate colors as perceived by men with normal sensory constitution as before.

In the face, then, of such remote contingencies we are uncertain what to say. And in such cases even Carnap's proposal is of no help, which he illustrates with the following example: In order to determine whether a person X regards the sentence (i) 'All ravens are black' as analytic or not, it is sufficient to put the following question before him: 'Mr. Smith caught a white raven yesterday, which I will be glad to show you. In the face of that fact, are you ready to withdraw your statement (i)?' Now if X answers: 'I would never have believed there are non-black ravens, and I still won't believe it until I have seen one with my own eyes. But in that case I shall naturally have to regard (i) as false', that makes it clear that X does not regard (i) as an analytic, but as a synthetic sentence. But if X answers: 'There can't be any such thing as a non-black raven. If a bird is not black, I do not call it a raven. So if Smith says he has found a white raven (and he isn't lying or joking) then he must understand either the word 'raven' or the word 'black' in a different sense from the one in which I understand it', it is then clear that X regards sentence (i) as analytic.[24]

In view of the uncertainty in the face of very unusual situations such an inquiry will neither elicit clear responses from individuals nor will there be a convergence toward a common opinion in a population.

As D. Lewis has emphasized in [69] we have to distinguish two concepts of analyticity here. On the one hand there is the predicate 'sentence A is analytic in language S' which may be defined by 'A is true in all worlds on which the interpretation of S is based', on the other hand there is the predicate 'Sentence A is analytic in the population P' which may be defined by 'A is analytic in that language S which is the language of P'.

In order to determine whether A is analytic in P we then first have to ascertain which language is spoken in P. Lewis believes that the use of a language in P is determined only for normal situations of communication so that there may be a set $\mathfrak{S}$ of precise languages (e.g. in the sense of intensional semantics) such that all S in $\mathfrak{S}$ are compatible with the normal usage in P although they differ for remote and unusual occasions. The languages in $\mathfrak{S}$ may then diverge, especially for worlds representing such unusual contingencies, contingencies that we normally do not contemplate. But sentences may be distinguished uniquely as analytical in P only if they are analytical in all languages in $\mathfrak{S}$, and Lewis believes that it is very well possible that there may not be such sentences at all. The indeterminacy of the concept 'analytic in P' as against 'analytic in S' therefore has its basis in the fact that the use of language in P is compatible with different logically precise languages.[25]

This analysis, however, is not quite adequate. It is not the case that all members of P speak well defined though different languages S – then Carnap's test would give clear results at least for the individual speakers. It seems to be more adequate to say that members of P speak essentially (i.e. not counting the peculiarities of their idiolects) the same language S, but that this language is only well defined for normal situations of communication and vague or undefined for other cases. Natural languages are not precise in the logical sense, and therefore the application of the concept 'analytic in S', which is exactly defined in the logical case, to natural languages yields no precise distinctions.

Quine's *third argument* against the distinction analytic-synthetic is this: According to Quine analytic sentences can not be sharply marked off from synthetic, because they are supposed to hold true on the basis of the meanings of their terms alone. But according to Quine the meaning of a term is not independent of which of the synthetic sentences that contain that term we accept as true. The meaning of a term changes with our assumptions about the world; consequently, questions of meaning and questions of fact can not be rigorously separated.

If my views about the world gradually change in such a way that I come to believe the same things about cats that I now believe about dogs, and about dogs the same things I now believe about cats – am I then supposed to say that the meanings of the words 'dog' and 'cat' have remained constant, and that only my views about the world have changed? But that would obviously be incorrect, for the characteristics and criteria of the concepts have changed completely: A dog is now an animal that meows, a cat an animal that barks, etc. It is more correct to say that together with my beliefs the meaning of the words has changed for me: A dog is now something other than it was before and therefore the definition of an animal as a dog no longer has the same content it had before.[26]

Here is a further argument: We do not learn linguistic expressions all by themselves, but in a context of sentences and situations. That holds especially for predicates, which we learn by example in [logically] singular contexts, such as 'This apple is red', 'This lemon is not red', and in general contexts such as 'All human beings die sometime', 'That is not a bird but a butterfly; birds have feathers, but butterflies do not'.

It is not so, then, that we observe and state facts and, as an activity entirely separate from that, establish the meanings of words, but rather learning language and experiencing the world stand in a very close relationship: The facts we accept determine the meanings we connect with our linguistic expressions.[27]

Finally, one can also argue in the following way: It is usually said that meaning is first attached to single terms, proper names and predicates, and that the meaning of a sentence is then a function of the meaning of its terms and the way they are combined in the sentence. Fundamentally, that idea is correct, especially where it is a matter of explaining how new facts can be communicated in sentences; for that can succeed only if the meaning of such sentences is determined by the meanings of the terms. In the context of language learning, however, the situation is the other way around in many respects: the primitive linguistic expressions are sentences. We analyze these sentences into proper names and predicates. The interpretation of the terms comes about, roughly speaking, somewhat as in the case of so-called implicit definitions: Certain sentences are marked out as true, certain others as false and an interpretation of the terms is sought for that attaches their assigned truth-values to all of the sentences in question. In that case, then, the meanings of the terms are determined by an analysis of the meanings of sentences, not the meanings of the sentences by a synthesis of the meanings of terms. And this determination of the meaning of the terms depends in a decisive way on which sentences we regard as true and which as false.

Now it is not so that the process of learning language ceases at a speci-

fic point in time and that we attach specific meanings to terms prior to
that time and that these meanings are then independent of our assumptions about the world. Instead, this process continues even after the
meanings of terms have become relatively independent, so that the dependence of term meanings on these assumptions goes on being the case.

The dependence of the meanings of terms on sentence contexts can be
ascertained for ordinary language from the fact that within certain limits
words can change their meaning according to the context in which they
occur. Therefore it can not be simply said of a sentence in ordinary language that the meanings of the terms determine the meaning of the sentence, but rather the meaning of the sentence also determines the meaning
of the terms.[28] What could perhaps be said is this: The meanings of the
terms pre-determine the meaning of the sentence within certain limits, but
the exact assessment of the sentence's sense – and with it the exact assessment of the meaning the terms have in the sentence – emerges only through
the interpretation of the entire sentence. Dependency of meaning on context of this sort does not exist solely in connection with ambiguous words.

Before we show that, some remarks should be added here on the problem of ambiguity and on the terminology that is relevant to it. In this connection we shall follow the ideas K. Heger has developed in [63] in part
using some of his examples.[29]

When it is said that one word is ambiguous or that several words have
the same meaning, the first thing that must be considered is how the expression 'word' is being used. If what one understands to be a word is a
specific expression together with its meaning, then it is immediately clear
that there can not be any ambiguous words, for whenever we have differ-
rent meanings before us, we also have different words *per definitionem*. If,
on the other hand, the meaning is not regarded as an integral component
of the word, there still remain various possibilities for defining a word.
(a) In the first place it is required that identical words represent the same
(e.g. phonetic or graphic) expression, i.e. that – according to the realization of the language to which one is referring – *homophony* or *homography*
is present. We have already emphasized that the two do not coincide,
and out of that arises an uncertainty in defining words, which can be
avoided, however, by specifying the word's form of realization. Add to
this, nevertheless, the fact that there are words that can be inflected whose

forms are constructed from different word stems (e.g. *go* – *went*, or in French, *beau* – *bel*). We speak of *allomorphy* in this case and the question is whether we wish to speak of two words here or of one. In the latter case, not even the weak condition (a) would be fulfilled. (b) One can add the further requirement that identical words also have identical syntactic-grammatical functions (in the sense of logical grammar, for example). On this view, the expression *murder*, as a verb and as a substantive, represents different words. Equally so the French *vers* in the sense of 'verse' and of '*contra*'. Naturally the criterion of identical grammatical function is precise only if account is taken of some specific grammar. (c) Finally, it can also be required that identical words have identical etymological roots. In that case, according to Heger, the German word *Kohl* in the sense of cabbage, derived from the Latin *caulis*, – and in the sense of nonsense, twaddle, from the Hebrew *gol*, for example, represents two different words. But this example also shows that the diachronic, i.e. historical criterion of identical etymon is questionable within the scope of a synchronic, systematic consideration of ambiguity. Those who use the German language no longer feel that there are two different roots concealed in 'Kohl' and therefore they see it not as two words, but as one.[30]

Let us assume that the concept 'word' can be clarified by such definitions without reference to meanings. In that case there can be ambiguous words. The two meanings of a word can have more or less in common, be more or less related. If they have no features in common, or they are unessential, one will speak of an *ambiguous* [*mehrdeutigen*] word (examples: 'pipe', 'bat'). If the meanings do include a group of characteristics in common, but typically different characteristics as well, then we speak of an *ambivalent* [*mehrwertigen*] word (examples: 'dark' as in 'a dark color' or 'a dark night', 'square' as in 'square in shape' or 'an area with a square shape').[31] 'Horse', on the other hand, as a generic concept covering 'stallion', 'mare', or 'pacer', 'trotter', etc., is not an ambivalent word, for as a rule we do not mean by 'horse' a pacer or a trotter, etc.; rather the word means a generic concept and there are many general statements about all kinds of horses, while statements about squares are as a rule either about places [such as a market-square] or square shapes or square numbers. Finally, one meaning can include all of the defining characteristics of the other, but not *vice versa*. Examples are: 'neck' (section of the vertebrate body between the trunk and the head – any narrow segment in front of the head of something) and 'turn red' (to change color to red – to blush). In the former case we have a metaphorical *extension* of the original sense of the word, in the second case a *contraction* of the word's meaning.

As a rule we speak of *homonymy* in connection with words that have more than one meaning and two (or more) different etymological roots, of *polysemy* in connection with words with more than one meaning but only one etymological root.

Now if we speak of meaning's *dependence on context*, then a linguistic context may be meant – the sentence or text in which the word occurs – or an extra-linguistic context, i.e. the circumstances in which the utterance is made. We shall return to the dependence of meaning on the circumstances of the utterance later on, here what we are concerned with at the outset is the dependence of meaning of words on the sentence context in which they stand, i.e. a consideration within the confines of *langue*, not of *parole*.

Dependence on context is demonstrated by the following sentences: (a) 'Fritz is smoking his pipe'. Here 'pipe' is synonymous with 'a small tube with a bowl at one end, used for smoking tobacco, opium, etc.' In this case the ambiguity of the word 'pipe' is eliminated by the context. (b) 'The monument is in the square'. Here 'square' is being used in the sense of a public place, and so the polyvalence of 'square' is eliminated by the context. (c) 'On hearing such praise, Fritz turned red'. Here 'turn red' is used in the sense of 'blush' and so the context brings about a narrowing of the meaning. (d) 'The bottle had a crack in its neck'. Here 'neck' is used in its expanded figurative sense.

But there is a dependence on context to be seen even in the case of words of which it can not be said that they are ambiguous or ambivalent. J. Lyons offers some examples of this in [69], p. 452*f*: (e) 'My dog has just had pups'. Here 'dog' is being used in the sense of 'bitch' and can be replaced by the latter word without any change in the meaning of the sentence. (f) 'I'm going to New York in my own car'; here 'go' is being used in the sense of 'drive' and can be replaced by this word.

Grammatical ambiguities can also be resolved by the context. Katz and Fodor in [63] offer the example, among others, of the two sentences: (g) 'Our store sells alligator shoes' and (h) 'Our store sells horse shoes'. You know that (g) is ordinarily to be understood in the sense of 'Our store sells shoes *made of* alligator hide' and (h) in the sense of 'Our store sells

shoes *for* horses' if you know that alligators do not ordinarily wear shoes
and that shoes are not customarily made out of horsehide.

Katz and Fodor now bring it out that this selection of interpretations
for (g) and (h) does not follow any purely linguistic criterion; the other
possible interpretations are not excluded by linguistic rules, but are improbable on the basis of factual information. It cannot be said that in the
context 'eating nuts', 'nuts' always means nuts that grow on trees, following purely linguistic rules. If there were a story of a humanoid metallic
monster who eats nuts and bolts, along with other more substantial fare,
we would be able to understand the expression 'eating nuts' differently in
this context. Both of these examples show, then, that general factual
information enters into the interpretation of linguistic expressions; that
dependence of meaning on context is not only a matter of linguistic regularities but that we interpret sentences against the background of certain
things we know or assume.

Now if it is true that the meaning of linguistic terms depends on our
assumptions about the world, as Quine maintains, then there is no sharp
boundary between analytic sentences, whose truth-value is determined on
the basis of the meanings of their terms alone, and synthetic sentences, for
which this does not hold.

Actually there are still differences in this connection, however. The
sentence 'All bachelors are unmarried' is more to be regarded as analytic
than 'Max is a bachelor'. Quine has no objection to a comparative concept of analyticity.[32] He represents the situation somewhat as follows: All
of our assumptions about the world, singular sentences and scientific
hypotheses and theories alike, analytic sentences (or meaning postulates)
and the theorems of logic alike, form an entire complex that can be confronted with experience only as a whole. Now if experience is incompatible
with the complex of our assumptions, then it is permissible in principle
to propose modification anywhere, not only in the singular sentences and
hypotheses or theories, but in the meaning postulates, indeed even in
logical theorems as well.[33] Basically, no assumption, no sentence in this
complex is incorrigible, i.e. immune to modification. Amendment of the
system follows various guidelines, such as simplicity and power of the resulting new system, the principle of conservatism, to make the fewest
changes possible and to change less secure assumptions in preference to
those that are more secure, and so on. If we call the sentences we are

more prepared to change *peripheral* – within the entire complex – and the sentences we are not so ready and willing to give up *central*, then meaning postulates, along with universally accepted fundamental laws of nature and logical theorems would be central sentences; and the central sentences would be more influential in determining meanings than the peripheral would be. But there are no sharp boundaries between modifiable sentences and non-modifiable ones, between those that determine meaning and those that do not.

The following comments on this presentation are to be made: For one thing, it is better to leave logical sentences and the meaning of logical expressions, mathematical as well, out of consideration here, since the situation is fundamentally different with them. For logical operators can be isolated and defined precisely without referring to empirical facts. These definitions are stipulations and as such do not depend upon our assumptions about the world. As against Quine, who denies that there is any sharp boundary between logical and non-logical expressions, so that we can only enumerate the operators used in our present logic, we can perceive such a boundary in the strict definability of these operators.[34]

Another point is that Quine's sketch remains very lacking in detail. In his effort to show that there is no absolute boundary between analytic and synthetic sentences, Quine obliterates the existing relative, but methodologically very important boundaries:

Quine's claim that there is no absolute boundary between analytic and synthetic expressions can be assumed to be sufficiently demonstrated by the arguments cited above. The insight that questions of meaning can not be rigorously separated from questions of fact, because the meaning of linguistic expressions depends on our assumptions about the world, is also extraordinarily important for an understanding of the way in which language functions. What is important for the methodological distinction between analytic and synthetic sentences, however, is not its absolute but its relative validity. When Quine says that even logical principles and meaning postulates are not immune to correction by experience, that is obviously true in quite a different sense than it would be in speaking of the hypothetical truth of general synthetic sentences. For example, if at a given point in time t the sentence $G(a)$ follows from system $S(t)$ of our assumptions about the world, with the aid of classical logic and meaning postulates, and if $G(a)$ turns out to be false on the basis of observation, then it obviously makes no sense to change the logic or the meaning of the predicate $G(x)$ (say by giving up the pertinent meaning postulates in $S(t)$) in such a way that $S(t)$ becomes compatible with $\neg G(a)$. For the result of that would be to change the meaning of the empirical sentence $G(a)$ so that possibly it would no longer reproduce the content of the observations.

If one wishes to formulate the question of whether certain assumptions fit with specific observations as a question about the compatibility of sentences, then in doing so one must take a language into account, interpreted in a definite way, with logical and descriptive constants that have a fixed meaning. Since the logical principles are based on the interpretation of the logical constants, a logic is also singled out accordingly. An (interpreted) language and a logic thus constitute the reference system within which the question is raised whether certain assumptions are compatible with specific observations or which assumptions must be modified in order to achieve such compatibility. Therefore what comes into question in adjusting the assumptions to experience is a modification only of sentences that can be modified without changing the reference system, thus without abrogating any laws of logic or any sentences whose truth follows from the interpretation of language. Thus it would obviously absurd to bring the sentence 'This raven is white' into agreement with the assumption 'All ravens are black' by re-interpreting the predicate 'white' into 'black' or 'all' into 'some'. It would be absurd because it would cancel out the presupposition of putting the question, the acceptance of a specific language and logic. Correction of assumptions on the basis of conflicting experience can only concern non-analytic sentences, then, with the referrence system held constant.

Naturally, one can change the interpretation of the language or choose another system of logic. But that is a change that experience does not make necessary – an incompatibility between observation sentences and assumptions, as indicated, exists only within the limits of a definite system of language and logic, and so cannot refute it. A change in the reference system is on quite a different level and is motivated by quite different considerations than is the abandonment of scientific hypotheses in the face of conflicting observations. It can be based, for example, on the fact that the language previously used has too limited an expressive capacity, that a re-interpretation of some terms bestows upon it a greater fruitfulness for the description of nature and permits general laws to be formulated more simply, etc.

It is important, then, to hold fast to this distinction between changing hypothetical assumptions and changing the reference system. Analytic sentences exist only relative to such a reference system, because the meanings of terms are fixed only within a reference system. The more precisely the interpretation of the language is specified, the sharper is the boundary between analytic and synthetic sentences with respect to this interpretation. Since the interpretation of descriptive terms in natural languages is fixed far less precisely than the interpretation of logical and mathematical terms, the analytic sentences that are not determined by logic or mathematics are also much less precisely determined. But practically speaking, the distinction between analytic – synthetic is sufficiently clear in most cases.[35]

If Quine insists that the meanings of words change along with our assumptions about the world, that is correct, viewed diachronically. But at every moment we have a definite understanding of language (even if it is of limited precision) which is the foundation of our statements about the world and there is relative to it a distinction (of limited precision) between analytic and synthetic sentences. That we can say anything about the world at all and communicate information about it depends on the fact that there are statements for which meaning and truth-value are independent of each other, that not all sentences have the character of meaning postulates, then; that there are definitely synthetic sentences; and that thus the boundary between analytic and synthetic sentences is sharp in at least some cases.[36]

3.3. Quine's Thesis of the Indeterminacy of Translation

We have portrayed the starting point of Quine's ideas on the philosophy of language, his pragmatic approach, by way of this quotation: "Language is a social art. In acquiring it, we have to depend entirely on intersubjectively available cues as to what to say and when. Hence there is no justification for collating linguistic meanings, unless in terms of men's dispositions to respond overtly to socially observable stimulations."[37]

From this view, that we learn language only by using it, there follows for Quine one of the fundamental theses of his book, *Word and Object*, the thesis of indeterminacy of translation.[38] Quine formulates this thesis as follows: "The infinite totality of sentences of any given speaker's language can be so permuted or mapped onto itself, that (a) the totality of the speaker's dispositions to verbal behavior remains invariant, and yet (b) the mapping is no mere correlation of sentences with equivalent sentences, in any plausible sense however loose." [39]

Although the term 'equivalent' is not explained in greater detail anywhere, it obviously stands for an identity of meaning defined in some way. What the thesis says, then, is this: The meanings of a language's expressions can not be determined unambiguously on the basis of its use; there are radically different interpretations all compatible with the use of a language.

This thesis can be reformulated in an especially perspicuous way if instead of the mapping of a language onto itself, one considers the translation of one language into another, which takes into account nothing but the criterion of word usage: "... manuals for translating one language into another can be set up in divergent ways, all compatible with the totality of speech dispositions, yet incompatible with one another." [40]

The thesis can best be made precise in this formulation by illustrating it in terms of two simple languages, L 1 and L 2. We will assume that L 1 and L 2 are languages in elementary predicate logic that differ only in their alphabet, not in their formal rules, i.e. how they draw the lines between expressions of different syntactic categories, the terms (proper names and predicates with various numbers of places) and sentences. [41] Let the expressions in L 1, or L 2, be interpreted along the lines of interpretation V 1, or V 2, which are defined over object domains γ_1, or γ_2, so that these sets include all of the objects it is possible to talk about in L 1 or L 2. [42] Now let X be a person who speaks language L 1 and learns the (to him) foreign language L 2 from the use which the members of the linguistic community – let Y serve as representative – make of the expressions in that language.

For the sake of simplification we will assume that X can read off the syntax (the grammar) of L 2 directly from its usage (which we are assuming to be identical with that of L 1). Furthermore, X is supposed to be able to infer from the usage the semantic character of the logical operators in L 2. [43]

In accord with these assumptions we can directly stipulate the following conditions for a translation:

(1)   A translation of L 2 into L 1 is a function ϕ, of which it is true
           that:

(a) ϕ coordinates to the terms and sentences of L 2 expressions of
       the same semantic category in L 1.[44]

(b) ϕ is operationally faithful with respect to the form rules com-
       mon to L 1 and L 2.[45]

(c) ϕ coordinates to the logical operators of L 2 equivalent opera-
       tors in L 1.

X can check these conditions (a) to (c) – this is our idealizing condition
– independently of any knowledge of the particular interpretation V 2 of
L 2.

The specifically semantic problem of translation can now be formulated
as follows: What additional criteria of translation arise for X from Y's
use of language, what can X infer about V 2 from Y's use of language?
Now what is decisive on this point is the sentences in L 2 that Y uses in
order to describe something which he and X can both directly observe,
since what is referred to is most distinct for such sentences.

We will assume along with Quine that X can establish whether a sentence Φ in L 2, which Y utters at a specific moment t, (partially) describes
X's field of perception W at t, i.e. refers to something X can perceive at t.[46]
X will then translate such a sentence Φ of L 2 into a sentence of L 1 that
likewise describes W.

We can then add in a last condition for the Quinean concept of translation:[47]

(d)   It is true of all sentences Φ of L 2 and all perceptual fields
           W of X that Φ describes W if and only if $\phi\Phi$ describes W.[48]

The thesis of indeterminacy of translation can then be expressed as
follows: For antecedently given ϕ and V 1, V 2 is not unambiguously determined by conditions (a) through (d).[49] Among other things, these conditions are compatible with γ_1 and γ_2 containing no common element and
interpretations V 2(α) and V 1$(\phi\alpha)$ being different for all terms α of L 2,
so that the translations of expressions in L 2 have entirely different
meanings from those expressions.

Now the validity of this thesis obviously depends on condition (d).
Without this condition it would be a triviality. The question is, then, to
what extent does (d) restrict translation.

Let us assume that Y uses a simple sentence such as 'a has the property F' to describe one of X's perceptual fields, that presents a rabbit sitting in a meadow, for example. Now X does not know which object Y uses 'a' to designate or which property 'F'. The perceptual field, i.e. the set of sensory stimuli X experiences at the moment in question, permits various (partial) descriptions and Y can just as well be using his sentence to describe the fact that the meadow is green as that the animal sitting in it is a rabbit. Now Y's subsequent use of language can be informative about such differences of meaning, for not all rabbits are sitting in green meadows and not every green meadow has a rabbit sitting in it. So if Y again says 'a has property F' when he is looking at a green meadow with no rabbit, the second possible interpretation is no longer open; but if Y says 'a has property F' when he is looking at a rabbit with no meadow, then the first possible interpretation is no longer open.[50]

But now if there are concomitant specifications, i.e. specifications that always enter into the picture together, then there is no longer any possibility of distinguishing between different meanings by way of language use. Quine offers as examples of concomitant specifications 'thing', 'thing part', and 'thing stage' ('thing at time t').[51]

Quine accordingly sees a difficulty for the interpretation of all expressions similar to the one Wittgenstein sees just for expressions in a private language, more exactly, for expressions that stand for private experiences, mental events and the like. Wittgenstein uses his beetle example to illustrate it:[52] "Suppose everyone had a box with something in it we call a 'beetle'. No one can look into anyone else's box.... In that case it might well be that everyone had something different in his box.... But if the word 'beetle' were to have a use for these people all the same? – Then it would not be the name of a thing. The thing in the box has no place in the language game at all... you can 'divide through' by the thing in the box; it cancels out, whatever it is."[53]

With Quine what corresponds to the box is the perceptual field and to the beetle the thing in the perceptual field, or the quality or relation designated by an expression of L 2. Quine's thesis thus goes further than Wittgenstein's statements on the determinability of the meaning of predicates by their use[54] to such an extent that according to it not even the meaning of proper names, indeed their references, can be unambiguously determined, that there is not even one case in which we can learn from the use of language what domain of objects a language is concerned with.[55]

The examples of concomitants that Quine offers do not make a very convincing impression, to be sure – as we shall see, that is in the nature of the case. But even if one does not assume that there are such concomitants, there remains the following difficulty for translation: Every one of X's perceptual fields admits of an infinite number of descriptions in principle, for along with a sentence Φ, for example, the sentence $\Phi \vee \Psi$ is also a description of W. Even the following simple geometric figure, for example, can be (partially) described by

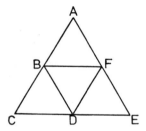

the sentences: 'Figure ACE is an equilateral triangle' or 'Figures ABF, BCD, DFB, FDE are equilateral triangles and together form an equilateral triangle', or 'Figure ABF is an equilateral triangle, figure $BCEF$ is a trapezoid and together the two form an equilateral triangle', or 'Figure ABF is an equilateral triangle' or 'Figures BDF and FDE have a side in common', or 'Figure ABF is not a trapezoid' – to cite only some of the possible descriptions.

Since the set of perceptual fields W available to X for the analysis of Y's use of language is only finite – X is supposed to determine V 2 on the basis of a finite number of observations of Y's use of language – that means that of an infinite number of hypotheses about V 2 that are possible according to (a) through (c), only a finite number can be ruled out on inductive grounds. All of the remaining hypotheses are equally probable, or better, equally improbable. This argument also shows, then, that in line with Quine's thesis V 2 is not unambiguously fixed by V 1 and ϕ, or that a translation ϕ is not unambiguously determined by V 1 and V 2.

Shifted back from the case of translation to the case of learning a language, what Quine's thesis says is this: Since we learn any language only by using it, we can always interpret its expressions in different ways as long as they are just in accord with usage.

But now it is nevertheless a fact that we can come to a very precise understanding about the meaning of words. We weigh the nuances of meaning of an English sentence and its German translation very precisely and we discuss the relationships and differences of meaning of German words in detail. There are not actually any competing English-German dictionaries offering genuine alternatives and there is no sentence that is not ambiguous in English as well for which there would be competing translations in German that were in no sense 'however loose' equivalent and between which we could not make a choice.

Quine too does speak of the different meanings of a word and distinguishes in language between his examples of concomitant specifications. Furthermore, it is precisely a basic pragmatic thesis that concepts are abstractions from predicates, that conceptual distinctions rest on linguistic distinctions. Thus wherever there is a conceptual distinction between possible interpretations of a word, it is also communicable in language. It can not be so, then, that the distinctions of meaning we ordinarily refer to can not be justified in terms of language use. Language use must therefore permit an essentially more precise determination of linguistic meanings than it appears to according to Quine's representations. In particular it must be possible for the criteria of adequate translation to be sharpened in essential ways, so that X can infer from Y's use of language what things, qualities and relations Y is talking about.

But how can that be explained? How can X know the meaning of the terms of L 2 and the domain of objects γ_2 from how Y uses the sentences of L 2 in concrete situations so as to apply them to observable things?

In such a situation there is a perceptual field given to X. Whether Y has the same or a similar perceptual field, X does not know. In principle it could be the case that Y has quite a different sort of sensory organization than X and experiences entirely different sensible stimuli. But for X it is a very natural and obvious, not to say self-evident, hypothesis, that Y has essentially the same perceptual field as himself. Quine too has to presuppose that, for otherwise X cannot observe Y's use of language at all. X obtains information about the meaning of a sentence Y uses only when he knows what that sentence refers to. But what Y uses his sentences to refer to is not X's perceptual field but his own. Here, as in what follows, the exception proves the rule: for example, the one perceives sound or light signals in frequency ranges that are not accessible to the other. But all that we need to do here is to explain how we understand each other in *most* cases, and not that we understand each other in *all* cases – which is indeed actually not so.

Now the same perceptual field does admit of different descriptions in general, however: Y can mean the one description by his sentence Φ and X the other, as the rabbit example above showed. But there are not as many descriptions of the perceptual field as you please, which X has to take account of in his interpretation of Φ. X's perceptual field is no mere 'swarm of sensations', no unorganized mass of sensory stimuli which X would first have to arrange into the form of things with qualities and relations. Instead, the perceptual field is structured to begin with. This fact is supported by extensive evidence in the psychology of perception. The aspects of the situations that strike upon the eye, the obvious descriptions that X has in mind without further deliberation, even though they may not be unambiguously determined, are only a few. Now it is another obvious and natural hypothesis for X, which can be supported or shaken by the knowledge X has of Y, that Y not only has the same sensory organization as X himself, but that there are biological, psychological, sociological features common to him and Y which result in the same aspects of the situation that strike on his eye also striking on Y's, and that Y with his sentence Φ expresses one of these aspects. The degrees of importance the various aspects have for X are effective in the sense that X can assign to his interpretations of Φ different degrees of (subjective) probability – taking account of his knowledge of Y. So X can rule out many possible interpretations with practical certainty from the beginning and he can make a choice among the rest inductively by way of Y's further use of language. The greater the common features shared by X and Y, the narrower an antecedent selection X can make among his hypotheses about the meaning of Φ.

Two examples of this: If a third person Z joins X, and Y says to X with a gesture in the direction of Z 'That is a', then X can be fairly sure that the expression 'a' designates Z, and not just the volume of space that Z exactly occupies, the third button on Z's vest, the sum-total of parts of Z or a momentary Z stage – unless Y is a philosopher, but that just isn't the rule. And if Y, seeing a group of young girls, applies the predicate 'F' to some of them who to X seem particularly attractive and denies it of others who to X seem less attractive, X can be fairly sure that 'F' is being used in the sense of some variation on the meaning of 'attractive' – unless Y is a misogynist, but that is not the rule either.

The interpretation of a predicate F of L 2, the use of which X has observed in examples, in the sense of a predicate of L 1, then also has the result that X can extend the predicate F beyond the examples Y has given him. Finally, it is also an easy matter for X, on the basis of the above reflections, to define the domain γ_2 of L 2 as the set of all such concrete things as are designated by proper names of L 2 which X has already learned. In the essentials, then, X will proceed upon the hypothesis that Y is talking of the same things that he ordinarily has in mind himself.[56]

But how can X interpret Y's sentences if he does not have mastery of any language himself and consequently has no stock of concepts for possible interpretations, if X is in the situation of the child just learning to speak? The particulars of this learning process are the business of developmental psychology. The only interesting aspect in our connection is the question of the conditions of possibility of understanding language in this situation. If it were so that to distinguish objects and their specific qualities would be possible at all only through the medium of language, then obviously one could never learn a language, since distinguishing linguistic expressions and comprehending situations to which they refer do presuppose such determinations also. Even the child who does not yet speak already has an environment in the sense of Jakob von Uexküll's environmental theory.[57] This environment is divided into things and events which are meaningful to the child – not in the sense of the meaning of a sign, but in the sense of an importance, a role they play in the total context of his life, a 'feeling tone', a 'valence' for the child. Even for the child the world is already structured in this way and his attention is directed to particular things and qualities in particular situations. The child incorporates a comprehension of these things and qualities into the first words he learns. There is certainly still a large margin of vagueness around these pre-linguistic features. Only with growing experience and mastery of language does the child learn to narrow them down. What is important is only that in the existence of pre-linguistic qualitative characterizations we can find a basis for the interpretation of linguistic expressions, for learning their use inductively by way of particular cases of their application.

The existence of pre-linguistic qualitative characterizations can still be established for the case of those who know a language as well. Thus we can identify certain colors, sounds, smells, etc., without having any simple descriptions in words available.

Quine also acknowledges the existence of pre-linguistic qualitative characterizations, when he says "In effect therefore we must credit the child with a sort of prelinguistic quality space." [58] Above and beyond that, however, what is decisive for the possibility of attaching subjective probabilities to interpretive hypotheses and so arriving inductively at an unambiguous identification of meanings is the significance particular aspects of the world have for us. This significance of things and qualities is what first makes it possible to go essentially beyond the limits of the Quinean thesis of indeterminacy of translation in attaching meanings. Now admittedly Quine has also assumed a "tendency to respond in different degrees to different differences" – for example, "more tendency to dissociate the ball from its surroundings than to dissociate its parts from one another" [59] – and he describes it as a presupposition for learning a language, but he did not take this tendency into account when he was establishing his indeterminacy thesis in [60].

Now there is an obvious objection to the effect that we have not interpreted Quine's statements in *Word and Object* correctly. For Quine would not express thesis (I) as we did, when we said: "The meanings of the expressions in a language are not unambiguously determined by its use," since for Quine differences in meaning are always differences in use.[60] Furthermore, Quine just does not assume in his reflections that languages L 1 and L 2 have an identical or even just an analogous syntactic structure.[61] He is not referring to languages that have wide-ranging cultural features in common that would suggest a translation along the lines of our discussion. Neither is Quine referring to such simple observation sentences as we considered, but rather to theoretical sentences such as "Neutrinos have no mass." [62] And finally, he is just not investigating the problem of translation in connection with such languages as English and German, which have special relationships as he views them.[63]

If we have thus considerably diverged from Quine in the details, we have nevertheless dealt with the central problem of the *indeterminacy* thesis. For so far as our formulation of thesis (I) is concerned, this thesis becomes trivially false if meaning and use are identified in the pragmatic way and non-equivalent sentences are consequently understood to have different uses. This thesis can also not be interpreted pragmatically in such a way that while the uses of the non-equivalent sentences are the same, the uses of the terms occurring in them are not, for a difference in the use of terms is nothing but a difference in the use of sentences in which they occur.[64]

Now Quine argues for thesis (II) in such a way that not all of the arguments can be carried over to case (I). But for Quine too (I) represents the more interesting claim.[65] To that extent the supplementary arguments for (II) have less weight. Quine says for example that a synonymous translation is not to be achieved when the syntactic structures of the two languages are entirely different, when the sentences of one language do not have the subject-predicate structure, for example, of the sentences of the other language. One can certainly grant to Quine that languages which are sufficiently different can not be translated into each other synonymously. But this difference no longer applies in the case of thesis (I). In the same way, strong cultural differences naturally result in considerable difficulties in translation, and one will always have to understand the translated sentences relative to a translation of the fundamental assumptions about the world the alien linguistic community starts out from. But this difficulty does not come into play in case (I) either.

For thesis (I), however, the following two arguments remain, in their essential features: In the first place, the synonymity of two sentences is never anything but stimulus synonymity for Quine, according to which two sentences count as *stimulus synonymous* when they are affirmed under the same stimulus conditions (we spoke of perceptual fields).[66] But what follows from stimulus synonymity for Quine is not synonymity in the usual sense.[67] What the argument we set forth above now comes to exactly is that one can get from stimulus synonymity to synonymity of sentences and with that to synonymity of the terms that occur within them.

Quine makes the further claim that for theoretic sentences stimulus synonymity cannot be defined at all.[68] But if, following our argument, one accepts synonymity of observation terms, then synonymity for theoretic terms[69] can be defined, for example, in this way: The series of theoretic terms $t_1, \ldots, t_n$ of a theory T 1 is synonymous with the series $s_1, \ldots, s_n$ of theory T 2 if the axioms of T 1 are transformed into the axioms of T 2 by substituting $s_i (i=1, ..., n)$ for t_i and possibly the substitution of other synonymous terms for observation terms.

For Quine, then, the decisive consideration is the claim that one can not go from stimulus synonymity to synonymity in the usual sense, and we have discussed this claim above.

NOTES

[1] Among the good discussions of Quine's ideas on semantics are Harman [67] and [68], for example.

[2] Quine [60], p. IX.

[3] In his reply to Chomsky's criticism in *Synthese* **19** (1968/69), pp. 274–283, Quine characteristically did not go into these points.

[4] In many points, Quine's remarks on the logical analysis of language (see e.g. [60], Chapters III–V) coincide with the program of logical grammar. See Chapter III.2 on this.

[5] See Quine [64c].

[6] See e.g. Tarski [35] and [44].

[7] On this point see Quine [60], §43, pp. 206f. – Such an argument occurs in Grice [56], p. 146

[8] Quine brings in examples such as the expression 'nothing', which is used like a proper name in the sentence 'His briefcase contained nothing', although it represents a quantifier ($\neg Vx$); and the expression 'sake', which is used in 'for the sake of' like an independent name, although it has no independent meaning. – While of course 'for the sake of' is a fully idiomatic expression, that is not true of 'meaningful': This composite is formed in a regular way out of components interpreted by themselves.

[9] One can even get along with the basic predicate $G(x, y)$ by itself, for since the field of $G(x, y)$ contains nothing but meaningful sentences and every sentence is synonymous with itself, we can define $S(x)$ by $S(x) := G(x, x)$.

[10] On this point, see also Kamlah and Lorenzen [67], p. 85f.

[11] Here again 'A' is a quasi-mention, i.e. to be understood as 'the mention of A'.

[12] The transition from 'say, that' to 'say*' also has the advantage that the sentence 'x says* "Es regnet" ', in contrast with 'x says that es regnet', can be regarded as a grammatically well-formed sentence.

[13] See e.g. Quine [60], § 44, and Quine [56].

[14] For Quine, who as we shall see holds the concept of synonymity to be not sufficiently clear – especially for expressions in different languages – this point involves a fundamental difficulty for these attempts at translation. He seeks to avoid it by not explicating 'say in Italian' at all. – Davidson's recommendation in [68] for translating (1) into a direct sentence appears to be less felicitous. It proposes that (1) be replaced by (5) 'The earth moves. Galileo said this.' – But what does 'this' identify? A sentence – then the translation is just as inadequate as (2) – or a proposition – then we have not gotten away from the realistic interpretation. – Quine makes still a further recommendation in [60], p. 215f. According to it, (1) is rendered by (6) 'Galileo said-that-the-earth-moves', where 'saying-that-the-earth-moves' is supposed to be a basic unanalyzable predicate. But how is that predicate to be defined? Surely by way of 'saying that the earth moves'. Another reason for holding this procedure to be basically not usable is that it would infinitely expand the number of basic predicates of the language. One could just as

well interpret all sentences as unanalyzable sentential constants – because the concepts 'predicate' and 'proper name' are thought to be not clear enough, perhaps – only then it would no longer be possible to give any explanation of how language works: how it is possible to communicate an infinite number of states of affairs with a finite number of linguistic conventions (with conventions concerning a finite number of linguistic expressions), particularly when they are new states. – Quine's remarks in [56] also belong in this context. What he wishes to do there is to replace the predicate 'a said that $F(b)$' with 'a said-F-of b' – a predicate that is not defined, despite the remarkable properties Quine ascribes to it (for example, 'a said that b had the property F' would not be true, but 'a said-F-of b' would be, if a ascribed the property F to someone he mistakenly took to be b). Finally, he wishes to replace it with 'a said-'F'-satisfied-by b' – a predicate that is also defined only for intensionalists, and for them by 'a attributed to b the property expressed by 'F'' (in the reference language). – With such a procedure, we must obviously ask what is supposed to be going on, when on the one hand talk of intensions is characterised as not clear, but on the other hand in order to avoid it predicates are introduced which either are not defined at all or are defined only by way of expressions that refer to intensions.

Quine's suggestion in [69b] would be worth mentioning, finally: to reconstruct a sentence like 'a believes that $F(b)$' along the lines of 'a believes the class of possible worlds in which $F(b)$ is true' – a suggestion that Quine himself treats with great reservations, for the range of worlds that come into the picture here is to be narrowed additionally by the fact that there is a wealth of further sentences that hold true in them which hold true in the real world and enter into the definition of 'b' and '$F(x)$'. Also, such classes of possible worlds, especially after the fashion of Quine's suggestion, are really no more simply defined than propositions.

These and similar attempts at reconstructing intensional contexts are quite artificial, however, and even Quine finally admits it, when he says: "There is, however, another objection to taking linguistic forms as objects of the attributary and propositional attitudes; viz., simply that that course is discouragingly artificial. With this objection I sympathize." ([58], p. 22).

[15] Quine has no objection to a comparative concept of synonymity of this sort. See [60], p. 203. – N. Goodman also accepts a comparative concept of synonymity in [49] and [52].

[16] See Quine [60], p. 203.

[17] This definition of analytic sentences is too narrow, to be sure, as the sentence 'If a is the father of b, then b is not the father of a' demonstrates, since it would surely be ordinarily viewed as analytic. For this reason Carnap defines analytic sentences in more general terms by recourse to meaning postulates. See also Stegmüller [69], p. 61.

[18] *Definitionally equivalent* is used to characterize two expressions that result one from the other upon replacement of defined terms by the corresponding definitions (or vice versa).

[19] The statements about synonymity in a lexicon are statements asserting synonymity, not *stipulations* about synonymity.

[20] This example is not a happy choice, of course, since in the sentence 'A is analytically equivalent to B' the sentences A and B are not used, but only mentioned. Instead we could have used the example 'It is necessary that $A \equiv B$'.

[21] See Quine [60], p. 42.

[22] For a discussion of Quine's arguments against intensional semantics see D. Lewis [69], p. 207.

23 The concept of analytic sentence is often taken more narrowly, so that only true statements fall under it. – Kant's definition in the *Critique of Pure Reason*, which encompasses nothing but sentences of the type $\wedge x(F(x) \supset G(x))$, is completely unsuitable.

24 Carnap brings in this example in [63], p. 920. Arne Naess has given further precise criteria by which synonymities and analytic propositions can be determined in [49] and [53]. For tests of synonymity of predicates see Carnap [56], p. 238f. – The criterion given by Carnap directly relates only to the analyticity concept of a single person, but it can be expanded for language communities as well. For more of Carnap's statements on the problem of analytic propositions see Carnap [52], [55] and [63].

25 Cf. D. Lewis [69], p. 201 and Schnelle's discussion in [73], p. 299 seq.

26 See also Harman [67] and Putnam [62b], where there are arguments along the same lines.

27 To some extent, the converse of this idea, that our language is also a co-determinant of our way of perceiving the world, will be discussed in Chapter IV.

28 In this vein, J. Stenzel says in [34], p. 16: "A word becomes determinate only as a consequence of the context of meaning always to be presupposed in any concrete language situation." See also Chapter II.4.3.

29 Heger later modified these ideas again in [69].

30 In the phenomenon of words merging, there is also the case in which an expression which has only one meaning has two etymological roots (e.g. French *haut* from Latin *altus* and Frankish *hōh*), or in the phenomenon of words *splitting* the case of two expressions with different meanings having the same etymological root, e.g. French *compter* and *conter*, from the Latin *computare*.

31 In this ambivalence, on which a polyvalence with respect to their grammatical functions can supervene, is revealed their plasticity. See also Chapter III.1.2 on this point.

32 See Quine [60], p. 203. – If a comparative concept of analyticity has already been admitted (x is no more analytic than y), then of course a classificatory concept (x is analytic) could be formally defined as: $1+1=2$ is at most as analytic as x.

33 Quine refers in this connection (e.g. in [51a], p. 41) to Duhem's argument (see Duhem [6], pp. 303–328), according to which it is possible to hold onto any scientific hypothesis H whatever even when there are conflicting observations. For an observation sentence E follows not from H alone; E follows from H, rather, only relative to a theory T (to which H belongs, or which says something about how the quantities in H are measured, etc.) and distinctive limiting conditions A. But if $T, H, A \vdash E$ holds, then what follows from $\neg E$ is not $\neg H$, but only $\neg(T \wedge H \wedge A)$. But that condition can be satisfied by $\neg T \wedge H \wedge A$ or $T \wedge H \wedge \neg A$ as well.

34 On the delimitation of the logical operators in Quine see e.g. [59], p. XIV. See also Tarski [55], p. 418f.

35 Putnam, too, has urged that while there is no absolute distinction between analytic and synthetic propositions, there is definitely a relative one [62b]. He sees the distinction in somewhat different terms from the way in which we have characterized it, however: For Putnam, an analytic proposition within a system of assumptions, e.g. within a theory T, is a basic proposition of T, one that could not be given up without giving up the whole theory T. Such propositions are, for example, Newton's axioms of mechanics or Maxwell's equations for electrodynamics. – This can be said in response: Propositions of this sort can have in T an analytic character in the usual sense of being true by virtue of meaning if they (partially) establish the interpretation of theoretical terms in T; but they can also be synthetic propositions in the usual sense, so that Putnam's characterization of analytic propositions deviates from the usual way of defining them. Only if T is

universally accepted as true, so that the basic laws of T constitute central assumptions about the world, for us an (at present) unproblematic foundation of understanding, and explaining other propositions, can it be supposed that they are characteristic for the meanings of the terms that occur in them. When Putnam in [62] offers the statement 'There is an infinite number of distinct, finite connected segments of space' as an example of a proposition which is analytic in the Euclidean geometry of classical physics, but non-analytic in the Riemannian geometry of relativity theory, and remarks that the analytic character of this proposition does not depend on the meaning of the terms, which are the same in both physical theories, the reply is that this proposition is not analytic either as a proposition of mathematical or of physical geometry. It is only when the expression 'segment of space' is interpreted as 'segment of Euclidean space' that it becomes analytic.

[36] On occasion, Quine's arguments against the acceptance of analytic propositions are interpreted as if Quine would not doubt the existence of a determinate set of analytic propositions, but would say that this set is empty. But the point Quine is making from the very beginning is that there are no sharp or systematically relevant boundaries between truths of fact and truths of meaning. – On the problem of analytic propositions see also Bohnert [63], Gewirth [53], Kemeny [63], Martin [52] and [59], Mates [51], Pap [58], Peach [52], Putnam [62], Wang [55] and White [50].

[37] Quine [60], p. IX.

[38] See Quine [60], Chapter II. See also Quine [58].

[39] Quine [60], p. 27.

[40] Quine [60], p. 27.

[41] See Chapter II.4.4 on the logical and semantical concepts applied here.

[42] It is sufficient to use an extensional semantics as a basis here, since Quine asserts not only an intensional but also an extensional difference of some translations that are possible in terms of linguistic usage.

[43] Quine says: "Truth functions can be translated" ([60], p. 68). We can go on beyond that and assume, for example, that the existence operator $Vx...$ (there is an x, such that...) can also be translated. For the presupposition for that is not that γ_1 and γ_2 are identical (Quine [60], p. 60f.), or that X knows γ_2, but instead $Vx...$ is already characterized as an existential quantifier in L2 if sentences of the form $A[a] \supset VxA[x]$ are regarded as analytic (Quine says: "Stimulus-analytic sentences can be recognized," [60], p. 68; a stimulus-analytic sentence in this connection is a sentence that is affirmed in every situation unless nothing is affirmed at all (see Quine [60], p. 55).), and if a sentence of the form $VxA[x] \supset C$ is always regarded as analytic when $A[a] \supset C$ is regarded as analytic (where a does not occur in C). Hintikka has proposed in [68] a semantic instead of a syntactic characterization of quantifiers. It starts out from the assumption that two languages can have as their basis a unitary domain of individuals, however, which Quine expressly denies in [60]. Neither is our suggestion affected by Quine's objection to Hintikka's proposal (*Synthese* 19 (1968/1969), 284–287) that it is possible for it to occur in practice that someone asserts a sentence $VxA(x)$ without being prepared to assert a sentence of the form $A(a)$. This is, to be sure, not a very weighty objection.

[44] I.e., φ correlates proper names to proper names, n-place predicates to n-place predicates and sentences to sentences.

[45] I.e.: If a term or sentence Φ in L2 is produced by combining terms or sentences $\psi_1,...,\psi_n$ in L2 in accord with a formal rule, then $\varphi\Phi$ should be produced by combining the expressions $\varphi\psi_1,...,\varphi\psi_n$ according to the same formal rule.

[46] If Φ describes W, that is to entail here that Φ is true.

[47] Our definition represents a simplification and modification of Quine's concept of translation. Since all that we are concerned with here is the thesis of indeterminacy of translations, we have taken up only those specifications of the Quinean concept in (I) on which that thesis is based.

[48] According to that it is not true of all sentences Φ in L2 that $V2(\Phi)=V1(\varphi\Phi)$, but only of sentences which describe a perceptual field W, particularly of observation sentences, then. On the other hand (d) asserts more than this condition for the case of such sentences. – If in (d) we speak of all perceptual fields of X, then there is an idealising assumption to the effect that in every perceptual situation X can check Y's use of language relative to that situation.

[49] In Quine [60] the thesis is formulated in such a way that L1 is a many-sorted language, so that L2 can be mapped onto several component languages of L1. The claim, then, is that for antecedently given V1 and V2 the mapping φ is not unambiguously fixed by conditions (a) through (d).

[50] Quine says: "Observation sentences can be translated. There is uncertainty, but the situation is the normal inductive one," [60], p. 68.

[51] See Quine [60], p. 53f., and Quine [58].

[52] See Chapter II.4.6 on this point.

[53] Wittgenstein [53], 293.

[54] See Chapter II.4.4.

[55] On the other hand, Quine's thesis is weaker than what Wittgenstein says about learning predicates when he assumes that we can learn the rule of use for observation predicates inductively, thus that we can assign to a predicate F in L2 a predicate φF in L1, such that for all proper names a in L2 it is true according to (d) that $V2(F(a))=$ $=V1(\varphi F(\varphi a))$.

[56] Naturally, we will not advance the hypothesis that translation of a foreign language is merely a process of statistical choice. On the contrary, there enter into it constructions that are creative through and through, similar to those of theory construction, especially in setting up grammatical rules, of which we have not spoken at all here. What is important, however, is that the translation hypotheses and theories can be inductively checked in every particular.

[57] See e.g. Uexküll [24] and [28].

[58] See Quine [60], p. 83, also Quine [69c], p. 123ff.

[59] See Quine [57], p. 218.

[60] See Quine [60], p. 26.

[61] See Quine [60], p. 53.

[62] See Quine [60], p. 76.

[63] See Quine [60], p. 28, 76.

[64] See Quine [60], p. 79.

[65] Quine [60], p. 78.

[66] Quine [60], p. 32f., 46.

[67] See Quine [60], p. 46.

[68] Quine [60], p. 46f.

[69] On the concept of theoretical terms see e.g. Stegmüller [70] or Kutschera [72], 3.3.

4. WITTGENSTEIN'S PHILOSOPHY OF LANGUAGE IN THE 'PHILOSOPHICAL INVESTIGATIONS'

After finishing the *Tractatus* in the period after the First World War, Wittgenstein had at first entirely withdrawn from philosophy, since he held the basic problems of philosophy to have been essentially solved and disposed of with the *Tractatus*. Wittgenstein did not turn back to philosophy until 1928. His attitude toward philosophical problems had already changed in many respects since the *Tractatus* and so he believed he could again accomplish creative philosophical work.[1] Particularly since about 1933 Wittgenstein's philosophical ideas changed radically. Above all he was again concerned with the problems of language, but he now arrived at views quite different from those he had advocated in the *Tractatus*. In the *Philosophical Investigations* [53] he engaged in sharp criticism of the basic ideas of the *Tractatus*. This work represents the pure pragmatic antithesis to the pure realistic semantics of the *Tractatus*.

In what follows we will discuss first of all what Wittgenstein asserts in [53] on the problem of meaning. But even these discussions will lead us to the epistemological theme of Chapter IV, since Wittgenstein's statements about the semantic function are ultimately based upon epistemological considerations.

The *Philosophical Investigations* are a collection of thoughts scarcely connected with each other in any systematic way. Wittgenstein did not wish to develop a semantic theory in them, but only to free us from 'the bewitchment of our intelligence by our language', i.e. to fight false conceptions of the function of language.[2] But since we are here concerned with systematic questions, our goal in what follows is not so much the most faithful possible recapitulation and interpretation of Wittgenstein's statements as the clarification of the problems he has raised.[3]

4.1. *The Abandonment of the* Tractatus' *Ontological Presuppositions*

In the *Tractatus* Wittgenstein had started from ontological presuppositions according to which the world is divided up into complex and ultimately into simple facts, which are once again composed of simple things (objects and attributes).[4] The task of the philosophical analysis of language was accordingly to provide an ideal language that is a true picture of that reality; in which the simple terms stand for (simple) things and sentence structure faithfully reproduces the structure of the facts pictured. Since our ordinary language is no such language – its sentence structure does not correspond to the way the facts pictured are objectively put together, its names do not stand for simple objects, its meanings are not precisely and exactly defined – it was accordingly the task of philosophical analysis to analyze the sentences of ordinary language, which do not satisfy the ideal of scientific exactitude, by means of sentences of the ideal language.

In his later philosophy Wittgenstein turns against these basic ideas. The most decisive factor is that he gives up the ontological presuppositions of the *Tractatus*: There is now no longer any reality in itself for Wittgenstein, no reality that is merely pictured by language, whose structures thus have to accommodate themselves to the ontological structures. Instead it is in the description in language that the world is first revealed to us. The world is never given to us in and of itself, but only in an interpretation in language.[5] This epistemological idea will occupy us more extensively in what follows. What we are immediately concerned with here is its far-reaching consequences for Wittgenstein's philosophy of language in the *Philosophical Investigations*:

(a) This idea cuts the ground out from under the realistic theory of linguistic meaning. For if the entities, the things and attributes are not given to us independently of language, then the meaning of linguistic expressions can not be explained by saying that such entities are conventionally assigned to them as meanings.[6] In that case, we can not start from the ontological structures either and attach isomorphic linguistic structures to them, but the ontological structures could rather be regarded the other way about as projections of the linguistic structures given primarily, in which we speak about the world.

(b) Furthermore, the idea cuts the ground out from under ontological and with it linguistic absolutism and atomism. For what it means is that there is no world built up in an unambiguous and definite manner (absolutism) out of elements (atomism), that instead the world is articulated for the first time in the linguistic description. How it can be articulated depends on the linguistic forms available for describing it.[7] The idea consequently contradicts the notion of replacing ordinary language with an ideal language, for precisely what had defined the ideal language was just that it was supposed to picture the structure of reality in and of itself.

But the structure of our world is only the structure of our language in which we describe it, i.e. in essential features the structure determined by the forms of ordinary language.

(c) With that, for Wittgenstein ordinary language now takes the place of an ideal language, an artificial language modelled on a logical calculus, in the center of philosophical attention. There is no more talk now of the real logical structure of language and the real meanings of linguistic expressions being hidden behind the inexact and vague formulations of ordinary language. Instead what is said now is that in principle ordinary language is in order just as it is – 'ordinary language is all right' – and Wittgenstein no longer sees the task of philosophical linguistic analysis in retreating from the formulas of ordinary language to sentences in an ideal language, but conversely in retreating from the scientific use, especially the philosophical use – for Wittgenstein almost always a misuse – of language back to the way words are utilized in ordinary language.[8]

This turn back in the direction of ordinary language marks the beginning of a new philosophical movement, *ordinary-language philosophy*, in the way it has been developed primarily at Oxford in Wittgenstein's wake as a counter-movement to the analysis of philosophical language, using the instruments of modern logic, as propagated by logical empiricism, for example. For it, as for Wittgenstein, most philosophical problems stemmed from a misuse or a misunderstanding of ordinary language and it is philosophy's task to take up the "fight against the bewitchment of our intelligence by our language" by attempting to understand better the way ordinary language works.

(d) Finally, Wittgenstein's epistemological idea of the world being put into order by language speaks against the ideal of linguistic precision that Wittgenstein had promulgated in the *Tractatus* with his demand for an ideal language. Along with the idea that there are well-defined objects and attributes in the world that come into question as exact meanings of linguistic expressions, Wittgenstein also gives up the idea that there is such a thing as absolute exactitude, particularly such a thing as absolute precision in the meanings of words. The ideal of exactitude in the *Tractatus* is for Wittgenstein a myth, a metaphysical fiction. Exactness is never anything but an exactness sufficient for a specific context, there is no absolute exactness.[9] And there is no *true* sense of a sentence, to be worked out with complete precision by means of analysis, one which is hidden to some extent behind its formulation in ordinary language, what is *really* intended by that formulation. Rather, the sense of any sentence is defined only within certain limits and it remains open how these limits are to be drawn closer together with a more precisely detailed definition.

The idea that reality is not given to us independently of its description in language is thus the guiding idea for a radical criticism of the basic ideas of the *Tractatus* and destroys their foundation completely.

4.2. *Language Games*

As we have already emphasized above, it is a basic characteristic of realistic semantics to see the semantic function of language in its representative or pictorial function alone and accordingly to identify the meaning content of the expression with its descriptive content. Accordingly realistic semantics is almost exclusively oriented toward declarative discourse and completely severs semantic considerations from inquiries as to how language is used in practice.

Now Wittgenstein pursues the pragmatic criticism of this realistic approach. For him speaking is in the first place a human activity like cutting wood, gymnastics, plowing, etc. This activity occurs in quite diverse contexts of situations and actions and must therefore be seen and analyzed against the background of these contexts. Wittgenstein speaks in this connection of various *forms of life*.[10] For him language is always part of a form of life, and since it can be part of various forms of life, its function has to be defined anew for each form of life. As many forms of life, as many contexts of action and situation as there are, there are that many different ways of using language, that many different *language games* as well. Language is used for giving orders, asking questions, describing objects, guessing, lying, telling jokes, making up stories, solving riddles, giving thanks, pleading, greeting, praying, to cite some of the examples Wittgenstein offers in [53], 23.[11]

Wittgenstein therefore wishes to study in the *Philosophical Investigations* the use of language in the pragmatic context and to relate all analyses of meaning to these contexts of use. The talk of 'language games' is supposed to place special emphasis on the aspect of language use represented by the fact that it follows specific rules in each of the various life contexts, that different systems of rules hold for the various language games. Indeed the rule-governed character of language is the presupposition of communicating by means of language: without firm rules for using a word it has no firm meaning.

What is fruitful about this idea of fitting language into its pragmatic context and studying it against that background is that the realistic semantics' overly abstract and overly narrow interpretation of language as a mere instrument for describing things is corrected, that the variety of modes of meaning is brought out and that the importance for semantics of the pragmatic background is emphasized. On the other hand the manner of speaking about language games may not be taken too literally. For in the first place, we can not overlook the fact that we use the same language in all action contexts, not different languages. That means, however, that words and language forms are invariant within certain limits as against the varying contexts of their use, and that their meanings are not simply different from one occasion of their being used to another, but remain more or less constant. And so analyses of meaning and comparisons of meanings of words can in fact often be carried out to a considerable degree independently of the context of their use. Nor could we lay down new rules of language use for every context of life, so that in every new situation and activity we would be without any language to begin with. Instead the serviceableness of our language depends precisely on the fact that it can be used in the most varied contexts and in new contexts as well.

According to Wittgenstein we should not let the external resemblance of words and language forms in different language games blind us to the fact that they have quite different functions in the various games, but this external resemblance is nevertheless definitely not just a matter of chance. Of course, there is a difference between the uses of language in different contexts, which has to be noted.[12] On the other hand, however, there is also a relationship, which ought equally to be noted. How, for example, is the use of the word 'door' in telling a joke differentiated from its use in thanking someone?[13]

What concerns Wittgenstein above all in his later philosophy is to stress differences, point out nuances and draw distinctions, to exhibit the value of the particular case as against the generalization. But generalizations – even if not too far-reaching – are necessary for a scientific systematization of the variety of experiences.

Furthermore, particular language games, in contrast to other games such as chess, football, etc., are not sharply set apart from each other and overlap. Questioning, describing, suggesting, asserting, proving, for example, are 'games' which are inseparably tied up with each other in many situational contexts.

Taken literally, Wittgenstein's assertions about words belonging to particular language games are most readily applicable to such words as '*Re*' and 'hand' which only occur in quite specific practical contexts (in this case in the card game skat) and in that context are used according to quite definite rules of play, but not to the mass of descriptive words in our language.

But so far as the principle intended by the talk of language games is concerned, expressing as it does the thesis that language is basically always to be understood and analyzed in terms of its use in specific practical situations and that the variety of semantic functions corresponds to the great diversity of such ways of applying language in practice, these assertions of Wittgenstein's contain a very important insight.[14]

4.3. *Word Usage and Word Meaning*

According to realistic semantics a word as a phonetic or graphic entity becomes meaningful by virtue of having a proposition, an object or a concept assigned to it as its meaning, so that along with meaningful words there are always antecedently existing objective, even if not necessarily concrete entities which are their meanings. If the ontological presuppositions of realistic semantics are given up, especially the underlying Platonism, this interpretation is no longer tenable. Concepts and propositions are in that case nothing but abstractions from predicates or sentences based on synonymity, and so they can not be called upon to explain the meaning of predicates and sentences. But then a new definition of the meaning of linguistic expressions or their synonymity must be given.

Wittgenstein holds that a word becomes meaningful by virtue of having a definite function in a language game, by being used in a definite way in that language game and for a definite purpose. According to Wittgenstein, then, for a word to be meaningful there does not need to be something which is its meaning. In this vein Wittgenstein says, "Don't look for the meaning, look for the use",[15] i.e. if one wishes to understand and explain the meaning of a word, one should not set out to look for concrete or abstract entities which are assigned to the word, which it designates, but one should look into how the word is used. It is not just that we can obtain information about the meaning of a word only from its use, but rather the meaning is nothing whatsoever except the word's use; besides the use there is nothing else that constitutes the meaning of the word. According to Wittgenstein, "for a large class of cases in which the word 'meaning' is used – even if not for all cases of its use – the word can be defined as follows: the meaning of a word is its use in the language." [16]

Wittgenstein illustrates this identification of meaning and use in [53], 454 by alluding to the meaning of non-linguistic signs, such as an arrow pointing the way. The arrow ' → ' does not mean a fact, a piece of advice, a direction, or the like, but is put up so that a person gets to where he wants to go if he follows it. It is this use that makes the arrow a meaningful sign; there is no need to assume a meaning-entity along with it, assigned by convention to the arrow as a sign.

This definition of meaning as use is simple and natural – simple, because the entire cosmos of propositions, concepts and the like, which remained doubtful in its ontological status, now becomes unnecessary. And natural, because there is certainly no dispute about the fact that a linguistic expression without firm rules for its use has no firm meaning and that there is at least a gross one-to-one correspondence between use and meaning.[17] It has the further advantage that by reducing semantics to pragmatics it brings into view the variety of meanings linguistic expressions have, the definitive role of the realization of language (*parole* in Saussure's terminology) for language as a system (*langue*), and the cultural achievement that is expressed in a language, of which one could scarcely speak if it were merely a system of assignments [of meanings]. This definition of meaning will also be essentially more in accord with many linguistic-empirical facts – some of which we shall be discussing below. Finally, this definition is also epistemologically much more satisfying than the realistic representative-image theory: since propositions and concepts, as things given independently of language, disappear, the problem of how these entities can be known also disappears and we have access to the phenomena that confirm the dependence of thought and experience on language.

The identification of use and meaning requires further explanations and distinctions, however, before it can be accepted as a basic systematic feature of semiotic. Although the term 'use' is a key word in Wittgenstein's philosophy of language, as it is for the whole pragmatic semantics, it remains quite vague for the most part and is used with a number of meanings. And little effort has been taken to make this term more precise.[18]

The first thing to be emphasized is that Wittgenstein does not understand the use of a word, along the lines of behavioristic semiotic, as a disposition to utter the word under certain circumstances, or to respond to it in a certain way. For Wittgenstein, 'use' is not a behavioristic term.

The use of a word is also not defined by counting up the occasions on which it is employed and reporting that so-and-so used the word on such-and-such an occasion, in this or that situation. I.e., what is meant by 'use' is not a *set of instances of use* but the *manner of being used*. This manner or way of being used can be defined by general rules of use which say that the word is used in cases of such and such a kind. It is one of the important accomplishments of language that it can be used to communicate new information. How language is employed for this purpose, i.e. what meaning sentences have when they are so used, is not revealed by historical instances of language use, however, which are indeed irrelevant to new facts, but only by general rules of use applicable in these cases as well.

Talk about the use of words does not refer to some actually occurrent use, either, but to their *correct* use in accord with a linguistic standard. If one wishes to identify the meaning of a word with its use, then one must refer to the rules for its correct use, i.e. to the generally accepted way in which it is used, not to mutually incompatible modes of usage that deviate from the general standard.[19]

Various objections have been made to the identification of meaning and use. A discussion of them will make the content of that definition clearer:

(a) It has sometimes been said that the formula 'meaning=use' is false because there are many ways in which words or sentences are used that have nothing at all to do with their meanings.[20] So, for example, we use expressions to insult, to amuse, to flatter or for aesthetic reasons (e.g. because they suit the rhythm of speech or because they are alliterative), without these ways of employing them being relevant to the meaning of these expressions.

This objection suggests an important distinction: The use of language occurs concretely in single speech acts, in *utterances* in the sense of Chapter I.1. These speech acts are related to specific situations and non-linguistic activities. But in these individually very diverse utterances we use the same language, the same words and sentences as expressions. What is meant by talking about the 'use' of expressions, then, is not actions but the outcomes of actions, phonetic or graphic expression-objects. One can say, 'I am using expression (-object) a' instead of 'I am performing the expression (-action) which has a as its phonetic result'. The use of an expression thus represents an utterance of that expression. Now we urged in Chapter I.1 that the meaning of an utterance of an expression a as opposed to the meaning of a itself often included supplementary features which emerge from the pragmatic context of the utterance. We called attention to indexical expressions in that connection; but the meaning of descriptive predicates can also be determined in more specific detail by the context of an utterance. Just as the intended sense of an ambiguous word can be picked out by its linguistic context ('She married a crook' – 'She carried a crook'), it can also be rendered specific by the pragmatic context of the utterance ('This crook is a very smooth one'). Such supplementary specification of meaning by the circumstances of utterance does not come about only in the case of ambiguous words. For example, if someone who wants to clip his hedge says to me: 'I need a pair of shears', what kind of shears is clear from the pragmatic context here. In this context, the utterances 'I need a pair of shears', and 'I need a pair of hedge-shears', have the same meaning, even though the two sentences (as expressions) are not generally synonymous. A third example is the dependence of what J. L. Austin calls the *illocutionary role* of an utterance on its context. The sentence 'It's raining' can be employed as a report, as a warning ('Don't go out without your umbrella') and as a request ('Close the window so the rain won't come in'). Which role it plays on a given occasion does not reside within the sentence itself, but is a function of the pragmatic context of the utterance.[21]

And so we must differentiate between the meaning of an expression and the meanings of the corresponding utterances. The meaning of the utterance is a function of the meaning of the expression and its pragmatic context: What belongs to the meaning of the expression is only what all the utterances have in common as regards meaning. The thesis 'use = meaning' is thus to be understood in such a way that the manner of use that is typical for all of the utterances determines the meaning of the corresponding expression. Between the way an expression is generally used and the particular occasions of its use there can then still be more or less specific forms of use which are typical for certain kinds of context. What corresponds to them are more specific meanings of the expression in such contexts.

So if the claim is advanced that there are many specific uses of a word that are irrelevant to its meaning, that is true enough, but it represents no objection to the thesis in question: not all of the characteristic features of a particular occasion of an expression's use are relevant to its meaning; often they do no more than define the meaning of the use on that occasion – often they are semantically entirely irrelevant.

The argument against identifying meaning and use has still another aspect, which is emphasized by Searle.[22] He points out that besides semantical criteria for the use of expressions there are also many pragmatic criteria for their use that are semantically quite irrelevant. In what we say we also take into account whether it is suitable in the situation, polite, appropriate, informative or expedient. How can we then distinguish between semantically relevant and irrelevant criteria in order to save the thesis meaning = use?

Again the decisive difference will be that semantic criteria for the use of an expression refer to all its applications while the other criteria are only brought in for some utterances. Criteria for the use of obscene expressions and their equivalents in medicinal terminology, for instance, are quite general and therefore we have here a difference in meaning in spite of an identity of descriptive content. On the other hand the fact that we cannot substitute the two expressions 'stairs' and 'series of steps for going up and down' in all situational contexts is no argument for a difference in meaning. That we do not express a warning 'Don't fall down the stairs!' by 'Don't fall down the series of steps for going up and down!' is explained simply by the fact that in warning a person against an imminent danger you have to be brief.[23]

(b) G. Pitcher, M. J. Charlesworth and P. Ziff have attempted to show by examples that the identification of meaning and use holds as a rough approximation at best.[24]

For example, Pitcher says that one can know the use of a word like 'Amen' without knowing its meaning, just as one can know the meaning of a word, such as the Latin 'ultor' (avenger), without knowing how it is used (in Latin). Charlesworth brings out the fact that an identification of meaning and use is impossible in the case of proper names, which definitely have a use but no meaning.[25]

All these counter-examples are not very convincing, however. The word 'Amen' is not used descriptively, but as a formula of confirmation, and as such what determines it as to its meaning is its use, not insights into its origin and its earlier meanings. Further, do I know the meaning of 'ultor' if I do not know Latin and so I am unable to cite any contexts in which it is used significantly and can take on various nuances of meaning? In reply to Charlesworth there is this to be said, that in identifying use and meaning for ostensive proper names what is to be understood by 'meaning' is the semantic function of the name, i.e. its reference.

With the explications that have been given, then, these objections do not speak against accepting the formula 'use = meaning' as a basic semantic hypothesis.

(c) A further objection reads as follows: If the meaning of a predicate, for example, is defined as the way in which it is used and this way of being used is determined by rules for its use, then little has been gained over the realistic position. Rules are no less abstract than concepts and therefore the formulation: 'The meaning of a predicate is the rule for its use' is no more or no less problematic than the formulation 'the meaning of a predicate is a concept'.

The pragmatic proposal, Wittgenstein's proposal in particular, does not amount to interpreting rules as the meanings of predicates, however, but to replacing the predicate 'x means y' by the predicates 'x is meaningful' and 'x and y are synonymous', along the lines of Quine's theory.[26] The first predicate is to be applied when the expression x is used in such a way that the way in which it is used is controlled by general rules and the second predicate when x is used in exactly the same way as y. An expression is not meaningful when there is a rule which it means, but when there is a fixed way of using it – there is no longer any need for a meaning, an additional entity it stands for. The rule of use is not a hypostasized something alongside of the rule-governed use, but consists in the fact that we generally use the expression in such and such a way.[27]

(d) A fourth objection is as follows: In many cases, especially in the case of words that are primarily used descriptively, the use of a word W is defined most simply and appropriately by saying: *W* is used for the purpose of expressing..., in the sense of ..., or as a designation for.... But if the use of *W* is defined by way of its meaning in this way, then it is circular to define the meaning of *W* the other way around by way of its use.[28] According to this view, the formula 'meaning = use' fits best with expressions that have no descriptive meaning, particularly performative utterances like 'Good morning', 'Beg pardon', 'I ask' (promise, assure, warn, etc.)..., which do not speak of or describe an act (greeting, excusing, asking, etc.) but with which we accomplish these acts.[29] What can be said here is ' "Good morning" is used as a greeting in the morning', ' "Beg pardon" is employed when one is asking to be excused', and so on. That is, in these cases the use of the expressions can be described without recurring to their meanings, but with descriptive expressions that is not the case.

This objection has some justification in two respects. If one attempts to give rules of use for descriptive words, one will for the most part refer to the meanings of the words. Thus, for example, one will say (a) 'the predicate "rot" is used in German as an expression for the quality "red" '. Such descriptions of use by referring to the meaning of words are also by far the simplest if appropriate synonymous expressions are already available and their meanings known. From the standpoint of the 'use-theory' one can say, however, that a description of the use of a word of this sort, by citing its meaning, is nothing but the clarification of the use of that word by using other words. That is, (a) says the same as (b): 'The predicate "rot" has a use in German corresponding to the use of "red" in English'.[30]

This sort of locution, that use is defined in terms of meaning, or the use of formula (a) instead of (b), is on this interpretation, viewed pragmatically, quite unproblematic.

On this understanding, the realistic sort of talk has its due also, and meaning can be defined as a concept or a proposition, for example, wherever linguistic expressions are available by which the concept or proposition can be represented as an abstraction after the manner of Chapter II.3.1. It is not so, then, that all of the statements made in realistic semantics are proved to be inadequate and false by the pragmatic approach identifying meaning and use. Their title as practically very useful forms of expression is preserved, rather – within the limits, to be sure, within which they are translatable into statements made in pragmatic semiotic. E.g., (a) as against (b) shows the advantage of realistic formulations: (a) avoids the difficulty of having to explain in greater detail the 'corresponding usage' of words in English and German. The terminology of realistic semantics is actually also essentially better developed and more precise than that of pragmatic semantics – for example, there is no formulation of general semantic rules for grammatical compounds in purely pragmatic language – so that for this reason alone it is indispensable in practice.

If we can adhere to the realistic way of speaking over wide areas, we still can not do so everywhere. The basic realistic thesis, that a predicate, for example, becomes meaningful by having a concept assigned to it, loses its sense on the pragmatic interpretation in cases in which there is no suitable predicate available for defining the concept in the first place. This formulation breaks down, then, when it is a matter of saying how linguistic meaning comes to be at the outset.

Because of the importance this problem of establishing predicate-meanings has for understanding the thesis of the identity of use and meaning, in the following section we will contrast Wittgenstein's pragmatic statements on the point with realistic statements and discuss them extensively.

First, however, we wish to evaluate the second aspect under which the objection that defining meaning by way of use is circular has a certain justification. Even if the circular definition of the meaning of, for example, the sentence, 'It is raining', (c): ' "It is raining" is used to express the fact that it is raining' is replaced by (d): ' "It is raining" is used to say that it is raining', the circularity is still there. For 'to say that it is raining' means to use the sentence 'It is raining' or some synonymous sentence, so that one can only understand definition (d) of the use of 'It is raining' if one is already acquainted with its use – just as one can only understand definition (c) of the meaning of 'It is raining' if one already understands the meaning of the words 'It is raining' that occur in the definition. But so far no one has been able to specify the use of a descriptive sentence like 'It is raining' without using that sentence or another one synonymous with it – falling back on the known identical usage of a synonymous sentence does not solve the problem of how to explain that use of the sentence in the first place.[31]

This objection is based upon a mistaken understanding of the 'use

theory', however. That theory is not a naturalistic theory of language –
such as behaviorism, for example – which wishes to reduce language to
the non-linguistic and define linguistic concepts in terms of general
behavioral concepts, for example. It does not wish to derive what saying,
asking, or arguing is from other distinctions. On the contrary, the theory,
particularly as Wittgenstein has stated it, must be understood as emphasizing the independence and distinctiveness of language. It does so precisely by seeking to explain the function of an expression not in the
realistic spirit as being attached to an entity independent of language and
capable of being apprehended without the mediation of language, but by
saying: meaning is immanent to language, it is first constituted in language
and is not anything alongside of language. Meaning is only disclosed in
use, in the realization of language, i.e. the distinctive work done by linguistic expressions, that of meaning something, lies in the particular way
in which they are employed. We understand language in its general functions as in the special functions of individual words by learning to use it,
not from outside as it were.

The thesis, then, is not that meaning can be reduced by definition to a
use that does not presuppose meaning and the latter to a form of behavior
that does not presuppose language – such reductive explications are not
possible in most cases – but that linguistic functions only reveal themselves in language use, which can be taught and, when an understanding
of language can already be presupposed, can be explicated by means of
descriptions in language.

X's question, 'What does the word a mean?', is answered by teaching
him the use of that word or, to the extent that the necessary expressions
are known, explaining it to him in language. The general question, 'What
is meaning?', is answered by saying that the expression 'to be meaningful'
marks the specific work done by linguistic expressions, which is based
upon the particular way they are used and is revealed only in use. That is
the thesis of meaning as use, not a claim of reducibility. It is thus much
weaker and, if you wish, more trivial than has frequently been assumed.

Finally, in reply to the argument that the use of a word is determined
by its meaning and so can not define the latter, the following comment is
to be made: When L. Antal, for example, says, "If words are used according to their meaning, then meaning comes before use, in the same way
as the use of a language presupposes the knowledge of that language," [32]

then it is obvious that what is being spoken of here is a specific use of an already meaningful word, which is determined by its meaning and does not define it. What Wittgenstein is referring to, however, as already emphasized, with his identification of meaning and use is not instances of use – his opinion is not that a meaningless expression would become meaningful by being used one or more times – instead he says that the meaning of a word becomes attached to it by way of general rules for using it. That the individual cases of using a meaningful word are determined by its meaning is clear. But according to Wittgenstein all that means is that they are determined by the general rules governing the word's use; a correct use is defined for the word, and it becomes meaningful in the various instances in which it is used only when those rules have been established.

4.4. *Meaning and Use of Predicates*

Let us assume that a person X, who is acquainted with the use and the meaning of a one-place predicate F unknown to us, wishes to teach us its meaning and use. How will X proceed? If a suitable one-place predicate G is already known to us, then X can say:

(a) F is used in the same way as G, or
(b) F means the same thing as (is synonymous with) G, or
(c) F means the concept that is expressed by (represented by) G.

The realistic accounts (b) and (c), viewed pragmatically, are only alternative formulations for (a) and so quite harmless. Since furthermore, as the realist sees it, the use of F is a use for expressing a concept, he will interpret (a) as an equivalent version of (b) or (c), so that in this case the two conceptions are compatible with each other.

But how is it when no such predicate G is available to us, none for which (a), (b) or (c) holds true? Now the realist cannot say that X explains the meaning of F to us by pointing out the concept for which F stands. For a concept can be directly specified only as the meaning of a predicate, which is not available in our case, but not by pointing, for one can not point to concepts as abstracta. The method of teaching by examples constitutes the only way for the realist as for the pragmatist: X teaches us the meaning, or the use of F by telling us that F belongs to, or can be applied to these objects and those objects, but not to these and those others. In this fashion we obtain two classes of objects, $K(F)$ and $\bar{K}(F)$, of which we know that F belongs to all of the elements of the first and to none of the elements of the second. Thus $K(F)$ and $\bar{K}(F)$ include examples for employing F correctly.[33]

Has the way in which F is used now been determined by means of such an exemplary display of F's use? Obviously that is the case only when the domain of objects $D(F)$ for which F is defined at all, of which it can be meaningfully affirmed or denied, then, coincides with the union of $K(F)$ and $\bar{K}(F)$. But now the cases of predicates F for which $D(F)$ can be given in the form of a finite list of objects are precisely the uninteresting special cases. For in the case of predicates that are defined by the fact that they belong to specified, enumerated objects and do not belong to other specified enumerated objects, every application has an analytic character. In order to make synthetic statements with F, and so be able to 'communicate new facts',[34] $D(F)$ must be an open, i.e. an infinite domain. But in that case, which we shall always have in mind in what follows, defining F for objects in $K(F)$ and $\bar{K}(F)$ tells us nothing about whether F can be applied to a new object not contained in $K(F)$ or $\bar{K}(F)$. Examples of using F do not distinguish any general criterion for the use of F. If $D(F)$ is infinite, then there are uncountably many concepts that pertain to all of the objects in $K(F)$, but to none of those in $\bar{K}(F)$, or of rules according to which F can be applied to all of the objects in $K(F)$ but to none of them in $\bar{K}(F)$.

The example Wittgenstein uses to illustrate this fact is the task of determining the formation rule for an infinite series of numbers of which only a finite number of initial elements are given. Such tasks are encountered in psychological intelligence tests, for example. The initial elements, 1, 4, 9, 16, say, of a series are given and the subject of the test is asked to write down the next number in the series. If he now writes down 25, the tester looks on him as intelligent, but if he writes 3, for example, he will get bad marks for intelligence. But most unjustly! 25 is no more correct than 3 or any other number, for there is no *one* correct continuation of the numbers 1, 4, 9, 16 into a series, but there are just as many possible continuations as there are numbers. A series is a function which assigns a number to every natural number (1, 2, ...), and what is asked for is a function $f(x)$ for which $f(1)=1$, $f(2)=4$, $f(3)=9$ and $f(4)=16$ hold true. One such function is $f(x)=x^2$, but another is given by the definition '$f(x) = x^2$ for $x \leqslant 4$ and $f(x) = 3$ for $x > 4$', for example. Any arbitrary continuation into a series is thus compatible with a finite initial section and likewise any arbitrary continuation of the application of F is compatible with the examples in $K(F)$ and $\bar{K}(F)$. How, then, is one supposed to infer from the definition by example which continuation is the correct one? That obviously has to be possible, for the learning of predicates by examples functions quite well enough in practice.

The only answer to the question of the correct continuation of a predicate beyond a finite set of examples that is found in the *Philosophical Investigations* is that the correct continuation is the one that is in accord with the use of the predicate by the linguistic community.

This statement is certainly correct to this extent: Linguistic expressions have meaning only by virtue of a convention which is expressed in the case of words in ordinary language by general (correct) language use. And so if the question is raised as to whether the predicate F can be applied to object a, what has to be done first of all is to fall back on the rule for the use of F as a linguistic convention. It provides a criterion of application R_F; whether or not a satisfies this criterion is a factual question. We will assume that a rule of use for F has the simple form:

(I) F may be applied to an object a if and only if $R_F(a)$.[35]

This statement gives us no answer to our question, however, for that question is: presupposed that there is a general rule for the use of F, how can this rule, in particular how can the criterion of application R_F be ascertained on the basis of individual cases?

Many of Wittgenstein's statements in the *Philosophical Investigations* suggest, however, that he sees more in the general use of language than just the condition of the correct use of a word. They suggest, with (I) for example, that he understands general linguistic usage to *be* the criterion as well, so that R_F is a criterion which refers to general usage. Thus he says that you teach words to someone by example and practice. "And in doing so, I am not telling him any less than I know myself." [36] If we pay attention to the fact that Wittgenstein makes a distinction between what one knows and what can be said, e.g. between the distinctions one can make and those that one can formulate in language, what this seems to imply is that someone who knows how a predicate F is used is only acquainted with the use of F in a set of examples (which is of course very large in comparison with the learner's), that the 'general rule' for the use of F with which he is acquainted consists in the fact that he knows that F is 'generally' used in such and such cases. Wittgenstein appears, then, often to have in mind instead of a *way* of using F determined by a general rule the instantial use of F over a large class of examples, and to see in it 'linguistic usage'.

Furthermore, in the *Philosophical Investigations* Wittgenstein rejects the possibility of private languages, i.e. of expressions introduced *privatim* – Wittgenstein is thinking above all of expressions that stand for a subject's private experiences, mental events, etc. – and one argument against them is that one could not speak of a correct use with respect to the words of a private language, since the general criterion of correct use – agreement with the usage of the linguistic community – is here inapplicable.[37] But if what one understands by this criterion is a general condition of adequacy that concerns the *way* a word is used, the general linguistic criterion (I), for example, then the usefulness of the criterion is independent of how many members there are in the language community, even should there be only one. Understood in this way, then, Wittgenstein's claim cannot be applied as an argument against private languages. Therefore it is natural to interpret it in such a way that Wittgenstein understands general linguistic usage, the usage of the other members of the language community, as the criterion for the use of words. For then in the case of words in a private language, this criterion of use becomes inapplicable, since there is no general usage, and one can now say with respect to the correct use of these expressions: "... what is correct is whatever is going to seem correct to me. And all that means is that there can not be any talk of 'correct' in this case." [38] Along these same lines, what Wittgenstein means by 'following a rule' is also a general practice. What is followed in it is what the language community consistently does.[39]

Now it is no doubt true that someone who wants to learn the use of a predicate F, first turns his attention to its use as employed by the language community, or his teacher X, and that he can be corrected and be approved in his own uses of F. But if he has grasped how F is used, i.e. the criterion of its use R_F has become clear to him, then he will be independent of others in his uses of F and will no longer need to pay any attention to what the others say. The question, whether F can be ascribed to a new object a, is no longer a question of language use for him, then – that has been fully established by his knowledge of convention (I)[40] – but a question of fact, the question whether condition R_F is fulfilled in a's case. If the language behavior of others were the criterion, every time F was applied to a new object, there would have to be a vote on whether F should be ascribed to a or not. All cases of using F for which F is determined, on which agreement has been reached, would then be components of the definition of F, however, without empirical content and so no new facts could be communicated by means of F.

But Wittgenstein did not intend his claim that even the criterion for applying words is a criterion of intersubjective agreement in word usage in this totally inadequate way. That is revealed by his comment that what is the same is not "what all or most men agree in regarding as the same.... For in order to verify sameness, naturally I do not make use of the agreement of mankind! – What criterion do you use, then? None at all. Using the word without a justification does not mean using it wrongly." [41]

Now here the capacity for learning a predicate by examples, generally, for following a rule makes its appearance as a basic human capacity that cannot be analyzed further. And Wittgenstein addresses himself to the problem in the *Philosophical Investigations* predominantly in this vein. We just can actually learn rules by example, but no more can be said about it. Why we follow the rule in this way and not another cannot be supported by further reasons: " 'How can he *know* how he has to continue on his own?' – Well, how do *I* know? – If that means: 'Do I have any reasons?', then the answer is: My reasons will soon fail me, and then I shall do without reasons." [42] And: " '... how am I able to follow a rule?' – If that is not a question about causes, then it is about the justification of my acting in the way that I do. If I have exhausted my reasons, then I have now reached bedrock and my spade turns back on itself. In that case, I am inclined to say: 'That's just the way I do' ".[43] And: "With what right do I say: 'Yes, that is red'? Well, I say it; and it cannot be justified. And for this language game, too, ... it is characteristic that it goes on with the peaceful agreement of all mankind." [44]

But it is quite unsatisfactory, as regards learning predicates from exemplary cases, which is after all a fundamental example of how language is acquired and how it functions, that we are supposed to rest content with this account, that what we have to do with here is a phenomenon not capable of being analyzed further, a basic process that no light can be shed upon.

From the realistic standpoint, it could be explained as follows: Of course it is true that a criterion R_F for using F is not unambiguously determined by examples of F's use taken from $K(F)$ and $\bar{K}(F)$, but the learner can consider various concepts or conditions R_F such as are compatible with $K(F)$ and $\bar{K}(F)$, i.e. that belong to all of the objects in $K(F)$ and to no object in $\bar{K}(F)$. By observing further instances of the use of F he can inductively confirm or overturn these interpretive hypotheses and so succeed in picking out a condition R_F by induction. Of course at the outset there is an infinite number of hypotheses that are compatible with $K(F)$ and $\bar{K}(F)$ and new instances of the use of F will confirm all of the hypotheses that are not refuted, so that an initial selection must be made from among the hypotheses which will make it practically certain from the beginning that only a finite number of them will have to be taken into account. But we have already explained in Chapter II.3.3 on what basis such an initial selection can be made.

This realistic approach now appears at first look to be pragmatically acceptable as well, if one is somewhat more sparing of realistic terminology and does not call the criterion of use a *concept* marked out by the illustrative classes $K(F)$ and $\bar{K}(F)$, but possibly a *distinction* identified inductively by means of those classes. On this view, we have at our disposal a capacity, independent of language, for making certain distinctions and these distinctions provide us with the criteria for using linguistic expressions.

Wittgenstein emphatically rejects such an interpretation of learning predicates, according to which the realistic way of speaking of concepts that are independent of language is simply replaced by talk of distinctions that are independent of language. It becomes clear in this connection that for Wittgenstein linguistic pragmatism is not just a different *façon de parler* from realism, but is based upon a fundamentally different understanding of the phenomena. Befitting the pragmatic theory of the priority of predicates over concepts, he refuses in the first place to explain the use of predicates by resorting to concepts. The use of a predicate F can not be explained by a concept R_F because concepts can only be obtained by abstraction from predicates. But the same thing also holds for distinctions. According to Wittgenstein we learn distinctions only by means of language and the capacity for distinguishing things only by means of predicates. He says: " 'How do I know that this color is red?' – One answer would be 'I have learned [English]'."[45] That is, in learning the predicate 'red' I am not learning the abstract rule, "The predicate 'red' may be applied to *a* if and only if *a* is red," but I am learning to orient myself in the world with the help of the word 'red', learning to distinguish things into red and non-red.[46]

There is an obvious reply to be made to that: If we did not have the capacity for making quality distinctions without language, then we could not, as was already stressed in Chapter II.3.3, learn any language either, for learning a language presupposes at least the possibility of distinguishing linguistic expressions one from another, and the situations in which they are applied, too. And so there would surely be no possibility of learning language entirely without the pre-linguistic or language-independent drawing of distinctions. Even granted that many distinctions are first conveyed by means of language or are made more precise by means of it, language is nevertheless certainly not the single source of all distinctions.[47]

This objection is true enough, but it is nevertheless incomplete. In order to understand that and to do justice to Wittgenstein's statements, we must have recourse to some epistemological considerations.[48]

Pre-linguistic distinctions, Quine's pre-linguistic qualities and Uexküll's significances and valences to which we referred in II.3.3 are of quite a different sort from most of the conceptual distinctions we formulate in language. They are related to a subject's private experiences, whereas linguistic predicates for the most part mark out distinctions that relate to things, to the world of objective, e.g. physical events.

Now what holds true objectively is basically also defined by the fact that it holds true intersubjectively. As a rule we are only prepared to accept a sentence about the world as true if an intersubjective agreement on its truth can be reached. But if intersubjective agreement is thus acknowledged to be a defining criterion of objective facts, then one must also say that objective distinctions are not immediately available to us directly on the basis of our own experience, but are obtained only by means of language.

We can not go into this general thesis more closely here or give arguments for it. Instead we will illustrate it using the predicate 'red' as an example. We ascribe this predicate to things and we use it to express an objective difference between things. The objective character of this distinction depends, however, on the fact that as a rule we agree in drawing this distinction – if we did not, we would not ascribe the quality of redness to things but to our own perceptions of things, varying from subject to subject. This intersubjective agreement is manifested by the fact that we agree in our use of the predicate 'red'. It is only by learning this predicate or another one with the same meaning that we come to be sure of the distinction between red and non-red as an objective distinction and know how this distinction is objectively applied.

In order for a person Y to be able to learn the predicate 'red' from the use that others make of it, Y must be able to observe a sufficiently pronounced similarity among the cases in which they apply this predicate. In accord with our earlier discussion in Chapter II.3.3, there is an adequate basis for that if we assume that Y can distinguish between things that have for him a certain experiential quality or valence, redness$_Y$, and other things. If completely disparate sensations in Y correspond to the different cases in which 'red' was applied, then he would not be able to learn the predicate's use, because he would have no criterion for employing it. The subjective attribute, redness$_Y$, must be a sufficiently trustworthy criterion for using the predicate 'red', then, so that it holds true as a rule that 'red' can be applied to an object a, if a is red_Y. The correlation between red_Y and red does not hold in all cases, however, i.e. the quality red_Y is neither a necessary nor a sufficient condition for red; not everything that looks red to Y is also red, and vice versa.

Thus while Y, before he has learned the use of 'red', has available to him only the experiential quality red_Y, he learns the distinction between red and $non\text{-}red$, i.e. the concept red, by means of the predicate 'red'. The foregoing quotation from the *Philosophical Investigations* can be understood along these lines, so that we only learn to distinguish between red and non-red things by way of the predicate 'red'.

The statements of Wittgenstein's that say that the criteria for using predicates are criteria of linguistic agreement can also be better understood now. Whether the predicate 'red' may be applied to an object a does not depend directly on the subjective criterion for its use, whether a looks red or not, but on whether a is objectively red, and what that means is – since what is true objectively is essentially defined in terms of holding true intersubjectively – on whether we agree in judging a to be red, and what that means, once again, is whether we agree in attaching the predicate 'red' to *a*. And so in its epistemological aspect, conditions as to linguistic agreement enter into even the criterion of use R_F we had considered above as a factual criterion in contrast with the general linguistic convention concerning the use of the predicate *F*.

In this vein Wittgenstein also says: "What is needed for communication by the medium of language is not only agreement in definitions, but also (strange as it may sound) agreement in judgments." [49] " 'So what you are saying is that human agreement decides what is true and what is false?' – What is true and false is what human beings *say*; and it is in *language* that human beings agree." [50] I.e., objective facts, like objective distinctions, are mediated by language, for it is by means of language that we mark out what holds true intersubjectively.

In the case of private phenomena, such as sensations and the like, where there is no possibility of direct intersubjective observation, and consequently agreement does not have the same relevance, the objective character of the facts ceases to apply and in that area we can therefore say along with Wittgenstein: "... what is correct is whatever is going to seem correct to me. And all that means is that there can be no talk about 'correct' [in the usual, objective sense] here." [51]

If a deeper and more accurate understanding of Wittgenstein's position becomes possible on the basis of these very simplified and abbreviated epistemological suggestions, they are yet to be supplemented in at least two points.

In the first place intersubjective validity, as manifested in agreement in linguistic usage, is not the sole criterion of objectivity. The domain of the objectively valid or true is fundamentally defined also as a domain subject to orderly laws that bind and regulate states and events and their consequences. For that reason, it is also an important criterion for accepting the truth of a sentence that it be in accord with generally accepted laws of nature, that it fit into the entire system of our fundamental assumptions about the world.

Now since this entire system is not determined just by arbitrary conventions but represents a system that has stood the test of organizing experience, the assertion that facts are marked out and distinguished by intersubjective linguistic agreement in judgment is by no means to be understood to mean that we define the set of facts by merely coming to an agreement. Conventions play an important role in our statements about the world; they are by no means established completely by convention, however, but have an empirical content that can not be overlooked.

A second remark aims in the same direction. The idea that even the criterion for using the predicate F, R_F, is subject as a factual criterion to the condition of intersubjective agreement in language, naturally does not cancel out the distinction between the general convention (I) concerning the use and the criterion for its use, R_F. R_F is established by way of convention (I). But the fact that R_F is satisfied in the case of a specified object a, or not satisfied, is not a matter of free convention all over again – there is no such convention contained in (I) ((I) does not determine how F is to be applied in a's case; the general rule for using 'red' does not determine which things are red) nor does any new convention enter into the scene here (no vote is taken on whether a should be called 'red' or not). Whether R_F is satisfied in the case of a is rather a question of fact, which we state on the basis of experience. It is a sufficient condition for something we state on the basis of experience to be counted a fact that as a rule it is possible to achieve an intersubjective agreement about it. The judgments in which we agree are not made on the basis of an agreement, however, but the agreement is founded on the fact that as a rule our experiences agree.

In this vein of thought, perhaps the one of Wittgenstein's pertinent assertions that comes closest to the mark is the passage in the *Philosophical Investigations* where he compares the way in which a predicate F is used with a method of measuring, and the application of F to a specific object a to a measurement, and says: "It is one thing to describe the method of measuring and another to discover and state the results of measurement." – Here, then, the general convention (I) concerning the use of F (the rule for measuring, which defines a physical quantity, for example) is distinguished from the applications of F to particular cases, which are carried out according to the criterion for applying F, R_F (the criterion of the value of the quantity to be measured given in the method of measuring), laid down on the basis of (I). – "But what we call 'measuring' is also determined by a certain constancy in the results of measurement." [52] – I.e., criterion R_F is capable of being used as a factual criterion only if we generally agree in the judgments in language to which it leads us. But agreement in the results of measurement is not a criterion for arriving at the values measurement gives, but of their reliability. And so agreement in judging that $F(a)$, or that $\neg F(a)$ is not a criterion for arriving at this judgment, but only a criterion of its reliability.

4.5. Speech Acts

Before going into two more specific themes concerning philosophy of language in the *Philosophical Investigations*, we will first of all pursue the fundamental theme 'What constitutes the meaning of linguistic expressions?' still further. The path we take in doing so was suggested by Wittgenstein, but J. L. Austin was the first to follow it up consistently and, after him, J. R. Searle and others in their theory of speech acts. This theory represents a decisive and important step beyond the use theory.

In the *Philosophical Investigations* Wittgenstein says: "*By itself* every sign looks dead. *What* brings it to life? – It *lives* in its use. Does it then have the breath of life within itself? – Or is its *use* its breath?"[53] And: "How does it come about that the arrow $\rangle\!\rangle\!\rightarrow$ *points*? Does it not already seem to carry within itself something over and beyond itself?" – "No, it is not the dead line; only what is mental, the meaning, can do that." – That is both true and false. The arrow is pointing only in the use that the living creature makes of it." [54] And in the *Blue Book* Wittgenstein says: "But if we had to name anything which is the life of the sign, we should have to say it was its use." [55] As early as the *Tractatus* Wittgenstein is advocating similar ideas, when he says: "What does not find expression in the signs is shown by their use. What the signs suppress their use expresses."[56] The fact that in the *Tractatus* Wittgenstein understands the sentence to be a fact, not an object, may be connected with this.[57]

If one wishes to understand what constitutes linguistic meanings – perhaps one can interpret these suggestions so – then one may not start out from expression objects, from sentences and words, but must begin with the utterance performances, the concrete speech acts.[58] What we understand is not abstract objects, but concrete actions; the meanings we attach to expression objects are secondary theoretical constructs, what is primary are the meanings of the speech acts.

What pertains to the meaning of an utterance as a speech act is everything we have to know in order to understand its use in the concrete situation. In this linguistic sense of 'meaning' it coincides with 'meaning' in that wider sense of the word we apply to non-linguistic actions as well, when for example we speak of the 'meaning' of an action in a ceremony or a game.

What differentiates the function of an action from the action itself? When I say 'Good morning', this action is a greeting and it has the function of a greeting; we can describe the action with the same word ('greeting') as its function. But there are many concrete details belonging to the action that are not essential to its function. The move in a game of chess has the same function whether I make it quickly or slowly, with my left hand or my right. Different actions can have the same functions, then. The like holds for speech acts. Instead of 'Good morning', I can say, 'A good morning', or 'I wish you a fine good morning', or, in case the person I am addressing knows German, 'Guten Morgen'. Phonetically different speech acts can therefore have the same meaning. What we intend by the meaning of a speech act coincides, however, with what we called its 'semantic aspect' in I.1. So we identify the meaning of an expression with its semantic aspect.[59]

The function of a linguistic utterance is based upon linguistic conventions. These conventions are general rules, thus refer not to individual actions but to *ways* of acting; not to utterances, then, but to expressions. A convention of this kind does not say, for example, that Fritz can greet Hans on January 1, 1973, in Munich by saying, 'Good morning', but contains the provision that in the morning anyone can greet anyone else (who understands English) with 'Good morning'. On the basis of this general convention a specific utterance of 'Good morning' then takes on the function of a greeting. The meaning of the utterance is thus defined by the expression and the circumstances of the utterance (who is speaking, who is being spoken to, etc.).

Consequently, one must differentiate, as we have in Chapter II.4.3, between the *meaning of the expression* as a form of action: the common function of all actions with this form, and the *meaning of the utterance*: the function of the particular act. The latter is a function of the former and the circumstances of the utterance; and so it includes additional features as compared with the former.[60]

In order to make what is here being understood by the 'semantic aspect' and 'meaning' of speech acts still clearer, we will briefly go into Austin's theory of the *illocutionary force* of utterances in [62a].

Austin points out there that a sentence like 'It is raining' can have quite different functions in different situations. As we have already set forth in Chapter II.4.3, it can be a report, but it can also be a warning ('Look out!

If you don't close the window, it will rain in'.) or a recommendation ('Take your umbrella with you if you are going out!'). This illocutionary force that particular utterances have (reporting, warning, recommending) frequently can not be read off from the sentence itself. The context not only indicates the reference of index expressions in such cases, but the role of the sentence in communication is revealed only by the pragmatic context in which it is used.

Austin is taking up in this connection Wittgenstein's ideas about the variety of ways in which language is used, the diverse language games. We do not use language just to assert, to ask or to command; on the contrary, there is a wealth of roles that language can assume, e.g. describing, telling, judging, confirming, testifying, protesting, retorting, supporting, suggesting, advising, explaining, elucidating, drawing conclusions, warning, demurring, recommending, promising, reporting, telling stories, thanking, praying, confessing, conceding, agreeing, criticizing, praising, blaming, greeting, proclaiming, excusing oneself, offering explanations, deriding – these are all roles that *declarative sentences* can have. We can use *interrogative sentences* not only to inquire but also, for example, for casting doubt, for requesting or ordering ('What are you waiting for?'), and for asserting (in the form of a rhetorical question). We can use *imperative sentences* not only for commanding, but also for wishing, prescribing, recommending, guiding, requesting, appealing, and asking ('Tell me whether you broke the pitcher!')

These distinctions are important if we wish to understand the communicative role of an utterance more precisely. They are by no means always and perfectly expressed in the sentence but in many cases they become clear from the context of the utterance. That led Austin to draw a fundamental distinction between *illocutionary force* and *meaning*.[61] In his account, meaning is never anything but the (descriptive) meaning of the expression. The illocutionary force of an utterance depends on the meaning of the expression uttered; the meaning of a sentence limits the set of illocutionary roles in which it can come into play, but it does not fix upon any one such role unambiguously. Further, with Austin certain results and presuppositions of a speech act are counted to its illocutionary force. He does distinguish between illocutionary and perlocutionary act (bringing about a result by means of a speech act), e.g. between expressing a warning and bringing it about that the hearer has been warned (and conducts himself accordingly). He urges, nevertheless, that certain results belong inseparably to the character of many illocutionary roles. For example, the obligation that follows from making a promise to do what has been promised belongs to [the nature of] promising. It belongs to the act of christening, accomplished by the formula 'I christen this ship the "Hamburg"', that as a result the ship is now called the 'Hamburg', i.e. that designating it in this way is binding. Since these results occur only given certain presuppositions, such necessary presuppositions also belong to the illocutionary act.[62]

In view of all that there is a distinct parallel between Austin's illocutionary force and our semantic aspect. But there are also two important differences and for that reason we have chosen another terminology. In order to fix the parallel still more clearly, we must distinguish between the *semantic aspect* of an utterance and its *performative mode* as the act type to which the utterance belongs. While performative modes are indicated by such verbs as 'assert', 'ask', 'warn', etc., the semantic aspect embraces the speech act's whole meaning. Austin's illocutionary force of an utterance, strictly speaking, corresponds not to its semantic aspect, but to its performative mode, then.

The first difference when illocutionary force and performative mode are being compared consists merely in the fact that we do not count the results of an action and its presuppositions as part of its performative mode. Many of the verbs by which we describe actions are *achievement verbs*[63], i.e. it is correct to apply them only if a certain result does occur or if certain presuppositions are the case. Thus we can say 'Hans knocks Fritz down' if Fritz does fall down after the blow, or 'The doctor cured Kuno's gastritis' if Kuno actually did suffer from gastritis and is healthy after the treatment. I.e. we often characterize the action proper ('Hans gives a Fritz blow', 'The doctor treats Kuno for gastritis') and its result, or its presuppositions at the same time. Naturally it is also possible to specify speech acts with respect to their presuppositions and results, but in the particular case such specifications go beyond the linguistically relevant aspect. The speech act is: promising, saying a christening formula; it remains the same whether the promise is made sincerely, whether an obligation is consequent upon it by virtue of general norms[64] or whether it is kept; or whether the speaker had a right to christen the ship or whether the ceremonial procedure is correct and successful. The function of the speech act does not encompass, then, everything that Austin calls its illocutionary role, so that caution is appropriate in using achievement verbs to characterize speech acts. In order to understand the performative mode 'saying the christening formula' or 'promising', it is necessary to know what 'christening' and 'promising' mean; one aspect of that is knowing the presuppositions, results and obligations that normally accompany such actions. The meaning of the individual speech act, however, is independent of whether such presuppositions are the case, the results occur, or the obligations are fulfilled. In the same way, the meaning of an assertion is independent of whether it is true or false, although it is part of the definition of the performative mode 'asserting' that only true assertions should be made.

The second important difference as compared with Austin is that we do not regard performative mode and meaning as two distinct, even though dependent parameters. Instead, we identify the meaning of an utterance with its semantic aspect and understand the performative mode to be the characteristic type of this aspect.[65] What makes this possible is that the concept of performative mode is narrower than Austin's concept of illocutionary force and that we do not, like Austin, start from the usual descriptive concept of meaning (according to which sentence meanings, for example, are propositions, which are coordinated with expression objects), but interpret meanings primarily as functions of action.

The performative mode can be explicitly indicated in language in the sentence itself. In particular, that is the case with what Austin calls *explicitly performatory expressions*, as for example:

(a)   'I congratulate you'.
(b)   'We invite you to settle your account'.
(c)   'I confirm the statement by Mr. X.'
(d)   'I am asking you if you will accept the nomination'.
(e)   'You are requested not to smoke'.

In these statements performative verbs ('congratulate', 'invite', 'confirm', 'ask', 'request') occur which indicate the sentence's performative mode. They are in either the first person singular or first person plural active indicative or, as in (e), in the corresponding passive, in which case the name of the speaker or speakers can be absent as well. The act of the speaker designated by the performative verb is accomplished in the utter-

ing of such a sentence. Uttering the sentences offered as examples does
not represent any description of speech acts, then – saying 'I congratulate
you' is congratulating, not describing or asserting.

Besides the performative verbs, however, there are also other expressions that serve to specify – whether partially or completely – the performative mode of a sentence. Conjectures are indicated by 'supposedly',
'probably', and 'perhaps', for example, rejoinders by 'but', 'yet',
'however', inferences by 'so', 'therefore', argumentation by 'since',
'because', etc. Further, there are verb forms (e.g. the subjunctive for
requesting, wishing, supposing), phonetic devices (e.g. intonation) and
so on. Punctuation marks ('.' after an assertion, '?' after a question,
and '!' after a command) also characterize the performative mode of a
sentence.

Now every sentence can be represented in an explicitly performative
form, e.g. in the pattern $P(a, b, A)$. P, the performative operator, is supposed to indicate the performative mode. Thus P stands for a performative verb, which can be very general, however. The sentence 'It is raining'
is largely undefined in its performative mode (we saw that it can be used,
for example, as a report, as a warning or as a request) so that it is not
possible to attach a specialized performative verb to it without changing
its sense. In the case of using words ironically or in jest, explicitly indicating the precise performative mode would even destroy it.[66] The sense
of a performative operator is often defined only within very wide limits,
then, and becomes determinate only in the context of an utterance. a and
b in $P(a, b, A)$ are supposed to be index expressions for the speaker or
speakers and the hearer or hearers. And A is supposed to be a sentence in
the form of a declarative sentence. Arguments a and b can even be missing. We rewrite the illustrative sentences as follows, then:

(a')   Congratulate (I, you)
(b')   Invite (we, you, you settle your bill)
(c')   Confirm (I, what Mr. X said is true)
(d')   Ask (I, you, you will accept the nomination)
(e')   Request (I, you, you do not smoke).

Sentences (c') and (e') show how sentences in which, unlike (d), there
is no complete declarative sentence occurring as a subordinate clause can
be brought into the form $P(a, b, A)$.

We call the expression A in P (a, b, A) the *descriptive component* of the sentence P (a, b, A). As such A represents only a part of the entire sentence and A is not tied up with any speech act of its own. In and of itself, then, A is meaningless in our present sense of 'meaning'. The fact that we give A the form of a declarative sentence, for the sake of simplicity, does not imply that A would have a performative function (of its own) and would represent, for example, an assertion. Nothing is asserted in sentence (d'), even though an expression in the form of a declarative sentence occurs in it.

Now how does the meaning of expressions as their performative aspect – we shall also speak of their *performative meaning* – relate to what are ordinarily called the 'meanings' of expressions as products of phonetic acts? When, for example, it is said that the name 'moon' means the moon, the predicate 'is red' means the property of being red, or the sentence 'This rose is yellow' means the fact that this rose is yellow? We will call this sort of meaning *descriptive meaning*. Having designated the performative sense of "meaning" as primary and fundamental, we are now concerned with characterizing descriptive meanings in terms of performative and defining their place in the semantics of speech acts.

If, as discussed above, sentences are given an explicitly performative form, then we obtain from the sentences:

(f)   You are closing the door.
(g)   Close the door!
(h)   Are you closing the door?
          the sentences
(f')   I say (assert) that you are closing the door, or
          Assert (I, you are closing the door)
(g')   I tell (order) you to close the door, or
          Order (I, you, you are closing the door)
(h')   I am asking whether you are closing the door, or
          Ask (I, you, you are closing the door)

These sentences have different performative modes, but a common descriptive component (f). So the attempt will be made to define the performative meanings of sentences in the form P (a, b, A) as functions of the (still to be specified) meanings of components a, b, and A, with such a function corresponding to each performative mode.

Let us consider first of all assertions in the narrower sense as descriptions of facts.

The performative meaning of sentence (f′) depends only on the descriptive meaning of (f) and the circumstances of its utterance, and plainly in a way that is typical of assertions. But we do not want to define the performative meaning of a declarative sentence, starting from its descriptive meaning. We want to go the other way and define its descriptive meaning in terms of its performative meaning. The descriptive meaning of such a sentence is also unambiguously determined by its performative meaning, however: assertions are speech acts that are true or false, and their truth-values depend only on the descriptive meaning of the descriptive components and the circumstances of their being uttered.[67] Therefore we can characterize this descriptive meaning by indicating the conditions under which the assertion is true. That leads to representing the descriptive meaning of (f), for example, as a function which maps possible worlds and circumstances of utterance onto truth-values. In this fashion descriptive sentence components are interpreted by reverting to properties (true – false) of the assertions as speech acts in which they occur.

Since we have given the descriptive components of all sentences the form of declarative sentences and by so doing let them all correspond to assertions, the descriptive meanings of all descriptive sentence components are accordingly fixed and determined.[68]

Since the performative meaning of a declarative sentence depends on its descriptive meaning alone, it is possible to regard descriptive semantics as the semantics of declarative sentences – not in the sense that the performative meanings of such sentences might be reduced to their descriptive meanings, but in such a way that the descriptive meaning of a sentence uniquely determines its performative meaning. The one-to-one correlation of descriptive and performative meanings in the case of declarative sentences makes it possible to define them in terms of each other.

The concept of descriptive meaning can be interpreted in the semantics of declarative sentences as an auxiliary concept that can also be dispensed with. In that event the semantics would have to be directly interpreted as the semantics of assertions, in which assertions as speech acts are said to be true or false depending on states of the world and circumstances of utterance.

Since the semantic aspect of every speech act can be described, its performative meaning can be characterized in terms of the descriptive meaning of a declarative sentence. Consequently the semantics of all speech acts can now be developed within the bounds of declarative sentences, i.e. within the bounds of descriptive semantics.[69]

For that purpose we assign to every utterance a *performative description*, which arises from a *performative version* of the utterance, i.e. from an explicitly performative formulation of the utterance, by interpreting it as an assertion and replacing the index expressions for speaker and hearer that occur in it with names, in case they do not coincide with the speaker and hearer of the performative description, and by introducing names, or index expressions for the relevant circumstances of its utterance.

Performative descriptions of utterances of sentences (f), (g) and (h) are, for example:

(f″)   Fritz asserts (now), that Hans is closing the door.
(g″)   I ordered you (yesterday) to close the door [or, less idiomatic in English, but more faithful to the example in the original: I ordered (yesterday) that you are closing the door.]
(h″)   I shall ask you (tomorrow) whether you are closing the door.

In contrast to (g′) and (h′), (g″) and (h″) are declarative sentences. They are not explicitly performative sentences, because the subject of the performative verb is not the index expression 'I', which stands for the one who is uttering the description (as in (f″)), or because the time of the speech act described does not coincide with the time of its description (as in (g″) and (h″)).

Generally speaking, explicitly performative sentences, e.g. (h′), will not be interpreted as performative descriptions. The description of a speech act is a different speech act from the one described. You can not ask a question and also describe it at one and the same time. To be sure, cases can be cited in which an utterance with an explicitly performative pattern serves as the description of another speech act occurring at the same time,[70] but in that case it is not a description of itself. So we must always draw a sharp distinction between the performance of a speech act and its description; no speech act is a description of itself.

The following would be performative versions of (f″), (g″) and (h″):

(f‴)   I say that Fritz says (now) that Hans is closing the door.

(g‴)   I say that I ordered you (yesterday) to close the door. [Or: that you are closing the door]

(h‴)   I say that I shall ask you (tomorrow) whether you are closing the door.

While an utterance is performed by a specific speaker under specific circumstances, an expression, specifically a sentence, is a form of speech activity, which can be performed by various speakers under diverse circumstances. Therefore performative descriptions of expressions are not rendered by sentences, but by predicates. Performative descriptions of sentences (f), (g) and (h) are along these lines:

(f⁗)   saying (asserting) that the hearer is closing the door.

(g⁗)   ordering the hearer to close the door [or: that the hearer is closing the door].

(h⁗)   asking whether the hearer is closing the door.

We can now regard the descriptive meaning of a performative description of an utterance as its performative meaning, and the same is the case with sentences. If Hans says 'Good morning' to Fritz and someone who hears him asks about the meaning of that utterance, what one will say is that Hans is greeting Fritz. The descriptive meaning of the description 'Hans is greeting Fritz' is used to give information as to the performative meaning of the utterance. And if someone asks what the expression 'Good morning' means, what one will say is that saying 'Good morning' is a greeting. I.e., the descriptive meaning of the description 'greeting' is used to give information as to the performative meaning of 'Good morning'.

If, as in Chapter III.2, one constructs a language L, in which all sentences are interpreted as declarative sentences, then it is not necessary to make the mode of assertion explicit in the sentences. The performative meaning of a sentence A of L follows from the descriptive meaning assigned to A in the semantics of L. In what way it follows from it is not fixed in that semantics, but belongs to its application. Within the bounds of the semantics, however, it is possible to correlate assertions and performative meanings. To do so, one goes from a sentence A to a performative description of A (as an expression). This might read $P(x, A)$, in which x is a variable for the speaker and the performative operator P represents the predicate 'saying' or 'asserting'. The descriptive meaning of $P(x, A)$ is different from that of A; A's descriptive meaning is something other than 'saying that *A*'. Assertion sentences thus have a descriptive and a performative meaning, but they are different. Interrogatives, imperatives, etc., on the other hand have no descriptive, but only a performative meaning. That we understand even the performative meaning of a sentence *A* to be a descriptive meaning is not capable of leading to confusion, for the performative meaning of *A* is not the descriptive meaning of *A* itself (if there is any), but the descriptive meaning of another expression *A'*, the performative description of *A*.[71]

These interim and still very sketchy remarks about performative and descriptive meanings, which we shall take up again in Chapter III.2, should be supplemented by four further comments:

(1) The possibility of characterizing the performative meaning of a non-declarative speech act in terms of the descriptive meaning of a description of the speech act naturally does not exclude other possibilities for semantic analysis. For example, questions can be semantically characterized in terms of the descriptive meanings of possible answers to them, and so a non-performative meaning can be attached to them analogous to the descriptive meaning of assertions, one which uniquely specifies their performative meaning.[72] While the description-approach sketched above has the advantage of simplicity and generality, approaches of this sort offer more detailed information for the analysis of particular kinds of speech act.

(2) One and the same utterance can have more than one semantic function, so that its performative mode contains more than one component. The sentence 'You have deceived me for the last time', for example, contains along with the component of assertion ('You have deceived me') the component of expressing a resolve ('I will not permit myself to be deceived by you again') and possibly also the component of demanding ('Justify your behavior!', 'Say you are sorry' or whatever). Descriptive, expressive and evocative modes of meaning, as we explained them in I.2 following K. Bühler in [34], can probably best be understood along these lines as components of the performative mode.

(3) The fact that a linguistic expression is not just a vocal sign has been the subject of frequent emphasis in linguistics, in agreement with W. von Humboldt, and word and sentence have been understood to be a union of sound and meaning. Most familiar is Saussure's equation *signe = signifiant + signifié*, i.e. the symbol consists of the (phonetic or graphic)

expression that signifies and the *significatum*, the meaning. But this union becomes intelligible only when one interprets expressions not as objects but as speech acts: only in speech is there a union between the act's phonetic form and its function; it is only in uttering 'Good morning' that greeting is accomplished by the production of sounds.

(4) So far we have been concerned only with the meaning of single sentences and this theme will continue to stand in the foreground. At this point, however, a few brief suggestions should be made about the problem of textual semantics, but of course they must be limited to a few points in passing.

A text is in the first instance a series of speech acts. The speaker can be the same person throughout (as with a report) or various speakers can enter in (as with a conversation). With texts, too, we differentiate between the utterance aspect and the expression aspect (the text as what is spoken in a specific situation by specific speakers as distinct from the form of that text), the phonetic aspect and the act or product aspect after the fashion of I.1.

Now by what criterion do we regard certain sequences of sentences as texts and others not? The first thing one will point to in this connection is that the contents of the sentences have a connection with each other, but that is a very vague characterization. It is probably more decisive that the sentence sequence has as a whole a definite illocutionary role of its own. Or in our terminology, that there is a performative mode which characterizes it all together as a story, report, discussion, proof, etc., while smaller segments of the sequence, particularly the individual sentences, can not be characterized in the same way. Now there are texts (e.g. reports) in which one could tie all of the sentences together with 'and' into one long sentence, which would have the same performative mode as the text. But not all texts are long sentences of this sort. Rather, in many texts (e.g. in discussions) the individual sentences – or parts of the texts – are characterized by their own diverse performative modes within the comprehensive performative mood of the entire text (thesis, counter-thesis, argument, rejoinder, challenge, etc.) Here for the first time the Wittgensteinian image of the language game, of speech acts following one on the other like moves in a game, becomes perfectly to the point. The performative mode of the text indicates which language game is being played, what rules govern the succession of individual moves, what moves are possible and consequently what function the individual moves have in the game.

Just as what we did above was to start out from a semantics of (describing) assertion sentences and interpret sentences with other performative modes by way of performative descriptions of these sentences as speech acts, we can now characterize all texts that do not have the character of reports, i.e. of sequences of sentences capable of being conjoined into one assertion sentence, in terms of performative descriptions, which are represented once again as sentences, or as predicates. The descriptive meaning of such descriptions can once again be regarded as the performative meaning of the texts as sequences of speech acts.

This is the way that looks in the example of a discussion: In an *ad hoc* sense laid down as our basis, a discussion is supposed to be made up of assertions, challenges to provide arguments for an assertion, and arguments. An argument for a sentence A is itself a text made up of several sentences of which A is the last and of premises (which count as new assertions) and logical consequences of sentences that came earlier in the argument. There are also supposed to be rules for the discussion, as for example the rule that when one of the participants asks for an argument to be given, one must be provided, that arguments can be called for only to support previous assertions by another participant and that an assertion A by one participant may be challenged only by the assertion of $\neg A$.

The following predicates are defined in terms of such rules:

$D(x, y, C)$ – there is a discussion between x and y as described by C

$B(x, t, E, C)$ – x gives an argument at t for E, as described by C

$T(x, t, C)$ – x asserts at t that C

$F(x, t, C)$ – x draws the conclusion at t that C

$A(x, y, t, C)$ – x calls on y at t to give an argument for his asserting that C.

A discussion that has the structure:

x asserts that C; thereupon y calls on x to give an argument for this assertion; x argues for his assertion by asserting that E and that C follows from it; thereupon y responds by asserting that $\neg E$

can thus be described by the predicate:

$$D(x, y, T(x, t_1, C) \wedge A(y, x, t_2, C) \wedge B(x, t_3, C, T(x, t_4, E) \wedge$$
$$\wedge F(x, t_5, C)) \wedge T(y, t_6, \neg E))$$

with variable x and y. In this description, t_1 through t_6, after the fashion of the relative temporal indicators, 'thereupon', 'then', etc., in the report of the discussion, give the order of the various speech acts.[73] If we use $\Phi(x, y)$ as an abbreviation for this predicate, then we interpret the descriptive meaning of $\Phi(x, y)$ as the performative meaning of the discussion as a text form (form of speech activity). If the constants a, b designate two participants in the discussion, then the descriptive meaning of $\Phi(a, b)$ is correspondingly the performative meaning of the discussion between these two as a text utterance.

In conclusion, let it be emphasized once again that the theory of speech acts, for which there are only scattered pointers in Wittgenstein, represents a distinct advance over the representation or picture theory and over the use theory of meaning in the *Philosophical Investigations*. If one starts out from expressions as (classes of) phonetic or graphic objects, then the difficulty in explicating their meaning lies in the fact that taken by themselves they do not mean anything more than stones or classes of numbers do. Meaning must first be assigned to them, be it along realistic lines or along pragmatic lines by way of rules of use. But interpreting words as marks for things is just as unnatural and distorted as interpreting them as pieces in a game. Speech acts, on the other hand, as conventional activities have meaning in a very natural sense not restricted just to the activities involved in speaking. We understand actions in a more immediate sense than objects. And we do not 'use' a sentence by going back to rules for employing it, which tell us that it can be used here, but we give voice to the sentence because (on the basis of linguistic conventions) we can accomplish what we want to by doing so. Performative meaning recommends itself as a more natural basic concept of semantics, with the help of which descriptive meanings can then be introduced as theoretical constructs.[74]

4.6. *Private Languages*

On one interpretation, a *private language expression* can be understood to be an expression that someone has introduced for his own use, one that does not belong to the intersubjective language spoken by a linguistic community. In this case we will speak of a *private expression*. But it can also be understood to be an expression – whether private or in common use – that stands for a private, inner experience of a subject, for a sensation, a feeling, a pain, say, to cite the example Wittgenstein brings up most frequently. In this case we will speak of an *expression for the private*. In the *Philosophical Investigations*, Wittgenstein denies the possibility of introducing such private language expressions. In doing so he does not draw any clear distinction between private expressions and expressions for the private, but his arguments are aimed at both. This doctrine of Wittgenstein's, insofar as it concerns expressions for the private, is of particular interest in connection with the philosophy of mind or consciousness, with behaviorism and phenomenalism. Insofar as it concerns private expressions it is also of significance in our context, as a thesis in the philosophy of language, however.

Wittgenstein's arguments against *private expressions* can be summarized as follows:

(1) An expression of this sort has meaning only if there are rules for using it correctly. But correct usage is not defined for private expressions, since on Wittgenstein's view the correct use of a word is always the use that is in accord with the way the word is employed by a language community. But where a word is not employed by a community but just by one individual, it is not possible to speak of that sort of correctness. According to Wittgenstein, following a rule is a social practice and consequently one can not follow a rule privatim.[75]

If we take into account the fact that according to Wittgenstein, as we saw in Chapter II.4.4, not only is the general linguistic convention concerning the criteria for using a word established by general usage, but that conditions of general usage enter into these criteria of use themselves, then the argument to the effect that there are no sufficient criteria for the use of private expressions becomes still sharper.

(2) But even if the latter argument is ignored, the criterion for applying a private predicate, for example, could not be anything but the fact that a new object a appears to me to be similar to the objects in $K(F)$ I used as examples in introducing F. An 'appears to be similar' of that sort is no criterion that can be used, however, because I can not put the correctness of this appearing-to-be to any test: "One would like to say: what is correct

is whatever is going to seem correct to me. And all that means is that there can not be any talk of 'correct' in this case." [76] This argument takes on particular force when F is a predicate for the private as well, e.g. for my sensations. For while objects can be put alongside each other and compared, that is not possible with sensations: earlier sensations can be compared with present sensations only in memory. But memory is unreliable and can only be tested by other memories. Someone who tests the correctness of one memory by means of another memory, however, is according to Wittgenstein like someone who buys several copies of the morning paper in order to assure himself that it is writing the truth.[77]

Thus while in applying a predicate F that is in general use one does have a wider criterion for an ascription of F being correct, viz. the linguistic usage of others, with private expressions one is referred to nothing but how things appear to oneself.

Wittgenstein's main arguments against *expressions for the private* read as follows, on the other hand:

(3) A predicate for the private, e.g. 'feeling a pain', since we can not directly observe the pain sensations of others, can be learned only by introspection, i.e. as it applies to our own pains. But then it is not possible to apply the predicate we have learned in that way to other persons as well. For if I learn "feeling a pain" only in terms of my own sensations, then for me 'pain' is synonymous with 'pain felt by me' and in that case it is nonsense to speak of another person's pain.[78] Nor can one say that someone else is feeling pains when he experiences the same sensations as I do when I am feeling pains, for I have no criterion for applying 'feeling pains' to others.[79]

(4) Even if we managed to apply expressions for the private like 'feeling pain' to others, it would nevertheless be impossible to embed them in the intersubjective language. For we can not compare our private sensations intersubjectively and so it would remain entirely unclear whether various people do not each mean something entirely different by 'feeling pain'. The meaning of 'feeling pain', as an intersubjective predicate, would remain totally undefined, because we would have no common criteria for applying that predicate.

How then is the meaning of such words as 'feeling pain' to be understood, words that are nevertheless actually part of our common language? According to Wittgenstein, one must first of all distinguish between statements such as 'I have a pain', which have no descriptive meaning, only expressive – like 'Ow' or a groan – and statements such as 'He has a pain'. The possibility of introducing statements of the latter type into the common language has its basis in the fact that there is something like natural pain behavior that all human beings exhibit when they have a pain, and according to Wittgenstein statements about someone else's pains are to be understood along behavioristic lines as statements about such pain behavior. If the mother observes such pain behavior in some third person, she says to the child: 'Now he has a pain', and in this way the child learns how to use the words 'having a pain' with pain behavior as the criterion for applying it. The words 'having a pain' are thus used as applied to pain behavior and therefore that behavior is what they mean. And so Wittgenstein can say, similarly as for the thing predicate 'red', "You learned the concept of pain when you learned the language." [80]

Wittgenstein also uses the beetle example we have already cited in II.3.3 to illustrate this idea: "Suppose everyone had a box with something in it we call a 'Beetle'. No one can look into anyone else's box.... In that case it might well be that everyone had something different in his box.... But if the word 'beetle' were to have a use for these people all the same? – Then it would not be the name of a thing. The thing in the box does not belong to the language game at all... you can 'divide through by' this thing in the box; it cancels out, whatever it is." [81]

The pain sensation is represented by the beetle here and what the example says is: just as the word 'beetle' as generally used does not refer to the possibly quite different things in the boxes, but only to the visible boxes themselves, for instance, so the word 'having a pain' does not refer to the possibly quite different pain sensations, but to the visible pain behavior.

The case is similar with other expressions for the private: they too are to be understood in a behavioristic way. To be sure, Wittgenstein does not offer any discussion of this program, only a few paltry hints. But the program has been carried out in detail by G. Ryle in [49], for example.

The following comments are to be made by way of a critique of Wittgenstein's arguments against private languages:

Ad 1: As we have already urged in Chapter II.4.4, whether a convention concerning the use of a word can function or not does not depend on the number who are subject to that convention. Even a single individual can adopt a resolution that he can make use of. There is no reason why one can not also follow a private rule. There is, to be sure, this much truth in Wittgenstein's argument, namely that absence of any way of checking one's own use of language against the linguistic usage of others would result in some uncertainty in the employment of private expressions, but that would not make the introduction of private words impossible. On the other hand, we have seen in Chapter II.4.4 that linguistic intersubjectivity is necessary for language to become a language about things, about objective facts. But this argument against the possibility of using private expressions collapses in precisely the case Wittgenstein has in mind, the case of private expressions for the private.

Ad 2: Faced with the question whether the use of a word is in accord with earlier and with the stipulated ways of using it, the individual is always ultimately thrown back on his own memories and impressions. That is true of the question whether we are using a word in the intersubjective language in accord with general usage as much as of the question of the use of private expressions. Ultimately we can never test the correctness of our impressions and memories except by means of impressions and memories, not of course by means of the same impressions and memories, but by means of other ones. And Wittgenstein's example of the morning paper is off the mark to this extent: We do not buy several copies of the same morning paper to convince ourselves of the truth of what is written in it, but we buy different morning papers. And where we have no possibilities for checking directly, that is an entirely sensible thing to do.

Furthermore, there is to be sure a distinct difference in the degree to which our sensations and objective 'public' facts can be checked, but it is just not the case that there are no distinctions within the realm of our sensations that will bear any weight – since our ultimate criteria are always experiences of our own [*Erlebniskriterien*], otherwise distinctions among things would not be possible either.

Ad 3: Even if we do learn predicates such as 'having a pain' primarily by introspection, Wittgenstein's argument is still not any valid objection to the possibility of applying these predicates to other persons. We learn predicates like 'red' also primarily by examples of red objects perceived by us. But it does not follow from that that for each person X 'red' is synonymous with 'perceived as red by X'. Rather we apply this predicate to objects not perceived by us too and understand it when it is applied by others to objects seen only by them. When a predicate F is learned from examples to which G also belongs, it can be the case, but it does not have to be, that F is understood in the sense of 'F and G'.

Ad 4: Wittgenstein's fourth argument holds not only for expressions for the private, but, as the discussions of Quine's thesis of indeterminacy of translation in Chapter II.3.3 have shown, for all linguistic expressions. We can say, as we did there: It is a natural assumption, to be checked by further observations, that in like situations the other person has sensations like my own. If he hits himself on the thumb with the hammer, I can reasonably assume that he has the same sensation as I do when I hit myself on the thumb, namely pain. And this assumption is supported by the fact that he exhibits the same reaction as I do on such occasions myself. If further the experiences he calls 'feeling pain' play the same role in his whole life and behavior, then the assumption that he means something different by this expression from what I mean by it has no sense. Wittgenstein's beetle example has its basis after all in the fact that the beetle in the box is an isolated phenomenon with no connection with any other visible phenomena. That can not be said of our experiences of sensations, feelings and the like, however, and to that extent this comparison is skewed.

This much is correct in Wittgenstein's argument, however: we could not introduce words for the private into intersubjective language unless there were intersubjectively observable causes, effects and criteria for private experiences.

Finally, it is to be granted Wittgenstein's reconstruction of the meanings of words for the private, that a distinction must be drawn between their descriptive use and their expressive (*Kundgabe*) and evocative use (*Appell*). But this distinction does not always coincide with the distinction between employing them in the second and third person as against a first person use: The sentence 'I feel such and such pains' said to a doctor is a descriptive sentence and the cry 'Ouch' can not be substituted for it in its semantic function. On the other side of the question, the sentence 'Fritz is in pain' may contain an appeal to the doctor to help Fritz.

Furthermore it does not follow from the fact that we often use behavioral criteria in employing the words 'feeling pain' that because of this it means those forms of behavior. When we say that someone has a pain what we mean is that he is having a certain sensation, not that he is be-

having in such and such a way or that he has a disposition so to behave –
what behavior or what behavioral disposition is analytically necessary
and sufficient for applying this predicate? If we say that as a rule the atmo-
spheric pressure increases according to the rising of the barometer needle,
it does not follow from this that what we mean by the sentence 'The atmo-
spheric pressure is increasing' is that the barometer is rising.

In summary we can say, then, that Wittgenstein's arguments against
private language expressions are not convincing. But they do illuminate
once again his endeavour to establish the connection between word
meaning and intersubjective word usage.

4.7. *Family Resemblances, Type Concepts and Linguistic Fields*

In the *Philosophical Investigations* Wittgenstein says that the objects to
which a one-place predicate *F* can be ascribed generally do not have any
quality in common (which all of the objects to which *F* can not be ascribed
do not have), but that there are only certain similarities among them: "I
can think of no better way of characterizing these similarities than by
using the term 'family resemblances'; for the various resemblances that
hold among the members of a family overlap and intersect each other in
the same way." [82]

Wittgenstein illustrates this in the case of the predicates 'game' and
'number'. He says: "Consider the proceedings we call 'games' for one
example. I mean board games, card games, ball games, games of combat,
and so on. What do these all have in common? – Do not say, 'There *has*
to be something common to them, or else they would not be called
'games' ' – but *look* and *see* whether they all have something in common.
– For if you look at them, you are surely not going to see something common to *all* of them, but you are going to see resemblances and relationships..." And after having pointed out such common features and relationships within particular groups of games and having shown that none
of these features are true of all games, he reaches this conclusion: "We
see a complicated network of resemblances that overlap and intersect
each other. Resemblances writ large and writ small." [83]

"And the kinds of numbers equally constitute a family, for another
example. Why do we call something a 'number'? Well, let us say, because it has a – direct – relationship to much that has previously been
called number; and by virtue of that, one can say, it acquires an indirect

relationship to other things we call by the *same* name. And we draw our concept out just as in spinning a thread we twist fibre onto fibre. And the strength of the thread does not lie in any one fibre running throughout its entire length, but in the fact that there are many overlapping fibres." [84]

Now these remarks of Wittgenstein's obviously can not be understood as saying that there is no property common to all games, for example – for the very property of being a game is one such property. If concepts or qualities, on the pragmatic interpretation, are determined by predicates, then there must be a quality corresponding to 'game' and 'number' as to other predicates. Nor can we interpret the remark in such a way that, as Bambrough proposed in [60], there is no predicate other than F that applies to precisely all the objects to which F applies – $\neg\neg F$ would be such a predicate – or there is no observable characteristic that belongs to precisely those objects – for the concept of observable characteristic can not be applied to abstracta such as numbers and besides that without being connected with any concrete scientific context it is much too vague.

More to the point is Bambrough's comment that in saying these things Wittgenstein is assuming a middle position between realism and nominalism in the philosophy of language. According to realism a predicate F is supposed to become meaningful by virtue of our assigning a concept independent of F to it and ascribing it to precisely the objects that fall under that concept. On that view, in Wittgenstein's example, the use of the predicate 'game' would be specified in such a way that we ascribe it to all affairs that are games – the criterion for applying 'game' would thus be the (antecedently given) property of being a game. For nominalism, on the other hand, the objects to which we ascribe F have nothing in common besides being called F, i.e. we do not use the word 'game' with an antecedently given conceptual criterion as a standard, but rather what is primary is the use of the predicate; if need be the concept of 'game' can be attained by abstraction from the predicate on the basis of identical usage.

Now the realistic approach leads – apart from the problems we pointed out earlier – to the difficulty that in fact we do not have at our disposal any sharply defined concept of a game, according to which we employ the word 'game'. If we were asked to say what a game is in general, we would be at a loss, even though we know how to use the word 'game' correctly. Nominalism, on the other hand, faces the problem that where there is no criterion for applying F, then the use of F is arbitrary, and a sentence saying that some affair is a game does not say anything about that affair except that it is called a 'game', i.e. such predications have no rational descriptive content.[85]

According to Wittgenstein, however, we apply a predicate F neither by using an antecedently given concept as a standard nor arbitrarily, without any criterion for applying it, but by using resemblances as a standard.

With his thesis of using predicates according to family resemblances Wittgenstein wishes to do justice to the following linguistic phenomena:

(1) Although we know how to use such a predicate as 'game', we can not, as was already stated, explain in general terms what a game is. A definition of 'game' such as might be in a dictionary, for example, is only a later attempt to describe an antecedently given linguistic usage, which is also determined by many accidental circumstances and arbitrary factors for which no further reason can be given. The definition of the concept is only a function of the word's use. This latter is not guided by an antecedently given concept, but concepts first arise, as the basic pragmatic thesis would have it, where the use of predicates has been firmly established.

But it is also an empirical fact, independent of pragmatism, that in applying the word 'game' to a new sort of affair, we are not guided by firm general criteria of games, but by relationships the new affairs manifest with those we are accustomed to calling 'games'.

(2) Predicates in ordinary language have a certain vagueness at their margins, they are *open* or *porous*, as it is also put.[86] If they stood for determinate concepts it could not be the case that there are objects within the domain for which they are defined of which one could either affirm or deny the predicate with equal justification. If e.g. 'red' stood for a determinate concept, we could never come to be in doubt, a doubt not capable of being resolved by factual information, about whether we should call an object 'red' or 'orange'.

(3) Ordinary predicates are in many respects highly *dependent on their contexts* for their meanings. We understand what a *mosquito-eating bat* is only if we know that the word 'bat' can designate an animal as well as a baseball or cricket bat – what occurs here is a typical ambiguity, different ways of using the same word, quite distinct from each other. We understand what a 'pitch-black night' is, on the other hand, on the basis of the resemblance in meaning between the use of 'pitch-black' in the sense of

'having the black color of pitch' and in the sense of 'very dark'. Consequently this way of using the expression requires no further explication.[87]

(4) The question of the *synonymity* of predicates is for the most part
not a matter of either-or, as it would have to be if predicates stood for
determinate concepts. Instead, it is a matter of more-or-less. We can
usually speak only of a resemblance of meaning between two predicates,
hardly ever of a strict identity of meaning.[88]

Wittgenstein can now explain these phenomena with his theory of
family resemblances:

For (1) that is obvious: If there is nothing but a family resemblance
among the objects that fall under F, this resemblance is the sole criterion
for applying F.

The marginal vagueness of F, as described in (2), arises from the fact
that an object can manifest resemblances both to objects to which F has
been ascribed and to objects of which it has been denied, and that these
resemblances may balance each other.

As to (3), the dependence of F on its context is made possible by the
fact that the F-objects spoken of in one context manifest specific resemblances to each other, and these then confer an additional meaning on F,
but they are different from the resemblances the F-objects spoken of in
another context manifest. This does not exclude the objects in both sets
from also being sufficiently similar to each other that they can all be
characterized by the one predicate F. Resemblances of meaning in different contexts permit words to be used metaphorically as well, without such
use always having to be explained anew in the new contexts.

Finally, as to (4), light is shed on the fact that the synonymity of two
predicates F and G is a matter of degree by noting that on the thesis of
family resemblances an F-object is an object sufficiently similar to the objects ordinarily called F and likewise for G-objects. The resemblances
specified in this way hold to a greater or a lesser degree, however, and consequently the description of an object as an F is more or less appropriate
than the description of it as a G, or more or less equivalent to it.

These examples already demonstrate the fruitfulness of the Wittgensteinian ideas. We shall see, however, that these ideas admit of still further
important applications in the philosophy of language. But before we go
into these any further, we will make an attempt at a more precise representation, since Wittgenstein's statements have only illustrative value. A

scientific use of the term 'family resemblance' presupposes more exact explication of the conceptual structures to which it is addressed.[89]

We will now give a logical model for the introduction of classificatory concepts on the basis of resemblances.[90] In doing so we shall refer, in order to have a concrete case before our minds, to the example of introducing color predicates such as 'blue', 'green', 'yellow', and 'red'. But features peculiar to this example are not supposed to enter into the model; instead it is supposed to be formulated in such general terms as to be assured of broad applicability.

The color predicates, according to Wittgenstein, are not defined as expressing classificatory concepts of blue, green, yellow and red already given in advance, but as being used by us on the basis of a resemblance between the objects to which they are supposed to be applied and objects that have already been distinguished as 'blue', 'green', 'yellow', 'red'. We will have to begin with a relation of color resemblance, then. Now this color-resemblance is no classificatory two-place relation, such that two objects from the class M of all colored objects, the field of the resemblance relation, must either resemble or not – for a resemblance relation of that sort would have to be reflexive, symmetric and transitive, i.e. an equivalence relation, which would as such already define the domains of the color concepts as equivalence classes, so that we would already have classificatory color concepts.[91]

A two-place comparative relation makes no sense as a resemblance relation. With a three-place comparative relation: *a resembles b at most as much as c resembles b*, the resemblances of two objects can only be compared with respect to a *tertium comparationis b*, not any arbitrarily selected resemblances of pairs of objects. Consequently one will begin with a four-place resemblance relation on M : *a and b resemble each other at most as much as c and d*, symbolically $a, b \leqslant . c, d$.[92]

This relation is supposed to satisfy the following axioms:

(A1) $a, b \leqslant . c, d \lor c, d \leqslant . a, b$

(A2) $a, b \leqslant . c, d \land c, d \leqslant . e, f \supset a, b \leqslant . e, f$

(A3) $a, b \leqslant . c, d \supset b, a \leqslant . c, d$

(A4) $a, b \leqslant . c, d \supset a, b \leqslant . d, c$

(A5) $a, b \leqslant . c, c$

(A6) $a, b \doteq a, a \supset a, c \doteq b, c$

We then define:

(d1) $a, b \doteq c, d := a, b \leqslant . c, d \wedge c, d \leqslant . ab$
(d2) $a, b \lessdot c, d := \neg c, d \leqslant . a, b$
(d3) $a \sim b := \wedge x(a, x \doteq b, x)$

(A1) to (A4) say that the relation $\{a, b\} \leqslant . \{c, d\} := a, b \leqslant . c, d$ between pair sets $\{a, b\}$ and $\{c, d\}$ is a comparative concept along the lines of a *weak ordering*. (A5) says that there are maximal elements for this relation (identity implies maximal resemblance). And (A6) says that two objects a and b with maximal resemblance are not distinguishable, i.e. $a \sim b$ holds. $\doteq$ and $\sim$ are both equivalence relations – sameness of color in our example – and the substitution principle $a \sim b \supset (A[a] \supset A[b])$, where $A[a]$ is a primary formula constructed with $\leqslant$. that contains a, holds.

On the basis of the relation $\leqslant$. on set M, color-resemblance in our example, n classificatory color concepts are now to be introduced. We represent them as classes $F_1, \ldots, F_n$. For that purpose we begin with classes $B_1, \ldots, B_n$ of objects in M given as *examples* of elements of $F_1, \ldots, F_n$. We also call these classes $B_i (i = 1, \ldots, n)$ *example-classes*. It is supposed to hold true of them that:

(B1) $B_i \neq \wedge$, i.e. the B_i are not empty (let $\wedge$ be the null class),

and

(B2) $a \in B_i \wedge b \in B_k \supset \neg a \sim b$ for $i \neq k$, i.e. different example classes do not contain any objects with the same color.

From that it follows immediately:

$$B_i \cap B_k = \wedge \text{ for } i \neq k.$$

The color classes F_i are now supposed to be defined as sets of objects that resemble the elements of B_i more than the elements of the classes B_k with $i \neq k$. I.e. we define:

(D1) $a \in F_i := \vee x(x \in B_i \wedge \wedge y(y \in \bigcup_{k \neq i} B_k \supset y, a \lessdot x, a))$.

$\bigcup_{k \neq i} B_k$ is the union of all example-classes, eliminating the elements of B_i.

According to (D1), then, F_i is defined as the set of objects a, which have a greater resemblance to *one* element of B_i than to any element of B_k with

$i \neq k$. A definition: $a \in F_i := \bigwedge xy(x \in B_i \wedge y \in \bigcup_{k \neq i} B_k \supset y, a \lessdot x, a)$, on which an object a belongs to class F_i only if it resembles *all* of the objects in B_i more than it does any of the objects in B_k with $k \neq i$, would be inadequate precisely in view of our example of color classes, because a red object lying on the Orange side resembles a yellow one more than it does a red object lying on the Violet side.

(D1) satisfies the two conditions:

(C1) $B_i \subset F_i,$

and

(C2) $a \in F_i \wedge b \in F_k \supset \neg\, a \sim b$ for $i \neq k$.

If the color classes F_i are defined in terms of the example classes B_i in this way, then the F_i depend entirely on the choice of examples. That generates the following problem: Actually the introduction of color predicates does not break down into two steps, so that first the example classes are presented and then the F_i determined exclusively by referring to those first examples. One is more inclined to say that every object in F_i can serve as an example of F_i. But then this would have to be true: If you substitute for the B_i in (D1) any sets F_i^*, for which $B_i \subset F_i^* \subset F_i$, then you obtain the same F_i, i.e. the F_i are invariant under any such expansion of the example-sets. But this condition is not universally true.

This does not make definition (D1) inadequate, however. For invariance with regard to expansions of the example classes actually only enters in when there is already a large number of widely scattered examples that indicate in particular the predicate F_i's limits of applicability.

If we give this definition: Two series of example classes $B_1, \ldots, B_n$ and $B'_1, \ldots, B'_n$ are called equivalent if they yield the same classes $F_1, \ldots, F_n$ on applying (D1) – so that F_i are invariant upon substitution of any other equivalent series of example classes for any given series – then it is clear that invariance of F_i with respect to the selection of B_i exists within very broad limits.

On certain conditions comparative relations can also be defined along these lines: *a is at most as typical a case of F_i as b is*. The following is a simple case, for example: If there is a sequence of objects $b_1, \ldots, b_n$ of M, such that the sequence $\{b_1\}, \ldots, \{b_n\}$ of unit classes of these objects is equivalent to the sequence of example classes $B_1, \ldots, B_n$, then we can construct a definition as follows:

(D2) $a \leqslant_i c := a \in F_i \wedge c \in F_i \wedge a, b_i \leqslant c, b_i.$

The b_i can then be called *pure cases* of F_i.

We will now show that two further linguistic phenomena besides family resemblances can be represented in our model of introducing classificatory predicates by means of a resemblance relation and example classes.

(a) Ordinary predicates are in many ways not purely classificatory concepts, but *type concepts*. A number is either a prime number or not. In this case it makes no sense to say that 3 is more, or less of a prime number than 5. To that degree, 'prime number' is a purely classificatory concept. The concept 'pyknic', on the other hand, is an example of a type concept. Here, too, it can be said that a specific man is a pyknic or is not a pyknic. But pyknics are not all equally pyknic; *the pyknic*, as a pure case, is rather rare, in fact. Most human beings who can be so described manifest other, atypical characteristics along with the pyknic features in their body structure. In this case, then, it does make sense to say: a is a more typical case of a pyknic than b, i.e. to be pyknic is not just a matter of either-or but also a matter of more-or-less.

C. G. Hempel and P. Oppenheim first presented a logical analysis of the structure of type concepts in [36]. They elaborated on the comparative character of the type concept. But since classificatory and comparative concepts represent different forms of concepts – a classificatory concept is a one-place concept, a comparative at least a two-place concept – comparative concepts can not be used for purposes of classification directly nor classificatory concepts for comparison. The usual type concepts unite the classificatory and the comparative aspects, however, insofar as they are used both in the way classificatory concepts $F(x)$ are and in the way comparative concepts defined on the set $\lambda \, xF(x)$ are. To that extent the Hempel-Oppenheim analysis is not entirely satisfactory. Hempel's differentiation between 'classificatory types' (as purely classificatory concepts) and 'extreme types' (as comparative concepts) does not do justice to these two aspects of type predicates either.[93]

Our model for introducing predicates by way of (D1) can now be looked upon as a model for introducing type concepts as well. For the F_i are classificatory concepts; but with the aid of the resemblance relation used in defining them in many cases a comparative concept in accord with (D2) is also established, so that it makes sense to say that one object in $\lambda\, x F_i(x)$ is a more typical case of F_i than another.

(b) The field concept in linguistics also impresses itself upon us in the context of our model. The basic idea of linguistic field theory goes back to W. v. Humboldt. The term 'linguistic field' was first introduced in 1924 by G. Ipsen, however, and later taken over by J. Trier in another sense. We shall refer in what follows to Trier's field concept, which is no doubt the most relevant for semiotic.[94]

According to Trier certain groups of words form a *word field*. What is characteristic of a word field is (1) that it is correlated with a semantic region [*Sinnbezirk*], i.e. there is some relationship of meaning among all the words in the field, and (2) that the meaning of one word depends on that of the other words in the field and can only be defined together with and in distinction from their meanings.

One example of a word field that has often been used is the field of color words. The correlated semantic region is the realm of color, and the meaning of 'red', for example, depends on whether the words 'orange', 'violet' are also in the field or only 'yellow' and 'blue'. Characterizing the meaning of 'red' requires, then, that the whole field to which it belongs be specified. Two different word fields correlated with the same semantic region represent two different ways of dividing this region up linguistically. That will be plain on comparing our system of basic color words with that of the Navahos, for example, in which one word takes over the function of our 'blue' and 'green', while two words correspond to our 'black'.[95]

Other examples of word fields are the levels in a grading scale – the predicate 'good' says one thing in the scale 'very good', 'good', 'satisfactory', 'adequate', 'inferior', 'unsatisfactory', and something else in the scale 'good', 'mediocre', 'bad' – or Trier's standard example of words in the region of intelligence. [The example contrasts the role of the word 'wize' in the Middle High German field of words '*wize*', '*witzig*', '*sinic*', '*bescheiden*', '*künstic*', '*listic*', '*kundig*', '*karc*', etc., with the role of the word '*weise*' in the New High German field of '*weise*', '*klug*', '*gescheit*', '*intelligent*', '*schlau*', '*gerissen*', etc.[96] For obvious reasons it can not be translated into English without ceasing to be Trier's example.]

Now our model of introducing classificatory concepts on the basis of a comparative resemblance structure with example classes represents this process of establishing the meaning of predicates in a word field. The field M of relation $\leqslant$. corresponds to the semantic region, which can be divided up into subdomains F_i in quite diverse ways. Also, from the perspective of (D1), we can apprehend the dependence of the F_i on the number n of classes into which M is divided and on the examples from B_k of the other color classes F_k with $k \neq i$, i.e. on where the other color classes are settled in M. I.e., we can see a dependence of the meanings of the F_i on each other: if one F_i is altered, then the others will be altered along with it.[97]

Our model contains within it, then, the three linguistically fundamental aspects of family resemblances, type concepts and linguistic fields, so that it can be looked upon as a basic model for introducing predicates. This model illustrates in a special case still another of Wittgenstein's theses, that we learn conceptual distinctions (here the classificatory predicates) only in learning language, his thesis of the world being divided up by language. If we consider the example again, it is clear that things do not fall into red, blue, yellow, and so on by themselves, but that we first introduce this differentiation with the assistance of language, by picking out example classes of color-resembling objects and designating them by a single word.

NOTES

[1] See Wright [55].

[2] See Wittgenstein [53], 109, 133.

[3] For an interpretation of the *Philosophical Investigations*, see also Pitcher [64] and [66], and Stegmüller [65], Chapter XI, Part II.

[4] See Chapter II.1.3.

[5] See Wittgenstein [53], 101–104, and 373, 379f. and 384.

[6] That is also true of those realistic theories according to which the entities to be pictured are ideal structures, such as concepts, or mental data, such as ideas (*Vorstellungen*). For mental reality, too, is revealed only by means of language and concepts are not given to us independently of language, but represent nothing but abstractions from linguistic givens.

[7] See Wittgenstein [53], 60–64 and 90.

[8] See Wittgenstein [53], 124.

[9] See Wittgenstein [53], 87, 88, 98, 99.

[10] See Wittgenstein [53], 7, 19, 23.

[11] Lying, to be sure, is not so much a distinct language game as an infraction of the rules of the game 'communication', which require that one assert only such declarative sentences as one is convinced are true.

[12] See Wittgenstein's comparison of words with tools in [53], 11.

[13] See also Chapter II.4.3.

[14] For criticism of the idea of language games see also Lenk [67].

[15] Alston, for example, gives this formulation in [63b], p. 84.

[16] Wittgenstein [53], 43. – On Wittgenstein's 'definition' of meaning as use see also Hallett [67].

[17] Wittgenstein says in [53], 560: "The meaning of the word is what is explained by the explanations of its meaning." In explaining a meaning what one explains is for the most part the word's use, however, and consequently the identification of meaning and use comes naturally.

[18] The vagueness and ambiguity of the concept 'use' has often been emphasized in the literature, See e.g. Alston [63a], Findlay [61], Ryle [60], Shwayder [60], Strawson [54] and Xenakis [54].

[19] See also the remarks in Pitcher [64] and Stegmüller [65], as well as G. Ryle's distinction in [53] between *use* (as correct, normal use) and *usage* (as the use that actually occurs). – We have already referred in 1.1 to the difficulties of ascertaining by empirical means the linguistic norms that are in force. – It has often been remarked that reasoning in support of assertions about correct linguistic use is often quite questionable precisely when it is advanced by ordinary-language-philosophers, among whom the armchair method of a scientifically uncultivated spontaneous linguistic intuition more often than not replaces empirical investigations. See e.g. Mates [58].

[20] See e.g. W. P. Alston in [63a] and P. F. Strawson in [54].

[21] See Chapter II.4.5.

[22] See Searle [69], p. 146ff. Searle alludes to G. Ryle's false analysis of the meaning of the word 'voluntarily' in [49], which arises out of a mixture of semantic and non-semantic criteria of use.

[23] See Searle [69], p. 155, and for the last example Chomsky [68].

[24] See Charlesworth [59], Pitcher [64] and Ziff [60], Chapter V. The example with 'ultor' is one of P. Ziff's, see [60], p. 189. – Ziff's further objections to the identification of use and meaning are based upon the error of understanding 'use' as nothing but syntactic use, the distribution of the words.

[25] Ryle's remark in [60], that meaning and use can be identified only for words, but not for sentences, because sentences are utterances, for which there is no general use as such, is entirely off the mark, since sentences are also expressions and the use even of new sentences is determined by the use of the words in them and the rules of grammar.

[26] See Chapter II.3.1.

[27] P. Ziff urges in [60], p. 34f. that it is better to speak of linguistic *regularities* than of *rules*, since rules are nothing but explicitly formulated norms for or descriptions of behavior. We speak of 'rules' here in a wider sense that does not imply explicit formulation.

[28] The fact that the use of words is a use for the expression of something has been given special prominence by M. J. Charlesworth in [59], p. 218 where he says: "linguistic use is defined in terms of meaning, so that meaning cannot be defined in terms of use" – and J. N. Findlay in [61], where he writes: "The reason why it is absurd to tell us not to attend to the meaning of expressions but to concentrate on their use, is perfectly simple: it is that the notion of use, as it ordinarily exists and is used, presupposes the notion of meaning… and that it therefore cannot be used to elucidate the latter, and much less replace it or to do duty for it." J. Wheatley expresses himself along similar lines in [63], p. 643.

[29] J. L. Austin first called attention to these forms of using language. See the article 'Performative Utterances' in Austin [61]. We shall return to the matter for more extended consideration in Chapter II.4.5.

[30] W. P. Alston has advanced some arguments in [63a] against the possibility of sub-

stituting explanations of use for explanations of meaning, arguments that represent for him objections to the possibility of identifying use and meaning. One argument, for instance, goes: If you say ' "*a*" is used in the same way as "*b*" ' you do not presuppose, as with ' "*a*" means *b*' that the other party knows the meaning, or the use of '*b*' – That may be. But instead of saying the latter, one can also say ' "*a*" means the same as "*b*" ' or in the place of the former, 'The word "*a*" is applied to (a) *b*'. The possibility of identification does not depend on such formulations. The rest of Alston's objections in [63a] are of a similar character, so that we will not go into them further here.

[31] D. Holdcroft has raised similar objections to explaining the meaning of an expression in terms of its use in [64]. – The idea comes easily to mind of sharpening this argument as follows: Since an explanation in language always presupposes the understanding of the language in which it is formulated, an explanation of language in language, e.g. an explanation of what a statement is formulated in the form of a statement, is circular and thus impossible. But the response to this would be: Naturally an explanation (in language) is not directed to someone who cannot yet speak, and does not understand the assertive function of a sentence, for example. The sense of such an explanation is not to teach language, but to deepen an understanding of language that is presupposed, e.g. a presupposed understanding of stating, by means of general definitions or explications. And there is no circularity in that.

[32] Antal [61], p. 217.

[33] Wittgenstein says: "How do I explain to someone the meaning of 'regular', 'uniform', 'the same'? – To one, let us say, who speaks only French, I shall explain those words in terms of the corresponding words in French. But someone who does not yet have these *concepts*, to him I shall explain the words by *examples* and by *practicing their use*." [53], 208.

[34] Wittgenstein [22], 4.027.

[35] Generally speaking, the use of F will be characterized by a system of rules with the form 'Under condition $T_{F_i}(a)$; F may be ascribed to a if (or: only if, or if and only if) $R_{F_i}(a)$ is true' $(i=1, ..., n)$.

[36] Wittgenstein [53], 208.

[37] See also Chapter II.4.6.

[38] Wittgenstein [53], 258. See also 202, *ibid.*

[39] See Wittgenstein [53], 199.

[40] *Diachronically*, i.e. considered in terms of its changes over time, language undergoes certain transformations, and in the process the rules of use for *langue* can be changed by some initially atypical instances of use from *parole*. But our argument is based upon a *synchronic* consideration of language, just as it is in a particular stage of development.

[41] Wittgenstein [56], p. 184.

[42] Wittgenstein [53], 211.

[43] Wittgenstein [53], 217.

[44] Wittgenstein [56], p. 184f.

[45] Wittgenstein [53], 381.

[46] Wittgenstein also attacks one of the crucial presuppositions of the question, which is supposed to be answered in terms of the notion of learning predicates inductively, namely the presupposition that it is possible to speak of a fully determinate meaning, or of a fully determinate general use of a predicate of ordinary language.

Wittgenstein refers in this connection first to the *openness* of these predicates: they are not, as we often assume when we are idealizing for logical purposes, defined in such a way for a determinate domain of objects that for each of those objects it is settled –

though it need not be decidable in every case – whether the predicate is to be affirmed or denied. Ordinary language predicates have a certain horizon of vagueness, rather, in which there are no longer any binding criteria of use. Thus while for many things there is no doubt as to whether they are to be described as 'red' or not, there are others that run more into orange or violet, for which it is no longer possible to say with compelling conviction whether they should continue to be described as 'red' or as 'orange', or 'violet'. And for the things we usually encounter, we ordinarily think of, it is clear whether or not they should be called an 'easy-chair'. But if we encounter something that has the shape and the solidity of an easy-chair, but changes its size all the time and appears and disappears inexplicably, then we would no longer know what we ought to say (see Wittgenstein [53], 80). These obscure cases can be disposed of by new linguistic conventions. In many cases, then, the question as to whether we can apply a word or not is not a question of fact, but of convention, of new stipulations about the use of language.

For another thing Wittgenstein points out the fact that it is not possible to assign to every predicate F a single property that belongs to precisely those things to which F can be applied. Instead, there is a sort of *family resemblance* among the objects to which a predicate can be applied, generally speaking, so that this is another reason that the use of a predicate can not be settled by a sharp conceptual criterion of application (see Wittgenstein [53], 65–67).

Neither observation, however, is a basis for any objection to the realistic notion of learning predicates inductively. For family resemblance this follows from the comments in II.4.7. Openness of predicates is understood from the realistic standpoint in the following way: a predicate F, defined in the first place only over a domain D and standing for a concept f in that domain, is supposed to be defined for an expanded domain D'. Now there are several continuations of f on D' and a new linguistic convention is necessary, to determine which of these concepts f' the predicate F defined on D' is supposed to stand for. Wittgenstein's easy-chair example depends in this way on the fact that the predicate 'easy-chair' is defined initially only for the usual concrete things, the things we ordinarily think of. But if some entirely new and unusual sort of thing turns up, then that predicate is no longer defined for them and new conventions are required for the expanded domain of application.

47 This objection can not be met by saying: in order to learn language, you must in fact be able to make certain distinctions. But what being able to make distinctions means is nothing but being able to learn distinguishing predicates. In this sense, the capacity to learn language naturally must be present in order for language to be learned, but that is a mere triviality. What the basis of the human capacity for being able to learn language, however, what its neurological presuppositions are, etc., that is no philosophical problem, for clearing it up contributes nothing to the clarification of what we are doing when we speak. (See e.g. the discussion of this point by J. Mittelstrass in [68].)

The fact that we can make certain distinctions in the sense that we can *learn* them is not what is relevant here. What is involved there is the fact that we can *apply* them so as to separate the expressions we are supposed to be learning as well as the learning situations. And a distinction cf that sort cannot be a distinction made by means of language.

48 These ideas will be formulated and argued in greater detail elsewhere.

49 Wittgenstein [53], 242.

50 Wittgenstein [53], 241.

51 Wittgenstein [53], 258. – The qualification in square brackets is not part of the quotation.

52 Wittgenstein [53], 242.

53 Wittgenstein [53], 432.

54 Wittgenstein [53], 454.

55 Wittgenstein [58], p. 4.

56 Wittgenstein [22], 3.262.

57 See Chapter II.1.3.

58 See also Searle [69], 1.4.

59 For the concept of meaning in the theory of speech acts cf. Grice [57], Searle's critique in [69], 2.6, and the discussion in Lewis [69], IV.5.

60 The supplementary specifications of the meaning of utterances as against the meaning of expressions are sometimes, but by no means always, the result of conventions. Thus Strawson in [64] stresses the point that the function of the sentence 'This is Mr. Smith' has, in the corresponding situation, a conventional character as an introduction (as opposed to an informative statement), while the function of the sentence 'It is raining' as a warning that you should take an umbrella along arises directly out of the circumstances of the utterance, not from conventions.

61 According to Austin, meaning belongs to the *locutionary* act, within which he distinguished three components: the *phonetic*, the *rhetic* (grammatical), and the *phatic* (descriptive-semantic).

62 Austin's theory of *infelicities* is supposed to serve for the analysis of these presuppositions of success of illocutionary acts.

63 The term stems from G. Ryle, cf. [49], p. 238.

64 For criticism of Searle, who in [69], Chapter 8 propounds the notion that the theory of speech acts is a setting within which it is possible to derive norm sentences (such as 'X ought to do F') logically from purely factual statements ('X promised to do F'), see for example Kutschera [73], 1.12. – For Searle the preeminent accomplishment of the theory of speech acts is that it provides a setting for a logical connection between factual statements and normative propositions and for an adequate treatment of presuppositions. (See [69], Part II). It is possible to have both of these in other ways as well, as the discussions in Kutschera [73], 5.3 and [74] demonstrate. Thus we do not see the significance of the theory of speech acts in these two points. We see it in something still more fundamental, that it opens up an adequate access to semantics.

65 Searle, too, urges in [68], p. 412, as does Cohen in [64], that the illocutionary role is part of the meaning.

66 While Austin stresses the impossibility of giving an explicitly performative formulation to all propositions, Searle in [68], p. 417f. mistakenly draws the opposite conclusion from his principle of universal expressibility (that anything that can be meant can also be said).

67 In setting out his differences with Austin, Searle in [68], p. 243 contests the notion that speech acts can be called 'true' or 'false'. But instead of saying 'The sentence is true, or false' we can also say 'An utterance of A is true, or false'. So this locution is unproblematic.

68 This idea is developed in greater detail in Chapter III.2.1. There we shall go into the descriptive meaning of terms, predicates, etc. – N.b: While the declarative sentence (f) (as an act) has a performative meaning and (as phonetic expression object) a descriptive meaning, in cases (g) and (h) descriptive meanings are defined only for the descriptive components.

69 D. Lewis in [70], p. 54ff. takes a similar approach to the interpretation of non-declarative sentences.

70 D. Lewis offers an example in [70], p. 60: Someone signs an order and talks about it at the same time.

71 D. Lewis in [70] ascribes the same meaning to explicitly performative sentences as performative versions of sentences and as performative descriptions of those sentences. He does not look upon the difference in performative mode between the two interpretations as a difference in meaning, but as a difference in the sentence's use. But these differences as differences of meaning are just what the semantics of performative modes is about.

72 See e.g. Keenan [72].

73 Relative temporal indicators of this sort can also be avoided by giving an *n*-tuple $\langle ,...,\rangle$ instead of the arguments of the functors D and B for the sequence of speech acts that make up the discussion or debate.

74 As the use-theory of meaning was a step beyond realistic semantics, and the theory of speech acts an improvement on use-theory, a decisive step forward has again been taken by D. Lewis in [69] in his analysis of linguistic conventions. Speech acts, according to Lewis, are ways to solve a problem of coordination between speaker and hearer, and they are only effective on the basis of a convention. The analysis of the coordination problem to be solved by them gives a deeper insight into the nature of their function and meaning than has been possible in the theories propounded by Austin or Searle. The theory of linguistic conventions, therefore, has to be regarded as the proper fundament of the theory of speech acts.

75 See Wittgenstein [53], 202.

76 Wittgenstein [53], 258.

77 Wittgenstein [53], 265.

78 See Wittgenstein [53], 302.

79 See Wittgenstein [53], 350.

80 Wittgenstein [53], 384. – Wittgenstein in [53], 312 also alluded to the following thought experiment: If for everyone there was always a pain sensation tied up with touching certain things, sensations we had only upon touching those things, then it would be conceivable that we would use an equivalent predicate 'to be painful' instead of the predicate 'to feel pains'. We would use it to describe the things in question and we would be able to say 'These things are painful'. This predicate would then describe not a sensation, but a property of things. (See also Strawson [54], p. 47f.) What Wittgenstein wishes to say is that 'to have pains' is only a psychological and not a physical predicate because the occurrence of pains depends on factors that are different from one individual to another, not because it stands for private sensations. – But in similar cases we very definitely are used to differentiating between properties of things that cause pain and the pain caused, e.g. between the heat of the fire and the pain sensations it can produce. Also, it does not follow at all from the fact that two predicates have the same extension that they have the same meaning, much less does it follow in the case before us, then, where the predicates' ranges of use are different.

81 Wittgenstein [53], 293.

82 Wittgenstein [53], 67.

83 Wittgenstein [53], 66.

84 Wittgenstein [53], 67.

85 Besides that, there is an infinite regress here: If precisely those things are supposed to have the property F which are called 'F', then the question arises, which things have the property of being called 'F'. Obviously, the things that are called 'called "F"', and so on.

[86] F. Waismann spoke in this connection of an *open texture* that empirical concepts have, in contrast with logico-mathematical concepts. See also Wittgenstein [53], 69–71, as well as 84, 87, 88 and 142. – See also note 46.

[87] On dependence of meaning on context and the polyvalence of words see Chapter II.3.2.

[88] See Chapter II.3.1 also.

[89] That such precision is not superfluous is already apparent from the problem of what similarities we attend to in applying a predicate. Obviously not just any similarity, for there is always a property with regard to which two objects *a* and *b* are similar to each other, so that all predicates would be universally applicable if we were not to specify the similarities more narrowly. We surely do not call an object 'red' because it is similar in size to other objects that have been so designated. On the other hand, the similarities are not defined by means of a classificatory concept, either: Whether *a* is called 'red' is not determined by its being similar in its red color to other objects so designated, else one would have to define the similarities by the concepts, and they were precisely what was supposed to be fixed and determined by similarities.

[90] On what follows see also the more comprehensive and detailed presentation in Kutschera [72a].

[91] For a similar reason, we cannot use Carnap's procedure in [28] for representing family resemblances. Carnap starts out there from a two-place relation of partial similarity *Ae*, that is supposed to hold between two objects if and only if a and b approximately agree in a quality. Then the qualities are defined with *Ae* as a starting point. Even if one ignores the serious shortcomings in the definition, that have been pointed out by Carnap himself and by N. Goodman in [51], such a procedure still has no more than formal significance: Intuitively, the relation *Ae* is no basic predicate, but is defined in terms of an approximate resemblance between two objects in a quality, i.e. the qualities are presupposed as being already known. Nor, for the practical handling of ordinary language predicates, can one assume that *Ae* is extensionally defined by citing all the pairs of objects to which *Ae* applies, as Carnap does.

[92] For comparative concepts see for instance the presentation in Stegmüller [70], Chapter I, and also Kutschera [72], 1.2.

[93] See Hempel [65], pp. 165–171. The 'ideal types' that Hempel discusses there do not belong in the context of our discussion.

[94] See Trier [34b] on this point, where Trier takes up a position critical of the field concepts of Ipsen, Porzig and Jolles. On Trier's field concept see also Trier [31], [32] and [34a]. Other field concepts are presented in Oehmann [51], p. 72ff.

[95] See Hoijer [54b], p. 96.

[96] Of course, it is problematic whether both groups of words belong to the same semantic region. The semantic region of the intellect itself is marked out from more inclusive regions, and Trier's way of drawing its boundaries is based upon the vocabulary of New High German. Just on the basis of his analyses, it can not be said that there would be a distinct linguistic field in Middle High German corresponding to that semantic region, for the word '*wize*' belongs to a comprehensive theory of virtue, a theory of ideal human types, not to a terminology for distinguishing pure intellectual capacities. See Trier [32], p. 422. Generally speaking, there is considerable difficulty in drawing the boundaries of regions of meanings for different word fields. The relationships are as simple as in the two model cases of colors and pitches only in a very small number of cases.

[97] Trier would like to apply the field account principally within the realm of the non-

physical [*undinglich*], see Trier [32], p. 420. He writes there: "Its view of [semantic regions as] a whole and of the proposed analysis and classifications of that whole and of the variations of the internal boundary lines will find the most to consider in the realm of objects that are not concrete things. Indeed, the field account must inevitably present itself as a simple, logical modification of a previously held referential account of onomasiology wherever a question is raised about referents in such a domain .... There is no referential account of cleverness as there can be a referential account of the sickle; a referential account of cleverness can exist only within a total and integral account of intellectual terminology." – But what is decisive for the question as to whether or not a linguistic field is to be assumed is surely not whether the semantic region falls within the realm of the concrete or of the abstract – abstract mathematical concepts are not field concepts, while color concepts, for example, do belong to a word field – but whether a resemblance field is linguistically broken down into classificatory concepts or not. Of course, the domain of the concrete is particularly rich in phenomena that are constant and already divided up beforehand in perceptual terms, phenomena to which classificatory concepts can very easily be attached: plants and animals offer a better basis for classificatory concepts than phenomena in the psychological realm.

CHAPTER III

THEORIES OF GRAMMAR

A language in which there is not just a finite number of messages that can be formulated must solve the task of determining an infinite set of possible messages with a finite number – practically the fewest possible – of conventions concerning the message content of particular linguistic expressions. The only way in which this can be done is by starting with a finite set of the minimal linguistic units, with their meanings determined by convention, and then building complex linguistic expressions by combining these minimal units in accord with a finite number of rules, which determine the meanings of the compounds from the meanings of their components.[1]

Now it is the task of the grammar of a language L to give the rules for forming all of the meaningful expressions in L by combining basic units of L. We limit ourselves in this connection to investigating how single sentences, particularly declarative, i.e., assertion sentences, are constructed. At the present time, the grammatical analysis of texts is still in its very beginnings and there do not yet appear to be any sufficiently general and thoroughly discussed theoretical approaches to that topic.

A grammar includes three components: a *syntactic* component, i.e., a system of rules according to which the set of grammatically correct sentences of a language L can be constructed from the words of L listed in its lexicon; a *semantic* component, i.e. a system of rules by which the meanings of sentences are determined from the meanings of the words, which are given in the lexicon; and a *phonological* component by which a phonetic interpretation can be assigned to every sentence of L. Here we will ignore the phonological component entirely, however, since it scarcely has any philosophical relevance.[2]

Now there is a close connection between syntax and semantics. Since the sentences have a communicative function, they must be formed syntactically in such a way that the rules for semantic interpretation always assign a meaning to the syntactically constructed expressions. In artificial logical languages this is achieved by having a rule for semantic interpretation corresponding to every syntactic formation rule. It determines the meaning of the composite expression on the basis of the meanings of the expressions that compose it. No such close parallel between syntax and semantics exists in natural languages. Despite that, a grammar should formulate syntactic and semantic rules in such a way that the connection between them becomes clear, that the semantic function of the syntactic structures, which *is* ultimately the point, is elaborated.

The philosophically interesting problem concerning grammar is the general question of how the combination of semantic elements in language works at all, not how the combination of the smallest units of meaning – the so-called *morphemes*, which we shall often identify with words in what follows, as a simplification – works in some specific language or how the formation rules for its sentences look in detail. But since it is by no means established beforehand that there are universal structures for compounding of meanings common to all existing, or even to all possible, languages,[3] we shall refer to specific languages, like English or German mostly.

The rules of composition are not explicitly formulated at the outset in the case of natural languages, but there are customs, regularities intuitively grasped and practiced, just as there are, for example, moral conventions and rules of social conduct. It is then the task of a grammar to make the regularities of linguistic usage explicit by means of a system of rules. If one assumes that the set $G(L)$ of grammatically well-formed sentences of a language L is fixed, then a grammar G for L (a system of syntactic and semantic rules) can be called syntactically or semantically *adequate*, if the set of expressions that are syntactically discriminated as sentences in G coincides with $G(L)$, or if over and beyond that G also interprets these expressions semantically as we do intuitively.[4] Naturally there can be more than one adequate grammar for L. In that case, the simplest of them will be given preference.[5] In particular, such grammars can also differ in the lexicon with which they begin, i.e., in their lists of grammatical elements (words, or morphemes), for what counts as grammatically simple depends on the particular grammatical analysis in each case.

Now the assumption that $G(L)$ is a determinate set with precise boundaries and that every sentence in this set has a determinate meaning represents an idealization. Actually the boundary between sentences we intuitively apprehend as well-formed and other expressions is not a sharp one.

There is rather a spectrum of expressions that are neither definitely well-formed nor definitely not well-formed, but only more or less well-formed. In this sense there are degrees of grammaticity.[6] In the same way, it is not always true of meaningful sentences that they can be described as having the same meaning or different meanings; instead, there is often only a greater or lesser similarity of meaning.[7] As a rule, however, we are in agreement as to whether an expression is a grammatically well-formed sentence or not and whether two sentences (in a certain context) can be regarded as synonymous or not. The idealization is thus reasonable and defensible in our present context.

As already stressed in I.1, along with the formulation of grammatical regularities in the form of explicit rules there is some sharpening as well: in grammar the set of well-formed sentences is defined more precisely than it is in linguistic usage and the like holds for the semantic interpretations. Grammar thus incorporates an explication of linguistic facts: the imprecisions of linguistic usage are put to good account in order to draw more precise boundaries appropriate for systematic purposes.[8] And so from the very outset it can not be expected that a grammar only describes, that it settles nothing over and above linguistic customs. On the contrary, if it is scientifically exact, it represents a clarification, which is forbidden to conflict with the intuitive regulative provisions of usage only where the latter are unambiguous.

There are essentially three types of theory of grammar: *traditional*, *logical* and *generative* grammar.[9] We will discuss these types in what follows. We begin our discussion with the traditional grammar, which nowadays, despite all the criticism directed against it and despite all the alternative approaches, still represents the dominant type of grammar. And so far no comparable representation of grammatical detail has been achieved elsewhere, so that at the present time the other grammars still have to refer back to it.

NOTES

[1] In the same way, we obtain names for all of the infinitely many natural numbers by constructing them out of a finite number of figures and specifying how the meaning of the groups of figures is a function of the meaning of the individual figures.

[2] See also I.1.

[3] We will go into the question of the universality of grammatical structures in Chapter IV.

[4] Instead of syntactic and semantic, Chomsky speaks of *strong* and *weak adequacy*.

[5] Making the concept of simplicity precise generates considerable difficulty, of course. See Kutschera [72], 4.2.

[6] See Chomsky [61b] on this point.

[7] See Chapter II.3.1.

[8] On the concept of explication see Kutschera [67], 6.3.

[9] We regard the corpus-grammatica of American structuralism as the antecedent of generative grammar.

1. Traditional grammar

What is called 'traditional' or 'classical' grammar nowadays is grammar as based upon the first grammatical distinctions made by Protagoras, Plato, and Aristotle in Greco-Roman antiquity, further developed in the medieval and modern periods and still taught in the schools today. The '*Duden-Grammatik*', Grebe [66], represents a good example of such a traditional grammar for German, in which the old grammar's basic scheme is preserved in spite of many modern approaches and modifications. We shall repeatedly refer to this work above all in presenting and criticizing traditional grammar.

Since the traditional grammar is well-known, it will be sufficient here to refer briefly to its basic features.

Classical grammar is divided, if we ignore the modern addition of phonology once again – the traditional grammar was above all a grammar of written language[1] – into a theory of words (*Wortlehre*) and a theory of sentences (*Satzlehre*). The *theory of words* embraces a division of words into categories – the theory of word types, a theory of the inflection of words and a theory of word formation.[2] The *theory of sentences* or *syntax* – the word is understood in a grammatical sense here, not in the sense defined in I.3 – embraces a theory of sentence parts and sentence structures and a theory of the forms and positions of words in a sentence.

1.1. *The Theory of Word Types or Parts of Speech*

In the theory of word types or parts of speech, the words of a language are supposed to be exhaustively classified into word categories. These categories are:

(1) *Substantives*: Substantives name objects (in the broadest sense of the word, thus including persons, living creatures and the like).[3] A further distinction is drawn between:

(a) *Proper names*, which designate individual objects, such as 'Socrates', 'the Zugspitze', 'England', 'Mars', etc.

(b) *Class names*, which designate classes of objects and 'at the same time each individual being or thing in the class',[4] such as 'human being', 'flower', 'chair', etc. Subordinate groups of class names are:

(α) *Collective terms*, which stand for aggregates or concrete collections, such as 'forest', 'herd', 'fleet', etc.,

(β) *Substance* or *mass terms*, such as 'water', 'gold', 'pepper', etc.

(2) *Verbs*: Verbs "say what is going on or what is the case."[5] They express activities, events or states of affairs.

(3) *Adjectives*: Adjectives tell us "what is the nature of a being or thing or how an event is taking place."[6] Their basic function is to express the position taken by the speaker concerning beings or things (substantives), to situations or events (verbs), to properties themselves (adjectives or participles) or even to the circumstantial features (adverbs), to indicate the impression that the beings, things, events, properties make on the speaker.

(4) *Articles*: Articles are modifiers of substantives, with the task of identifying the object named by the substantive as a specific individual object or as representative of a class.[7]

(5) *Pronouns*: Pronouns represent a substantive, refer to it or accompany it.[8] Personal pronouns represent a substantive; possessive pronouns indicate a relationship of ownership or attachment; demonstrative pronouns a relationship of time or position; relative pronouns indicate that a verbal expression pertains to a substantive; interrogative pronouns a question about a being or thing;[9] indefinite pronouns, finally, "designate a being or thing in an entirely general and indefinite way, if the speaker does not wish to or cannot describe it in more specific terms. We also count number words that express a number or amount in an entirely unspecified way within this group."[10] Indefinite pronouns of this type are 'all', 'another', 'both', 'one', 'some', 'a few', 'something', 'each', 'someone', 'no one', 'none', 'many', 'several', 'nothing', 'whole', 'much', 'little', 'which', 'who'.

(6) *Numeralia*: Number words are modifiers of substantives that give numerical support to their capacity for differentiating between unity and plurality.[11] Number words are words for specific numbers (cardinal numbers, ordinal numbers, fractions, etc.), distributive number words ('every three', 'every three times'), multiplicative number words ('single', 'double'), number words of recurrence ('once', 'sometimes', 'never', 'another time') and classificatory number words ('same', 'diverse').

(7) *Adverbs*: "It is the adverb's task to characterize the states or situations (*Umstände*) named in the sentence in terms of their most general outlines."[12] Classifying in greater detail: adverbs of place ('here', 'to the right', 'inside of'), of time ('yesterday', 'never', 'at the same time'), of modality ('gladly', 'in vain', 'somewhat', 'twice as', 'firstly', 'very',

'enough', 'not', 'never', 'perhaps', 'probably') and of reason ('therefore', 'consequently', 'therewith', 'otherwise', 'nevertheless').

(8) *Prepositions*: For the most part prepositions designate relationships between the being or thing named by the substantive and an event or state (verb), another being or thing (substantive) or an attitude or opinion (adjective).[13] "It is the principal task of the preposition to attach a substantive subject to it to another word."[14] They are differentiated as prepositions of space ('on', 'toward', 'over'), of time ('until', 'since', 'from'), of modality ('exclusive of', 'except', 'notwithstanding') and of reason ('on the occasion of', 'thanks to', 'through', 'under', 'by means of').

(9) *Conjunctions*: Conjunctions connect sentences or parts of sentences and express a relationship that holds between words or sentences in thought.[15]

(10) *Interjections*: Interjections express feelings or commands. They stand outside the sentence frame.[16] Since they are not components of sentences, but self-contained exclamations, they are of no grammatical interest and for that reason we shall ignore them in what follows.

Now these specifications of verbal categories cannot be used for constructing a grammar with precision, for in the first place they are too vague for us to be able to attach any exact sense to them or to achieve any well-defined classification of words with them. To be sure, they are illustrated by examples and counter-examples, but frequently these are not in accord with the general definitions. In the second place, the classification is not disjunctive, i.e., one and the same word can belong to different categories. And thirdly, the classification is not based on any one unitary point of view and words in the same category do not have either the same semantic nor the same syntactic function.

The following points suffice to establish the first claim:

Ad (1): Only proper names, but not class names, can be said to name objects. 'Human' is neither a name for the class of humans (otherwise the word would be a proper name) nor a common name for all humans (you can not say 'human is mortal' instead of 'Socrates is mortal') nor a name for indeterminate humans, for there are no creatures in addition to specific individual humans who would be indeterminate or unspecific humans. Also, what object is the substantive 'unicorn', for example, supposed to name? Can we say further that substantives like 'truth' or 'beauty' name objects? And finally, how do things stand with substantives like 'event', 'action', 'state'?

Ad (2): Verbs do not say 'what is going on'; only sentences can do that. What kind of an event is "sleep" really supposed to express, for example?

Ad (3): It is not only adjectives that say 'what the nature of a being or thing is or how an event is taking place'. That can also be expressed by substantives, verbs or adverbs. Furthermore, purely descriptive adjectives, such as e.g. the word 'red', in the sentence 'This rose is red', do not entail any taking of a position on the part of the speaker. That holds true only of evaluative adjectives like 'beautiful', 'delightful', 'unpleasant', etc. Finally, the word 'presumably' in 'Presumably Hans is coming today' expresses the speaker's attitude towards an event without that making it an adjective.

Ad (7): What is a state or situation? In the sentence 'Fritz ran fast' does 'fast' express a situation, or 'not' in 'Fritz did not run'? A state or situation is a fact and facts are expressed by sentences. And what are the 'general outlines'?

Ad (8): 'Loves' also expresses a relation between two persons, without being a preposition.

Ad (9): That a word connects other words or parts of a sentence is something that can be said of almost any word. Likewise that it expresses 'relationship in thought'.

In support of the second statement it is sufficient to point out that Grebe himself says there are no firm boundaries to be drawn between articles, pronouns and number words.[17] But they also overlap with adverbs, as shown by words like 'somewhat' and 'twice', for example.

As to the third point; according to Grebe, the classification of words into categories is determined by the particular way "in which they enter into manifesting the world by means of language, or by the presence or absence of a realm of forms."[18] But those are two entirely different viewpoints: a semantic viewpoint, according to which words are classified according to their meanings – it is scarcely possible to understand anything else in this context by the very vague and general expression 'manifesting the world by means of language' – and a syntactic viewpoint.

But a strictly semantic or syntactic definition of these word categories is not possible either, because many particles,[19] for example, do not have any independent semantic function and because the characterization of words in terms of certain syntactic functions is only the outcome of a grammatical theory. Even the distinctions drawn among cases are in many respects a theoretical construction, since there are often no morphological or semantic distinctions corresponding to them.[20] In Chapter III.2 we shall see that on a very simple and natural definition of the syntactic functions, words with the same syntactic function occur in entirely different categories and words in the same category have entirely different syntactic functions. For example, the adverbs 'not' and 'presumably' are quite as much as the conjunctions 'and' and 'therefore' expressions with which one can construct new sentences out of sentences; while the adverbs 'fast' and 'gladly' represent expressions with which one can create sentences out of predicates and names just as much as do the verbs 'love' and 'believe'.

In the *theory of the inflection of words* distinctions are made between gender, number and case in connection with forms of substantives, adjectives, articles, pronouns and numerals, as well as person, number, mood, tense and voice or diathesis (in [English and] German: active and passive) in connection with verbs, and positive, comparative and superlative forms of adjectives. An account is given of how these forms are constructed for various classes of words as well. These inflections themselves are peculiar to a language and are of no interest to us here. What is interesting to us, on the other hand, is the function these forms have. What traditional grammar has to say about them is once again most unsatisfactory. For example, in addition to the grammatical functions of case, which of course are not always represented by their own special case forms, a distinction is often drawn between the *subjective* function (of indicating the subject of the sentence, i.e., the object of the sentence is saying something about (nominative)), the *objective* function (indicating the direct object of the activity expressed by the sentence predicate (usually accusative)), the *indirect-objective* function (indicating the indirect object which is collaterally a target of the activity asserted by the sentence predicate (usually dative)), the *possessive* function (indicating the relation of possessing (with the genitive)), the *instrumental* function (indicating a means used in connection with the activity expressed by the sentence predicate, as in *'Fritz beat Hans with* a stick' (the ablative in Latin, for example)), the *agentative* function (to indicate something that causes an event, but which is not the subject of the sentence, 'Hans was visited *by Fritz*'), and the *comitative* function (to indicate someone accompanying the active subject, as in 'Hans met his wife and visited Fritz *with her*').[21]

It is already becoming clear that one and the same case can have entirely different functions in different contexts. Thus, for example, the German dative can have an indirect-objective function, an instrumental, an agentative and a comitative. But these functions can scarcely be ascribed to the case alone, for the same function can be expressed by different cases. So there is no clear connection between these functions and case.

Furthermore, a number of such function systems have been advanced and whatever claim to completeness any of them can make is solely on account of the vagueness with which they define their functions. The distinction between direct and indirect object, for example, has no basis in the proceeding sketched out by a sentence like 'Fritz gave Hans the book', so far as the facts of the matter are concerned. Its basis is rather in the grammatical distinction between accusative and dative object and therefore it cannot be the basis of the latter.

Attempts to start from the individual case and attach various semantic functions to it also miscarry, as e.g. the discussion of functional analyses of the genitive in Groot [56] demonstrates convincingly.[22] And so we can say that no unambiguous and independent functions can be attached to the morphologically distinct cases.

The *theory of word formation* by way of combination ('underarm', 'dogfood') or derivation ('fly' – 'flight', 'idea' – 'ideal', 'kind' – 'unkind', 'do' – 'outdo') studies how it is possible in language to obtain new words from words. It belongs, however, – even from the standpoint of the older grammar – partly to lexicography, i.e., to the description and analysis of the vocabulary rather than to grammar as a theory of combination. For the newly formed words often have an independent semantic function not derivable from the meanings of the component words.[23] For example, the word '*Junggeselle*' (bachelor), as far as meaning is concerned, has nothing to do with either '*jung*' (young) or '*Geselle*' (fellow). ['Cockpit', unlike 'airplane', has nothing to do with either of its components.] And even where the meaning of a compound word is defined by the meanings of the component words (as in 'underarm' – 'the part under the arm', 'birthplace' – 'the place of birth', 'skyblue' – 'blue like the sky'), these combinations do not always follow any general rules, but each one of them is a unique formation exhibiting only more or less loose analogies to other formations.

In other cases, however, there are semantic rules which do permit the introduction of new formations into the language without their having first to be defined.[24] And so we can say that word formation belongs in part to lexicography, in part to grammar.

1.2. *The Theory of Sentences [or Syntax]*

The traditional *theory of sentences* says that there is one basic form of sentence, which can be expanded by means of supplementations, and that sentences constructed in this way can be combined into sentence sequences.

The basic form of every sentence consists in subject and predicate. The *subject* indicates the object or objects of which something is supposed to be asserted in the sentence. What is supposed to be said of that object or those objects is the content of the *predicate*.

The subject without any supplementation is a substantive ('*Fritz* is coming', '*Men* are mortal'), a pronoun ('*I* am sick', '*They* are lying'), an infinitive ('*To err* is human'), a clause (*Satz*) ('*That Fritz is coming* makes Hans happy') or a series of words ('*Fritz and Hans and Max* are coming')[25] [or a participle ('*Smoking* is forbidden')]. The unsupplemented predicate is a verb ('Fritz *turns*'), or an auxiliary verb [('to be', 'to have' in their various forms)], combined as copula with an adjective ('Fritz *is sick*') or a substantive ('Fritz *is a jurist*', 'Fish *are vertebrates*'),[26] or a series of predicates ('Fritz *laughs and sings*').

The supplementations are supplements to the subject, to the predicate or supplements to other supplements. The following supplementary components of a sentence are differentiated in the traditional grammar: object, attribute and adverbial modification.

The *attribute* involves a more detailed characterization of a substantive, pronoun, adjective or adverb. What is concerned can be single words ('*Two* trees were felled', '*The* tree was felled'), word groups ('Half *of his great wealth* he inherited', 'His pleasure *at the gift* was great') or clauses ('The tree *that stands in the garden* was trimmed').

An *object* indicates which object or objects the subject's (or subjects') activity asserted in the predicate relates to ('The horse is pulling *the cart*', 'Hans strikes *Fritz*', 'Hans gives *the book to Fritz*', 'I make sport *of him*'); and to that extent it is regarded as a supplement of the predicate.

An *adverbial modification* states where, when, how or why an action takes place, and so characterizes the content of predicative components of sentences as to form and manner ('The ocean is *especially* cold *today*', 'He is trying *with all his might*', 'Fritz skis *just as well as Hans*', '*Out of diffidence* he *probably* will *not* protest').

Sentence sequences arise from the combination of complete sentences, e.g., by means of coordinating conjunctions like 'and', 'or', 'but', 'although', 'therefore', etc.

Finally, the traditional theory of combining words in a sentence and imbedding them in it embraces the theory of word position and congruence and of the forms of sentence components. To a large extent, it foregoes general statements and essentially restricts itself to describing the regularities of actual linguistic usage. The role of congruence is seen in its marking out expressions as belonging together; word position can determine sentence structure and, as e.g. in 'Hans loves Mary', make the distinction between subject and object where that distinction is not made by case endings and prepositions.

The traditional model of syntax, its theory of sentence components in particular, is inadequate for the following reasons:

In the first place, the definitions of subject and predicate are unsatisfactory: The grammatical subject of the sentence does not always designate or does not always designate only the object or objects of which something is said in the sentence. Thus in 'Fritz loves Bertha' something is said about both Fritz and Bertha, in 'Fritz comes to Bertha with Hans' something is said about Fritz, Hans, and Bertha, and in the sentence 'No one loves Kuno', 'Not a thing will be revealed by Kuno' it would surely seem to be Kuno more than anyone or anything else who is being spoken of. To the extent that what a sentence speaks of is definitely settled, then – and this is a thoroughly problematic question[27] – we can not say that sentences speak of the objects their grammatical subjects designate.[28] It is a similar matter with the predicate: If there is already some obscurity about the subject-matter of a sentence, this is also true of what is asserted of it. Furthermore, the objects and adverbial specifications contained in it also make essential contributions to determining what the sentence says, as the following examples demonstrate.

The most striking flaw in the traditional theory of sentences surely consists in the fact that the subject-predicate kernel of a sentence is very often not a meaningful sentence. The kernel 'Regensburg lies' in 'Regensburg lies on the Danube' is not a reasonable sentence, for by itself 'lying' means something entirely different from 'lying on' (it expresses the opposite of 'standing' or 'sitting', and these expressions can not be applied to cities.) Likewise the sentence kernel 'Hans gives' in 'Hans gives Fritz a book' is not a meaningful sentence.

For this reason the object or objects of the sentence are often counted as part of the predicate. But that is not enough, for adverbial specifications can also essentially alter the content of a sentence. Thus 'singing' in 'Fritz sings' [used as what is sometimes called the narrative present in English] means something different from what it means in 'Fritz sings for the pleasure of it', for the former sentence makes an assertion about an action going on at that moment, but the latter makes an assertion about a disposition. The 'supplementations' are by no means additions that can always be omitted, but often are just as important elements of the sentence as subject and predicate.

For this reason the attempt has often been made to replace the one subject-predicate schema with a number of basic forms of sentence, *sentence models* or *sentence designs*, and to define supplements relative to them.[29] But this attempt is not very convincing, either.

So far no unity has been achieved as to the identification of certain basic sentence designs. The reason for this is the inadequacy of the so-called *method of reduction (Abstrichmethode)*[30] for investigating such designs. Every assertion is taken to be an assertion about 'a something-or-other', of which an assertion 'with a relatively definite character' is made. According to the method of reduction it is supposed to be possible to free this kernel of the assertion by striking out the assertion's supplements, in such a way that 'whatever posit is intended' by the sentence is still contained in this kernel. So in the sentence 'The farmer plows his field early in the morning', we can strike the expression 'in the morning' as a supplement that can be dispensed with, but not 'his field', because in this case plowing-a-field is what is meant to be posited and just not plowing.[31]

What 'posit' the speaker intends can not be inferred from the sentence as such, however. It may plainly and simply be the case that the primary intent does lie in the specification of nothing but plowing (the emphasis then falls on 'plows' and says that the farmer is not about the business of harrowing, say), or in specifying that the plowing is going on in the early morning, not just before noon, say (the emphasis then falls on 'early').

In general, one will have to assume that the speaker wishes to say everything he does say in the sentence, i.e., that nothing specified in the sentence is non-essential.

It is a further basic flaw in this method that it defines sentence designs
in terms of the traditional categories (e.g. subject-predicate-supplement-
type-prepositional object), to which, as we have seen, there correspond no
single grammatical functions of expressions (and so the sentence design
identified embraces such different sentences as 'Fritz laughs heartily at
Hans' and 'No one laughs openly at himself'). But sentence designs could
only have a determinate grammatical function if they are composed in the
same way of components that have the same function. Even the characterization of these sentence structure functions proves to be correspondingly
imprecise, then.[32]

In summary, then, we can say this: The traditional grammar does bring
out a wealth of linguistic regularities, but for the most part those regularities do not hold rigorously, but hold only in typical cases that are
pointed out as examples. In other cases, also pointed out only in examples,
cases that are very numerous, they do not hold. In most cases, statements
intended to gather together in one general linguistic rule the regularities
of linguistic usage illustrated by examples either remain too vague or do
not hold without restriction. And so this grammar is far from providing
a rigorous system of rules for forming sentences.

Something else is lacking, too, however: an exact functional analysis
of words and parts of speech that defines what is accomplished by them
semantically and tells us how the meaning of the sentence is determined
by the meanings of the words. What is particularly wanting is a sufficiently
precise conceptual *instrumentarium*. For functional analysis, the traditional grammatical categories are inadequate and too vague. The problem of
functional analysis is taken up in logical grammar. Since a solution of
this problem, as will yet be demonstrated, is also a presupposition of the
feasibility of generative grammar, we turn first to logical grammar in the
next chapter.

At this point in the discussion, however, we can already say the following: the advantage that has often been claimed for traditional grammar as
against other grammars is its proximity to language. This consists in the
fact that it analyzes grammatical composites (sentences) according to the

words (or morphemes) of which they are constructed. The elements of its analyses are thus the expressions out of which the sentences are compounded in a purely external syntactical manner. (These 'natural building blocks', however, usually do not have any fixed semantic function in natural languages, one that is independent of context.) Natural languages are not constructed atomistically: The meaning of a sentence is on the one hand determined by the meanings of the words of which it is composed, to be sure – without the whole being determined by the parts in this way it would not be possible to construct an infinite number of sentences with a finite set of words – but conversely the specific meaning of the individual words in the sentence is determined by the context, by the relationship in which they stand to the other words in the sentence. Words have a certain indeterminacy of meaning, then, which is eliminated only in their context. That we not only understand the sense of the sentence on the basis of the meanings of the words, but conversely understand word meaning on the basis of sentence meaning is also shown by the fact that we actually learn and use words only in context. This *plasticity* of words, as we will call it, is also illustrated by the fact that we very commonly have to respond to the question 'What does this word mean?' by countering with the question 'In what context?' It is a property that different words possess in different degrees and may not be confused with the ambiguity of words – although there are no firm boundaries in that respect, of course. On the whole, it contributes significantly to the expressiveness of natural languages.[33]

The plasticity of words involves a certain difficulty for the construction of a grammar as a rigorous system of rules, however: precise and sufficiently simple grammatical rules will always have to be formed in such a way that they determine the meaning of compound expressions as a function of its components and ignore an additional determination of the meanings of the components by their context. I.e. they will have an atomistic character. The elements of analysis for such grammars will in many respects not coincide with the 'natural' building blocks of language, words (morphemes), therefore, but must be semantically determinate word groups or parts of words or even constructs that do not themselves occur in the language. But in virtue of that the grammatical analyses become 'artificial', grammar becomes a theoretical construction, fundamentally different from the mere description of superficial, i.e. directly observable linguistic facts and generalization from them. The words of Roger Bacon *'philosophus grammaticam invenit'* hold true of this interpretation of grammar as a theoretical construction.[34] To be sure, this theoretical construction must have an empirical linguistic content and it must prove itself to be an adequate and fruitful theory in terms of that content.

As a consequence, for natural languages there is a certain incompatibility between the demands of proximity to the language and of precision, and the root of the vaguenesses and inadequacies of traditional grammar probably lies in the fact that it wants to relate a precise system of rules – the construction of which must be the goal of a scientific grammar – to the natural building blocks of language, which in many ways just have no firm, context-independent function.

NOTES

1 See also Lyons [69], p. 38ff.
2 The theory of how the vocabulary is divided up, e.g. into word fields, belongs to the theory of meaning.
3 See Grebe [66], p. 65, 134.
4 Grebe [66], p. 135.
5 Grebe [66], p. 64.
6 Grege [66], p. 65.
7 See Grebe [66], p. 66, 152.
8 See Grebe [66], p. 66, 246.
9 See Grebe [66], p. 246.
10 Grebe [66], p. 272.
11 See Grebe [66], p. 66, 282.
12 Grebe [66], p. 302.
13 Grebe [66], p. 67.
14 Grebe [66], p. 315.
15 See Grebe [66], p. 67, 334.
16 See Grebe [66], p. 67.
17 See Grebe [66], p. 247.
18 See Grebe [66], p. 64. – This definition, which is generally the customary one in traditional grammar, goes back to Dionysius Thrax, by whom the substantive is defined as a word that has case and designates persons or things, the verb as a word that does not have case but does have person, number and tense, which designates an action or passion, etc.
19 Particles are the non-inflected words, i.e. adverbs, prepositions, conjunctions and interjections.
20 See also Lyons [69], p. 291f. as well as Beckmann [63].
21 See Lyons [69], p. 295f.
22 See also Fillmore [68], p. 7. – Fillmore makes a study of semantically determined depth case in this work.
23 See also Grebe [66], p. 348.

[24] See also Brekle [70a] and Marchand [69].

[25] See Grebe [66], p. 527, 543.

[26] While the older traditional grammar views the auxiliary verb 'to be' in the last three examples as a dependent component of the predicate, as we indicated, in Grebe [66], for example, there occurs the notion that "to be" is an independent predicate here, while 'sick' in the first example is an adverbial supplement and 'a jurist' or 'vertebrates' in the last two sentences are adjunctions in the so-called 'nominative of identification' (See op. cit., p. 540ff., 472f., 531). But this notion is hardly tenable. For the unsupplemented component expression in the first sentence 'Fritz is' is not a complete and meaningful sentence. To be sure, the word 'is' can also be used in the sense of 'exists', but in that case the supplement is impossible. We can not say: 'Fritz exists', – 'How does he exist?' – 'Sickly!' Likewise, there can be no talk of identification in the second and third cases. 'To be' can not be interpreted as having the meaning of the predicate 'to be identical with' in those cases, for Fritz is not identical with a jurist (which one? !), all jurists or the class of jurists and the same holds for the third sentence. Therefore the older conception of the auxiliary as copula is more adequate. – Auxiliaries that are used in constructing verb forms ('Fritz *has slept*') count as part of the verb.

[27] See Goodman [61], for example.

[28] See also Lyons [69], p. 343f., as well as the discussion of *sema* and *rhema*, or of *topic* and *comment*. There are references and bibliographical information in Lyons [69], 8.1.2 and in Brekle [70a], 3.5 and 4.2.1.3.

[29] For the terminology and the idea of sentence design see Weisgerber [63a], p. 264. –

[30] See Weisgerber [62], V. II, p. 372, and Grebe [66], p. 468ff.

[31] The example and terminology are taken from Grebe [66], p. 468ff.

[32] A quotation on this point: "While the subject of the unsupplemented sentence was something the statement touched on directly ['Nobody is perfect'?], and the subject of the identification sentence was something simply held up for comparison ['Fritz is an unknown'?], here [i.e. in a sentence with an accusative object] the subject is the agent, whose action expressed in the predicate is purposefully directed to another being or thing ['Snow covers the earth'?]." Grebe [66], p. 473.

[33] See also Lyons [69], p. 406, 410, as well as Chapter II.3.2.

[34] Cited in Robins [51], p. 76, Note 2.

2. LOGICAL GRAMMAR

In modern logic, as built on foundations laid down by G. Boole, A. de Morgan and especially G. Frege from the middle of the 19th century on, artificial languages are constructed in order to avoid the vagueness, ambiguities and lack of rigorous and simple general grammatical structures that are characteristic of natural language. The syntax of these artificial languages follows simple and exact rules and, following Leibniz's idea of a *characteristica universalis*, is built up in such a close relationship to semantics that the syntactic form of expressions reflects the structure of their meanings. There is a grammar, a syntax and a semantics for such artificial languages; they meet all the requirements of exactitude. It is natural to ask whether such logical models of grammar can not be applied to natural languages as well.

Now such an application cannot proceed in such a way as to employ the syntactic and semantic concepts for a logical language L in the analysis of a natural language S directly – S just is not a language constructed "with the edge of a logical ruler" (Frege). The attempt, rather, will be to present an interpretation M of L and an analyzing relation $R(X, Y)$ which correlates to every expression Y of S a grammatically well-formed expression X of L that has the same meaning. In doing so, several expressions of L will be correlated to an ambiguous expression in S. The domain consisting of the items that have the first position in R, i.e. the set of expressions A of L for which there is an expression A' of S with $R(A, A')$, is thus a subset of the grammatically well-formed expressions of L and the relation R is many-many, since there cannot only be more than one A with $R(A, A')$ for one A' but also more than one A' with $R(A, A')$ for one A – the same proposition can often be expressed by more than one sentence in S. If we are successful in arriving at a general definition of R then the grammar of L gives us the two fundamental grammatical specifications of S as well:

(1)   An expression A' of S is grammatically well-formed if and only if there is an expression A of L with $R(A, A')$.

(2)   An expression A' of S has meaning α if and only if there is an expression A of L with $R(A, A')$ that has the meaning α.

In this way, using L and R, we obtain a *logical grammar* for S.

In what follows we shall do no more than construct a logical language L with sufficient power of expression and offer some examples of the analysis of expressions in natural language. We cannot attempt to define R for a natural language or even an interesting fragment of a natural language[1], for that requires detailed and lengthy analyses, and all we are concerned with here is presenting the basic ideas of logical grammar. Of course part of what belongs to that enterprise is a sketch of the structure of a logical language L that has a rich stock of expressions and in carrying this out we must also burden the reader with some technical details and a knowledge of elementary logic is useful for understanding them. What justifies making this demand of the reader is that logical systems like L are still not very well known and that they have an eminent interest for the philosophy of language since they offer the possibility of linguistic analyses that satisfy modern criteria of exactitude.

The works of R. Montague form the basis of the following exposition, especially his essay 'Universal Grammar' of 1970, in which a powerful and intuitively satisfying semantics of intensional logic was developed for the first time. Our language L coincides in essential respects with the language L_0 presented there. For other approaches see, for instance, D. Lewis [70] and Cresswell [73].

2.1. The Structure of Logical Language L

2.1.1. *The syntax of language L.* L is constructed in two steps. First the syntax of L is specified. The main task is to define the notion of well-formed expression, or *term*, as we shall say. Then in the semantics we define the concept of an interpretation of L. Instead of the traditional word categories we define logical categories as follows:

(*Logical*) *Categories*:

(a) σ, v are (basic) categories.
(b)   If τ, ρ are categories, then $\tau(\rho)$ is also a category.
(c)   If τ is a category, then $\iota(\tau)$ is also a category.

σ is the category of sentences, v that of proper names (names of objects). There is no need to assume any further basic categories besides σ and v, although that could easily be done. $\tau(\rho)$ is the category of a functor that generates expressions of category τ out of expressions of category ρ. $\iota(\tau)$ is the category of intensions of expressions of category τ.

$\sigma(v)$, then, is the category of a one-place predicate (such as ' is human') which generates sentences out of names, $v(v)$ is the category of a one-place functor (such as 'the father of') which generates a new name out of a name, $\sigma(\sigma)$ is the category of a sentential operator (such as 'not') which generates a new sentence out of a sentence. A two-place predicate (such as 'hits') which generates a sentence from two names, has the category $(\sigma(v))(v)$ – we can also write $\sigma(v, v)$ for this – a two-place predicate (such as 'believes that') which generates a sentence out of a name and a sentence has the category $(\sigma(v))(\sigma)$ – we can also write $\sigma(v, \sigma)$ for that; $\sigma(\sigma(v))$ is the category of an expression (such as 'all' and 'some') which generates a sentence out of a one-place predicate, $v(\sigma(v))$ is the category of an expression (such as 'the thing which') which generates a name out of a predicate, etc.

The *alphabet* of L consists of the basic symbols λ, μ, $\equiv$, δ, (,) and a denumerably infinite number of constants and variables for each category τ.

As the occasion arises, we shall indicate the category of an expression by putting an index above it.

An expression of L is a finite sequence of basic symbols of L. If $*$ is a symbol that does not occur in L, and if $A[*]$ is a finite sequence of basic symbols of L and this symbol, then $A[a]$ is the expression generated from $A[*]$ by replacing all occurrences of $*$ by a. If the symbol $*$ does not occur in $A[*]$, then $A[a]=A[*]$. The set of grammatically well-formed expressions or *terms* of L is specified by the following rules:

2.1.1.1. *Terms of L*

(a) Constants of category τ of L are terms of category τ of L.

(b) If F is a term of category $\tau(\rho)$ $(\tau \neq \iota)$ and if a is a term of category ρ of L, then $F(a)$ is a term of category τ of L.[2]

(c) If a and b are terms of L of the same category, then $a \equiv b$ is a term of L of category σ.

(d) If $A[a]$ is a term of category τ, a a constant of category ρ, x a variable of category ρ of L which does not occur in $A[a]$, then $\lambda x(A[x])$ is a term of category $\tau(\rho)$ of L.

(e) If A is a term of category τ of L then $\mu(A)$ is a term of category $\iota(\tau)$ of L.

(f) If A is a term of category $\iota(\tau)$ of L, then $\delta(A)$ is a term of category τ of L.

Sentences of L are terms of L of category σ, *proper names* of L are terms of L of category v.

Parentheses that are not necessary to delimit the scope of an operator λ, μ, or δ unambiguously may be omitted in what follows.

Let L_1 be that part of language L in which the operators μ and δ do not occur and the only constants and variables belong to those categories constructible according to rules (a), (b) alone.

2.1.2. *Extensions.* We shall build the semantics of L up in several stages, and consider first of all the case in which the expressions of L have nothing but extensions assigned to them. In this connection, we restrict ourselves to sublanguage L_1.

Let A^B be the set of functions defined over domain B and taking values from range A.[3]

2.1.2.1. Let $E_{\tau,U}$ be the *set of possible extensions* of the terms of L_1 of category τ, relative to object domain U. We set:

(a) $E_{v,U} = U$

(b) $E_{\sigma,U} = \{t,f\}$

(c) $E_{\tau(\rho),U} = E_{\tau,U}^{E_{\rho,U}}$

't' represents the truth-value 'true' and 'f' the truth-value 'false'.

2.1.2.2. An *extensional interpretation* of L_1 over the (non-empty) object domain U is a one-place function M, for which:

(a) $M(a) \in E_{\tau,U}$ for all constants a of category τ.

(b) $M(F(a)) = M(F)(M(a))$ for all terms constructed in accord with 2.1.1.1b.

(c) $M(a \equiv b) = t$ iff $M(a) = M(b)$ for all terms constructed in accord with 2.1.1.1.c.

(d) $M(\lambda x A[x])$ is that function f from $E_{\tau(\rho),U}$ for which: $f(M'(b)) = = M'(A[b])$ for all $M' =_b M$. The term $\lambda x A[x]$ is to be constructed from $A[a]$ in accord with 2.1.1.1.d, and the constant b of the same category as a should not occur in $A[a]$.

$M' =_b M$ says that the extensional interpretation M' coincides with M with the possible exception of the values $M(b)$ and $M'(b)$. I.e., M' is based upon the same object domain as M and $M(c) = M'(c)$ is true for all constants $c \neq b$.

The term $\lambda x A[x]$ stands for what Frege called a *Wertverlauf* (value-distribution), i.e. for the function which takes the value $A[a]$ for the argument a, taken as a class of pairs consisting of an argument and the corresponding value of the function. Therefore we have $\lambda x A[x](a) \equiv A[a]$. If $A[a]$ is a sentence, then $\lambda x A[x]$ is a one-place predicate. Concepts may be represented, according to Frege, as functions with the range $\{t, f\}$. This allows a strong simplification in the formalism. Classes as extensions of concepts correspond then to the *Wertverläufe* of such functions. Therefore predicates are in effect assigned classes by 2.1.2.2.d, as usual in extensional semantics.

The following definitions show how rich the type-theoretical language L_1 is.[4] Here $\wedge$ is to be the universal ('For all things...'), $\vee$ the existential quantifier ('For some things...'), $\neg$ the negation, $\wedge$ the conjunction, $\vee$ the disjunction, $\supset$ the implication sign, and $\in$ represents the relation of being an element of a set.

2.1.2.3. *Definitions.* We can now define the usual logical operators in terms of the operator $\equiv$, for example:

(a) $\wedge x^\tau(A) := \lambda x^\tau A \equiv \lambda x^\tau(x^\tau \equiv x^\tau)$

(b) $\neg A := A \equiv \wedge x^\sigma(x^\sigma)$.

(c) $A \wedge B := \wedge x^{\sigma(\sigma)}(B \equiv (x^{\sigma(\sigma)}(A) \equiv x^{\sigma(\sigma)}(B)))$

(d) $A \vee B := \neg(\neg A \wedge \neg B)$

(e) $A \supset B := \neg A \vee B$

(f) $\vee x^\tau A := \neg \wedge x^\tau \neg A$.

(g) $a^\rho \in b^{\sigma(\rho)} := b^{\sigma(\rho)}(a^\rho)$.

It is often suitable to operate with names that do not name any (real) object, and so have, in the sense specified in II.1.2, no referent, names such as 'Odysseus' or names for persons no longer living, such as 'Socrates' or 'Eisenhower'. While in many contexts the use of such names makes no sense (What, for example, does 'Socrates is sick' mean, uttered at a time in which Socrates is no longer alive?), in other contexts (such as 'Hans is dreaming of Odysseus', 'Nixon remembers Eisenhower' or 'Eva believes that Socrates is a living philosopher') they can be used in a perfectly intelligible manner. But if a is such a name, one that has no referent, then the principle $A[a] \supset \vee x A[x]$ should not hold and $\wedge x A[x] \supset A[a]$ should be equally invalid.

Now if we regard U as the set of 'possible objects'[5] and single out a non-empty set U' within U as 'existing objects', then we can use a constant E of category $\sigma(v)$, for which we have

(e) $M(E) = U'$

and define

(h) $\bigwedge . x^v A[x^v] := \bigwedge x(E(x^v) \supset A[x^v])$

(i) $\bigvee . x^v A[x^v] := \neg \bigwedge . x^v \neg A[x^v]$.

These new quantifiers then refer only to existing objects so that we have $A[a] \wedge E(a) \supset \bigvee . xA[x]$, but not $A[a] \supset \bigvee . xA[x]$, and $\bigwedge . xA[x] \wedge E(a) \supset A[a]$, but not $\bigwedge . xA[x] \supset A[a]$.

2.1.3. *Intensions.* We shall now consider the assignme ntof intensions, too, to the expressions of L and to do so we move from L_1 to L. L can be characterized as a type-theoretical *language of modalities*, then. The construction of a semantics for such an intensional language is to be seen as the decisive step in determining a logical grammar, since natural languages are very rich in intensional contexts, so that an extensional logical language does not represent any suitable instrument for their analysis.

On R. Carnap's understanding of it the intension of an expression is that function which establishes its extension relative to possible worlds.[6] A world is defined in terms of the set of objects that belong to it and their attributes. So if what attribute a predicate means is a settled matter, then its extension for every world is settled as well. But the converse also holds if we understand attributes in such a way that they can only be distinguished if they have different extensions in at least one world. Understood in this way, attributes are the intensions of predicates.

Apparently not all objects existing in one world also exist in all others. Are there any objects at all which belong to different worlds? According to what criteria may an object a in world i be said to be identical with an object b in world j? Or can we only speak of similarities or correspondencies between objects of different worlds?

These problems have been extensively discussed in the literature. There are three proposed solutions.

(1) The simplest approach, which we shall take in what follows, is to take objects as individuals which may be identified or distinguished independently of their attributes. Then there may be the same objects in different worlds. We shall even assume that all the worlds have the same

set U of possible objects. This still leaves the chance to assign the worlds different sets U_i of objects existing in them.

(2) The second approach arises from the idea that we can identify objects only by means of the attributes they have. In fact we should say that two objects that have different *essential* properties cannot be identical. So what is, say a planet in one world cannot be a rabbit in another. In correspondence to the Leibniz-principle according to which (in one world) an object a is identical with b iff they have the same properties, we should therefore have a criterion for *trans-world identity*.

We can, however, still use the first approach even if we consider coincidence of essential properties as a necessary condition for identity. For this coincidence may be understood not as a defining criterion for identity but as a principle for choosing the admissible worlds. Then essential predicates would have the same extension in all worlds. The identity of the objects in different worlds may furthermore be guaranteed by the coincidence of other essential properties besides those expressed in L.

(3) The third approach is to give each world its own domain of objects so that no object occurs in two worlds at once. In place of trans-world identity we then have a *counterpart relation*, a relation not of identity but only of correspondence between objects in different worlds. This makes for higher generality but the simplicity of the first approach is to be preferred as long as this generality cannot be put to use.[7]

In every case there must be a relation of direct or trans-world identity or of correspondence between the objects of different worlds so that the definition of intensions makes sense. If the name a were to refer to quite different things α_i, which have nothing to do with each other, in different worlds i then the function $f(i) = \alpha_i$ cannot be understood as an intension of a in any sense, however loose.

Now let I be a set of worlds with the common domain U of possible objects and domains U_i of existing objects ($i \in I$), such that $U_i \subset U$. We shall interpret proper names as standard names in the sense of II.1.5, i.e. they are to have the same reference in all worlds.

According to Carnap's idea, for every term A of L there will be an extension $E_i(A)$, and the intension of A – represented in the object language by $\mu(A)$ – is the value distribution $\lambda^* i E_i(A)$. 'λ^*', as distinguished from the symbol 'λ' of the object language, is to be the metalinguistic symbol for functional abstraction.

The extension of a function expression, such as 'It is necessary that p', for example, often depends not only on the extension but on the intension of the argument. We assign to the argument place in the functor 'It is necessary that -' the category $\iota(\sigma)$ for propositions (as intensions of sentences), then, instead of the category σ for sentences. But since we can express the intension of 'p' in L by '$\mu(p)$', we can also say that extensions of function expressions always depend only on the extension of their arguments, along Fregean lines, if we write 'It is necessary $(\mu(p))$' for 'It is necessary that p'. The word 'that' can often be interpreted as the ordinary language equivalent of 'μ' (applied to sentences). Following this procedure, however, one must introduce special extensions of type $\iota(\tau)$.

We complete the specifications in 2.1.2.1 with this:

(d) $E_{\iota(\tau),U} = E_{\tau,U}{}^I$

and give the following definition:

2.1.3.1. An *intensional interpretation* of L over the (non-empty) world domain I with object domain U and (non-empty) domains U_i with $U_i \subset U$ is a two-place function $M_i(a)$ such that for all $i \in I$:

(a) $M_i(a) \in E_{\tau,U}$ for all constants a of L of category τ.

(b) $M_i(a) = M_j(a)$ for all constants a of category v and all $j \in I$.

(c) $M_i(F(a)) = M_i(F)(M_i(a))$ for all terms constructed in accord with 2.1.1.1b.

(d) $M_i(a \equiv b) = t$ iff $M_i(a) = M_i(b)$ for all terms, in accord with 2.1.1.1c.

(e) $M_i(E) = U_i$.

(f) $M_i(\lambda x A[x])$ is that function f from $E_{\tau(\rho),U}$, for which: $f(M_i'(b)) = M_i'(A[b])$ for all M' with $M' = {}_b M$ and $M_i'(b) = M_j'(b)$ for all $j' \in I$; the term $\lambda x A[x]$ is to be constructed in accord with 2.1.1.1d and the constant b of the same category as x is not to occur in $\lambda x A[x]$.

(g) $M_i(\mu(A)) = \lambda*iM_i(A)$[8]

(h) $M_i(\delta(A)) = M_i(A)(i)$.

Now what $M' = {}_b M$ says is that the intensional interpretations M, M' are at most distinguished with respect to the values $M_i(b)$ and $M_i'(b)$ for any number of $i \in I$.

$M_i(A)$ is the *extension* of the term A in world i, $\lambda i*M_i(A)$ its *intension*.

Definition 2.1.3.1 requires some explanation:

(1) If the variable x in $\lambda x(A[x])$ does not appear within the scope of an occurrence of μ, then we can also give the following definition: $M_i(\lambda x A[x])$

is that function f from $E_{\tau(\rho),U}$ for which $f(M_i'(b)) = M_i'(A[b])$ is true for all M' with $M' = {}_bM$; since in that case for all M', M'' with $M' = {}_bM$, $M'' = {}_bM$ and $M_i'(b) = M_i''(b)$: $M_i'(A[b]) = M_i''(A[b])$.

But that does not hold true if $\lambda x A[x]$ is e.g. the expression $\lambda x^v G^{\sigma(\iota(\sigma))}$ $(\mu(F^{\sigma(v)}(x^v)))$, for $\mu(F(a))$ can also depend on the intension of a, i.e. on the values $M_j(a)$ with $j \neq i$, even if it does not have to depend on these values in every case. Now if there is such dependence, then the expression $\lambda x G(\mu(F(x)))$, which is supposed to be a function taken from $E_{\sigma(v),U}$, has no sense. But the formation of terms $\lambda x A[x]$ cannot be restricted to cases in which x does not occur within the scope of an occurrence of μ. For there are also interpretations of G and F, for which the truth value of $G(\mu(F(a)))$ does not depend on the intension of a, but only on its extension. Deontic contexts, such as $O(\mu(F(a)))$ ($F(a)$ is obligatory), are of this sort, for example.[9] In such contexts, we can not renounce the formation of terms like $\lambda x A[x]$, $\bigwedge x A[x]$, $\bigvee x A[x]$. And so the formation of terms $\lambda x A[x]$ in general must be syntactically permitted, and they must then be so interpreted as to have their normal sense when the dependence in question is not present. But condition (f) provides for that. The problem can be solved better when partial interpretations are used.[10]

(2) The operator δ is required in order to be able to construct the term $\lambda x^{\iota(v)} G^{\sigma(\iota(\sigma))}(\mu(F^{\sigma(v)}(\delta(x^{\iota(v)}))))$, for example, and with it the sentence $\bigwedge x G(\mu(F(\delta(x))))$ – for all intensions of type $\iota(v)$ it holds that G, applied to the intension of F, applied to the extension of x, is true. While $\lambda x G(\mu(F(x)))$ is a function belonging to $E_{\sigma(v),U}$, $\lambda x G(\mu(F(\delta(x))))$ is a function belonging to $E_{\sigma(\iota(v)),U}$.

We can now supplement the definitions in 2.1.3 by defining modal operators in L, as for example:

$$NA := \mu(A) \equiv \mu(\bigwedge x^v(x^v \equiv x^v)) \quad \text{(It is necessary that } A)$$
$$MA := \neg N \neg A. \quad \text{(It is possible that } A)$$

2.1.4. *Pragmatic referents.* So far we have constructed a semantics of *expressions.* It is the intent of this section that a semantic characterization be given of utterances as well. Semantics can not be concerned only with expressions, but must also take utterances into account, for the meaning of an utterance, as we have already pointed out in Chapter I.1 and II, by no means always coincides with the meaning of the expression that is uttered, but is often specified more precisely by the pragmatic circumstances of the utterance. That becomes clear, for example, in the fact that a determinate extension can not be correlated with the expression but only with the utterance. Our earlier illustrations of this phenomenon concerned index expressions and descriptive predicates as examples.

According to Montague the relevant pragmatic parameters of an utterance can be condensed in the index j (j is thus an n-tuple of parameters), the _point of reference_ of the utterance. Let J be the set of these points of reference. One can then interpret utterances as pairs $\langle A, j \rangle$ of an expression A and an index j, following Y. Bar-Hillel, and assign extensions and intensions to such pairs; or the parameter j is included as an additional argument in the interpretation M, or M_i, of expressions. The two approaches are of equal value.

We give the following definitions:

A pragmatic extensional interpretation of L_1 over the (non-empty) object domain U and the (non-empty) index set J is a two-place function $M_j(x)$, such that for all $j \in J$ $M_j(x)$ is an extensional interpretation of L_1 over U as defined in 2.1.2.2.

Pragmatic intensional interpretations are defined in a corresponding manner.

We designate $M_{i,j}(A)$ as the _extension of the utterance_ $\langle A, j \rangle$ relative to i and $\lambda^* i M_{i,j}(A)$ as the _intension of the utterance_ $\langle A, j \rangle$. And we call $\lambda^* j M_{i,j}(A)$ the _extension of the term_ A relative to i and $\lambda^* ij M_{i,j}(A)$ the _intension of the term_ A.

If a term A does not depend on its pragmatic context, then $M_j(A) = M_{j'}(A)$, or $M_{i,j}(A) = M_{i,j'}(A)$, respectively for all $j, j' \in J$. On this condition the extensions, and likewise the intensions of all of the utterances of A are the same. The extension of A is the function with the constant value $M(A) = M_j(A)$, and analogously for intensions.

The problem of applying this logical schema for pragmatic interpretations concerns whether and how meaningfully boundaries can be placed around the set of pragmatic parameters to be taken account of by the index j. The speaker, the person(s) addressed, the person(s) or (objects) spoken of (as referents of 3rd person personal pronouns or of demonstrative pronouns), the place and the time of the utterance surely belong to it, but as a rule that is not enough, as is shown by the example of the dependence of the meaning even of descriptive expressions on pragmatic context that was discussed previously.

This characterisation of an intensional logical language will suffice here. For an application of intensional logic in analyses of sentences of natural languages we would have to supplement the semantics of L, for instance by introducing partial interpretations for dealing with syntactically well-formed but meaningless expressions, or by bringing in anormal (logically impossible) worlds to determine a more narrow concept of meaning than that of intension. But since we do not intend to give systematic analyses our definitions are sufficient in so much as they illustrate how logical languages may be constructed syntactically and semantically, and that is all we wanted to do here. For more details we have to refer to the literature.[11]

2.2. *The Logical Analysis of Sentences in Natural Language*

We shall now illustrate by a few examples how to analyze natural language sentences in L. We confine ourselves to an analysis of the *logical form* of such sentences, i.e. we do not refer to a specific interpretation of L, but only coordinate analysing sentences B of L to English sentences A, so that for a suitable interpretation of L B becomes synonymous with A. This means that we only describe the structure of A with the help of the logical categories introduced in the last chapter.[12]

So that we do not have to specify the categories of constants of L all over again in every example, we stipulate that the symbols in the left hand column of the following table belong to the categories indicated in the right hand column:

a, b, c, d	constants and
x, y, z	variables of categories v and $\iota(v)$
p, q	constants and
r, s	variables of categories σ and $\iota(\sigma)$
F, G, H, I	constants and
f, g, h	variables of categories $\sigma(v)$,
	$\sigma(v, v), \ldots, \sigma(\iota(v)), \ldots, \sigma(\sigma)$,
	$\sigma(\sigma, \sigma), \ldots, \sigma(\iota(\sigma)), \ldots, \sigma(v, \sigma), \ldots$,
U, V	constants and
u, v	variables of categories $v(v)$,
	$v(v, v), \ldots, v(\iota(v))$
M, N	constants of categories $\sigma(\sigma(v)), \sigma(v, \sigma(v)), \sigma(\sigma, v(v))$,
	$\sigma(\iota(\sigma(v)))$
T, W	constants of categories $v(\sigma(v)), v(v(v)), v(v, \sigma(v)), \ldots$

These provisions are sufficient to identify the categories of the constants in the contexts that follow. We shall write, as discussed in III, 2.1, '$\sigma(v, v)$' for '$(\sigma(v))(v)$' and '$F(a, b)$' for '$(F(a))(b)$' and use analogous abbreviations for other many-place categories and predicates.

In order to bring the following examples into some system, we shall go through the categories of traditional grammar referred to in III.1 and show how they can be represented from the point of view of logical grammar. For the sake of perspicuity we shall also make use of the logical operators defined in III.2.1.

Let us first consider the traditional theory of words. If we study word types with regard to the logical categories that occur within them, what emerges is the following:

(1) *Substantives*: Proper names are names in the logical sense. Articles in front of proper names are part of these ('the Zugspitze', 'the moon'). Class terms, on the other hand, are predicates, mostly one-place predicates like 'man' (category $\sigma(v)$), but also predicates with more than one place, such as 'gift from – to' (category $\sigma(v, v, v)$), predicates of predicates, such as 'type of sport' (category $\sigma(\iota(\sigma(v)))$), sentential predicates such as 'surprise' (category $\sigma(\iota(\sigma))$) and function expressions such as 'content' (category $v(v)$). Collectives are one-place predicates that are applied to names of aggregates of objects and even mass terms are one-place predicates.

From the above it follows that the analyses for the following examples are the expressions of L given after each of them:

(1) Socrates is a man – $F(a)$.[13]
(2) This vase is a gift from Fritz to Hans – $F(a, b, c)$.
(3) It is a surprise that Fritz is coming – $G(\mu(F(a)))$.
(4) Skiing is a type of sport – $M(\mu(F))$.
(5) This bar is gold – $F(a)$.
(6) The content of this bottle is water – $F(U(a))$.

(2) *Verbs*: Verbs are predicates, too, primarily predicates of one or more places belonging to category $\sigma(v, ..., v)$, such as 'run' ($\sigma(v)$), 'hit' ($\sigma(v, v)$, 'lie between – and' ($\sigma(v, v, v)$)), but also predicates of categories $\sigma(v, \iota(\sigma))$ and $\sigma(v, \iota(\sigma(v)))$ such as 'believe' and 'can'.

Reflexive verbs such as 'enjoy oneself', 'bestir oneself', 'perjure oneself', etc., which have come to be firmly tied to the relative pronoun, count as one-place predicates. Impersonal verbs such as 'rain', 'thunder', etc., which occur only in company with the pronoun 'it', can not be considered one-place predicates, but only as sentence constants. The pronoun 'it' does not play the role of a proper name here, for it makes no sense to ask 'What is raining?' or 'What is thundering?'[14]

(7)　　　Fritz runs – $F(a)$

(8)　　　Klais lies between Garmisch and Mittenwald – $F(a, b, c)$

(9)　　　Fritz believes that it is raining – $F(a, \mu(p))$.

(10)　　　Fritz can play tennis – $M(a, \mu(F))$.

(11)　　　Fritz is hunting a rabbit – $\vee x(F(x) \wedge G(a, x))$ or $M(a, \mu(F))$.

The first reading says that there is a particular rabbit Fritz is hunting. The second reading says, on the other hand, that Fritz is on a rabbit hunt, i.e. he does not want to bag a particular rabbit, but just some rabbit or other. In the latter sense 'hunt' is a predicate of category $\sigma(v, \iota(\sigma(v)))$.

(12)　　　Fritz wants to catch a fish and eat it – $I(a, \mu(\vee x(F(x) \wedge \\ \wedge G(a, x) \wedge H(a, x)))$[15]

Here 'want' is a predicate of category $\sigma(v, \iota(\sigma))$. The relation between 'it' and 'a fish' is established by the variable x. If one were to regard 'want' as a predicate of category $\sigma(v, \iota(\sigma(v)))$ and the sentence as the conjunction of 'Fritz wants to catch a fish' and 'he wants to eat it', this relation would remain open if Fritz does not want to catch a particular fish.

(3) *Adjectives*: Adjectives are also predicates, for the most part one-place predicates of category $\sigma(v)$, such as 'big', 'heavy', 'red', or of category $\sigma(v, v)$, such as 'larger than', 'friendly to', but there are also adjectives which are predicates of category $\sigma(\iota(\sigma))$, such as 'pleasant' (applied to facts), or $\sigma(\iota(\sigma(v)))$, such as 'fast', 'intentionally'.

(13)　　　Hans is bigger than Fritz – $F(a, b)$

(14)　　　It is pleasant that the sun is shining – $G(\mu(F(a)))$.

(15)　　　Hans is running fast – $\vee f(M(f) \wedge f(a) \wedge N(f))$.

The adjective 'fast' does not refer to the fact, that Hans is running, in this case – and so we can not write $G(\mu(F(a)))$; it is not the fact that is fast but the activity of running. But we can not write $M(\mu(F))$ either, since part of the sentence's content is that Fritz is running. The sentence is thus to be analyzed along the lines of 'Fritz is engaged in an activity of running (M) and this activity is fast (N)'.

(4) *Articles*: Articles have very different functions depending on the context in which they stand: Definite articles are parts of names ('the Zugspitze'); [in inflected languages], they express the number and case of the substantive (this is becoming especially important in German, with its declined endings in the process of being reduced or eliminated)[16]; they serve as index expressions or so as to express identification [by way of a definite description] ('the father of Fritz', meaning 'that particular person who is father of Fritz') and in such cases are expressions belonging to category $v(\sigma(v))$ or, in the case of descriptive identifications of one-place concepts, to category $\sigma(v, \sigma(\sigma(v)))$. Or they may serve to express generalization ('The lion is a mammal' as meaning 'All lions are mammals') and they are then expressions belonging to category $\sigma(\sigma(v))$.

The principal function of the indefinite article is to express particularization ('A locksmith came') – they are expressions belonging to category $\sigma(\sigma(v))$ in such cases – but they can also serve to express generalization ('A lion is a mammal' as meaning 'All lions are mammals') – then they have the same category – and together with the copula they serve to express the predicative use of substantives ('Fritz is a gardener') – in such cases they have no semantic function of their own, but serve as connectors.

(16)   The dog Fritz rescued is injured – $F(\iota x(H(x) \wedge G(x, a)))$.
(17)   The (a) lion is a mammal, or: (All) lions are mammals – $\wedge x(F(x) \supset G(x))$.
(18)   A locksmith is coming – $\vee x(F(x) \wedge G(x))$.
(19)   Fritz is a gardener – $F(a)$.

(5) *Pronouns*: *Personal pronouns* stand for proper names that were already introduced in the context concerned or which are determined by the context of utterance ('Fritz is a student and he is studying law', 'I am tired') – used in this way they serve as proper names and can be replaced by proper names – or they serve, like demonstratives, as index expressions, or they have the same function as variables in L, i.e. they occupy the places for arguments in an expression which as a function of these arguments is the argument of another expression.[17] The same holds true for reflexive pronouns, to the extent that they are not, as is the case with reflexive verbs, fixed components of verbs. The personal pronoun 'it' can also, as was already mentioned above, occur as a fixed component of an impersonal verb.

Reciprocal pronouns ('one another', 'each other', 'mutual') that occur in sentences such as 'Fritz and Inge love one another', 'Hans and Fritz are standing next to each other', 'Max and Hans have given utterance to mutual denunciations', serve as abbreviations of sentences with the same predicates – in unabbreviated form, the sentences read 'Fritz loves Inge and Inge loves Fritz', 'Hans is standing next to Fritz and Fritz is standing next to Hans', 'Max has denounced Hans and Hans has denounced Max'.

Demonstrative pronouns ('this', 'that', 'that particular', 'such', 'so', 'him (her, it, etc.) self' [in their reflective use]) serve first and foremost as index expressions. But demonstrative pronouns also function like personal pronouns as substitutes for proper names, as for example in the sentence 'Bei dem Kampf zwischen Fritz und Hans wurde jenem das Nasenbein gebrochen, diesem der Unterkiefer'. [Literally: 'In the fight between Fritz and Hans, that one suffered a broken nose and this one a broken jaw'. In English we would have to use 'the former' and 'the latter' in the place of '*jener*' ('that one') and '*dieser*' ('this one'), since the demonstrative pronouns themselves do not accomplish the discrimination of referent fixed by their German usage. That is accomplished in English by referring explicitly to the order of previous reference. In the sentence immediately preceding this one, it should be noted, the word 'that' does have the function discussed in the text. We could, with only some subtle change of emphasis, use the personal pronoun 'it' instead. The same point could have been illustrated with 'this' in the place of 'that'. In each of the three cases, 'this', 'that' or 'it' would be standing in for 'the discrimination of referent ...' An example (two, in fact) closer to that (here = 'the one') in the original text might be: 'Hans gave Fritz a black eye but that (1) was not the worst of it. He also shamed him in front of Inge. That (2) was the real blow that ended their friendship'.] The (non-reflexive) pronouns formed with '-self', 'himself', 'herself', 'itself', serve principally to place emphasis on the fact that one particular thing and no other is meant, as in 'Hans said so himself', 'Do it yourself'. When they have these functions, they contribute to the sentence's expressive aspects ('my information is authentic', 'I will not do it for you').

Relative pronouns ('who', 'which', 'that') function like variables in definite description expressions ('the man *who* met me') or like personal pronouns ('Anna, who entered the room, saw Fritz' – in this case the attributive sentence is to be understood conjunctively, i.e. as meaning 'Anna entered the room and Anna saw Fritz'). The expressions 'who' and 'what' have a generalizing character in, for example, the sentences 'Who dares, wins' (meaning 'Everyone who dares wins') and 'What is red is not green' (meaning 'Everything which is red is not green').

Interrogative pronouns ('who', 'what', 'which') function like relative pronouns in declarative sentences. For example, the interrogative pronoun in the sentence 'Hans believed what Fritz told him' can be replaced by a relative pronoun: 'Hans believed that which Fritz told him'. In grammar expressions such as 'all', 'each', 'none', 'nothing', 'one', 'some', 'something', 'many', 'few', 'a few', 'several' are counted as *indefinite pronouns*. Like the logical quantifiers, all of these words belong to category $\sigma(\sigma(v))$. Further, the expressions 'another' ['someone else'] and 'both' are numbered among the indefinite pronouns. The expression 'another' or 'someone else' can be rendered logically by means of a particularization (so, for example, the sentence 'Fritz praised Hans and *someone else* censured him' can be rendered by 'Fritz praised Hans and there is a person who is distinct from Fritz and who censured Hans'). And so that expression belongs to category $\sigma(\sigma(v))$. The expression 'both' stands for two proper names, as in 'Fritz and Hans are studying medicine and both are in their fifth semester' (meaning 'Fritz is studying medicine and Hans is studying medicine and Fritz is in the fifth semester and Hans is in the fifth semester').

The *possessive pronouns* ('my', 'your', 'his', 'her', 'its', 'our', 'their') viewed logically stand for function expressions (e.g. of category $v(v)$) or identifications (definite descriptions) with or without supplementary constants expressing a property, origin, or some other sort of relationship ('*his* father' can be rendered by 'the person who is father in relation to him', '*his* hat' can be replaced by 'the hat that belongs to him'). The only personal pronouns these function expressions contain are pronouns for which, according to the preceding discussion, proper names, or variables, are to be substituted.

(20)   Fritz is a student and he is an engineer – $F(a) \wedge G(a)$.
(21)   It is only a coward who takes flight – $\bigwedge x(F(x) \supset G(x))$.
(22)   Max praises himself – $F(a, a)$
(23)   Max and Manfred hate each other – $F(a, b) \wedge F(b, a)$
(24)   Who dares, wins – $\bigwedge x(F(x) \supset G(x))$

(25)   The man who married Eva is a cousin of Max – $F(\imath x G(x, a), b)$
(26)   Hans believes what Max told him – $F(a, \imath r G(b, r))$ – here r is
        a variable belonging to category $\imath(\sigma)$.
(27)   Nothing is perfect – $\neg \bigvee x F(x)$.
(28)   Some logicians are philosophers – $\bigvee x(F(x) \wedge G(x))$
(29)   Fritz is an engineer and his father is a doctor – $F(a) \wedge G(v(a))$.

(6) *Numeralia*: The principal occurrence of words for cardinal numbers
('one', 'two',...) is in combination with substantives, as in the sentence
'There are two books on the table'. In such a context cardinal number
words belong to category $\sigma(\sigma(v))$.[18] In mathematical statements such as
'$2+2=4$', on the other hand, cardinal number expressions serve as names
of numbers, i.e. they belong to category v. Words for ordinal numbers
('the first', 'the second',...) also occur primarily in connection with substantives and have in such cases the category $v(\sigma(v))$, as in the expression
'The first man who set foot on the moon'. Recurrence number words
('once', 'twice',...) indicate the number of events of the same kind, as in
the sentence 'Max failed the examination twice', and so they belong to
category $\sigma(\sigma(v))$ in the example. Number words of indefinite recurrence
('often', 'sometimes', 'never', 'several times') belong to the same category.

(30)   Two books have been damaged – $M(\lambda x(F(x) \wedge G(x)))$.
(31)   The third contestant is a Berliner – $F(T(\lambda x G(x)))$.
(32)   Sometimes it rains – $M(\lambda x F(x))$.

(7) *Adverbs*:
Adverbs of place and time: Indications as to time refer to events, they
express temporal relations between events (such as 'simultaneously',
'while', 'when', 'earlier than', 'before', 'later than', 'after', etc.) – Adverbs
of time, which stand for such temporal relationships, are of category
$\sigma(\sigma, \sigma)$, then – or they indicate either points or periods of time in which
events are occurring or have occurred ('now', 'today', 'yesterday'), or
relations between such points or periods of time ('before', 'after', etc.) –
in such cases they can be represented either as sentential operators of
category $\sigma(\sigma)$ or as names for temporal points or periods (category v),
which function as the arguments of predicates with which the events in
question are expressed or as the argument of a relation between points of
time and events (category $\sigma(v, \sigma)$).

In representing indications of time as names for points in time adverbs of time can also function as quantifiers, such as 'always', 'never', 'sometimes', 'frequently', 'often', 'since', 'before', etc. and they then have category $\sigma(\sigma(v))$. They can also be represented as sentential operators (category $\sigma(\sigma)$), however. Which form of representation is adopted depends on general applicability and systematic simplicity and on how far one is willing to diverge from the language. Representation by means of temporal parameters, as is usual in the physical sciences, for example, seems to be at a considerable remove from natural language, but it is systematically simple and it can be applied universally. Representation by means of sentential operators, on the other hand, is closer to language but generally more complicated.[19]

The like holds for adverbs of place. At the same time it should be noted of them that indications of place do not refer to events only but can refer to objects as well.

Adverbs of modality: They have very diverse functions and serve as sentential operators (category $\sigma(\sigma)$), such as 'perhaps', 'fortunately', 'possibly', 'not'. They can also serve as expressions belonging to category $\sigma(\sigma(v))$, such as 'at least', 'at most', or as sentential operators of category $\sigma(\sigma, \sigma)$, such as 'even', 'also', 'rather', and as independent components of comparative statements, such as 'so', 'very', 'all too', 'especially', or finally as predicates. For example, 'gladly' is a predicate belonging to category $\sigma(v, \sigma(v))$, for in the sentence 'Fritz gladly goes to the theatre', this word does not characterize the activity of going to the theatre, but an attitude of Fritz's toward the activity of going to the theatre, so that this sentence could also be rendered as 'Fritz likes to go to the theatre'.

Adverbs of reason: These are sentential operators that belong to category $\sigma(\sigma, \sigma)$, such as 'therefore', 'consequently', 'accordingly', 'otherwise', 'nevertheless', 'besides', or to category $\sigma(\sigma(v), v)$, as the instrumental 'with'.[20]

(33)   Hans came yesterday – $F(a, b)$

(34)   Max visits Fritz before he visits Hans – $G(\mu(F(a, b)), \mu(F(a, c)))$.

(35)   The car was stolen while Fritz was asleep – $N(\lambda x F(a, x), \lambda x G(b, x))$.

The sentence says that the time interval in which the car was stolen falls

within the time interval in which Fritz was asleep. So 'while' is a predicate
of category $\sigma(\sigma(v), \sigma(v))$ in this case.

(36)   Perhaps Fritz is sick – $F(a, \mu(G(b)))$.

Although 'perhaps' is an expression with which new sentences can be constructed out of sentences, this word is not used descriptively (it is not the
fact that Fritz is sick that is characterised by 'perhaps'), but serves an
expressive purpose and indicates the sentence's performative mode. And
so we offer a performative version of the sentence ('I regard it as possible
that Fritz is sick').

(37)   At least four books are missing – $M(\lambda x(F(x) \wedge G(x)))$.
(38)   Fritz gladly goes to the theatre – $M(a, \mu(f))$.
(39)   Fritz is not coming because he is sick – $H(\mu(\neg F(a)), \mu(G(a)))$.

8. *Prepositions*: They are either dependent components of predicates,
such as 'on' in 'Regensburg is situated on the Danube', or like adverbs
they express space and time relationships, as do 'within', 'around', 'outside', 'behind', etc., or sentential operators belonging to category $\sigma(\sigma, \sigma)$,
such as 'despite', 'without prejudice to', 'except'. The instrumental 'with',
as we shall demonstrate at length below, is a functor of category $\sigma(v, \sigma(v))$.

(40)   Regensburg is situated on the Danube – $F(a, b)$.
(41)   The building is closed outside of business hours – $\wedge x(\neg F(x) \supset$
          $\supset G(a, x))$.

9. *Conjunctions*: Conjunctions are predominantly sentential operators
belonging to category $\sigma(\iota(\sigma))$, such as 'necessarily', 'probably', 'hardly',
'presumably', or operators of category $\sigma(\sigma, \sigma)$ such as 'and', 'besides',
'likewise', 'not only – but also', 'or', 'either – or', 'otherwise', 'but', 'if –
then', 'if and only if', 'insofar as', 'so', 'consequently', 'therefore', 'because', 'all the more since', 'if only', 'for', 'in order that', 'so that'. They
are also expressions for temporal relations, such as 'as long as', 'while',
'after', or dependent components of comparatives like 'just as – so', 'as',
'all the more', 'the – the', 'the same as', or connectives like 'that' and
'whether'.

In this connection we need to check whether the conjunctions are (also)
used after the manner of performative operators (such as 'presumably')

or not (e.g., 'necessarily'); in the former case what should be logically analyzed is an explicitly performative version of the sentence.

(42)   Eva is young and beautiful – $F(a) \wedge G(a)$
(43)   Fritz is going either to Rome or to Naples – $I(F(a, b), F(a, c))$.
(44)   Max asks whether he may go – $F(a, \mu(M(a, \mu(G))))$.
(45)   Max comes whenever Fritz calls him – $\wedge x(F(a, b, x) \supset G(b, x))$.

We see, then, if we make a review of the various types of words or parts of speech in relation to the logical categories of the expressions that fall under them, that word classes and logical categories are not at all parallel. These brief reflections underscore still more emphatically the absence of any homogeneity of grammatical function among the expressions traditionally grouped together under one and the same word type.

Let us now consider *inflection* from the point of view of logical analysis:

As a rule, the *gender* of a substantive does not have any independent logical function. The grammatical gender of words does not coincide with the natural gender of the objects they designate, or which belong to the set of concepts they express. Grammatical gender probably arose originally by transference of the distinction 'masculine – feminine' onto the world of things, but it also conforms sometimes to pure syntactical principles. For example, in German all words that end in '-*ling*' are masculine, all words that end in '-*heit*' or '-*keit*' are feminine. Grammatical gender can even be contradictory to natural gender, as exemplified by the expression '*das Weib*'. And so the principal grammatical function of gender consists in making clear which expressions in the sentence belong together, the function, then, of an (often unnecessary) connective.[21]

As *connectives* we here designate those linguistic means which indicate connections between expressions in a sentence, or determine the scope of functors, distinguish their arguments etc. – which, in other words, indicate the structure of a sentence. In L these are brackets and commas, besides the order of the expressions.

On occasion, however, gender does still have a semantic function, when it alone characterizes human beings or animals as masculine or feminine.[22] In these cases it can be rendered by means of special constants or what it specifies semantically can be assimilated into the meaning of the substantive.

In German the forms taken by *number* are singular and plural. Besides them Indogermanic formerly had the dual as a special form for expressing two in number. In accordance with their meanings names are always in the singular. In the normal forms of sentences, however, common nouns are also always in the singular. We must therefore inquire whether sentences that contain a plural can always be translated synonymously into sentences that contain only singular forms.

The linguistic plural expresses the fact that the predicate relates to a number of things. It occurs, for example, in the following sentences:

(a)   Fritz and Hans are football players.
(b)   Some Austrians are Tyrolians.
(c)   The French were engaged in battle with the Prussians at Jena.
(d)   Fritz and Hans are brothers.
(e)   Erna and Karl love each other.

In sentences (a) and (b) the predicate is distributive, i.e. it concerns each and every individual thing mentioned in the sentence. With that in mind, we can translate these sentences into the following expressions, in which only the singular occurs:

(a′)   Fritz is a football player and Hans is a football player.
(b′)   For (at least) one man it is the case that: He is an Austrian and he is a Tyrolian.

In sentences (c) through (e), on the other hand, the predicate is not distributive, i.e. these sentences can not be reformulated into the expressions:

(c′)   For every individual x and for every individual y it is true that: If x is a Frenchman and y is a Prussian, then x was engaged in battle with y at Jena.
(d′)   Fritz is a brother and Hans is a brother.
(e′)   Erna loves herself and Fritz loves himself.

What is meant by (c) is rather that the French army was engaged with the Prussian army at Jena, i.e. we must replace the plural 'the French', or 'the Prussians' with the singular 'the French army', or 'the Prussian army' and by so doing we obtain as the correct translation into the singular the sentence:

(c″)   The French army was engaged in battle with the Prussian army at Jena.[23]

In sentences (d) and (e), however, there are two-place predicates, which can be linguistically analyzed by using conjunction.[24] These expressions also involve abbreviations. Therefore we can render the sentences as follows:

(d″)   Fritz is brother of Hans (and Hans is brother of Fritz).

(e″)   Erna loves Karl and Karl loves Erna.

These translations show that the plural has no independent logical function.

The principal function of *case* is just to establish the relationship between the individual words in the sentence. Congruence, which has to do with gender and number, determines which adjectives belong to which substantives and which verbs to which substantives. In particular, case establishes whether a substantive is functioning as subject or object of the sentence and distinguishes its various objects. In the analyzing terms of sentences this function is taken over by the position of the terms in the sentence. For example, while in German one can say not only '*Erna liebt Hans*' but also '*Den Hans liebt die Erna*', so that it is necessary for case to establish who loves whom; after specifying that in the two-place predicate 'loves (x, y)' 'x' represents the subject, 'y' the object of the love, the only form that remains a possibility is 'love (Erna, Hans)', but not 'love (Hans, Erna)'. For that reason case is also superfluous here. In the expression, 'father's mother', case determines which part is the argument and which part the function constant, while this distinction is effected in the normal form 'mother (father)' by word position and parentheses.

Viewed logically, then, case has the function of specifying the connection of the expressions in the sentence, i.e. case belongs among the connectives.[25]

Along with that, however, case can also have a semantic function. For example, 'So-and-so's picture' can mean the same as 'the picture that belongs to so-and-so', 'the picture that so-and-so painted', or 'the picture that represents so-and-so'. Here the genitive has three different semantic functions, which are rendered by relational constants in the analyzing expression of L.[26]

With adjectives the formation of *comparative forms* is also counted as a matter of inflection: From certain adjectives, e.g. 'tall', 'light', 'pretty', 'old', 'bright', but not from other adjectives such as 'red', 'written', 'dead', 'silent', comparative forms can be constituted, such as 'taller', 'lighter', 'prettiest', 'very useful', and so on. We shall take the adjective 'tall' as an example.

Viewed logically, what we are concerned with in the case of the positive (the basic form) is a one-place classificatory predicate belonging to category $\sigma(v)$. In grammar, however, the form of comparison 'just as tall as', which is a two-place predicate in category $\sigma(v, v)$, is also counted as falling within the positive. In the case of the comparative form 'taller than' we also have to do with a two-place predicate. 'Less (more) tall than' is also a comparative form. The superlative 'the tallest' or 'tallest', as well as the elative 'very tall', are once again one-place predicates of category $\sigma(v)$. In contexts such as 'Hans is the tallest student' or 'Fritz is a very tall boy', on the other hand, superlative and elative have category $\sigma(\sigma(v))$.

There is no logical formation of comparative forms as complex predicates with the positive as argument corresponding to the formation of comparative forms to the positive in language, i.e., what we are concerned with here is not the formation of new expressions from others by combining them logically.[27] From a logical point of view, the formation of comparative forms belongs, then, to the lexical part of the theory of word formation.

In the case of verbs, besides person (the speaker, the one spoken to, the one spoken of) which can be read off from congruence with the subject, and number, which was discussed above, there are still the following to be considered as inflected forms: tense, mood and voice (active and passive).

Tenses (in German: present, preterite, perfect, pluperfect, (1) and (2) future) serve primarily to indicate time in terms of past, present and future, and can be rendered by time parameters or sentential operators. In this connection it is to be noted that these time indications are index expressions, for on each occasion they relate to the point in time at which the statement is made as the present.[28] If this point in time is indicated by the sentence itself, then the time indications as given by tense have a relational character. The present can serve as the basic form for the logical analysis, since it is also used for the representation of facts that are timeless or do not depend on time.[29] Also polyadic temporal relations are expressed by tense, particularly by the pluperfect and (2) future, as for example in the sentences 'Fritz had just entered the room, when the telephone rang', 'When you arrive in Rome, Max will already have left the city'.

In addition, the distinction of preterite – perfect also marks a distinction in the speaker's relationship to the event described in terms of aspect or participation. A sentence in the perfect contains a reference to the speaker and his present situation that a sentence in the preterite does not contain. Generally speaking tense can also have a modal character, the future in particular often expressing expectations and aims.[30] Such expectations and intentions are to be rendered by performative predicates.

Finally, tense forms can also be used to express the beginning (Aorist), duration, frequency and repetition of events. In such cases they are to be rendered, as in example (35), by quantifying over points in time, for instance.

The basic *mood* that utterances have is the *indicative*. The *subjunctive*, which has become quite rare in present-day German,[31] primarily serves the purpose of *Kundgabe* [expressing the speaker's attitude] and can be represented in that function by performative predicates. It serves to express obligation ('Be that issue left unresolved' – 'That issue ought to be left unresolved'), exhortation ('May we attain to peace and calm' – 'We desire to attain peace and calm'), concession ('Be it so, then!' – 'It should be so!'). Besides these functions, however, the subjunctive also serves to express irrealia, as for example in the sentence 'If Hans had put on the brakes in time, the accident would not have happened' – or to express the content of a position that is maintained, as in the sentence 'Fritz claims not to have been responsible for the accident'. [The subjunctive is not used for this purpose in English; it is used, however, to express the content of a question, e,g. 'Fritz asked if it were the case that Hans had not put on the brakes', or of a demand, as in 'Fritz demanded that Hans be charged with criminal negligence'].

The *imperative*, finally, serves to express command, and so in logical analysis it too is rendered by a performative operator.[32]

The *infinite* (i.e., indeterminate as to person and number) *verb forms*, the infinitive and participle, finally, have the following function: The infinitive is used when a verb assumes the role of argument ('Max loves to ski'). [In English, the participle is used for the same purpose ('Max loves skiing').] The (1) and (2) *participle* are used especially in attribution as forms of an adjectival use of the verb ('the blossoming tree', – 'the fallen tree').[33] The *gerundive* ('the action to be done' – 'the action that should be done') can be expressed by combining the passive with the sentential operator, 'should'.

The formation of the *passive* from transitive verbs ('Hans strikes Fritz' – 'Fritz is struck by Hans') is usually interpreted as the formation of the converse relation.[34] That interpretation, however, does not do justice to the fact that there is an impersonal passive for intransitive (i.e., one-place) verbs ('*lachen*' – '*Es wird gelacht*' [Literally, 'to laugh' – 'It is laughed'; there is no such use of the passive voice of intransitive verbs in English]), while there is no converse for monadic predicates. Of course, one can say: '*Es wird gelacht*' means the same as '*Jemand lacht*' ['Someone is laughing'], so that the impersonal passive takes on the role of particularization. There is still a question, however, as to whether this is an adequate interpretation or whether impersonal passive sentences are not to be interpreted as independent sentential constants (in analogy with '*Es regnet*' ['It is raining']) and passive forms of transitive verbs as independent monadic predicate constants. On that view, the expression 'by Hans' in the sentence 'Fritz is struck by Hans' would be an adverbial qualification of 'Fritz is struck'. Depending on how one interprets the passive, then, one arrives at quite different analyses of the structures of sentences in the passive mood.[35]

Now how does the traditional *theory of sentences* look from the standpoint of logical grammar?

The syntax of the logical language L is differentiated from traditional syntax in virtue of the fact that it replaces the traditional sentence schema subject – predicate, which can be expanded by supplementations, with the substitution of arguments of categories $\tau_1, ..., \tau_m (m \geqslant 1)$ in a predicate of category $\sigma(\tau_1, ..., \tau_m)$ as a basic logical schema. This *logical predicate* replaces the traditional grammatical predicate. It is differentiated from the latter by the fact that it can contain expressions the traditional grammar counts as supplementation (e.g., prepositions, as in 'to lie between ... and ...'), and that it does not always contain the constants that traditionally count as predicate (in (17) the traditional predicate is 'are mammals'; the logical predicate is 'all'). Furthermore, the expression that serves as analysans can contain constants that do not occur in the original sentence themselves and these new constants can even play the logical role of predicate (cp. example (17)).

The traditional *sentence subject* is usually viewed logically as one of the arguments of the logical predicate, but in logical analysis it loses its distinctive role in relation to the other arguments, for example the sentence objects. But in many cases the subject of the sentence does not even have the role of an argument of the predicate, as for example in the normal forms of 'All lions are mammals' and 'Hans ran fast'.

Objects of sentences for the most part function as arguments of the logical predicate ('Eva loves *Kuno*', 'Max gives *Fritz the book*', 'Hans is helping *Fritz*', 'Hans is caring for *the wounded*'), but they can also be components of the argument, as for example in (34).

As viewed by logic, *attributes* too can have quite a variety of functions: They are conjunctive sentence parts (as in 'The *pale* winter sun stands low in the sky' – 'the winter sun is pale and stands low in the sky', or in 'Hans, *who was coming in the door*, saw Fritz' – 'Hans was coming in the door and saw Fritz'), or identifying descriptions (as in 'The *red* car belongs to Maria' – 'The car that is red belongs to Maria', or in 'The rejoicing *over the victory* did not last long' – 'That rejoicing which was a rejoicing over the victory did not last long') or predicates of predicates (as in 'The rose is *pale* rose' – 'The rose color this rose has is pale', or in 'Kunigunde is *frightfully* ugly' i.e. 'The quality of ugliness Kunigunde possesses is frightful'), or predicates of sentences, or parts of predicates of sentences (as in 'Max travels by train *very often*' – 'It is very often the case that Max travels by train', or in 'Hans lived in Munich for *five years*' – 'During a period that lasted five years it was the case that Hans lived in Munich') or as argument of the logical predicate (as in 'To suffer injustice is better *than to commit injustice*', or in 'To the right of his house there stands a church').

Finally, adverbial modifications, like adverbs, when viewed logically are predicates of sentences or predicates of predicates, but they are also predicates of sentences with arguments or the like as well.

Taken all in all, then, no uniform logical function can be assigned to the traditional categories of sentence components.

Since the treatment of adverbial modifications in translating sentences in ordinary language into logical formulae is an excellent example of how complicated logic can be, it would be well to offer three more typical examples.

Let us consider first of all sentence (15) 'Hans runs fast'. In that sentence the word 'fast', as we have already insisted, does not characterize the proposition that Hans is running, and so it is not a sentential operator of category $\sigma(\sigma)$; instead it specifies the nature and manner of the activ-

ity of running, which is described as fast running. Therefore sentence
(15) can also be formulated in the following way: 'Hans is engaged in an
activity of running and that activity is fast' or 'There is an activity f of
which it is true that: f is an activity of running and Hans is engaged in f
and f is fast' – as a formula of logic written: $\bigvee f(L^*(f) \wedge f(a) \wedge S(f))$,
where 'a' stands for 'Hans', 'S' for 'fast' and 'L^*' for 'activity of running'.[36] In this case $L^*(f)$ is a predicate belonging to category $\sigma(\sigma(v))$.
The predicate 'running' – $L(x)$ in symbols – on the other hand, belongs
to category $\sigma(v)$. These predicates are connected as follows: $\bigwedge x(L(x) \equiv$
$\equiv \bigvee f(L^*(f) \wedge f(x)))$. Thus $L(x)$ can be defined by way of $L^*(f)$ but not
conversely,[37] and to that extent no expression that contains the predicate $L(x)$ can be assigned to (15) as analysans. It also becomes clear
from this that adverbial modification is not, as it seems to be at first
glance, a supplementation added on to the sentence 'Hans runs', but that
'running' is a different predicate here.

The situation is similar with adverbial modifications that indicate instruments used or ends pursued, as the following two examples demonstrate:

(46)   Hans strikes Fritz with a stick – There is a thing x, of which it
         is true that: x is a stick and there is an activity f, of which it is
         true that: f is an activity of striking and f applies to Hans and
         Fritz and f is accomplished by means of x – $\bigvee x(F(x) \wedge$
         $\wedge \bigvee f(M(f) \wedge f(a, b) \wedge N(f, x)))$.

(47)   Max works to earn money – There is an activity f, of which it
         is true that: f is an activity of working and f applies to Max
         and f is an activity of which earning money is the purpose –
         $\bigvee f(M(f) \wedge f(a) \wedge N(f, G))$.

The examples given for the logical forms of natural language sentences
cannot be more than indications of how to analyze such sentences in L;
how an analyzing relation $R(X, Y)$ between the sentences of a natural
language S and sentences of L would look.

These examples, however, suffice to illustrate the following points:

(1) The logical analysans of a natural language sentence A is not uniquely determined. This became apparent, for instance, in the analysis of
temporal adverbs. For the same sentence A there may then be several
sentences $B_1, ..., B_n$ of L with $R(B_1, A), ..., R(B_n, A)$ even if A is not am-

biguous. Therefore it would be expedient to standardize the logical analyses so that we may speak of *the* analyzing term of unambiguous sentences.

(2) The logical structure of an analyzing term of L for a sentence A of S is often very different from the grammatical structure of A. If we call the former the *deep structure* of A, the latter its *surface structure*, then deep structure can be very far from the way a sentence is constructed in language. A consequence of this is that there are no simple and systematic connections between logical categories and the traditional grammatical categories that aim at surface structures.

(3) Deep structures are theoretical constructs, in our case constructs in the framework of a logical theory of grammar. Instead of L we could also have taken another logical language L' which would then determine different deep structures. If we try to diminish the distance between surface and deep structure, then also other, less orthodox logical languages gain in interest.[38] And it may very well be the case that different logical languages are suitable for the analysis of different natural languages.[39]

(4) The deep structure of a sentence is often much more complicated than its surface structure. That is illustrated for instance by our examples (46) and (47).[40]

(5) The plasticity of natural languages cannot be modelled by the rigid logical languages. The same expression of a natural language may have quite different syntactical and semantical functions in different contexts. They must be assigned different logical categories in these contexts. The same expression can also function as a (descriptive) constant in one sentence and as a connective in another. The constants of L, moreover, not only correspond to words of S, but may represent parts of words or groups of words in S. We already mentioned, for instance, that 'to lie' occurs as a 1-place predicate in 'The cat lies on a mat', as a 2-place predicate in 'Regensburg lies on the Danube', and as a 3-place predicate in 'Klais lies between Garmisch and Mittenwald'. In fact there is no semantic connection between 'lie' as a 1-place and as a 2-place predicate, at most a partial homonymy: while 'lie' is the opposite of 'stand' or 'sit', 'lie on' expresses a situation, and may be applied also to objects, like cities, of which we cannot say that they lie, stand or sit. Finally the analysans may have to contain constants or functors which do not correspond to expressions in the analysandum. In the analysans of the sentence 'Lions are mammals', for instance, we have to put in an expression for 'all'.

Natural languages are just not constructed 'with a logical ruler'[41], their regularities have not arisen from systematic considerations – least of all by those according to which L is constructed – but have developed in all their peculiarities and accidental features in a long historical process.

The examples point out the astonishing semantic and syntactic polyvalence of the words and forms of natural languages – astonishing primarily, because the number of constants of a logical language like L with equal expressive power is reduced considerably, without making the statements less intelligible as a rule.

(6) At present the value of logical grammar, in the absence of a general definition of analyzing relations R for natural languages, consists less in the fact that it is possible to present a syntax and semantics for such languages within the framework it provides than in specific analyses of sentences in natural language. For example, if what we are concerned with is to describe the ambiguities of sentences in a systematic fashion and not just list the various possible interpretations by means of paraphrases, the concepts of traditional grammar are often insufficient. Let us consider an example of a sentence that is structurally ambiguous: 'Hans had a book stolen'.[42] In this case the ambiguity of 'had' is at work ('caused to' and 'happened to'), so that it is possible to interpret this sentence along the lines of 'Hans was the victim of a theft of a book' (which in its turn could be read either as 'of one of his books' or as 'of a book that was in his possession but that did not belong to him') or 'Hans caused someone to steal a book for him' (which is again ambiguous in a way roughly parallel to the ambiguity of the former interpretation. I.e., Hans might have caused someone to steal one of his own books for him – presumably for the sake of recovering from an insurance company – or, the more natural interpretation, he caused someone to steal a book he did not own, but wanted, for him.) On the former interpretation of 'had', Hans is an innocent victim; on the latter, he is an unscrupulous instigator of either a theft or a fraud. Since the 'had' of 'Had such-and-such happen to' is of category $\sigma(v, \iota(\sigma))$, while the 'had' of 'caused someone to' belongs to category $\sigma(v, v, \iota(\sigma(v)))$, this semantic ambiguity is also the source of a structural ambiguity. [The foregoing example has been modified to fit the author's presentation of it as closely as possible while using English rather than German idioms. Hence it is not precisely the example chosen by the author for his German text, since that can not be rendered literally in English,

nor is it Chomsky's original example in English (although it, too, turned on the ambiguity of 'had'), since Kutschera's treatment is significantly different in some respects.]

And so the sentences in L that provide the analyses are:

$$\bigvee x(F(x) \wedge M(a, \mu(\bigvee yG(y, x, a)))),$$

and

$$\bigvee x(F(x) \wedge \bigvee yM(a, y, \mu(\lambda zG(z, x, a))))).^{43}$$

(7) After many grammatical details have disappeared in logical analysis (such as accent and position, case, and the distinction between subject, adjective, verb), the final question arises, whether logical semantics is capable of reproducing all of the discriminations of meaning in natural languages. For reasons discussed below we cannot maintain that all semantically relevant differences many be represented in L. What we will do, however, is to illustrate by an example that the difficulties are not as great as they are sometimes represented to be: The two sentences (a) 'Hans patted his friend on the shoulder' and (b) 'Hans patted his friend's shoulder' both have the same normal form (at least at the first look). Weisgerber urges that in the first sentence there is exemplified a sentence type or sentence structure [in German] that he calls an 'advertive action sentence' ['*zugewandten Betätigungssatz*'].[44] He regards the function specifically accomplished by such sentences as lying in the fact that the event to which they refer is not identified as a goal-directed activity but as an activity of the subject adverted to the person cited as dative object. The role of the dative as being that of a case that expresses 'the inward concern of the person referred to by the verbal concept' and as 'more subjective, warmer, more inward than the genitive, which simply states objectively a relation of possession',[45] is therefore essential to this sentence structure, according to Weisgerber.

But apart from the fact that Weisgerber's statements are very imprecise and, as he himself confesses, remain incomplete and that these sentence structures also occur in cases in which there can be no talk of an 'advertive activity' (as in 'The stone hit his friend on the head', 'Hans slapped his friend in the face' alongside of 'Hans gave his friend a slap in the face') [These examples depend on the dative case being used in the first and the last, and so the point can not be made as clearly in English.], the difference in meaning between the two sentences can be represented as follows:

'patting someone on the shoulder' is a conventional form of expression, which is only conditionally tied up with the predicate 'patting', since the prevalent component of meaning lies in the expression of appreciation or approval, not the expression of the activity of patting. But this constant does not occur in the second sentence (b), which consequently does not also express appreciation or approval, but only the activity of patting and so has a different meaning from (a). Similarly with Weisgerber's other examples, such as 'Hans looks Fritz in the face', etc.

The difficulties of a *semantical* analysis of natural language sentences with an *interpreted* logical language L did not appear in our examples because we aimed at a purely syntactical analysis with the help of an uninterpreted L. The following remarks may be made on this point:

(8) We have analyzed only assertions. Although we have indicated in II.4.5 how to interpret other types of sentences in the framework of descriptive semantics with the help of performatory operators we still should have to develop the procedures for the analysis of imperatives, questions, etc. in L.

(9) In the semantics of L we have treated meanings as intensions. For the reasons discussed in II.1.5 such a meaning-concept is too weak. We have indicated how to narrow intensions by admitting logically inconsistent worlds, but at present there is no really satisfactory and technically well defined procedure to handle meanings in intensional semantics.

(10) Natural languages contain many expressions which are grammatically wellformed but meaningless; which are assembled from meaningful words or morphemes according to the syntactical rules but derive no meaning under the semantical determinations. Let us take five typical examples of such wellformed but meaningless expressions:

(a) *Incompletely defined functors*: Many predicates are not defined for all syntactically permissible arguments. Thus the verb 'to run' is defined for animals with locomotive appendages, for humans, machines, fluids and for noses, not however for plants, minerals or numbers. And the German verb 'lachen' is defined only for humans and the sun. The sentence 'Der Mond lacht', though constructed grammatically just as 'Die Sonne lacht', has unlike this sentence no meaning.

(b) *Non-existent objects*: Sentences about objects which do not exist or no longer exist form a significant sub-category of example (a). The sentences 'Odysseus is (now) shaving himself' and 'Eisenhower is (now) sick' are meaningless but not the sentences 'Professor Snell is dreaming of Odysseus' or 'Nixon remembers Eisenhower'. Thus many predicates are defined for non-existent objects while others are not. Since the question of whether a human being is alive or dead is purely empirical, syntax cannot refer to this distinction.

(c) *Invalid presuppositions*: A presupposition of a statement or utterance A is a state of affairs which is not itself asserted in A, but which must be the case if both A and the (colloquial) negation of A are to be meaningful. Thus the sentence 'John gave up smoking' presupposes that John previously smoked. 'Jack knows that there is a university in Regensburg' presupposes that Regensburg does indeed have a university. The utterance 'As a doctor I realise how dangerous this symptom is' presupposes that the speaker is a physician. These presuppositions are not part of the content of the sentences but rather preconditions to them being meaningful at all. Such presuppositions, being again matters of empirical fact, cannot be accounted for by syntax.

Invalid presuppositions also appear in the following special cases:

(d) *Definite descriptions with unfulfilled normality conditions*: Description terms as 'Russell's book' or 'George VI's son' have no meaning because the describing predicate fails to apply to exactly one object as the normality condition of descriptions requires. Whether this condition holds or not is again an empirical question, not a syntactic one.

(e) *Empty generalisations*: In ordinary discourse the sentence 'All of John's children have red hair' is meaningless if John does not have any children. In general a sentence of the form 'All A's are B' is only meaningful if there are A's. Such a sentence thus presupposes the sentence 'A's exist'. This should not be understood in every case to mean that there must exist 'real objects' which are A's – sentences like 'All Greek Gods were assimilated into the Roman Pantheon' indicate to the contrary that they can also be possible objects. These presuppositions of descriptions and generalisations were first noticed by P. F. Strawson.

In the semantics of L we have assigned all well-formed expressions A of L an intension which for every world i determines the extension of A in i. To analyze expressions in natural languages which for some worlds have no extensions, or for functors which are not defined for all syntactically permissible arguments we have to define *partial interpretations* of L.[46]

(11) Natural languages contain many vague and ambiguous expressions or regularities. This is true in the syntactical domain – there are degrees of grammaticalness, of well-formedness of sentences, the grammatical categories apply more or less to an expression – and much more so in the semantical domain. A logical analysis, especially a semantical analysis of natural language sentences with the exact concepts of logic and precise logical interpretation therefore often implies an explication more than an interpretation, and hence a modification of these sentences.

Of course the first aim in developing a logical grammar is to have a functioning syntactic and semantic system at all. And for that the price of a certain modification may be very well worth paying. But in a second step one will have to try to replace some classificatory concepts by comparative ones; for instance comparative concepts of well-formedness or of synonymity. With these concepts the vagueness of natural languages can be mirrored exactly, since it is based on the comparative or typological character of grammatical categories and rules. Because it is possible to describe in a logically exact way even what is vague and not exact, there is no justification to think that a logical analysis is inadequate in principle, then. At present, however, as far as I know, there has been no attempt to develop such comparative concepts in the framework of logical grammar.

We can sum up these remarks then by saying: Logical grammar is a step in the right direction. The logical analysis of natural language is fruitful even now, but there is still a lot to be done before we can claim that an adequate logical analysis of natural languages is possible.

NOTES

[1] See e.g. Montague [70] and [70a].

[2] For $F(a_1)\!\ldots\!(a_n)$ we shall sometimes write $F(a_1, ..., a_n)$.

[3] $(A^B)^C$ can be represented by $A^{B \times C}$, but not $A^{(B^C)}$: $(A^B)^C$ is the set of functions h on C with $h(x) = g$ for $x \in C$ and $g \in A^B$. If $y \in B$, then $g(y) \in A$, and so $h(x)(y) \in A$, and for that we can also write $h(x, y) \in A$. $A^{(B^C)}$, on the other hand, is the set of functions h, which assign values drawn from A to functions g of C into B: $h(g) \in A$.

[4] See Montague [70], p. 387. The definitions of negation and conjunction were given by A. Tarski in [23].

[5] This form of expression is very problematical, since 'possible' is not an adjective, but a sentential adverb. The procedure sketched in what follows simply amounts to assigning a referent to the term that has no referent, but making a distinction between existing objects existing in one world and others.

[6] See Chapter II.1.5.

[7] See D. Lewis [68] on counterpart theory.

[8] Since $\lambda^*iM_i(A) \neq \lambda^*i\,(\lambda^*iM_i(A))$, the expressions $\mu(A)$ and $\mu(\mu(A))$ do not have the same extension. The fact that there may be no relevant distinction in natural language corresponding to this formal difference in meaning is no objection to the interpretation of $\mu(A)$.

[9] See Kutschera [73a], Chapter 1.

[10] Montague in [70] interprets variables, too, along the lines of condition (a) and in (d) requires instead of $M'_i(b) = M'_j(b)$ for all $j \in I$, that $M'_j(b) = M_j(x)$ should hold for all $j \neq i$. But then such simple logical principles as $\lambda xA\,[x] \equiv \lambda yA\,[y]$ are no longer valid.

[11] For partial interpretations cf. Kutschera [74], for anormal worlds Montague [70], for intensional logic in general Cresswell [73].

[12] Logical categories of this sort were first developed by K. Ajdukiewicz and S. Lesniewski. They are used for grammatical purposes also in Bar-Hillel [53] and [60b], in Curry [61] and in Lambeck [61].

[13] The predicative character of class words is linguistically clear in sentences in which such a word is a part of the grammatical predicate, as in (1), but not in sentences in which the class term is the subject of the sentence, as in 'Man is mortal'. Superficially considered, 'Man' has the same place here as "Socrates" in (1). For that reason, the substantive has sometimes been denied any predicative character generally and (1) has been interpreted as an identification of Socrates with a man, so that 'is' (in the sense of identity) would be the predicate all by itself (see III.1.2, Note 26). But this conception, as we have seen, is untenable. It is necessary to take the opposite course and interpret class terms serving as subjects of sentences predicatively also, as becomes clear in the following formulation of the second sentence: 'For every thing it is true that if it is a man, it is mortal'.

[14] See Grebe [66], p. 457ff., 472.

[15] Montague discusses this example in [70a].

[16] See Grebe [66], p. 176. On p. 152ff. there is also an explanation of how the article arises through the blurring of declined endings. For example, if someone says '*Ich ziehe Wein Wasser vor* [I prefer wine to water/water to wine]' that is ambiguous, since the arguments taken by '*vorziehen* [prefer]' are distinguished by case as dative and accusative object, but the accusative and dative of "wine" and "water" read the same. Consequently, articles are used here to distinguish between the sentences '*Ich ziehe dem Wein (das) Wasser vor*' and '*Ich ziehe (den) Wein dem Wasser vor*'. [In English, one way of resolving the notoriously ambiguous oracle: 'The Medes the Persians will subdue', would be to insert the nominative form of the pronoun in apposition before whichever noun was intended to be agent of the subduing and so the subject of the sentence.]

[17] Cf. sentence (21) below or the sentence 'Hans saw a lion and Fritz killed him'.

[18] See the representation of enumerative statements by means of quantifiers and identity, e.g. in Kutschera [67], 3.1. The statement that there are (precisely) two things – symbolically $\bigvee^{=2}xF(x)$ – is represented as follows: $\bigvee xy(F(x) \wedge F(y) \wedge x \neq y \,\dot{\vee}$ $\wedge\, xyz(F(x) \wedge F(y) \wedge F(z) \supset x = y \vee x = z \vee y = z)$. In our context it is of no importance how the operator $\bigvee^{=2}$ is defined in terms of other logical operators, only that what is involved is an expression that generates sentences out of predicates belonging to the category $\sigma(v)$ that can be substituted for $F(x)$, one which belongs to category $\sigma(\sigma(v))$, then.

[19] It becomes clear here, for example, that the logical analysis of expressions is not unambiguous. – On the logical systematization of statements of time and place see also Rescher [68] and the literature cited there.

[20] See example (46).

21 Johann Werner Meiner also makes a point of that in his *Versuch einer an der menschlichen Sprache abgebildeten Vernunftlehre oder Philosophie und allgemeine Sprachlehre*, Leipzig 1781, in the Preface, p. XLVIIIf.: "On the other hand, when a language does not assign any fixed and definite position to the modifying word, as in the Latin and Greek languages, where it is equally correct to place the modifying word before or after the substantive; it then becomes doubtful which of the two substantives that a modifying word stands between it belongs to. It is then necessary to make such [relationship] clear by means of visible and audible signs. That is the true reason for gender in language, and not at all the two genders of animals, as heretofore believed." – H. Brekle called my attention to this passage.

22 See Lyons [69], p. 287. Lyons offers examples such as le chat (tomcat) – la chatte (cat); ragazzo (boy) – ragazza (girl).

23 It becomes clear in this case that the plural is not always used to express plural number but also to express collectives. See also Lyons [66], p. 281f.

24 This is a method that is often used – particularly in primitive languages – for rendering relations in terms of conjunctions and representing the sentence '*a* loves *b*', for example by '*a* and *b* love', or the sentence '*a* gives *b* a book' by '*a* gives and *b* receives and a book is given'.

25 Lyons says in [66], p. 218, along these same lines: 'Case is not present in "deep structure" at all, but is merely the inflectional "realisation" of particular syntactic relationships'. – On the concept of 'deep structure' see III.3.1.

26 According to Ch. Fillmore in [68], semantic or 'deep cases' play a corresponding role.

27 Logically, it would be better to regard the concepts 'just as tall as' or 'taller than' as more basic than 'tall', since 'tall' can be defined with those concepts as starting points, e.g. as 'taller than *a*', where *a* is a comparison object or standard, or by 'taller than most things', or in other ways. The superlative 'tallest' can be represented with the aid of a definite description as 'that object which is taller than all others'. And the elative 'very tall' could be defined e.g. in terms of a reference to standard object *b* as 'taller than *b*'.

28 See also Lyons [69], p. 305.

29 The use of the present along with time parameters also occurs in the historical present ('Socrates dies in 399 B.C.') or the use of the present to express the future ('I come tomorrow').

30 It is variously urged that tenses primarily express point of view and express objective temporal relationships only secondarily. See Lyons [69], p. 311, 313ff., Weinrich [64], Weisgerber [62], V. II, p. 327, Grebe [66], p. 103f., as well as IV.3.

31 See Grebe [66], p. 97.

32 Reichenbach in [47], 57 takes the indicative along with the subjunctive to be a means of expressing the speaker's attitude toward the sentence. The indicative is supposed to express an affirmation, just as the subjunctive expresses denial (in irrealia), wish, warning or abstention from judgment ('Fritz said he was innocent'). But the assertive character is common to all declarative sentences, even if the indicative does not occur in them. Thus the sentence 'If he were your friend, he would help you' is an affirmation, too, one that Reichenbach characterises as a non-affirmation. And conversely, the indicative enters into sentences that have no assertive force as well, as for example in the dependent clause, 'Hans claims that he is innocent'. To that extent, to describe the indicative as the basic form of statement is surely more correct.

33 In compounds with auxiliary verbs the (2) participle is the component of a verbal form all the same, as in the sentence 'The tree has been felled'.

34 The converse relation to $F(x, y)$, $F^{-1}(x, y)$ is defined by $F^{-1}(x, y) := F(y, x)$.

[35] See Weisgerber [63b] and Chapter IV.3.

[36] One could also try to transform sentence (15) into the sentence: 'That activity f, of which it is true that f is an activity of running and Hans is doing it, is fast' – $S(\iota f(L^*(x) \wedge f(x) \wedge f(a)))$. But this description is meaningful only when Hans is running, otherwise the meaning of the new formulation is undefined while the existence proposition will be simply false. Thus the representation of (15) as an existential proposition is more adequate.

[37] Of course it is true that $L^*(f) \supset \wedge x(f(x) \supset L(x))$, but the converse is not true, else every empty predicate would express e.g. an activity of running.

[38] See D. Lewis [70] and Cresswell [73].

[39] To be sure, logical grammar is often referred to as *universal* or *rational* grammar, see e.g. the title of the Port Royal Grammar by Arnauld and Lancelot [60] and the work by Montague cited. E. Husserl even speaks of an *a priori* grammar. What is bound up with these expressions is the idea that there is only one grammar for all languages, just as there is only one logic. Thus Roger Bacon, for example, says that the grammar of all languages is substantially the same, even if it may be subject to accidental variations: "Grammatica una et eadem est secundum substantiam in omnibus linguis, licet accidentaliter varietur." ([57], p. 278). And K. Becker writes ([42], p. 5): "To derive these basic relationships common to all languages out of the idea of language as an organised instrument of human nature and to demonstrate them by comparing differing languages is the task of universal grammar."

[40] Wittgenstein says in the *Tractatus*: "Ordinary language is a part of the human organism and no less complicated than it is. It is humanly impossible to get the logic of language out of it directly. Language disguises thought. And in just such a way that it is impossible to draw any conclusions from the external form of the costume, the disguise, about the form of the disguised thought; because the costume's external form is made for purposes quite distinct from that of making known the form of the body. The implicit adjustments for understanding ordinary language are immensely complicated." ([22], 4.002)

[41] Thus Frege in an unpublished letter to Husserl dated Nov. 1, 1906.

[42] Chomsky brings this example in in [65], p. 21.

[43] A structural ambiguity exists only where there is a semantic ambiguity. The converse does not hold, however. The sentence 'Hans sings', for example, has the same logical structure whether the verb 'to sing' is understood in the sense of 'to give forth words with a melodic intonation' or in the sense of 'to make statements to the police concerning the participation of others in a crime in which one had had a part one-self', for in either case 'to sing' belongs to category $\sigma(\nu)$. – There is another example of semantic ambiguity in the sentence 'Later on the letter by Hans was read' [A literal rendering of the idiomatically correct example in German]. (This example is brought in by Bierwisch in [66], p. 102.) In 'the letter by Hans', 'by' indicates the letter's origin, and so stands for the predicate 'written by', while in 'by Hans was read' the word identifies the subject performing the activity [of reading]. Chomsky in [65], p. 22 cites the example of the two sentences in English, 'I persuaded John to leave' – 'I expected John to leave', which on superficial inspection have the same structure, although 'persuade' is a predicate belonging to category $\sigma(\nu, \nu, \iota(\sigma(\nu)))$ and 'expect', on the other hand, belongs to category $\sigma(\nu, \iota(\sigma))$.

[44] See Weisgerber [63a], p. 262ff. See also Grebe [66], p. 491.

[45] Thus A. Weiss, cited in Weisgerber [63a], p. 291.

[46] Cf. Kutschera [74].

3. Generative Grammar

3.1. *Generative Syntax*

On its syntactic side, which we will take up first, generative grammar starts out from the problem of constructing the grammar of a language L as a system of rules by which the set of grammatically correct sentences of L can be engendered. Hence its name. It lays particular emphasis on the requirement that the syntactical rules form a system of really exact rules and in this respect it intends to go beyond the traditional grammar which, as we have seen, does not provide any precise and complete rules, but only illustrates regularities of sentence structure by example and counterexample without precisely delimiting the range within which these rules are valid.

The conceptual-technical presuppositions necessary for making generative systems of rules precise were created around 1930, through the development of the theory of recursive functions and its formalization in terms of Semi-Thue systems, Turing machines, etc. Generative grammar aims at making use of this mathematical apparatus in carrying out its task.

The first requirement imposed on a generative syntax is that it should provide a procedure for the recursive enumeration of the set $G(S)$ of syntactically well-formed (grammatically correct) sentences of a language S, i.e. a routinely applicable general procedure firmly fixed in every detail by explicit rules, with which one after the other every expression in $G(S)$ can be effectively generated. Since all recursively enumerable sets of expressions can be generated by Semi-Thue-Systems, we can represent a generative syntax as a Semi-Thue-System, for example.[1]

A *Semi-Thue-System* T is defined over a finite alphabet $A = \{S_1, ..., S_n\}$ ($n \geqslant 1$), i.e. over a set of basic symbols $S_1, ..., S_n$. We define as an *expression* or *word* on A a finite sequence of signs drawn from A and possibly the empty sign (symbolized by $\square$), which when it is put into a particular place indicates that there is no sign in that place. Where W is a word it is then true that $W\square = \square W = W$. The definition of T is now accomplished by giving a finite set of pairs $\langle R_i, R_i' \rangle$ of expressions on A, T's *defining relations*.

Let $W_1 W_2$ be the expression that arises from the concatenation of W_1 and W_2.[2] We then say that in T a word W is *directly transformable* into a word W' – symbolically $W \Rightarrow W'$ – if there is a defining relation $\langle R_i, R_i' \rangle$ of T and (possibly empty) words U and V such that $W = UR_iV$ and $W' =$

$= UR_i'V$ both hold. And we say that in T a word W is *transformable* into a word W' – symbolically $W \to W'$ – if there is a finite series of words $W_0, W_1, \ldots, W_m$ such that $W_0 = W$ and $W_m = W'$ and $W_k \Rightarrow W_{k+1}$ all hold for $k = 0, \ldots, m-1$. Such a sequence is also called a *derivation* of W' from W. If some of the words of A are laid down as axioms (one is sufficient), then those words that can be derived from an axiom can be designated as *provable*.

But it is not only required that the set $G(S)$ of well-formed sentences of S be recursively enumerable, but that it also be decidable, i.e., that there be an algorithm, a routinely applicable procedure firmly fixed in every detail, by which for any expression it can be determined in a finite number of steps whether or not it belongs to $G(S)$. The communicative function of the sentences in a language surely requires at a minimum that it be possible to know definitely whether or not they are grammatically correct. If we start out from Semi-Thue-Systems, then, we can limit ourselves to such systems as are decidable.

But now the set of Semi-Thue-Systems that produce decidable sets of sentences is not recursively enumerable, so that it is impossible in particular to offer any fixed schematism for decidable Semi-Thue-Systems of that sort.[3]

With a view to the remarks that follow, it is reasonable to delimit decidable Semi-Thue-Systems by imposing the following requirements on the systems considered:

(I) It should hold true of all defining relations $\langle R_i, R_i' \rangle$ that R_i' is at least as long an expression as R_i. Such systems are decidable, as can easily be seen.[4]

Systems that satisfy requirement (I) can now be formulated in such a way that:

(II) All defining relations have the form $\langle UAV, UZV \rangle$, where A is a single symbol and U and V, but not Z can be empty.

For a relation $\langle C_1 \ldots C_m, D_1 \ldots D_n \rangle (n \geq m)$ the relations $\langle C_1 \ldots C_m, D_1 C_2 \ldots C_m \rangle$, $\langle D_1 C_2 \ldots C_m, D_1 D_2 C_3 \ldots C_m \rangle, \ldots, \langle D_1 \ldots D_{m-1} C_m, D_1 \ldots D_n \rangle$ can then be substituted.

A further restriction on Semi-Thue-Systems going beyond (II), or (I), contains the condition:

(III) All defining relations have the form $\langle A, Z \rangle$, where A is a single symbol and Z is not empty.

Defining relations of this sort, in contrast to *context-bound* relations $\langle XAY, XZY \rangle$ with XY not empty, according to which Z can be substituted for A only in the context XAY, are identified as *context-free*.[5]

A further restriction vis-à-vis (III) is:

(IV) All defining relations have the form $\langle A, XB \rangle$ or $\langle A, Y \rangle$, where the set of words on A is to be composed of two disjunct parts, the *terminal vocabulary* V_T and the non-terminal vocabulary V_N, and A, B are single symbols from V_N, X and Y expressions on V_T, of which X but not Y can be empty.[6]

Derivations that satisfy (II) can be written in tree form as well.[7] For example, if

$$ABCDE$$
$$AB'B''CDE$$
$$A'B'B''CDE$$
$$A'B'B''CD'D''D'''E$$
$$A'B'B''CD'D^+D^{++}D'''E$$

is a derivation in T, this derivation can also be written in the form

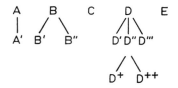

But syntax is not just a question of providing rules for the recursive enumeration of sets $G(S)$. The fact is that the sentences of $G(S)$ are supposed to be interpreted in semantics, and this semantic interpretation also must take the form of a system of rules. Since we wish to interpret all of the sentences of $G(S)$,[8] we shall consequently find it useful, as has already been urged in the introduction to this chapter, to frame the syntactic rules so that the way they are set up syntactically will correspond to their semantic structure.

Perhaps it is this principle that is behind the somewhat vague requirement of generative grammar that in the syntax sentences are to be assigned a structure that is supposed to correspond to the 'intuitive structure', in terms of which the sentence is understood by speaker and hearer.[9] Syntax, then, should not only make it certain that a sentence such as 'Hans had a book stolen', can be generated, but that there should be as many syntactic structures coordinated to it as there are possible interpretations of that sentence.

In grammar this requirement that sentences be given a syntactic structure is now often interpreted so as to mean that every sentence must be analyzed into connected parts which can then be classified as expressions of a definite type, e.g. according to word or sentence categories. Those expressions can then be analyzed further and the parts classified once again. Lees describes this as follows: '... the linguist... has assumed that the sentences of a language may each be analyzed into a linearly con-catenated sequence of immediate constituents, and that this bracketing or parsing operation may be performed at various levels of generality to yield a hierarchical branching-diagram, such that any unit at any level is just a certain continuous string within some sentence or else a class of such strings drawn from different but grammatically equivalent sentences.'[10]

Thus, for example, the sentence 'The man hits the brown dog' will be analyzed as follows:

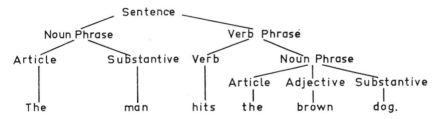

Such a hierarchical analysis of a sentence in terms of its components is also called a *phrase-marker* or *structural description* ('SD' for short).

Now the basic idea of generative grammar is the characterization of the syntactic structure of a sentence in terms of its derivation within a Semi-Thue-System of Type (II). In such a system the derivations become SD's if we proceed as follows: Category symbols such as S (for sentence), N (for noun), V (for verb), At (for article), Aj (for adjective), Av (for adverb), Pr (for preposition), Np (for noun phrase), Vp (for verb phrase), etc., are introduced into the alphabet A of system T. These category symbols constitute the non-terminal vocabulary V_N of A and count as single symbols as intended in (II). The words (or morphemes) of language S, the sentences of which are to be generated, constitute the terminal vocabulary of A, V_T. The symbol S counts as an axiom of T. Rules of structure such as $\langle S, NpVp \rangle$, $\langle Np, AtN \rangle$, $\langle Np, AtAjN \rangle$, $\langle Vp, VNp \rangle$, for example, and rules of substitution such as $\langle At, the \rangle$, $\langle N, man \rangle$, $\langle N, dog \rangle$, $\langle V, hits \rangle$, $\langle Aj, brown \rangle$, for example, are given as defining relations. The expressions of V_T occur only as second constituents in the defining relations, so that every derivation in T ends with a sequence of words of S.

In that case the SD given above for the sentence 'The man hits the brown dog' can be constructed as a derivation in T.

One naturally arrives, then, by way of the desired SD, to systems of syntactic rules presented as Semi-Thue-Systems of type (II). For this reason, within the domain of generative grammar such systems are also called *general* SD-*grammars*, contrasted to systems of type (III), which are called *simple* SD-*grammars*.

The detailed elaboration of simple SD-syntax leads to formidable complications and difficulties, however. Thus, for example, gender, number and case are to be provided for every substantive, person, number, mood, tense and voice for every verb. For example, it is not generally possible to substitute 'man' for N, but depending on the context either 'man's' or 'men'. For V it is not possible always to substitute 'jump', but 'jumps', 'jumped', 'would jump', and so on, too. Consequently, further specifications must be added to the category symbols and the rules of substitution will read, for example, not $\langle V, jump \rangle$, but $\langle V(3.\ person, plural, indicative, present, active), jumps \rangle$. On top of that we have the fact that congruence must be taken into consideration in connection with the category rules. That is, we have to replace the rule $\langle S, NV \rangle$, for example, with $\langle S, N$ (nominative, plural), V(3. person, plural, indicative, present, active)$\rangle$, and so on.

Further complications arise when one takes into account the fact that not all predicates are defined for all substitutions. For example, 'hard' is defined only for concrete and tangible things [*Konkreta*], 'smile' only for human beings and the sun, 'run' only for the higher animals, machines, water faucets and noses, 'whinny' only occurs in connection with horses, 'meow' in connection with cats, and so on. That is, we would now have to add specifications of a semantical character for every substantive and verb, that say whether it is defined for concrete or abstract items, animate or inanimate, animal, human, etc., and we would have to pay attention to the agreement of these specifications in making substitutions.[11] But that is definitely doomed to failure by the fact that the number of such semantic categories can not be delimited in any rational manner. But as a consequence, the program of constructing the syntax in such a way that the set of well-formed sentences in S coincides with the set of semantically well-interpreted sentences in S is also compromised.

There are other arguments besides, quite fundamental ones, that count against the feasibility of a pure SD-syntax, and they have led Harris and Chomsky to a modification of that type of grammar. The two most important considerations are these:[12]

(1) The basic idea of SD-syntax is that all of the grammatically connected expressions in a sentence form a closed contextual unit. But that is often not the case, as the example 'The girls called Hans up' shows. Here 'call up' is the verb, which does not constitute a connected unit, however, but is divided in two by the object of the sentence, 'Hans'. Now the SD-syntax does not contain any possibility for classifying disconnected parts of a sentence as one sentence component. Nor does it contain any mechanism that would permit us to deal with transformations of the sentence, i.e. first of all to form:

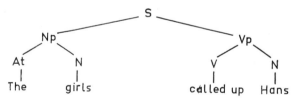

in order then to transform the latter sentence so that it will be grammatically correct. Therefore the only way in which it can analyze the sentence is:

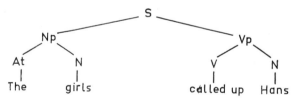

But that is inadequate, since 'up' is not an independent preposition here but a constituent of the verb 'call up'. Furthermore, the future is expressed as 'The girls will Fritz call-up' ['Die Mädeln werden Fritz anrufen'. The example, so far as the future tense is concerned, depends on the fact that the German verb '*anrufen*' has a separable prefix. The point can not be made in English in the same way.], so that we would obtain different structural descriptions of the sentence for present and future.[13]

(2) SD-syntax can not adequately render the phenomenon of reflexive reference, i.e. the structures of sentences like (a) 'Hans is sleeping and so is Fritz' and (b) 'Fritz is sleeping and he is snoring' are not correctly represented, since there is no way of expressing the reference of 'so' back to 'is sleeping' and of 'he' back to 'Fritz'. The SD's of these two sentences do not make clear the connection between the sentence 'Hans is sleeping and Fritz is sleeping' and (a) or 'Fritz is sleeping and Fritz is snoring' and (b).

To these two objections we could add still others, although in most cases they come to the same thing, that SD-syntax can not give an adequate expression to that structure of the sentence we are concerned with in semantic interpretation, because it cuts sentences into parts that are attached to each other in surface structure instead of analyzing them in terms of the expressions' semantic function.[14]

On account of these inadequacies of the SD-syntax, Harris and Chomsky have developed a syntax with *transformation-rules, T-syntax* for short. In it transformation rules are permitted along with the SD rules for construction. These rules generate a sentence out of one or more SD (such as do not end with a well-formed sentence of S).[15] The syntax of these transformationally generated sentences is supposed to be represented by the transformational structure, i.e. by the derivation of the sentences from the SD using rules of transformation.[16]

One can now distinguish two stages in the development of this T-syntax: in the first stage, represented by Chomsky's works [57] and [61a], for example, the rules of transformation are given a significantly larger domain of application than in the second stage, which is exemplified by [65]. Above all, in the first stage even sentence sequences are generated by transformation rules and the embedding of subordinate clauses in the primary sentence is accomplished by means of transformation rules. That requires transformation rules with more than one argument.[17]

At the second stage only transformation rules with one argument are used. Different tasks are now assigned to the SD part and the transformation part of syntax: For every sentence, besides its syntactic *surface structure*, which is grasped by traditional grammar, for example, there is a *depth structure*, which determines the sentence's semantic interpretation.[18] Now it is the task of the SD part to generate the depth-structure of sentences, which need not be grammatically well-formed sentences, and the task of the transformation rules is to generate wellformed sentences out of the terminal expressions of the SD.[19] For that purpose one-place transformation rules, which generate one expression out of another, are sufficient.[20] The transformational structure is no longer of any importance now, for the task of the SD was above all else to present the semantic structure of a sentence (so that with the aid of the SD, for example, one can differentiate between the possible meanings of ambiguous sentences). The transformation rules, however, leave the interpretation of the expressions invariant and to that extent one can identify the depth-structure of a sentence with the SD of those expressions from which the sentence can be obtained by means of transformation rules.

By means of a transformation rule of the form $\langle X$ – finite present or preterite form of 'to call up' – object – Y, X – finite present or preterite form of 'to call' – object – 'up' – $Y\rangle$ we can then produce from the last lines of the SD

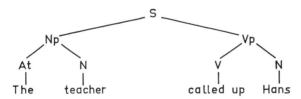

the sentence 'The teacher called Hans up'.

Besides the approaches to a generative grammar sketched here, SD-Syntax and its supplementary transformation rules, there are still further systems, but they have not attained the same importance in the discussion [of this matter].

Many of these systems have been shown to be inadequate and for others proofs of equivalence have been given. Thus in Bar-Hillel [60b] it is demonstrated that SD-grammars (or (III)-systems) are equivalent to the *categorical grammars* of Bar-Hillel [21] (i.e. that the same sets of sentences can be produced by them) and in particular to *restricted* categorical grammars. Furthermore Chomsky proved in [59a] that the so-called *finite state systems*[22] are equivalent to the (IV)-systems and the latter equivalent once again to *deterministic* and to *non-deterministic finite automata*.[23] We had already made reference to Harman's system in [63].[24] We will not go into these systems here, but make a critical comment on T-syntax instead.

It appears to us to be a fundamental defect of this syntax that the SD of the sentences make use of the traditional grammatical categories, which, as we saw in III.1 and III.2 are neither adequate nor precisely defined. Now since the depth structure of a sentence is supposed to determine its semantic interpretation, as far as we are concerned nothing seems to count against identifying the depth structure of a sentence with the logical structure of a sentence in L that analyzes it and so describing depth structure in terms of logical categories.[25]

If that is done, then the SD-part of generative grammar simply amounts to giving the rules for generating sentences in L. Since the sentences of L are unambiguous with respect to their semantic structure, it is not necessary to attach structural descriptions to them, in the form of derivations, for example.

The transformational part of generative grammar is determined by the analyzing relation R for S: A sentence B of S can be generated out of a sentence A of L if and only if $R(A, B)$ is true. If it is possible to define R inductively so that for every A the set of B with $R(A, B)$ is recursively enumerable, then the transformations are also defined thereby, with a precision appropriate to the standards of generative grammar.

In specifying the analyzing relation, likewise the transformation rules, all the grammatical distinctions such as gender, case, construction of inflected forms and the like naturally play a role that can be ignored in logical analysis. Experience will have to tell the extent to which we have to introduce new categories beside the logical ones in this connection. Generally speaking, all of the distinctions relevant to sentence construction in S that are included in the so-called *substitution-categories* may be important, which we can define as follows:

Two expressions X and Y in S are said to be *isogenic* if and only if for all expressions $A[Z]$ it is true that: $A[X]$ is a sentence in S if and only if $A[Y]$ is a sentence in S.[26]

The equivalence classes pertaining to the relation of isogeny are then substitution categories,[27] which *per definitionem* cover exactly the distinctions that are syntactically relevant in *S*.

As against generative grammar, besides the advantage of superior precision, logical grammar also has the advantage of greater simplicity, for the replacement of the derivations in Semi-Thue-Systems by sentences in *L* makes the SD-part essentially simpler and would hardly make the transformational part any more complicated. Since the end-products of the SD have to render unambiguously the semantic structure of the sentence, they will hardly be less complicated or closer to surface structure than the analyzing sentences of *L*; i.e. the transformation rules will look just about as complicated as the definition of the relation *R*. Besides that, as we shall see immediately, a workable generative semantics can be constructed on the basis of this syntax, in contrast with *T*-syntax.

It is possible, furthermore, to attain yet another decided simplification, if we give up the requirement that the set of well-formed expressions that can be constructed in the syntax coincide with the set of semantically interpretable sentences in *S*. We have seen above that Chomsky's recommendation that semantic categories be included in the SD leads to great difficulties. But it does no harm if we permit within the syntax of *S* sentences such as 'Prime numbers laugh', or 'The moon is hitting the sun', for example, which are well-formed in terms of grammatical categories but have no sense. For the nonsensical character of these sentences is a purely semantic phenomenon based solely on semantic considerations. Those sentences can be singled out and set aside in the semantics, then.[28]

3.2. *Generative Semantics*

A semantics within the confines of generative grammar was first developed by Katz and Fodor in [63] and by Katz in [64a] and by Katz and Postal in [64b].[29]

This semantics starts out from a *T*-syntax of a language *S*. Let *G* be the class of those syntactic categories (or category symbols) that are used in this syntax for describing expressions in *S*, and let *K* be a finite class of semantic categories (or category symbols) by means of which the meanings of words in *S* are supposed to be characterized. The following can serve as semantic categories of this sort, for example: *activity, state, concrete/-abstract entities, living creature, inanimate thing, animal, human, male, adult*, etc. Now in the lexicon of *S* there should be associated with every word one, or in case of ambiguity more than one, set of category symbols $\{w_1, \ldots, w_n\}$ drawn from G and K. These constitute a syntactic and semantic characterization of the word. In addition, there is a *distinctor*, i.e. a statement concerning the meaning of the word that distinguishes its meaning from all related meanings insofar as the semantic categories do not do that already, and also a *selector*, which specifies the range within which the word is defined. For example, the following *readings are ascribed to* the English word 'ball':

(a)   ball – {*N, Social Activity, Large, Assembly*} [For the purpose of social dancing]
(b)   ball – {*N, Physical Object*} [Having globular shape]
(c)   ball – {*N, Physical Object*} [Solid missile for projection by engine of war].

These readings thus define the different possible interpretations of a word. The distinctor stands within square brackets.

Now let X be a sentence with which an SD (depth structure) B is associated. X will then be assigned an interpretation by way of applying the following rules.

(1) A rule of substitution E coordinates every word W with the set of those readings of W in the lexicon that have syntactic characteristics compatible with the syntactic characteristics of W in B. If this set is empty, then W and consequently X is meaningless.

(2) One now goes through the SD B from bottom to top and specifies by means of a projection rule R the set of readings anew at each branching. We can illustrate this best by means of an example that Katz and Fodor introduce in [63]: The starting point is the following structural description:

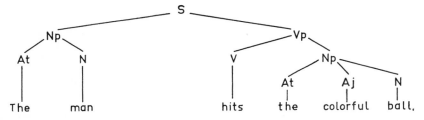

In the lexicon the following readings will be attached to the words other than 'ball' that occur in this sentence, with the selector in pointed brackets.

(d)   The – {At} [*Some contextually definite*]

(e)   colorful – {Aj, *Color*} [*Abounding in contrast or variety of bright colors*] ⟨*Physical object or social activity*⟩

(f)   colorful – {Aj, *Evaluative*} [*Having distinctive character, vividness, or picturesqueness*] ⟨*Aesthetic object or Social activity*⟩

(g)   man – {N, *Physical object, Human, Adult, Male*}

(h)   hits – {V(transitive), *Action, Instancy, Intensity*} [*Collides with an impact*] ⟨Subject: *Higher animal or Improper part or Physical object*; Object: *Physical object*⟩

(i)   hits – {V(transitive), *Action, Instancy, Intensity*} [*Strikes with a blow or missile*] ⟨Subject: *Human or Higher animal*; Object: *Physical object*; Instrument: *Physical object*⟩

The next step is to construct the set of readings of 'colorful ball'. For that there is a projection rule R_1 concerning certain connections between expressions, among them the attributive connection, by which we obtain the following readings from the sets {e, f} and {a, b, c}:

(j)   colorful ball – {Np, *Social Activity, Large, Assembly, Color*} [[*Abounding in contrast or variety of bright colors*] [*For the purpose of social dancing*]]

(k)   colorful ball – {Np, *Physical object, Color*} [[*Abounding in contrast or variety of bright colors*] [*Having globular shape*]]

(l)   Colorful ball – {Np, *Physical object, Color*} [[*Abounding in contrast or variety of bright colors*] [*Solid missile for projection by engine of war*]]

(m)   Colorful ball – {Np, *Social activity, Large, Assembly, Evaluative*} [[*Having distinctive character, vividness or picturesqueness*] [*For the purpose of social dancing*]]

Of the six possible readings, then, the combinations (f)–(b) and (f)–(c) are inapplicable, since the selector of (f) is incompatible with the category symbol *Physical Object*. The attributive rule thus immediately picks out the mutually compatible readings and eliminates the nonsensical attributive combinations.

Within the compatible readings we then go on to combine the semantic categories and likewise the distinctors.

By means of a projection rule R_2 we can connect the article and substantive expressions. We thus obtain from readings {d} and {g} the reading

(n)   The man – {Np} [*Some contextually definite*] {*Physical object,*
         Human, Adult, Male}

and from {d} and {j, k, l, m} the readings

(o)   The colorful ball – {Np} [*Some contextually definite*] {*Social*
         activity, Large, Assembly, Color} ⟦*Abounding in contrast or*
         variety of bright colors] [*For the purpose of social dancing*⟧

(p)   The colorful ball – {Np} [*Some contextually definite*] {*Phy-*
         sical object, Color} ⟦*Abounding in contrast or variety of bright*
         colors] [*Having globular shape*⟧

(q)   The colorful ball – {Np} [*Some contextually definite*] {*Phy-*
         sical object, Color} ⟦*Abounding in contrast or variety of bright*
         colors] [*Solid missile for projection by engine of war*⟧

(r)   The colorful ball – {Np} [*Some contextually definite*] {*Social*
         activity, Large, Assembly, Evaluative} ⟦*Having distinctive*
         character, vividness or picturesqueness] [*For the purpose of*
         social dancing⟧

By means of a projection rule R_2 we can then connect a transitive verb
with its object. We obtain accordingly from readings {h, i} and {o, p, q, r}
the readings

(s)   Hits the colorful ball – {Vp, *Action, Instancy, Intensity*} [*Col-*
         lides with an impact] [*Some contextually definite*] {*Physical*
         object, Color} ⟦*Abounding in contrast or variety of bright*
         colors] [*Having globular shape*⟧ ⟨Subject: *Higher animal or*
         Improper Part or Physical object⟩

(t)   Hits the colorful ball – {Vp, *Action, Instancy, Intensity*} [*Col-*
         lides with an impact] [*Some contextually definite*] {*Physical*
         object, Color} ⟦*Abounding in contrast or variety of bright colors*]
         [*Solid missile for projection by engine of war*⟧ ⟨Subject: *Higher*
         animal or Improper Part or Physical object⟩

(u)   Hits the colorful ball – {Vp, *Action, Instancy, Intensity*}
         [*Strikes with a blow or missile*] [*Some contextually definite*]
         {*Physical object, Color*} ⟦*Abounding in contrast or variety of*
         bright colors] [*Having globular shape*⟧ ⟨Subject: *Human or*
         Higher Animal⟩ Vp,

(v)   Hits the colorful ball – {Vp, *Action, Instancy, Intensity*}
           [*Strikes with a blow or missile*] [*Some contextually definite*]
           {*Physical object, Color*} ⟦*Abounding in contrast or variety of
           bright colors*] [*Solid missile for projection by engine of war*⟧
           ⟨Subject: *Human or Higher Animal*⟩

Now the combinations (h)–(o), (h)–(r), (i)–(o), (i)–(r) are inapplicable
here on account of the selection specifications in (h) and (i). Moreover,
as is already the case with R_2, the semantic characteristics and the distinctors are not connected up with each other as with R_1.

Finally, by means of a projection rule R_2 we can connect subject with
predicate. This gives us from readings {n} and {s, t, u, v} these readings:

(w)   The man hits the colorful ball – {S} [*Some contextually def-
           inite*] {*Physical Object, Human, Adult, Male*} {*Action, In-
           stancy, Intensity*} [*Collides with an impact*] [*Some contextual-
           ly definite*] {*Physical object, Color*} ⟦*Abounding in contrast or
           variety of bright colors*] [*Having globular shape*⟧

(x)   The man hits the colorful ball – {S} [*Some contextually def-
           inite*] {*Physical object, Human, Adult, Male*} {*Action, In-
           stancy, Intensity*} [*Collides with an impact*] [*Some contextual-
           ly definite*] {*Physical object, Color*} ⟦*Abounding in contrast or
           variety of bright colors*] [*Solid missile for projection by engine
           of war*⟧

(y)   The man hits the colorful ball – {S} [*Some contextually def-
           inite*] {*Physical object, Human, Adult, Male*} {*Action, Instancy,
           Intensity*} [*Strikes with a blow or missile*] [*Some contextually
           definite*] {*Physical object, Color*} ⟦*Abounding in contrast or
           variety of bright colors*] [*Having globular shape*⟧

(z)   The man hits the colorful ball – {S} [*Some contextually def-
           inite*] {*Physical object, Human, Adult, Male*} {*Action, Instancy,
           Intensity*} [*Strikes as a blow or missile*] [*Some contextually
           definite*] {*Physical object, Color*} ⟦*Abounding in contrast or
           variety of bright colors*] [*Solid missile for projection by engine
           of war*⟧.

Now the set {w, x, y, z} is the set of possible readings of the sentence
'The man hits the colorful ball'. If this set were empty, the sentence would

be meaningless, if it included only one reading the sentence would be unambiguous. But since four readings are now associated with the sentence, it is ambiguous in four ways, i.e. there are four possible meanings for the sentence. If the sets of readings for two sentences X_1 and X_2 contain no reading in common, then these two sentences are distinct in meaning; if they contain n readings in common, then the two sentences are synonymous in n ways. If they contain precisely the same readings, then the two sentences are fully synonymous.

Since the transformation rules on the second stage of the development of T-syntax are so defined as to leave the meaning of the expressions invariant, the semantic rules always apply solely to the SD of a sentence, which gives its depth structure.

Even this short sketch of Katz and Fodor's semantic approach clearly reveals its fundamental defects.

In the first place, how the set of semantic categories is to be determined is left completely open. Now the authors' intent, to be sure, is not so much to provide a semantics for a specified language as to set forth the general outlines of a semantic theory, but even in such outlines it would be necessary to say how these categories are to be understood: Are they characteristics of the concepts to be characterized or properties of those concepts? The two accounts have entirely different logical status: A *characteristic* (*Merkmal*) G of a concept F of category $\sigma(v)$ is a concept of the same category such that $\bigwedge x(F(x) \equiv G(x) \wedge ...)$. A *property* (*Eigenschaft*) of $F(x)$, on the other hand, is a concept $M(f)$ of category $\sigma(\sigma(v))$ such that $M(F)$ is true. Both characteristics and properties occur in Katz and Fodor's work. For example, the word 'bachelor' is supposed to be defined by way of the category Human, and so in terms of a characteristic, but 'light' (as an adjective) by way of the categories *Color*, or *Weight*, i.e. by way of properties. Furthermore, if the categories are always taken to be one-place concepts, in specifying them for transitive verbs, for example, they will have to be properties for the most part. Finally, there can be no question of anything but properties in the case of proper names and function expressions.

Let us now consider the projection rules, first of all R_1. This rule has the form $W_1 - \{K_1\}\ [D_1]\ \langle S_1 \rangle,\ W_2 - \{K_2\}\ [D_2]\ \langle S_2 \rangle \Rightarrow W_1 W_2 - \{K_1, K_2\}\ [\![D_1][D_2]\!]\ \langle S_2 \rangle$.

Now the question is, whatever is the expression in the conclusion supposed to mean: If W_1 and W_2 are one-place predicates and $\{K_1\}$ and $\{K_2\}$ groups of characteristics, then $\{K_1, K_2\}$ could represent the conjunction of those characteristics. So in that case, W_1W_2 would be interpreted as the conjunction of two one-place predicates. This interpretation would surely enter into the question for many attributive combinations, such as 'red ball' in the sense of 'x is red and x is a ball', but this would by no means be true for all cases of applying R_1, among which Katz and Fodor in fact also count the construction adverb–verb, for example. But one can not interpret 'to sing badly' as 'to be bad and to sing'. Furthermore, even in the case of constructions in the form adjective + substantive – insofar as they can be interpreted conjunctively at all – this interpretation of $\{K_1, K_2\}$ will not hold up generally, for we saw that not only characteristics but also properties occur in $\{K_1\}$ and $\{K_2\}$. One can not infer $M(\lambda x(F(x) \wedge G(x)))$ from $M(F)$, however. For example, it is true that 'red' is a color predicate, but 'red ball' is no color predicate. Finally, in III.2.2 we saw that by no means all attributive constructions are capable of being interpreted as conjunctive connections.

We lack any reasonable interpretation of $\{K_1, K_2\}$, then. But we miss still more an interpretation of $[\![D_1]\!] [\![D_2]\!]$. Such an expression is never defined. If it were supposed to be equivalent to $[D_1 \wedge D_2]$, that again would require D_1 and D_2 to be characteristics, and again that works only with conjunctive constructions. Otherwise the expression remains completely unintelligible.

It becomes still worse with the other rules. Here, in the conclusions there occur expressions like $W_1W_2 - \{K_1\} [D_1] \{K_2\} [D_2]$, which remain entirely undefined. A reasonable interpretation of such expressions is nowhere in sight, not even is it distinguished from expressions of the form $\{K_1, K_2\} [\![D_1]\!] [\![D_2]\!]$. It is simply left up to the reader, who knows the interpretation of W_1W_2 anyway, once again to figure it out from the variegated succession of semantic fragments that are offered. Naturally that sort of thing no longer has anything to do with scientific precision. Compare, for example, readings (y) and (z): You are able to learn semantic information from them only because you already know what they are supposed to mean, and because you do not permit yourself to be led astray in what you know by even the most extraordinary way of writing.

The most elementary semantic insights are also absent here: things, concepts of different types, function expressions and sentences are not differentiated semantically, there is no account of how concepts apply to objects, etc.[30]

Although the semantics of Katz and Fodor is only a prototypical form of generative semantics that has been superseded in the meantime, it is nevertheless well suited to illustrate the shortcomings of that semantics. So far a really precise semantics, capable of accomplishing anything, exists only within the confines of logical grammar. There, too, as we indicated in III.2.1, such fundamental problems as the partial definition of predicates in natural language, for example, admit of satisfactory solutions.[31] Therefore at the present time logical grammar constitutes the best approach to the development of exact grammar-models for natural languages.

3.3. *Innate Ideas*

In connection with generative grammar, we will, in the form of a short excursus, go into a hypothesis that really does not belong to the theory of grammar, but to epistemology. However, it should be mentioned at this point because it is based upon generative grammar.

This *hypothesis of innate ideas*, abbreviated IH (*Innateness Hypothesis*), has been advocated by Chomsky especially.[32] It states that the occurrence of language learning in humans is differentiated from other learning processes, e.g. learning to play chess, by the fact that certain items of information about language that enter into the process of learning language are built into the human mind (or human brain). On this view, we have an innate linguistic capacity, but not an innate capacity for playing chess. Everything we know about chess we have learned from experience, but we know more about language than we have learned from experience – indeed, according to Chomsky, more than we could ever learn by way of experience.

More exactly, the information about language that is independent of experience is supposed to be the content of general language theory.[33] What belongs to general language theory are the general properties of grammars: that (a) every grammar contains an SD component and (b) transformation rules, that (c) every grammar contains certain syntactic and semantic categories, 'proper name', 'sentence', 'verb', etc., for example, that (d) certain general semantic rules belong to every grammar and that (e) the phonological component of every grammar interprets sentences over a certain finite basic stock of phonetic signs. Further, it includes an evaluation of different grammars that generate the same set of sentences, in terms of their degree of simplicity, for example.

Now what is explicitly formulated in general language theory, the general properties of grammars, for example, is supposed to be built into the way the human *Language Acquisition Device* works – LAD for short – so that the LAD functions in such a way that we select one specific grammar from all those possible, namely the simplest of those grammars that fit the linguistic data presented in experience. I.e., the LAD provides us with no information concerning the language we consciously use, but it steers the process of language acquisition and our linguistic behavior without our having been aware of the way in which it works nor being able to know how it works by introspection. The talk of 'innate ideas' is to be understood as nothing but a historical allusion then – actually Chomsky's hypothesis is essentially different from the presentations of rationalism in the 17th and 18th centuries from Descartes to Leibniz.[34] Chomsky does not offer any more precise account of the manner in which the LAD functions, but in his IH merely hints at a cybernetic model of this LAD.

According to Chomsky, what the IH *accomplishes* consists in the fact that it explains:

(1) The extensive similarity among all human languages (on the basis of the specifics common to all grammars, the so-called (formal) *linguistic universals*), as they are stated in (a) through (e).[35]

(2) The species-specific character of languages (apes can not learn them, even though they do possess a general learning ability and intelligence).

(3) The independence of the mastery of language from intelligence (children learn language at an age in which their general intellectual capacities are still quite undeveloped) and – most extensively – from the linguistic data presented, which can be quite different from one individual to another.

(4) The ease with which language is learned (language is an extraordinarily complicated system of rules – think of Chomsky's generative syntax – which is learned by children in a relatively short time, however).

(5) That language is learned at all: an infinite set of sentences, as marked out by a grammar, on the basis of merely finite linguistic data. According

to Chomsky, that cannot be explained in terms of a general capacity for learning, for in learning a language not only the surface structure but the depth structure, too, which is not apparent in the data at all, must be analyzed.

There is the following to be said in criticizing this hypothesis, however:

(A) The content of the hypothesis is not rendered sufficiently precise so long as we are not told exactly which items of information the LAD contains, or what it does.

(B) As to what the LAD accomplishes, this much can be established: In the first place, the IH cannot be directly tested. To do that one would have to produce a language that does not conform to the LAD schema and would have to show that human beings could not learn it or at least not learn it as an initial language, i.e. one would have to give children practical trials with this language exclusively and show that they could not master it within a reasonable time, even though it was essentially no more complicated than our own. But no such language has yet been produced and according to Chomsky it may be that no such language can be produced by us at all.[36]

All that is left, then, is to judge the IH in terms of its *explanatory value*.[37] How does it stand in that respect?

This is to be said in response to (1): the general validity of formal universals, for which the IH is supposed to provide a basis, can also be explained independently of the IH:

(a) It is not correct that every syntax contains an SD-component and a *T*-component: the generation of sentences in logical grammar is not something done with an SD-grammar. Nor do SD-grammars show up in other systems of generative grammar. All we can say, then, is that for every language there is an SD-grammar, supplemented by transformation rules, that generates all the sentences of that language. But that is trivial, because the transformation rules – in the general terms, as Chomsky considers them – have the form of the defining relationships of general Semi-Thue-Systems, so that every Semi-Thue-System can also be written in the form of a (II)-system with transformation rules. But since the sentences of any language have to be recursively enumerable, they can be generated by means of such systems.

(b) That e.g. the syntactic category 'proper name' occurs universally is in the first place empirically questionable; but if it actually is the case, that can be explained as a consequence of the power and usefulness of languages with proper names.[38] But the category 'proper name' together with the actually universal category 'sentence' already suffice to define all of the logical categories.[39]

(c) The semantic rules, not specified in any greater detail by Chomsky, emerge simply out of the demand for defining semantic interpretations parallel to the fundamental syntactic rules.

(d) The finite stock of basic phonetic signs is explained, according to Putnam, [67], by the identity of human linguistic organs.

Finally, according to Putnam many features common to languages are easily explained by taking all human languages to have descended from the same source.

In response to (2), this is to be said: The species-specific character of the ability to learn languages is also explained by a species-specific higher intelligence in humans.

And to (3): There is not a strict independence of language from intelligence. Less intelligent human beings learn language less perfectly than the intelligent, their vocabulary and their grammatical abilities lag behind the others.[40] The extensive independence from linguistic data arises from the fact that those data have to constitute a very large and representative set of linguistic examples; otherwise one can certainly not count on any independence.

In response to (4) Putnam urges in [67]: The language of which the normal adult is master is the one that every normal adult can learn. But what every normal adult can learn can not be described as 'complicated'. Especially, when we consider that one needs 9 to 10 years in order to master a language to some extent, the grammar would have to be essentially still more complicated than it actually is, for learning it to be astonishing.[41] Besides, it is not permissible to identify the complexity of linguistic habits with the complexity of explicitly formulated grammatical rules that give those linguistic habits some precision and surely not at all with the complexity of Chomsky's generative grammar.

In response to (5), finally, we can say this – and this is the main objection to Chomsky's argument: As long as there are no precise, fully worked out theories in learning, we may not claim that general learning capacity is incapable of explaining language learning.[42] That the mastery of an infinite number of sentences can not be attained from a finite amount of data is false, for we can learn just a finite number of rules. The chess player, too, learns how to conduct himself correctly in (practically) infinitely many situations on the board with the few general rules of play. Despite that one does not assume any innate knowledge of chess.

Taking all of that into account, the IH has no explanatory value either: It explains nothing that can not be more simply explained in other ways. But since the hypothesis can not be directly tested either, there is then no reason of any kind for accepting it and building upon it farreaching views about the theory of knowledge.

NOTES

[1] On the concepts of recursive function, recursive enumerability and Semi-Thue-System see e.g. Hermes [61] and Davis [58].

[2] In view of the associativity of concatenation $W_1(W_2W_3)=(W_1W_2)W_3$ it is also acceptable to put together a sequence of several expressions without parentheses.

[3] It is generally true that the set of decidable sets of words is not recursively denumerable. For along with a recursive enumeration of these sets you would also have an (effective) enumeration M_1, M_2,... for them. If so, where A_1, A_2,... is an effective enumeration of words, it would be possible to define a decidable set M as follows: $A_i \in M \equiv \neg A_i \in M_i$. But then, in contradiction with the assumption, M would not be one of the enumerated sets, since for $M=M_k$ we obtain $A_k \in M_k \equiv \neg A_k \in M_k$.

[4] If T is a system of this sort on A and X is an expression on A, then there is a finite number of expressions Y of the same length as X, from which X can be derived in T. It can be determined which possibilities for Y there are. Y is investigated in the same way, etc. In every case in which you do not encounter one of T's axioms anyway, an expression Z which is shorter than X must turn up as a premise. In this way, the length of the expressions from which X can be derived is reduced step by step, so that it is possible after a finite number of steps to reach a decision about the derivability of X.

[5] Chomsky proves in [59a], Theorem 4, that (III) represents vis-a-vis (II) a genuine limitation, i.e. that there are word sets that can be generated by way of systems of type (II), but not by systems of type (III), – See also Postal [64b].

[6] In [59a] (Theorem 7), Chomsky proves that there are word sets that can be generated by (III)-systems, but not by (IV)-systems. – In particular, those word sets that are *self-imbedding*, i.e. that contain rules of the type $A \rightarrow XAY$, are of this kind (Theorem 11).

[7] On the other hand, this is not true of other Semi-Thue-Systems, e.g. the systems given by Harman in [63], in which the defining relations have the form $\langle A, X \rangle$ and $\langle AB, XBY \rangle$, where A and B are single signs and X, Y can also be empty.

[8] We will later relax this requirement.

[9] See e.g. Chomsky [65], p. 24. Chomsky calls a grammar of this sort 'descriptively adequate'.

[10] Lees [57], p. 385.

[11] This is Chomsky's suggestion in [65], Chapter II, § 2.

[12] See e.g. Postal [64a], p. 73ff. as well.

[13] Harman's systems in [63], cited above in note 7, have been tried for the purpose of making such transformations possible. As Chomsky has stated in [65], such systems no longer provide any structural descriptions, however. For example, we obtain the derivation:

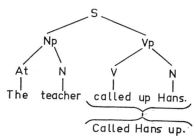

The words in the expression 'called Hans up' are no longer classified as to category in this case and have to be identified as substantive and verb components by supplementary specifications.

[14] See also Postal [64b]. – Many other objections often raised against SD-syntax are of no great weight. The objection, for example, that the connections between active and passive, assertion and related question, and similar connections are not expressed. It is not the task of syntax to bring out clearly every semantic connection, although a syntax with rules corresponding to the rules of semantic interpretation does at least make the basic semantic relations much clearer than SD-syntax does.

[15] It is often required that a transformation rule generate not only a sentence, but an appropriate SD. But if this SD is supposed to satisfy the general requirement that it adequately represent the sentence's grammatical structure, then all of the sentences generated by transformation can also be generated in the SD-syntax without transformation rules. In that case the only point of transformation rules would be to call attention to relationships and connections between SD, e.g. to generate questions from assertions in a simple way, etc. But calling attention to such semantic connections is not, as already remarked above, the primary goal of syntax. The essential part of the justification for introducing transformation rules is that there are sentences which syntax has to generate, to which no SD can be attached, e.g. in the case of discontinuous expressions. Therefore, there will just not be adequate structural descriptions for every sentence that can be generated by transformation rules and hence it will not be possible to lay down a general requirement that transformation rules generate SD. On the other hand, you then run into difficulties in repeated applications of transformation rules, for the arguments of these rules are supposed to be not sentences, but SD!

[16] Now if the arguments of a transformation rule are always supposed to be structural descriptions – in the usual sense as constituent structures and transformation structures – then the problem arises of defining these transformation rules in such general terms that they are defined for all of these arguments. That problem has never been solved, as far as I know.

[17] See the example Chomsky cites in [66a], p. 30ff., for one, as well as [62a].

[18] The distinction between deep and surface structure can be illustrated by examples of ambiguous sentences in which identical sentences have different deep structures ('Hans

had a book stolen' and 'Later the letter by Hans was read' [See above note 43 to Chapter III.2]), or in sentences such as 'Fritz laughs often' and 'Fritz laughs happily', where sentences with the same surface structure (proper name – verb – adverb) have different depth structures. We have already discussed these examples in Chapter III.2.2.– See also Postal [64c]. – On the history of the concept of depth structure see Chomsky [66b].

[19] See e.g. Chomsky [64], p. 85.

[20] This avoids the difficulties in defining transformation rules that were mentioned above. It is also possible to incorporate into the definition of the transformation rules specifications that refer to the deep-structural classification of the expressions in their arguments. These specifications do remain invariant in relation to transformations.

[21] On their definition see Bar-Hillel [53].

[22] On their definition see Chomsky [59].

[23] See Bar-Hillel, Theorems 1 and 2.

[24] For discussion of other generative grammars see also Postal [64a], Chomsky [62b] and Chomsky [56].

[25] Bierwisch also emphasizes in [66], p. 145f. the relation between depth structure and logical structure. He does not take them to be identical, to be sure, but to be closely related. These ideas have been more extensively developed first by E. Bach in [68], by G. Lakoff in [70] and by J. McCawley in [68].

[26] The representation A [Z] was explained in III.2.

[27] These and similarly defined substitution categories were introduced by Bloomfield, Harris and Bar-Hillel. See e.g. Bar-Hillel [50].

[28] Curry also expresses himself along these lines in [61], while Putnam takes the position in [61] that there are no sharp boundaries between syntactic and semantic irregularities. – Perhaps there are none from the point of view of language, but that does not speak against drawing such boundaries in grammar.

[29] See also the presentation in Katz [66].

[30] This lack is still more obvious in Abraham and Kiefer [66]. Here distinctors and selectors are omitted in the readings and what shows up as a single rule of projection is a rule that corresponds to Katz and Fodor's rule R_1 in so far as it combines characteristics (?) of the components of the new expression conjunctively. At best, however, it can be used to identify conjunctive combinations of one-place predicates, but not names, sentences, polyadic predicates, functors or functor-argument constructions.

[31] See Chapter III.2.1.6 on this point.

[32] See Chomsky [66b] and [67].

[33] On the definition of general language theory see e.g. Chomsky [61a], p. 120 or Postal [64a], p. 3f.

[34] Chomsky takes up the historical parallels to his hypothesis in [66b].

[35] Chomsky draws the distinction between *formal – substantial* categories in [65], Chapter I, § 5.

[36] See also Goodman's discussions of the point in [67].

[37] Even if the IH would explain certain phenomena for which we have no other satisfactory explanation, it would not follow from this, as Goodman emphasizes in [67], that it is correct or even just acceptable. The latter would be true only if it did not raise more problems than it solved.

[38] See the remarks in Chapter IV.3.

[39] See also Putnam [67].

[40] The question is, of course, whether we are not obliged to say that persons of lesser

intellectual gifts do master *another language*, namely the everyday language they speak, just as well as others master cultivated speech.

[41] Putnam says: "Nine or ten years is enough time to become pretty darn good at *anything*," [67], p. 20. Of course, we have to draw some distinctions here: As a rule, a child has mastered simple sentence structures by five years, but needs more than ten years to learn more complex sentence forms; here again there is the question of whether it is not a matter of different language systems.

[42] Along these lines, Putnam in [67], too.

CHAPTER IV

LANGUAGE AND REALITY

1. THE THESIS OF THE ROLE LANGUAGE PLAYS IN EXPERIENCE

A thesis concerning the role language plays in experience was first set forth on a scientific basis by Wilhelm von Humboldt, whose ideas continue to have an effect up to the present, especially in German linguistic theory.

For Humboldt language is not only a means of expressing or communicating what is in thought, but thought and language form an inseparable unity: "The most obvious, but the most limited view of language is that which considers it a mere means of understanding each other. ... But language is through and through not just a means of understanding, but the imprint of the speaker's mind and his view of the world; association in society is the essential vehicle of its development, but it is by far not the sole purpose it works toward...."[1] He speaks of the "inseparability of human consciousness and human language"[2] and says: "Language is the formative organ of thought. Intellectual activity, mental through and through, passing by all inwardly and somehow without a trace, becomes external and perceptible to the sense by virtue of sound in speech. It and language are therefore one and inseparable from each other. But in itself, too, it is bound to the necessity of entering into a connection with the sound of words; else thinking can not attain clarity, the idea not become a concept."[3] "The concept may ... no more loose itself from the word, than the man can lay aside the features of his face. The word is its own particular shaping and, if it wishes to depart therefrom, only in other words can it find itself again."[4]

The concept is first formed by means of the word; concept and sound pattern are not brought together in the word: "From the first element on, production of language is a synthetical process in the most genuine sense of the word, where the synthesis engenders something that does not lie within any of the connected parts by themselves."[5]

Accordingly, it is only with the help of language that we apprehend the world, the things, distinctions, properties and relations within it; and we apprehend them in a particular way with a particular language: Every language contains a view of the world [*Weltansicht*] and its structure, a distinctive ontology: "The mutual dependence of the thought and the word on each other makes it clear that languages are not really instruments for representing the truth already known, but far more of revealing the previously unknown. Their differences are not a matter of sounds and symbols, but differences in their very world views."[6] "Here too we find that the way of representing language as if it did no more than describe objects perceived in and of themselves is far from exhausting its full and deep content. Just as concepts are not possible without language, so there would be no objects for the soul without it, since every external object obtains its essential determination only through the mediation of a concept. The entire manner of the subjective perception of objects merges into the structure and use of language. For it is out of this perception that the word arises and it is not an imprint struck from the object in and of itself but from the image of it created in the soul. Since subjectivity is unavoidably mixed in with all objective perception, even independently of language each human individuality can be viewed as a unique and distinctive standpoint in viewing the world. It becomes still more so, however, because of language, since the word, vis-a-vis the soul, makes of itself an object once again and introduces a new distinctive feature separate from the subject, so that now the concept includes a threefold aspect, the impression of the object, the way in which this is taken up by the subject, the influence of the word, as speech sound."[7] "Subjective activity constitutes an object in thought. For no class of ideas can be regarded as merely a passive reception and contemplation of an object already present. The activity of the senses must be synthetically combined with the mind's inward functioning, and out of that combination the idea emerges a separate thing, becomes, vis-a-vis the subjective faculty, object and returns as such, newly perceived, into the former. For that, however, language is indispensable."[8] "The concept first attains its clearness and distinctness by means of being mirrored from another intelligence. It is created, as we saw in the foregoing, by loosing itself from the turbulent mass of ideas and constituting itself as an object vis-a-vis the subject. Yet it does not suffice for this rupture to occur within the subject alone, objectivity is not brought to fulfillment until the thinker of the ideas beholds the thought really outside of himself, which is possible only in another being, like him, thinking and having ideas. But between one intelligence and another the only intermediary is language, and so its necessity for the complete realization of the thought is a consequence of this too." [9]

"But language is not world view just because, since every concept must be grasped by it, it must equal the entire compass of the world, but also because it is only its transformation of the objects that makes the mind capable of insight into the connectedness that is inseparable from the concept of the world. For it is only by transducing reality's impression on the senses and the sensation over into its own realm of articulated sounds made ready beforehand as organ of thinking that it enables us to unite objects with clear and pure ideas, and so shedding light upon the way the world hangs together. Man primarily lives with objects just as language brings them to him, and his sensation and action depend on his ideas, even exclusively so. By the same act by which man spins language out of himself, he spins himself into it, and every language draws a circle around the nation to which it belongs, a circle that can be crossed only insofar as one at the same time steps over into the circle of another language." [10]

Humboldt speaks of the "transformation of the world into language" [11] and says: "The distinctive feature of language is that, mediating between men and outer objects, it fastens onto sounds a world of thought." [12] "But the path it takes is always different and its constructions arise from the interaction of external impressions and inner feeling, tied to the general goal that language pursues, binding subjectivity with objectivity in the creation of an ideal, but neither entirely inner nor entirely outer world." [13]

For Humboldt it is true that languages: "... remodel, each with the power that dwells within it, the common land that lies before us into the property of mind." [14]

This world view that belongs to a language bears the stamp of the life will, or, as we also say, the *cultural will* of the *nation* that speaks that language; conversely, the peculiar nature and the character of a culture manifests itself in the *potency of language*, for language and culture, language and life are bound up in the most intimate way:

"Language lives and moves in nationality and the deepest secret of its being manifests itself precisely in the fact that it comes forth out of the apparently confused mass of individualities, within which no one of them need be singled out. It receives its whole form from this natural working, dark and obscure, of unconsciously concurring tendencies, since whatever comes of individual aim, no matter how well calculated, does nothing but play around their outskirts, so to speak, in visible impotence." [15] "From every language, therefore, conclusions can be drawn about the national character." [16] For Humboldt, then, a language is a "spiritual individuality" [17] and this individuality is that of the nation: "Basically the language is ... the nation itself, and strictly, genuinely the nation." [18] "The language, however, has just this power to thank for its origin, or more correctly: the particular national power and strength can be externally expressed only in the particular national language, these sounds, these linkages of analogy, these symbolic hints, these specific principles of inward development. It is this that we may well call, but always improperly and loosely, the making of language by the nation." [19] "We can, as generally acknowledged, assume that the diverse languages constitute the organs of the nations' distinctive ways of thinking and feeling, that a large number of objects [of thought] are first brought forth by the words that designate them, and have their being only in [those words] ..." [20]

If culture is the maker of language, then it is a power over the individual that determines his thinking and his experience in the form of its world view and so has a part in shaping his experience:

"The idea that the various languages do nothing more than describe in different words the same vast number of objects and concepts existing independently of them and that the words are arranged according to different principles, which apart from their influence on understanding have no further significance, is too natural to man for him to be able easily to free himself from it before he has reflected more deeply on language. He disdains what appears in the particular to be so small and negligible as to be mere grammatical fussiness, and forgets that the cumulative mass of those particularities, all unknown to himself, constrains him and rules him all the same. Always living, moving, acting in [a world of] objects he takes subjectivity too little into account; the concept comes hard to him of a power given by nature itself, a power that is not fortuitous nor whimsical nor arbitrary but so transforming all, according to its own inward principles, that the apparent object itself is only a subjective notion, yet one that has every right to lay claim to universal validity." [21] "But thinking is not just dependent on language in general, but to a certain extent it is determined by each individual one as well." [22] "For the influence of the individual view of the object on the moulding of the word also determines, as long as it remains a living force, the way the word recalls the object." [23] "But language, as the work of the nation, and of time past, is something foreign to the individual; on the one side he is bound by it, but on the other he is enriched, invigorated and stimulated by all that earlier generations have deposited in it." [24] "When one considers what a binding influence over each generation of a people everything their language has experienced throughout all the preceding centuries has... it will be clear how slight is the power of the individual as against the mighty force of language." [25] And therefore it is true: "(1) that language attains an individuality through the influences that work upon it, an individuality that really becomes its nature, to the extent that it now reacts upon it and can be used willingly only within its limits. (2) that its reactive force is the more definitive as what is brought to bear upon the individual by means of whole epochs and nations is working within it, whose very individuality, inclined in the same direction by the likeness of the influences affecting it, is scarcely capable of resisting." [26] "But man does not speak because he wants to speak that way, but because he has to speak that way; the way he speaks is a compulsion of his intellectual nature; it is free, to be sure, because it is his own, original nature, but there is no bridge leading him in a unifying consciousness from each momentary appearance to that unknown fundamental presence." [27]

This influence of language on thinking is the result of the conceptual system or vocabulary, but also of the forms of grammar: "It is only on more precise consideration, but then clearly and distinctly, that we find the character of the diverse world views of peoples adhering to the value and weight of words. I have already remarked in the foregoing... that it is scarcely possible for different individuals uniformly to take up some word into their idea, unless it be momentarily used merely as a material sign of its concept. We can say, therefore, quite flatly that there is something in each one that can not be differentiated once again by means of words and that the words of diverse languages, even if they designate roughly the same concepts, are never true synonyms." [28] "Yet it would be one-sided to think that the distinctive quality of the nation's spirit and character is revealed in concept formation alone; it exerts a similar large influence on the way discourse is structured and can equally be known in it." [29]

For Humboldt, grammatical form is even the primary respect in which different languages are distinguished from each other. [30]

In view of all this, the usefulness of comparative studies of language lies in the fact that by learning new languages we become acquainted with new world views and ways of thinking and thereby widen the limits of our own horizon. It is precisely through the study of the most diverse languages that the broadest perspective rises, for: "Difference in structure, even where it is quite substantial enough, is nevertheless often insufficiently recognized and appreciated as long as we are concerned with a small number of languages not totally different one from the other." [31]

But Humboldt sees very clearly, too, the difficulties that stand in the way of comparing languages or the world views they are based upon.

In the first place, according to him, every language, no matter how 'primitive' it may be in particular detail, has a universal character, i.e. every thought or concept can be expressed in it, even if it is with difficulty and only in approximations. I.e., it would never be possible to say: This concept or that thought can not be rendered here at all, this and that do not enter into the ontology of this language:

"But in both the language and the concepts of any people, no matter how culturally undeveloped, there resides, and this is by far the more decisive point here, a totality commensurate with the full range of the unrestricted human cultural potential, out of which can be engendered, with no outside aid, every detail that humanity encompasses." [32] "Experience with translation from very disparate languages, and with the use of the roughest and most undeveloped of them in teaching the most arcane doctrines of a revealed religion [in the case of Bible translation], does show that, even if with greatly variable success, any sequence of ideas can be expressed in every one of them. But this is not merely a consequence of the general relatedness of everything, and of the flexibility of the concepts, and their signs. For the languages themselves and the influence they have on the nations proves nothing but what follows from them naturally; not what they can be compelled to, but what they invite and encourage." [23] "In translating phrases in such languages with such and such a form, therefore, it is necessary to keep very much in mind the fact that those translations, so far as they have to do with grammatical forms, are almost always false, and their grammatical aspect is quite different from the one presented by the speaker in saying them. If we wished to avoid this, we would have to use in translating only the grammatical forms present in the original language; but then we would come up against cases where we would have to give up translating at all." [34] "Nor is it simply indifferent whether one language accomplishes by periphrasis what another language expresses in one word; not with grammatical forms, since in the case of periphrasis, they no longer present the appearance of modified ideas, but that of specifying the modification, contrary to the concept of a mere form; not in the designation of the concepts, either. The principle of segmentation necessarily suffers when what presents itself as a unit in concept does not appear to be so in expression, and all of the word's vivid effectiveness, as an individual, falls by the wayside for the concept that lacks any such expression." [35]

There are always translations, then, but they are for the most part inexact. But since there are no generally valid and sharp criteria for precision of translation, the differences in meaning are often very difficult to assess.

For Humboldt language is furthermore an organism, i.e. a structure, the individual parts of which must always be viewed in terms of their function in the whole. And it has an inner dynamics that cannot be adequately caught by descriptions of momentary linguistic situations. This implies an additional difficulty for grasping the peculiar character of languages and for making comparisons between them.

Humboldt says: "There are no isolated phenomena in language; each element in it proclaims itself to be a part of a whole." [36] And: "Language is not at all something spread out there, a stuff made up of the mass of words and rules it offers, but something ongoing, an ideal process, as life is a corporeal one." [37] "The direct, immediate exhalation of an organic being in its sensual and intellectual status, it shares the nature of everything organic, that each thing within it exists only through the other and all of them only through the one all-pervasive power that permeates the whole." [38]

The diversity of languages does not lie in their details, which viewed in isolation can always be interpreted in such a way that they are similar to each other, but in the languages' entirety. Only with regard to the diversity of the whole structures do the details also reveal themselves to be diverse. But it is very difficult to attain a perspective on languages in their entireties and to catch their characteristic and distinctive features in statements that are general and yet sufficiently precise: "But the spirit that forms language knows how to master the technical grammatical instruments and to give them differing value so that neither their presence nor their absence will lead to generally definitive and certain conclusions about the essence of the language form. Therefore if we run through any given language, it is hard to find a single point it would not be possible to conceive in another way, with no damage to the essential nature of its language form, and we will be forced to return to the overall impression. Here the exact opposite comes into play; the most decided individuality strikes the eye clearly, impresses itself compellingly on our feeling. If one goes back to the material and the technical aspect of language from here, there is scarcely anything else to do but take all and everything together, just as concrete as it is, as making up the language form, understanding this in a sense that would really exclude any possibility of alteration within the same language form. Languages can be compared, most adequately, to human physiognomies in this respect. Individuality is obtrusively present, similarities are recognized, but there is no measuring, nor any description of component parts as to particular detail or their connection with each other that is capable of summing up into one concept the distinctive character. It is based on the whole and on the way it is apprehended, once again an individual matter, and thus every physiognomy is sure to take on a different look for every individual. Since language, in whatever form you may take it up, is always a spiritual exhalation of an individual national life, both must be realized in it. No matter how much you isolate it, pin it down, embody it, there is always something more, precisely the most important thing about it, wherein there is the unity and the breath of life of a living being."[39] "Within language, the character of the whole sweeps the individual along with it every time. If you forget to hold fast to this basic principle in arriving at judgments about languages, you are mistaking their very nature and every genuine difference among them as well. For they do not ever diverge from one another to such an extent that there should be no particular resemblances even between the most disparate of them."[40] "Language offers us an infinitude of particular details, in words, rules, analogies and exceptions of every kind. We are more than slightly perplexed as to how we are to bring this mass of detail – which seems to us a confusing chaos still, despite the order into which it has already been brought going unnoticed – into some judgment comparing it with the unified image of human intellectual capacity. Even if we find ourselves in possession of the necessary lexical and grammatical details of two important language stems, e.g. Sanskrit and Semitic; that will still not take us very far in our effort to sum up the character of each of them in such a way that we can make fruitful comparisons between them and specify their proper places in the general enterprise of language creation, as measured by their relation to the spiritual-intellectual capacity of the nations. What is still required is a special seeking out of the common sources of the individual particularities, the gathering together of the scattered features into the picture of an organic whole. That is the only way to enable us to get a firm hold on the particulars." [41]

Current discussion of the thesis that language plays a role in experience has been prompted, at least in Anglo-Saxon world, more by the works of Edward Sapir (1884–1935) and Benjamin Lee Whorf (1897–1941) than by Humboldt.

Sapir, one of the most influential American linguists, expressed the thesis of language's role in experience as follows: "Human beings do not live in the objective world alone, nor alone in the world of social activity as ordinarily understood, but are very much at the mercy of the particular language which has become the medium of expression for their society. It is quite an illusion to imagine that one adjusts to reality essentially without the use of language and that language is merely an incidental means of solving specific problems of communication and reflection. The fact of the matter is that the 'real world' is to a large extent unconciously built up on the language of the group." [42] "The relation between language and experience is often misunderstood. Language is not merely a more or less systematic inventory of the various items of experience which seem relevant to the individual, as is so often naively assumed, but is also a selfcontained, creative symbolic organization, which not only refers to experience largely acquired without its help but actually defines experience for us by reason of its formal completeness and because of our unconscious projection of its implicit expectations into the field of experience."[43]

Whorf, who took up these ideas of Sapir's and developed them further, formulates his principle of relativity in this way: He refers to the realistic conception and says: "Natural logic says that talking is merely an incidental process concerned strictly with communication, not with formulation of ideas. Talking, or the use of language, is supposed only to 'express' what is essentially already formulated nonlinguistically. Formulation is an independent process, called thought or thinking, and is supposed to be largely indifferent to the nature of particular languages. Languages have grammars, which are assumed to be merely norms of conventional and social correctness, but the use of language is supposed to be guided not so much by them as by correct, rational, or intelligent thinking."[44]

Against this realistic interpretation Whorf now urges: "It was found that the background linguistic system (in other words, the grammar) of each language is not merely a reproducing instrument for voicing ideas but rather is itself the shaper of ideas, the program and guide for the individual's mental activity, for his analysis of impressions, for his synthesis of his mental stock in trade. Formulation of ideas is not an independent process, strictly rational in the old sense, but is part of a particular grammar, and differs, from slightly to greatly, between different grammars. We dissect nature along lines laid down by our native languages. The categories and types that we isolate from the world of phenomena we do not find there because they stare every observer in the face; on the contrary, the world is presented in a kaleidoscopic flux of impressions which has to be organized by our minds – and this means largely by the linguistic systems in our minds. We cut nature up, organize it into concepts, and ascribe significances as we do, largely because we are parties to an agreement to organize it in this way – an agreement that holds throughout our speech community and is codified in the patterns of our language. The agreement is, of course, an implicit and unstated one, but its terms are absolutely obligatory; we cannot talk at all except by subscribing to the organization and classification of data which the agreement decrees."[45]

Further: "We are thus introduced to a new principle of relativity, which holds that all observers are not led by the same physical evidence to the same picture of the universe, unless their linguistic backgrounds are similar, or can in some way be calibrated."[46] Or: "From this fact proceeds what I have called the 'linguistic relativity principle', which means, in informal terms, that users of markedly different grammars are pointed by their grammars toward different types of observations and different evaluations of externally similar acts of observation, and hence are not equivalent as observers but must arrive at somewhat different views of the world."[47]

In many passages Whorf emphasizes this influence of language on thinking and experience so strongly that he speaks of determination or compulsion by language: "This study shows that the forms of a person's thoughts are controlled by inexorable laws of pattern of which he is unconscious. These patterns are the unperceived intricate systematizations of his own language – shown readily enough by a candid comparison and contrast with other languages, especially those of a different linguistic family."[48] "Thinking follows a network of tracks laid down in a given language.... The individual is utterly unaware of their organization and is constrained completely within its unbreakable bonds."[49]

No more than Humboldt do Sapir and Whorf take the view that the world view of a culture is determined by its language alone, however. They urge rather that though the individual bears the stamp in his thinking and his world view of the language that he learns and accepts – although he also has a certain share in the formation of the language – the many individuals as a social culture create the language through their own particular way of coming to grips with the world in which they live. – "Which was first: the language patterns or the cultural norms? In main they have grown up together, constantly influencing each other. But in this partnership the nature of the language is the factor that limits free plasticity and rigidifies channels of development in the more autocratic way. This is so because a language is a system, not just an assemblage of norms. Large systematic outlines can change to something really new only very slowly, while many other cultural innovations are made with comparative quickness. Language thus represents the mass mind; it is affected by inventions and innovations, but affected little and slowly, whereas TO inventors and innovators it legislates with the decree immediate."[50]

Whorf does not view the connection between language and culture and language and world view as being as close as it is in Humboldt's view.

In particular, he does not believe that one would obtain all the information about a culture and its world view out of language, or conversely that the basic structures of the language would already be implied in the world view. So Whorf denies "that there is anything so definite as a 'correlation' between culture and language"[51] and insists: "there are connections but not correlations or diagnostic correspondencies between culture norms and linguistic patterns."[52]

For Whorf, as for Humboldt, the general significance of comparative linguistic research lies in the fact that it widens our horizons by showing us the relativity of our world view, which is mediated by our language: "One significant contribution to science from the linguistic point of view may be the greater development of our sense of perspective. We shall no longer be able to see a few dialects of the Indo-European family, and the rationalizing techniques elaborated from their patterns, as the apex of the evolution of the human mind, nor their present wide spread as due to any survival from fitness or to anything but a few events of history – events that could be called fortunate only from the parochial point of view of the favored parties. They, and our own thought processes with them, can no longer be envisioned as spanning the gamut of reason and knowledge but only as one constellation in a galactic expanse."[53]

In the next two sections, we will discuss some arguments for the relativity thesis drawn from linguistics, in order to make clear their concrete content, and then in Chapter IV.4 we shall go into the aspects of that thesis that have to do with the philosophy of language and theory of knowledge.

NOTES

[1] Humboldt [03], V. VI, p. 22f.
[2] Humboldt [03], V. VI, p. 16.
[3] Humboldt [03], V. VII, p. 33.
[4] Humboldt [03], V. VII, p. 100.
[5] Humboldt [03], V. VII, p. 94.
[6] Humboldt [03], V. IV, p. 27.
[7] Humboldt [03], V. VI, p. 179.
[8] Humboldt [03], V. VII, p. 55.
[9] Humboldt [03], V. VI, p. 160.
[10] Humboldt [03], V. VI, p. 179f.
[11] Humboldt [03], V. VI, p. 28.
[12] Humboldt [03], V. V, p. 110.
[13] Humboldt [03], V. VII, p. 115.
[14] Humboldt [03], V. IV, p. 420.
[15] Humboldt [03], V. VI, p. 189.

16 Humboldt [03], V. VII, p. 172.
17 Humboldt [03], V. VI, p. 151.
18 Humboldt [03], V. VII, p. 641.
19 Humboldt [03], V. VI, p. 127.
20 Humboldt [03], V. VII, p. 640.
21 Humboldt [03], V. VI, p. 119.
22 Humboldt [03], V. IV, p. 22.
23 Humboldt [03], V. IV, p. 29.
24 Humboldt [03], V. V, p. 27.
25 Humboldt [03], V. VI, p. 182.
26 Humboldt [03], V. IV, p. 423f.
27 Humboldt [03], V. VI, p. 127.
28 Humboldt [03], V. VII, p. 190.
29 Humboldt [03], V. VII, p. 92.
30 Cp. Humboldt [03], V. VI, p. 249f.
31 Humboldt [03], V. VI, p. 121.
32 Humboldt [03], V. VII, p. 28.
33 Humboldt [03], V. VI, p. 16f.
34 Humboldt [03], V. IV, p. 293.
35 Humboldt [03], V. IV, p. 20f.
36 Humboldt [03], V. IV, p. 14f.
37 Humboldt [03], V. VI, p. 146.
38 Humboldt [03], V. IV, p. 3.
39 Humboldt [03], V. VI, p. 245.
40 Humboldt [03], V. VI, p. 266.
41 Humboldt [03], V. VII, p. 44f.
42 Sapir [29], p. 209.
43 Cited by P. Henle in [65], p. 1.
44 Whorf [56], p. 207f.
45 Whorf [56], p. 212f.
46 Whorf [56], p. 214.
47 Whorf [56], p. 221.
48 Whorf [56], p. 252.
49 Whorf [56], p. 256.
50 Whorf [56], p. 156. – P. Henle also has this to say along the same lines: "In neither case have we claimed, nor would we want to claim, that language is the sole influence or even the primary influence. In neither case have we claimed that the causal relationship does not also run in the other direction as well. Because of the enduring character of languages and the fact that a population changes in time, it may well be that language considered in the large is molded by environmental conditions, social organisation, and prevalent modes of thought. This would not prevent language being an influence on thought in the development of the individual, and this is all we have claimed." ([65], p. 16f.)
51 Whorf [56], p. 139.
52 Whorf [56], p. 159.
53 Whorf [56], p. 218f. – For presentation and discussion of the Whorfian relativity theory, see also the contributions in Hoijer [54a] and Henle [65]. – For references to standpoints similar to what we have presented with respect to Humboldt's and Whorf's statements in this section, see Basilius [52].

2. THE ROLE OF VOCABULARY

If one wishes to give to language a role in experience, one can make reference to vocabulary or to grammar. Vocabulary's part can be understood more easily, but from the point of view of Humboldt and Whorf [it is] altogether less important than that of grammar.

We will treat the relativity thesis for vocabulary in terms of an example of diverse arrangements of one semantic region into word fields, one which has played an important role in the discussion of this thesis: the example of diverse word fields in the differentiation of colors.[1]

Most languages have only a few basic words available for the classification of the extraordinarily large number of distinguishable shades of color. Now to a considerable degree the classifications of colors realized by means of these basic words partially diverge from each other. For example, the language of the Navaho Indians has two color words for our 'black', which designate the black of night (darkness) and the black of coal (black color), say, but they have only one word in the place of our 'blue' and 'green', on the other hand.[2]

Now if we assume that the distinction blue – green cannot be reproduced in Navaho in some simple way, e.g. by auxiliary adjectives (*cold blue-or-green=blue, warm blue-or-green=green*, say, or *sky blue-or-green =blue, grassy blue-or-green=green*), according to Whorf that would mean that the Navahos typically do not distinguish between blue and green in color experience, and that the division of the color region in language determines the differences in the way we perceive colors.

Max Black criticized Whorf's claim that a classification example of that sort implies an influence of language on experience in [59]. What he says there is: The Navahos are able to distinguish colors, e.g. blue and green, just as well as we are, i.e. they have at their disposal the same concepts as possibilities of differentiation as we do. It is only that among the various distinctions that can be made, the ones they can express in linguistically simple ways are different from the ones we can express in that way. There are no empirical grounds of any kind for taking the view that different color vocabularies have an influence on how colors are perceived. What this case has to do with is simply a difference in classification, not a difference in perception.[3]

But one must make a distinction here: Whorf does not deny that the

Navahos have the capacity for distinguishing colors just as precisely as we do, in particular that they are in a position to distinguish between blue and green. He does not say that the Navahos are color blind with respect to the distinction blue – green. But that does not make it possible to maintain that 'they have at their disposal the concepts' blue and green – a way of putting it that Black takes over from H. H. Price. You do not already have a concept at your disposal when you are capable of learning a distinction, but only when you have learned it. We can scarcely say of a layman in mathematics, for example, that he has at this disposal the concept of perfect number, even though he does have the capacity for learning the distinction between perfect and imperfect numbers. He has that concept at his disposal only when he has learned that a perfect number is a number n, for which the sum of its whole number divisors $= 2 \cdot n$, i.e. when the concept, or the use of the predicate 'perfect number' has been explained to him. Beforehand, however, he does not make that distinction and is entirely incapable of making it. He does not just lack the means of making the distinction.

To begin with, then, it is not a matter of the capacity of being able to make distinctions in the sense of being capable of learning them, but of the distinctions that are actually made.[4] It is also not a matter of distinctions that are made on occasion, but of the distinctions that are made systematically and often.

Now what Whorf claims is that distinctions for which there are no simple and stereotyped forms of linguistic expression are not that sort of common and systematic distinctions. This surely has the highest degree of plausibility, for one would construct simple forms of expression for common distinctions for reasons of economy.

Perceptions, observations, generally speaking, experiences, furthermore, are not isolated from other activities, but are intimately entangled in the totality of all we do: Distinctions we establish in observation cause us to conduct ourselves differently, and conversely, we do not make just any and every distinction in observation, but direct our attention to the distinctions that are relevant to what we do. But since our life and activity is very firmly linked up with society and since we use language to coordinate our common activities, distinctions within experience are not things that would be only partially and imperfectly expressed; on the contrary, every functioning language must be capable of expressing all of the distinctions that are practically relevant for the members of its linguistic community. The variety of the distinctions that are systematic, regular and important, even when they have not first been learned through language, will essentially coincide with the language's diverse possibilities of expression.

But that is to say: there is a close connection between means of making distinctions in language and the contents of experience. In the color example, then, it is not so that we only classify and express the same color perceptions in different ways in language, but rather different forms of color perception correspond to the various ways of dividing and arranging the semantic region of color into word fields.

Of course the example of color word fields is not suited for the illustration of more radical differences of apprehension or understanding. Those become much clearer when one considers other world fields, from the psychological or intellectual domain, for example. Here we make distinctions between e.g. 'sorrowful', 'melancholy', and 'dejected', or 'wise', 'intelligent', and 'clever', for which in other languages there are no simple stereotyped possibilities of expression, simply because those distinctions are not made as a rule in the relevant cultures. And it would be extremely peculiar to say that the people who belong to those cultures perceive, just as we do, that a man is intelligent but not wise, or melancholy but not sorrowful, but just can not express it in words or do express it in words that when translated back into our language mean something quite different – why should their linguistic behavior be so awkward? It is surely more sensible to say: They do not express those distinctions because they do not make them.

Furthermore, we can extract from a people's juridical language the distinctions they make in matters juridical and from the vocabulary of a language a great deal about a people's cultural forms and living conditions. For example, the Nootka Indians of the northwest coast of America have a large number of very specific words for sea animals, while other inland tribes have available instead detailed designations for berries and edible plants. The Paiute Indians, who live in the desert, have very exact terms for topographical particulars – a very important matter for orientation in a uniform landscape, and so on.[5]

It is in this sense that E. Sapir says that the vocabulary of a language is a "complex inventory of all the ideas, interests, and occupations that take up the attention of the community."[6]

The alleged role of language in experience is not, then, a matter of which distinctions could be made or happen to be made on occasion, but of which distinctions are typically made; nor is it a matter of what can be expressed in a language at all, but rather of what can be expressed in simple and stereotyped locutions.[7] In the latter sense, however, we can regard a close connection between vocabulary and experience as having sufficient evidence in its favor.

Nevertheless, the thesis of the role of language in experience is not proved thereby. For the fact that the distinctions that are typically drawn in the experience, as generally within the life of a linguistic community are expressed in its language, that the various cultures' ways of understanding and experiencing the world are reflected in their languages has hardly been contested, but what has been contested is that language conversely has an influence on experience, on the apprehension of the world, and, if it is not the only influence, is nevertheless a codeterminant of the form and shape of experience. And only that gives us the full content of the relativity thesis.

On this point, however, Humboldt, and Whorf as well, as we saw above, draw some distinctions. Neither one of them advocates the thesis that a people gets a language from somewhere or other, which then determines its typical forms of experience, action and life, nor would it be the least bit plausible. Rather, language is shaped out of the confrontation with the material, social and religious requirements and circumstances of a people. By and large, language is a part of culture and is formed by the powers that form that culture also. Equally, by and large, the human beings who belong to a people form its culture, and not *vice versa*.

If, on the other hand, one considers the individual, it makes sense to say that he is shaped by the culture into which he is born, and it also makes sense to say that the language he acquires participates in determining his way of experiencing. Along with words he learns certain differences, certain forms that determine the experienced world in a way that is relevant and important for the society and culture to which he belongs, and consequently for him as well. Along with these differences he learns to orient himself in the world and to interpret the objects of his experience. The world reveals itself to him in these differences. Because we learn distinctions and determinations already made, language influences the way and manner in which the individual perceives and experiences, and what he perceives. Perception does not consist just in having the senses stimulated, but in the perception of something as specifically characterized in such and such a way.

Naturally, not even for the individual is there total dependence on language, such that he would not be in a position to make other distinctions besides those that can be simply expressed in language. For in the first place an adequate and expressive language is so plastic that new distinctions can be formulated in it as well. For another thing, the individual can introduce new expressions and mark new differences in language which expand or alter the language. For example, that is what occurs constantly in scientific work, where when new domains of objects are revealed, a new terminology for describing them must be developed. On the large view, however, the individual follows the language as he finds it rather than shaping it anew, and therefore it can be said, following Humboldt, Sapir and Whorf, that our language determines the form and manner of our experience.[8]

But it is also an error when M. Black says in [59] that there are no empirical arguments for a correlation between perception and language. In a very careful empirical-psychological study – one, moreover, which in its general statements about the Whorfian thesis belongs among the works on that theme that are most worth reading – R. W. Brown and E. H. Lenneberg have proved in [54] that there is a connection between the recognition of colors and linguistic *codability*. This is defined in terms of the simplicity (brevity) of the color designation, its availability (the speed with which it is named) and its reliability (individual and interpersonal agreement in using it). It is shown that colors are recognized the more easily, the greater their codability. And E. H. Lenneberg and J. M. Roberts proved in [53] that the Zuni Indians, who have in their language only one designation for yellow and orange, confuse these two colors more frequently than English-speaking Americans do. Interestingly, the success of bilingual Zuni, who also know English, in recognizing these two colors falls between the success of monolingual Zuni and that of Americans who speak English only.

These studies lend support to the intimate involvement of language with experience and the role played by language in experience by showing that we recognize colors – and we may say by way of generalization: objects – not so much by way of a comparison between present sense-impressions and earlier ones as by comparing earlier designations with present ones, and so with the help of linguistic classifications. Success in recognition within some specific domain depends upon the means of linguistic classification for the domain and for that reason success can vary conspicuously from language to language.

NOTES

[1] See also Oehmann [51], p. 123ff., and Gipper [69], Chapter 5 on this point.

[2] See e.g. Hoijer [54b], p. 96.

[3] See Black [59], p. 231.

[4] P. Henle also makes statements along these lines in [64], p. 7f. and H. Hoijer in [54b], p. 96. See also C. F. Hockett's assertions in Hoijer [54a], p. 122.

[5] See Henle [65], p. 5.

[6] Sapir [12], p. 228.

[7] Humboldt also makes this point in the passages cited.

[8] In Whorf, it is true, there are also many statements, as was emphasized in Chapter IV.1, according to which language does not just suggest a certain world view to us but forces one upon us. In this connection he refers primarily to grammar, which on his view leaves a much stronger imprint on our experience than vocabulary. – P. Henle gives a very weak formulation for the relativity thesis, when he says: "Neither finally have we argued that there is any compulsive influence of language upon thought, that language makes impossible all but certain modes of perception and organisation of expression. Since perception and experience are ordinarily manifested only through language, the point being made here may be made in another way. In natural languages, the elements we have been considering – vocabulary, inflection and modes of sentence structure – do not make it impossible to express certain things, they merely make it more difficult to express them." ([65], p. 17). But that lies on the border of triviality and need not be discussed. What is expressible in a simple way in a language naturally depends on the language's expressive resources. Whorf says, for example, that we not only always *express* ourselves in the simplest way that is possible in our language, but that we *see* the matter in the way the forms of our language suggest.

3. THE ROLE OF GRAMMAR

In arguing for his relativity thesis Whorf places particular emphasis on linguistic *background phenomena*, i.e. on the basic grammatical structures of language and their role in determining experience. For the most part we do not notice these basic structures, because we take them for granted as obvious and use them continuously. Whorf says: "that the phenomena of a language are to its own speakers largely of a background character and so are outside the critical consciousness and control of the speaker."[1] "... we all hold an illusion about talking, an illusion that talking is quite untrammeled and spontaneous and merely 'expresses' whatever we wish to have it express. This illusory appearance results from the fact that the obligatory phenomena within the apparently free flow of talk are so completely automatic that speaker and listener are bound unconsciously as though in the grip of a law of nature. The phenomena of language are background phenomena, of which the talkers are unaware or, at the most, very dimly aware – as they are of the motes of dust in the air of a room, though the linguistic phenomena govern the talkers more as gravitation than as dust would. These automatic, involuntary patterns of language are not the same for all men but are specific for each language and constitute the formalized side of the language, or its 'grammar' – a term that includes much more than the grammar we learned in the textbooks of our school days."[2]

We shall show in what follows, however, that the influence of grammar on experience is much more difficult to confirm than is that of vocabulary.

Out of the many examples of the diversity of basic linguistic forms that Whorf gives, we cite three:

(1) When we start out from our own language, the categories *substantive – adjective – verb* appear to us to be fundamental grammatical categories, and we customarily associate those word types with basic ontological categories, by distinguishing between *things* (or persons), *attributes* (or states) and *activities* (or processes). These ontological distinctions, we say, produce the distinctions among types of words and therefore we expect those same distinctions to be expressed in every language. But that is not the case. In the language of the Hopi Indians, for example, all of the predicates by which events of short duration are expressed are verbs. Thus the substantives 'lightning', 'cloud', 'flame', 'meteor', 'smoke cloud', etc., do not exist, only verbs corresponding to

them. What is said, for example, is not 'The flames are making a bright light', but 'It's burning brightly', and so on. In Nootka, on the other hand, all predicates take the form of verbs.[3] According to Whorf that shows that nature itself is not divided into things, states and processes, but that we have imposed those distinctions on the world with our language, so that those categories are only forms of interpreting reality.[4]

Similarly, for us the distinction between class terms and substance terms is essential and we also distinguish between things and the substance of which they are composed. But the fact that in Hopi, for example, substance terms are treated like class terms – so that depending on the context one can say, for example, 'a water' for 'a glass of water' or 'a lake', or 'a gold' for 'a golden object' – shows that this distinction, too, is only induced by language.[5]

The fact is that the distinctions *substance – attribute – verb* on the one hand and *class terms* and *substance terms* on the other prove not to be fundamental in the logical analysis of grammar nor do those distinctions actually follow any clear criterion: One can just as well say 'Lightning flashes' as 'It lightens [*Es blitzt*]', 'A strong wind is blowing' as 'It is storming', and so on. And the expressions 'golden object' or 'made of gold' as class terms accomplish the same thing as 'gold' as a substance term. However, as for the most part we use a substantive to express the complex of basic enduring features that belong to an object existing over a long period of time and an adjective, on the other hand, for particular attributes or states, often accidental or momentary, the use of a substantive instead of an adjective suggests a different interpretation: If instead of saying 'This rose is red' you say 'This rose has a share of redness', that can be understood just as well as the former case. But that the latter formulation suggests another meaning is clearly shown by the philosophical questions that have been joined to that formulation.[6] If you speak not of temporal relationships ('earlier than', 'simultaneous with') but of 'the time', and if you say, e.g. 'The time has gone by' instead of 'It is late', these changed locutions raise entirely new problems.[7] That is to say, despite their equivalence in particular cases, the use of substantives, adjectives or verbs still commonly suggests a different interpretation.

(2) Whorf contrasts the *time concept* as it is expressed in our temporal adverbs and prepositions and the tense forms of verbs, and the idea of an 'objective, steadily flowing time', with the time concept of the Hopi. He

writes: "After long and careful study and analysis, the Hopi language is seen to contain no words, grammatical forms, constructions or expressions that refer directly to what we call 'time' or to past, present, or future, or to enduring or lasting." [8] According to Whorf, the Hopi have only three basic forms of statement. One form refers to what is objectively real or realized, whether in the present or the past, another to the subject realm, to wishes, intentions, expectations and ideas, and the third form is the form of statements that are universally and timelessly true. Statements in the future are rendered by statements of the second type, and so have to do with expectations and intentions of a subject concerning something that is yet to be realized. Statements about the past that no longer have any connection with the present, and so are in the preterite, are rendered by means of statements of the first type with an adjunct that characterizes them as from memory. Thus according to Whorf our division of time has only a very indirect counterpart in the Hopi language. There is only the difference between facts and expectations as viewed by the individual subject and between facts that refer to what is experienced in the present and those for which such a connection exists only by way of recollection. Therefore Whorf says that the Hopi lack a time category as well as time expressions corresponding to our own and that therefore the Hopi's world picture is basically different from ours.

Unfortunately Whorf's statements concerning the distinction between the realms of objective and subjective phenomena are not extensive enough to permit any very precise idea of what it is. What is to be regretted most of all is that Whorf does not even succeed in characterizing precisely the time concept on which the Indoeuropean languages, or our world picture is based. When he speaks of a "kinetic one-dimensional uniformly and perpetually flowing time" [9] that is anything but illuminating, so that one asks oneself the question whether 'Hopi time' was really defined precisely, if there was no such success even for 'European time'.

Add to this the fact that the function of time cannot be represented simply by way of reference to physical time even for European languages. Weinrich in particular showed that in [64].[10] Although an interesting problem has been laid out here and interesting points made, it still does not provide any firm support for the linguistic relativity principle.

(3) The third example of Whorf's illustrations of his thesis concerns the fundamental structure of European languages, namely the *subject-pred-*

icate structure of sentences. According to Whorf every language carries out an "artificial chopping up of the continuous spread and flow of existence in a different way,"[11] in that whenever something is specified in language certain events, things and states are isolated out of the stream of sense-data, and the subject-predicate structure of the European languages indicates a particular form of this organization.

M. Black has rightly criticized this formulation:[12] Reality is not 'sliced up' in being formulated in language, it is only that partial aspects come to be represented. Furthermore, according to Whorf there is no 'reality in itself' at all, but what is real is always relative to a language. And finally, the 'stream of sense-data', 'the welter of sensations' is itself an abstraction from our already organized experiences.

But this can be said: In our experiences what is experienced is always interpreted in some way, and what Whorf says is that the subject-predicate structure is a specific form of interpretation. According to Whorf, we first of all isolate particular events and interpret those events in the form that there are one or more things (or persons) which are involved in an activity (or a state). Even when to do so is scarcely adequate considered in terms of the situation, we apply this schema: We speak of things where we have no relatively firmly delineated bodies such as stones, tables or creatures before us and so lack any sharp criteria of identity, as the words 'heaven', 'wave', 'cloud', 'marsh', 'plain', and so on will witness, and we consistently understand all events in such a way that 'things' enter in as agents or bearers of states and processes. Even sentences such as 'It is raining', which are constructed with impersonal verbs and have no genuine subject, have at least the grammatical form of subject-predicate sentences. The Hopi, in contrast, can use verbs without subjects, i.e. grammatically impersonal constructions are possible, too, and the set of impersonal sentences is essentially larger as against the European languages.[13] But the Nootka language, according to Whorf, lacks subjects and predicates entirely: there complex sentences are formed by means of suffixes from simple sentences serving as basic constants of the language.[14]

Without a more exact knowledge of Nootka grammar than Whorf's statements provide, no more exact representation of the views that are basic to that language can be given. This point – the linguistic analysis of events into things and states – is so important, however, that we will come back to it again in more detail below.

These three examples of the way in which Whorf supports his relativity thesis give an impression of the arguments with which the problem of the influence of language on experience is discussed in linguistics. They offer a series of quite interesting suggestions and pointers, but they are incapable of lending support to the thesis adequately in all particulars. That also becomes clear from the discussion of the following criticisms, which do not concern Whorf's particular examples, but his argument's basic ideas.

One objection takes this form: If Whorf were correct in saying that our language fixes our interpretation of the world, then we would be totally incapable of establishing that there are languages with radically different interpretation schemata and ways of understanding the world, as Whorf says we can, for we would remain always imprisoned within the world view of our own language and would therefore be totally unable to grasp and fully work out an understanding of a radically different language. In particular, every attempt to translate the sentences of that language into our own would lead to a totally inadequate result. A translation of such languages would then either be false or would contradict the relativity thesis.

There is actually a serious difficulty here, but one which both Humboldt and Whorf have seen. Whorf writes as follows: "In order to describe the structure of the universe according to the Hopi, it is necessary to attempt – insofar as it is possible – to make explicit this metaphysics, properly describable only in the Hopi language, by means of an approximation expressed in our own language, somewhat inadequately it is true, yet by availing ourselves of such concepts as we have worked up into relative consonance with the system underlying the Hopi view of the universe."[15] And: "They [these abstractions] are not, as far as I can consciously avoid it, projections of other systems upon the Hopi language and culture made by me in my attempt at an objective analysis."[16]

This difficulty also becomes clear in all of Whorf's attempts to express in the English language the peculiar nature of the quite different Indian languages which are supposed to provide him with the primary examples in support of his thesis. Here the reader who does not know those languages actually has the feeling most of the time that they are matters of more or less superficial syntactical differences, but not basic differences of language form and interpretation of the world.

For example, when Whorf says that the Nootka do not have any knowledge of the subject-predicate structure, but can form sentences only out of sentences and then illustrates this claim by citing a Nootka sentence that means the same as 'He invites people to a feast' and reads in literal translation 'boil-ed-eat-ers-go-for-he-does', that is not at all convincing, since even in the literal translation what are being combined into a sentence are proper names and predicates.[17]

But the reason for this is that single examples are not sufficient to grasp the peculiar nature of a foreign language. For that a thorough study of the language, especially of its grammar, is indispensable. For a single linguistic phenomenon, a grammatical form or a word field, as Humboldt emphasized, should always be viewed against the background of the entire language and also against the background of the whole culture to which the language belongs and its world picture. Really very different languages can never be compared in their detail, in the structure of single sentences, but only as a whole.

But this difficulty does not imply any fundamental objection to the relativity thesis. For our language does not compel – as Whorf sometimes formulates it overly sharply – a conception of the world upon us, but suggests it to us and we are able – by learning a new, quite different language, for example – to open up other conceptions of the world and so come to know the relativity of our own conceptions.

The following objection weighs more heavily: A language's basic grammatical structures remain constant as it develops in an essentially higher degree than its vocabulary, and they survive for long periods of time, during which the culture, the apprehension of the world and the interpretation of reality often change radically. The influence of those linguistic structures on experience relates, then, either to quite fundamental components of the conception of the world, which remain invariant during the change in the culture – as Whorf does say – or it has only an indirect and limited effect, i.e. there are no unambiguously well-defined forms of interpretation corresponding to the grammatical forms.

The three examples we introduced above and with which Whorf wishes to confirm the role of grammar in experience, prove only such an indirect influence of grammar, for example. We have already seen above that in German [or English] substantives, adjectives or verbs can often be replaced by expressions belonging to other categories without any great shift in the statement's sense. Whether one says 'The leaves are yellowing' or 'The leaves are (are becoming) yellow', 'Fritz lives in Munich' or

'Fritz is a resident of Munich' does not make such a great difference that one could speak of diverse interpretations in this case. The fact is only that in most cases we have synonymous adjectives [or descriptive nouns] for the verbs and that there are always nuances of meaning in which the substitutions, where they are possible, differ. The efforts, by L. Weisgerber[18] for example, to catch these differences generally and exactly show, however, how hard it is to arrive at binding assertions here. What is to be said of the time concept is that our time concept nowadays is to a great extent that of physics, although we express it linguistically in forms in which the subjective aspect they originally contained is still clearly demonstrable. And the subject-predicate structure of such sentences as 'It is raining' does not mislead us into bringing a thing which performs an activity or in which a process is realized into the picture.

In addition, there is the following: Just as, when we consider vocabularies, comparing different word fields often makes for difficulties, because the semantic regions related to them do not coincide – we had brought that out above in Trier's example for the region of the intellect – so comparing grammatical forms of different languages makes for serious difficulties: If in doing so one starts out from syntactically determinate forms related by descent from a common origin, then one discovers that the same forms often have quite different semantic functions – as will become quite clear below in the case of the passive. On the other hand, if the set of forms is defined in terms of their semantic function, or of the *results* they effect, in Weisgerber's sense, then it will be trivial that semantically equivalent forms bring about the same result for the interpretation of experience. Grammatical forms, too, are to be analyzed in each case with the background of the whole language behind them. It is clear, then, that in some respects the functions of syntactically determinate forms are changed very much during the course of a language's development, just as the meaning of particular words can change. There is, then, no direct influence of syntactic forms on our experience, because the interpretation of them can shift, no more than there is an influence of syntactic word patterns on our experience. In the one case there is only the influence of the concepts as interpreted words and in the other there is only the influence of conceptual forms as interpreted grammatical forms. In particular, a considerable phase shift between the semantic and the syntactic change in these forms can come into play.

These critical remarks are no arguments against the relativity thesis itself; they only restrict it as against many of Whorf's assertions and point out the difficulties in proving it, as Humboldt had already seen, more clearly than Whorf.

Because this thesis has such an import and interest just for philosophy, we will discuss somewhat more extensively in what follows two cases of grammatical interpretation schemata that may be especially important for epistemology: the interpretation schema *active-passive* and the schema *subject-predicate*.

In discussing the interpretation schemata of active and passive sentences we shall draw upon the studies of L. Weisgerber.[19] Weisgerber begins with the fact that the range of forms of passive sentences encompasses significantly more than sentences with verbs constructed with passive endings. Along with the simple passive forms that can be constructed from transitive verbs of action especially, where the accusative object can appear without restriction as the subject in the related passive forms (as in 'I praise you' – 'You are praised by me'), within the range of the passive there are also active verbs that can be substituted for passive forms ('He was given a cuff on the ear' – 'He got a cuff on the ear', 'The bill was read' – 'The bill came to a reading', [and in German only] *'Der Ring wurde gefunden'* – *'Der Ring hat sich gefunden'*, *'Die Tür wurde geöffnet'* – *'Die Tür öffnete sich'*, and so on). Furthermore, the impersonal passive, which can be constructed with intransitive verbs as well (*'Fritz lacht'* – *'Es wird gelacht'*) is very close to the impersonal active (*'Es wird getanzt'* – *'Man tanzt'* ['A ballet is danced' – 'One dances a ballet'], *'Es wird über Apollo 13 gesprochen'* – *'Man spricht über Apollo 13'*, *'Es wird geklopft'* – *'Man klopft'*). The converse also holds: Where no 'one'-form ['*man*'-Form] of the active is possible, neither is an impersonal passive possible (neither *'Man blüht'* nor *'Es wird geblüht'*). Correspondingly, event verbs used only in the third person with a non-personal subject, such as 'happen', *'gelingen'*, *'misslingen'*, 'occur', 'take place', etc., do not form a passive either. Finally, we note in considering forms that not all transitive verbs form a passive, e.g. 'have', 'become', etc. [a number of examples from the German are omitted.]

If one now attempts to define the semantic function of the passive, the obvious interpretation on first glance – since we usually think first of all of transitive verbs of action in connection with the passive – is that the passive sentence is the converse in subject-object relationship of the active sentence, i.e. that the sentence 'Hans was struck by Fritz' has essentially the same content as 'Fritz struck Hans', only that the event was seen more from Hans' standpoint in the first case and more from Fritz's in the second.[20] J. Wackernagel says in this vein: "The passive has been correctly described as a linguistic luxury, because the passive sentence represents nothing but the converse of the normal active sentence."[21] But this interpretation, expressed in the designation 'passive', will not do justice to all of the linguistic data and grammatical facts that were pointed out above.

Weisgerber opposed to this conception the following account. On the whole, it is quite convincing: He distinguishes between two types of sentences: The first type interprets an event or state as the act of an agent-subject, as an occurrence brought about or supported by such a subject or as a state caused by him. In particular, those active sentences that have a definite personal or non-personal subject belong to this type, such as 'Fritz is laughing', 'Fritz is watching Hans', 'The ball rolls', etc. The second type does not interpret an event or state in this fashion, i.e. even where a definite subject or object is involved, it does not interpret it as agent-subject. Here is where impersonal active sentences such as 'It is raining', or 'One sings the Marseillaise', and active sentences such as 'A mishap occurred' or 'Fritz owns (has, gets) a bicycle', especially belong.

If sentences of the first sentence type are designated as *action sentences* and those of the second type as *action-free sentences*, then the action sentence is typical for Indogermanic. In German, action sentences predominate in a ratio of about 10:1, i.e. we have at our disposal many more linguistic forms for interpreting an event along the lines of an action event. Now in Weisgerber's view the passive, which was developed only relatively late in the various Indogermanic languages, is a form to compensate for this predominance of action sentences, a form for transforming action sentences into action-free sentences, so that the predominantly active stock of words can be used for expressing action-free sentences as well. For this reason the passive is constructed on such verbs as function in action sentences, and so on verbs of action especially, but not on forms that are only formally active, which do not express any action, such as 'happen', 'have', etc. Further, as a consequence the passive stands very close to the impersonal active sentences: '*Man lacht*' coincides in meaning

to a broad extent with '*Es wird gelacht*'. Weisgerber sees the transformation of an active sentence into a passive one in the following way: '*Fritz
lacht*' → '*Man lacht*' → '*Es wird gelacht*' [literally, 'Fritz is laughing →
→ 'One is laughing' → 'It is laughed'], ... etc. I.e., the definite agent-subject is eliminated and in the passive even that indefinite reference to an
agent-subject often still concealed in the word '*man*' ['one'] is set aside.[22]

In connection with sentences with transitive verbs the transition to
the passive is then to be understood as follows: '*Fritz schlägt Hans*' →
→ '*Man schlägt Hans*' → '*Hans wird von Fritz geschlagen*' [literally,
'Fritz strikes Hans' → 'One strikes Hans' → 'Hans is struck by Fritz'].
I.e. in this case one starts out from an event interpreted as an act of the
agent-subject Fritz directed at Hans, from there one goes to an agent-free
interpretation of the event, and from there to a specification of the event
as an event caused by Fritz. I.e. 'Fritz' functions in the passive sentence as
part of a specification of the circumstances (like 'stick' in 'Hans was struck
with a stick'). The addition of 'by Fritz' is only an adverbial supplement
to the sentence, then, which in citing a subject causing has the practical
effect of rescinding the elimination of the agent-subject that was achieved
by means of the passive. This interpretation shows how difficult it is to
understand the passive from this case, according to Weisgerber a typical
case of a passive sentence.

Now this interpretation of Weisgerber's has much in its favor, since
in particular it explains the near relationship between the active and the
passive impersonal construction and about covers the range of forms
sketched above. Of course the expressions 'action sentence' and 'action-
free sentence' certainly require still more extensive and careful definition.

What is the outcome of this study for the relativity thesis now? In the
active and the passive sentence – more generally, in the action sentence
and the action-free sentence – it points to two forms of interpretation of
our experience. These forms of interpretation are not entirely bound up
with the related linguistic forms, however, in such a way that whenever
we use an action sentence, for example, we assume a (human, animal
or superhuman) subject and interpret what happens as the act of that
subject. Thus we say 'The one ball bumps into the other' without regarding the ball as an active subject. But the language form nevertheless often
suggests such an interpretation. That is apparent, for example, in the
old way of talking in physics about the '*vis viva*', the 'live force' (kinetic

energy) within the first ball, with which it works on the second, or in the interpretation of biological phenomena by assuming an entelechy. To that extent the strong predominance of the world of active forms in Indogermanic generally is a clear indication of a world view clothed in linguistic tradition, according to which reality is represented predominantly as something going on that is dominated and determined by agent-subjects.

We said above that there can be a phase shift between linguistic forms and their interpretation, so that the forms of expression can lose their original meaning. Something of that sort is certainly true of action sentences insofar as they have no human or animal subjects, since nowadays we view the world more as passive, i.e. in the form of states and changes of state, than in the form of subject-determined events. That complicates the proof of a connection between language form and resulting interpretation very much and it is probably responsible for the fact that Weisgerber's account of the function of active and passive does not apply in many particular instances. On the whole and especially in historical perspective, however, that connection is very clear.

Weisgerber's distinctions become still clearer when we view them against the background of the language as a whole and the related world of ideas, in contrasting our language world with others. H. Hartmann in [54] has studied the range of passive forms in Celtic and Aryan languages, especially Irish, in which the passive is especially pronounced, and has placed them in relationship to the world picture and the religious ideas of the culture that stands behind these languages. In view of his observations, which are extraordinarily informative in their very detail, he too reaches the conclusion that the construction and use of passive forms for expressing facts that have only an active formulation in German is connected with the fact that the Indogermanic idea of the freely and autonomously active subject as the origin and bearer of an event withdraws behind the idea of man as a part of the cosmos, of a total cosmic power that works in him and through him.[23] That we have to do here with two different forms of interpretation of the event also becomes especially clear from the rules for applying active and passive in Irish. For example, Hartmann says this about the expression of following an order: "The passive... has a place only when someone finds himself under some compulsion and sees that he is forced to give way to it. If his obstinate rejection of the demand is supposed to be expressed nevertheless, or at least the freedom of his own decision is not wrested away from him entirely, then the active is used for this purpose." [24]

The subject-predicate schema our sentences have is the most general and consequently in Whorf's sense also the most powerful interpretation schema in our language.

By far the largest number of simple sentences in our language have the subject-predicate-(object-) structure, i.e. they consist of proper names, which stand for definite objects (be they concrete or abstract, things, persons or other subjects), and a predicate, which ascribes to these objects an attribute (be they qualities, relations, states, processes or actions). The objects are taken to be more or less enduring givens, which maintain their identity throughout their various momentary states, as their attributes change, things which subsist beneath the phenomena in which the event is realized and which function as bearers of the states.

We ordinarily interpret all events and facts along these lines in an object-attribute structure. That this interpretation is not self-evidently true, that we cannot naively project this predication schema into ontology, already becomes clear in the cases in which we use this linguistic form even though there can be no talk of identifiable objects. In this vein, we say, for example 'The wind is blowing', 'The sky is blue', 'The ocean roars', 'The rain is falling', 'His will is inflexible', 'His sorrow is profound', etc.

Besides that, in verbs used impersonally we have a means of representing what happens in a way other than the object-attribute form: The sentences: 'It is raining', 'It is freezing', 'It is windy', '*Es klopft*', '*Es wird getanzt*', '*Es wird gepflügt*', etc., have, to be sure, a subject-predicate structure in terms of formal grammar, but it is quite clear in these cases that the pronoun 'it' ['*Es*'] does not stand for a definite object, that we cannot interpret these sentences as statements about objects. In the case of sentences with impersonal verbs it makes no sense to ask after something that supports what happens: 'Who is raining?'. 'What is freezing?'; and that is equally true of the sentences 'It is windy', 'It is cold', in which the adjectives are used impersonally. In the case of the other sentences it does of course make sense to ask about a subject ('*Wer klopft?*') ['Who knocks?'], '*Wer tanzt?*' ['Who is dancing?'], '*Wer pflügt?*' ['Who is plowing?'], but it is not a question of existence sentences ('There is some-one who knocks' etc.); on the contrary, the addition of a subject acting would have the character of an adverbial supplementation here: In the sentence '*Es klopft*' an event is depicted in which there is no mention of persons or things, and that event is more closely described by citing the agent, when one says, for example, '*Es wird geklopft von Fritz*'.[25]

The possibility of forming impersonal sentences shows that not every-thing that happens has to be interpreted in terms of the object-attribute schema. The fact that we make only relatively infrequent use of this pos-sibility, that formally speaking even impersonal sentences have the sub-ject-predicate-(object-) structure and that we use substantives even where we are not concerned with identifiable objects proves how overpowering that interpretation is.

We have seen above that Whorf assumes predication in this sense to be unknown to the Nootka language. That would be very significant further evidence that the object-attribute schema has to do with a form of interpretation but not with a pre-existent ontological structure.[26] Still, since Whorf's claim can only be tested and rendered precise by someone who has a mastery of that language, we will reflect a bit on how a simple language that has no subject-predicate-(object-) structure might look.

The basic units of this descriptive language – let us call it T – which we are supposed to be able to use for communication just as well as our own language – let us call it S – are simple declarative sentences. Now while such sentences are analyzed in S into proper names and predicates, and so have the logical form $F(a)$, $G(a, b)$, or $H(a, b, c)$, for example, that analysis is not supposed to be possible in T. In terms of content, then, the sentences of T would correspond to impersonal sentences of S and so say, e.g., 'It is raining', '*Es wird gegessen*', '*Es wird gekämpft*', 'It is cold', etc.

But now it is not the case that a sentence constant of T can simply be coordinated with every simple sentence of S, otherwise special basic constants would have to be introduced for all of the facts that can be represented in S in the form $F(a)$, $F(b)$, ... or as $G(a, b)$, $G(b, a)$, ..., so that T would be much too uneconomical. Where S, for example, gets along with five constants for expressing the 64 sentences that can be con-structed with one three-place predicate constant and four object constants, T would require 64 to do that.

But if we let sentence constants of T correspond to predicate constants of S, in such a way, say, that to a predicate constant $F(x)$ there corresponds in T a sentence with the content 'There is something F-ish there', or 'F-ness is here' – so that to 'is red', for example, there corresponds 'Redness occurs', to the predicate '*lacht*' the sentence '*Es wird gelacht*' – and if we let sentence constants of T correspond to object constants of S, such that a sentence with the content 'a participates' (is present), corresponds to the object constant 'a', then simple sentences in S of the form 'a has the property F' can be translated into 'F-ness is present and a participates'. To be sure, conjunction must be understood in a stronger sense than that of sentential logic, so that the sentences bound up together by this 'and' express specific accounts of the same fact.[27]

In this fashion the simple sentences of S with n constants in the form cited can be represented by sentences in T with the same number of constants.

It becomes more difficult when we consider sentences with polyadic predicates in S, e.g. the sentence $F(a, b)$, which could mean the same, say, as 'Fritz hits Hans'. Since conjunction is commutative, one can not simply construct in its place in T the sentence 'There is hitting and Fritz participates and Hans participates'. Instead, in this case we must distinguish between the subject and the object of the event, e.g. divide the sentence 'a participates' into 'a participates actively' and 'a participates passively' and then say 'There is hitting and Fritz participates actively and Hans participates passively'.

The inferiority of language T in comparison with S is already becoming clear at this point. It becomes still more so when instrumental participation, etc., is also introduced.

Sentences that express quantifications can then be introduced, too, for example, 'All participate' or 'Some participate' and so analogies to simple sentences of predicate logic can be constructed. Constructing analogues in T to multiply quantified sentences in S, on the other hand, would create great difficulties. S is thus considerably richer expressively than is T, in which sentences consist of combinations of elementary sentences.

The language of set theory, on the other hand, is an example of a language not inferior to S in wealth of expression and in which there are no predicate constants, but only object constants and logical operators, in which one might say, then, a different form of interpretation is expressed than in S. The disadvantage of such linguistic constructions naturally lies in the fact that we still interpret them with the assistance of our own language, so that they can not lend support to the thesis that other kinds of grammatical forms often express a different sort of interpretation. They may be suited, however, to make somewhat clearer the possibility of such other kinds of interpretation forms and to get a better view of the distinctive character of the predication schema and what it does.

In the case of the subject-predicate-(object-) structure of sentences, the role of language in experience consists in the fact that with language we learn to systematize and represent our experiences in the schema object-attribute. Thus we learn, for example, to describe a fact as 'The rose is red', and not as 'The redness roses', or 'Redness is present and the rose participates in it'. Such descriptions would imply an entirely different systematization of phenomena, an entirely different ontology. By virtue of the fact that there is available a certain stock of linguistic expressions and forms that serve one particular interpretation and ordering of the phenomena, that simple and stereotyped expressions and forms for other interpretations are not available, language establishes the shape and form of our apprehension and interpretation of what is experienced, within a certain compass. For so long as we get along with the linguistic instruments available, there is no reason for us to look around for new instruments. A modification of the basic forms of our language would carry with it such far-reaching consequences for our conceptual apparatus and our beliefs about the world that it would be something to be realized only after a long look and only by the linguistic community as a whole.

On this basis, the object-attribute schema, stand our logic and our concept and theory construction in the sciences. To that extent it is not an exaggeration to say that e.g. our mathematics and natural science and with them our world picture that bears the imprint of natural science have this basic linguistic foundation as their presupposition. In this vein Whorf says: "Thus the world view of modern science arises by higher specialization of the basic grammar of the Western Indo-European languages. Science of course was not caused by this grammar; it was simply colored by it." [28]

To be sure this linguistic basis is itself modified: Our logical conceptions once again shape our understanding of our language. Logical grammar is not our language's 'natural' grammar, but nevertheless it rests upon the same predication schema that is basic to it as well.

NOTES

[1] Whorf [56], p. 211.

[2] Whorf [56], p. 221.

[3] This claim of Whorf's does not quite fit his other statements, of course, which say that all sentential components in these languages are sentences themselves, combined by sentential operators (as sentence suffixes).

[4] See Whorf [56], p. 215f.

[5] See Whorf [56], p. 141f.

[6] Take account, say, of the Platonic theory of Ideas, in which what corresponds to the shift from adjective to substantive is a shift from an attribute to an object, the Idea.

[7] See also Wittgenstein's statements about time in [53], 90, as well as Waismann's amusing remarks in [56], p. 348ff. – Wittgenstein's battle against the 'bewitchment of our intelligence by our language' is definitely also a struggle against the naive conception of language that projects the surface structures of grammar onto reality without further thought.

[8] Whorf [56], p. 57.

[9] Whorf [56], p. 59.

[10] See also Weisgerber [62], V. II, p. 327, as well as note 30 to Chapter III.2.

[11] Whorf [56], p. 253. On this point see also p. 41f. and 213f.

[12] See Black [59], p. 231 and 236f.

[13] See Whorf [56], p. 253f., 262.

[14] See Whorf [56], p. 241f. on this, as well as what is said about the sentence structure of Japanese in P. Hartmann [52] and Weisgerber [62], V. II, p. 353f.

[15] Whorf [56], p. 58.

[16] Whorf [56], p. 59. – See also Fearing [54], p. 53ff., as well as Köhler [37].

[17] See Whorf [56], p. 241f.

[18] See e.g. Weisgerber [62], V. II, p. 300ff. – See also Snell [52], P. Hartmann [56] and Brinkmann [50].

[19] See Weisgerber [63b] and [63a], p. 232ff.

[20] That would then correspond to another topicalisation, i.e. to another division of the state of affairs into *topic* and *comment*, into object and something said about that object.

[21] Wackernagel [24], V. I, p. 135.

[22] Along similar lines H. Hartmann says: "If the person involved in the action is unknown or unimportant or for some special reason is kept in the background, then the passive comes into the picture; on the other hand, if someone in the present or the past is being described as active or as having an effect, then as a rule we make use of the active form." ([54], p. 12)

[23] See H. Hartmann [54], pp. 33, 39 and 62.

[24] H. Hartmann [54], p. 29.

[25] The 'one [*man*]' in impersonal sentences can also be often understood as the existential or as the universal quantifier, to be sure.

[26] P. Hartmann has called attention to a language type in Japanese as in other East Asian languages in which sentences do not have any subject-predicate structure. He calls these languages 'referring [*referierende*]' and says: "Event designation is always the main content of the Japanese sentence. As such, it is what appears as the only sentence component in the nominative representation. All other members of the sentence can be looked upon as attributes of this event designation." ([52], p. 96) I.e. mention of the subject, like mention of the object is an expendable supplement to the

simple sentence as a pure event sentence. This 'subjectlessness [*Subjektlosigkeit*]', perhaps better: this secondary role of the subject, is a property of all East Asian languages, according to Hartmann. The English sentence 'The man sees the mountain' takes, for example, the form in Japanese of 'the man's the-mountain-seeing', where 'seeing' (in the sense of 'there is seeing') is the event designation, which can also stand by itself. This event is first supplementarily described as a 'mountain-seeing' ('A mountain is seen') and then as a mountain-seeing by the man ('A mountain is seen by the man'). (See [52], p. 23.) – For Hartmann a different sort of world view is expressed by this different sort of sentence construction.

27 The English 'and' [German '*und*'], as against the logical conjunction, also includes a relationship of content or an affinity between the sentences connected.

28 Whorf [56], p. 221.

4. THE EPISTEMOLOGICAL PROBLEMATIC OF
THE RELATIVITY THESIS

So far in this chapter we have discussed the thesis as to the role of language in experience primarily in terms of the formulations and arguments laid out for it in the general theory of language. We will now place this thesis within our specifically philosophical discussion of the problem of meaning and discuss its relevance to epistemology.

The relativity thesis can be divided into two claims:

(1) There is a correlation between language and world view of such a kind that typical and profound differences in world view correspond to typical and profound differences in linguistic forms.

(2) The world view depends on the language; the forms of interpreting experience are imparted by language.

While the second claim says that the language we speak influences the forms of our experience, and so implies an effect of language on experience, the first claim says only that there are correspondences between linguistic forms and forms of world view, without stating whether the former is determined by the latter or the latter by the former. The first claim is weaker than the second, for there can be a correlation between language and world view not based upon any influence of language on experience; but one can not assume that language has that sort of influence if there are no distinct differences in experience corresponding to even typical and profound differences in linguistic forms. Only the second claim expresses the full content of the relativity thesis as Humboldt, Whorf and Sapir understood it.

The empirical work of comparative studies of language and of the history of language initially discloses nothing but correlations between forms of language and forms of experience. In order to establish an influence above and beyond that, one can either bring to bear empirical-psychological studies that show, for example, that certain forms of experience depend on linguistic parameters and how they do[1], or one can rely on studies in the philosophy of language. Such arguments from the philosophy of language emerge directly out of the discussion of Wittgenstein's ideas in the 'Philosophical Investigations' in Chapter II.4. And a way of founding the relativity thesis on the philosophy of language is to be expected only within the confines of a pragmatic theory of meaning with a Wittgensteinian stamp.

From the standpoint of realistic semantics what one would say is this: If words and grammatical forms become meaningful by our assigning to them as their meanings objects, concepts or propositions that are independent of language, then the thesis of the role of language in experience is false. It is false in a trivial way if what we understand by language are only the vocal or written linguistic expressions, for these expressions surely have no influence on our experience by themselves. Nor can an influence of a purely syntactical character ever be maintained, it can never be anything but an influence exerted by an interpreted meaningful language. But on the realistic understanding a meaningful expression is an expression for an entity independent of language. So even if one does not take concepts and propositions to be 'objectively real' attributes and facts occurring in the world, and experience to be a true copy of reality in consciousness, but rather understands them in conceptualist terms as ways of interpreting, still the linguistic expressions do not determine those ways of interpreting. On the contrary, they are defined as meaningful expressions only in terms of them, as expressions of these ways of interpreting. First there are the ways of interpreting and then the words and sentences explicated through them. There is then no influence of a sign on what is signified.

If the realistic premises of this argument are accepted, one will not be able to say very much in the way of objection to it.

The thesis that language plays a part in experience has its place only within the confines of pragmatic meaning theory. Indeed it has already become clear from the quotations cited in IV.1 from Humboldt, Sapir and Whorf that they advocate a pragmatic theory of meaning,[2] and that with them the relativity thesis grows out of that theory of meaning. Only if the linguistic apparatus is regarded as not just a way of expressing forms of interpretation, but as defining those forms in the first place, if we learn the differentiations and specifications in terms of which we articulate what is experienced, and if language is a means of bringing order into the world, does it make sense to say that our ways of conceiving and apprehending are shaped by our language and that different languages can represent different ways of interpreting [the world]. The pragmatic theory of meaning, however, not only provides the conditions under which the relativity thesis can be accepted, but with its doctrine of the mediation of conceptual determinations by language it even implies that thesis. That there are languages to which distinctly or quite fundamentally different ways of interpretation correspond, that the differences that hold among languages are thus not all insignificant for our world view and that the relativity thesis has something more than just theoretical significance in principle, is to be proved separately, to be sure, and doing that requires the empirical work of comparative linguistics.

Now the relativity thesis raises a series of epistemological problems, which we will discuss in what follows. Since the thesis follows from the pragmatic theory of meaning, these problems also have to do with that theory.

Realistic semantics, as a theory of the assignment of objects, concepts and propositions to linguistic expressions, entails no epistemological problematic of its own. For the assignments have a conventional character; there are no objectively correct assignments that could possibly be hidden from us; the assignments have no influence on what is assigned and it is presupposed of the entities to be assigned that they antecedently exist. The question as to which ontological status these entities have, whether they belong to a world 'an sich', i.e. independent of our knowledge, the physical world of concrete things or an ideal sphere of abstract concepts, classes and the like, such as Platonism assumes, or whether it is a matter of things constructed by the intellect, understood conceptually, or of ideas, and of how these entities are known, is not of great significance for the basic ideas of realistic semantics itself.

We became acquainted in II.1.3 with Wittgenstein's semantics in the *Tractatus* as an example of a realistic theory. But Wittgenstein also developed in the *Tractatus* an epistemological position which gave E. Stenius occasion to speak of a *transcendental-linguistic* approach, of an analogy in philosophy of language to Kant's transcendental philosophy in the '*Critique of Pure Reason*'.[3] We want to reflect, therefore, on whether there is not after all some question of an epistemological problematic that concerns realistic semantics in general.

Wittgenstein depends on the picture theory of language, which we discussed in II.1.3, as the support for his statements on epistemology. We saw there, by way of a quotation from his letter to Bertrand Russell dated August 8, 1919, that his semantic theory serves him only as a foundation for his central concern in the *Tractatus*, his distinction between what can be said by means of sentences and what can only be shown. What can be *said* or *represented* by a sentence is the fact, which a (true) sentence pictures by virtue of its structure and the isomorphy correlation. What on the contrary can not be represented by sentences are e.g. the correspondences between the syntactic structure of the sentence and the ontological structure of the facts pictured. These structures and correspondences are *shown* in the sentence, but they can not be represented by it, for knowledge of these structures and correlations is the presupposition of our understanding language at all.[4] But what is a presupposition of all understanding of language can not be explicated by means of language. Someone who does not yet know English cannot learn the language from the Oxford Dictionary, and no more can anyone say by means of a sentence, which according to the picture theory has to be grasped as a fact itself, and which means a fact, what a fact is. It is to no avail in this connection to switch to a metalanguage wherein the sentences can represent the way in which the sentences in the object language function, for the metalanguage, just as much as the object language and any other language, would have to presuppose the ontology and the picturing function, but could not communicate them. When we speak, we are always 'inside the language' and we can not somehow observe it from the outside.[5]

For Wittgenstein it follows from this that the statements in the *Tractatus* that are concerned with the ontological structure of reality are also senseless, because they attempt to say what cannot be said. But that does not make them valueless, for they are illuminating and help us see what can not be said: "My propositions are illuminating by virtue of the fact that anyone who understands me knows at the end that they are nonsensical, when by means of them – on them – he has climbed on beyond them. (He must throw the ladder away, as it were, after he has climbed up it) – he must surmount these propositions, and then he will see the world correctly."[6]

With the radicality so distinctive of him, Wittgenstein then draws the conclusion that a philosophy as a system of theoretical propositions about the ontological structures of reality and the basic forms of language is not possible. Even in the *Tractatus* philosophy for him is not a theoretical science, but has only maieutic and therapeutic functions.[7]

Philosophy, in particular the philosophy of language, is naturally not a natural science, as behaviorism, for example, intends.[8] It does not impart to us totally new facts about language, it does not intend to understand language for the first time by means of language, but it does intend to analyze systematically the antecedent understanding of language (that aids us in understanding its own statements as well), so that we can better comprehend the way in which the language functions. But that its limits are drawn so narrowly as Wittgenstein says, with his reference point the semantic picture theory of the *Tractatus* cannot be maintained in the face of the fact that this picture theory is a much too restricted theory and even when limited to simple descriptive sentences a thoroughly dubious one.

Wittgenstein's theses are statements about the limits of language's capacity for successful representation. That the world is as we judge it to be in language, or as it turns out to be in our statements, Wittgenstein does not doubt. When he says: "The limits of my language indicate the limits of my world," [9] he does not mean to suggest that the world is always mediated through language and that for that reason it would make no sense to speak of the world as it already is prior to any conceptual-linguistic specification. Just as for Kant the *a priori* concepts [*Verstandesbegriffe*] refer exclusively to possible experience and cannot be applied beyond experience (in rational metaphysics, for example: in rational psychology, cosmology or theology as it is represented in the transcendental dialectic) so for Wittgenstein the representational function of language relates only to empirical facts. To that extent the analogy holds. But it does not go so far that language also has a role in the limits of its applicability, as Kant assumes there is a part played by reason in experience. At the limits of its applicability language has according to Wittgenstein a purely pictorial function, so that the title 'transcendental lingualism' is not quite adequate for his position in the *Tractatus*.

The question as to the extent in which we can describe the way language functions with linguistic means is not, as we have seen in section 2.4.3, just a problem that applies to realistic semantics in particular, however. Beyond that, Wittgenstein's statements about the limits of language can be separated from the realistic semantics of the *Tractatus* as well. What Wittgenstein intends by the proposition cited above, "The limits of my language indicate the limits of my world", as the explanation that follows in the *Tractatus* shows, is that in a language one can never speak of the things that belong to the ontology of that language, that the only questions about existence it makes sense to formulate in it are, as Carnap formulated it later, *internal,* but not *external* ones.[10] But that is equally true, as we shall see below, of the pragmatic conception of language, indeed it is true in a still stronger sense because of the correlation between language and world view.

That pragmatic theories of meaning, as compared with realistic, imply a distinctive and inseparable epistemological component has already become clear in the discussions in the second chapter. There are already epistemological considerations with which pragmatic criticism attacks the presuppositions of the realistic semantics, when it urges that concepts can not be indicated, differentiated or defined without using predicates and that there is no 'knowledge' of concepts not mediated by language. But the relativity thesis points out the most important problematic for these theories of meaning: If language is not only a means for the *expression* of properties, distinctions and facts discovered beforehand, but *defines* them, then one cannot say that the world, i.e. the concrete things, states, processes, etc., are determinate in and of themselves [*an sich*], and so prior to having been established by language in any way. Nor can we say that we express their antecedent determinateness more or less correctly in our statements about them. On the contrary, nothing like a determinate world ever comes to be except by way of linguistic interpretation, the world is always mediated by language.

Thus the thesis of the part played by language in experience parallels Kant's transcendental-philosophical thesis of the role played by reason in experience: As for Kant, experience arises out of an indefinite 'welter of sensations' only through the application of the categories of the understanding and the world as it is in itself remains unknowable in principle, so experience here comes to be only through the application of language and its categories and statements about the 'objective' world in itself, i.e. not mediated through linguistic interpretation have no sense.

But while for Kant the concepts of the understanding pertain to a reason as organized universally among all human beings, so that experiential knowledge is at least intersubjectively valid, according to the relativity thesis there are fundamentally different, but in principle equally correct forms of experiential knowledge.

The thesis of the role played by language in experience implies, then, a still more radical relativization of our knowledge than Kant's thesis of the role of reason in experience.

The relativity thesis immediately takes on the color of the remarkable and unusual: The real world on which our knowledge is always directed so far as its intention is concerned does not exist at all; our knowledge is under the dominion of our language and never shows us anything except what the forms of that language permit; there is no correct world picture, but only various equally warranted world pictures belonging to various languages. So the relativity thesis appears to be a fundamentally skeptical thesis.

But those are all false or misleading formulations:

(1) In the first place, we urged in II.4.5 that even from the pragmatic point of view language cannot be conceived as a game played with expressions, but must be understood as a system of speech acts. That a game played with expressions should determine our knowledge would in fact be remarkable and unusual. Not at all remarkable and unusual, on the other hand, is the close connection between speech acts and experiences. Speech activities encompass very much more than utterances of words. Declaratives are speech acts, because we can only make them within linguistic forms. But making a declaration does not consist just in the utterance of words, but encompasses all of the features we take on when we know and judge. So it does not make sense to look upon speech acts and acts of determining something of a cognitive character as two acts independent of each other; they form a unity within which determining something cognitively, i.e. judging, is always realized in language and within which when we are asserting declarative sentences we are always judging. There is then nothing astonishing in saying that we can never make judgments except by means of (linguistic) declaratives and that therefore the possibilities of making judgments (in language) define our possibilities of knowledge. Only when language is looked upon as merely an instrument of expression, when language is freed from its close interrelationship with our whole behavior and knowledge, does the relativity thesis become dubious.

The non-trivial character of this thesis resides solely in how closely, (in contrast to the so very natural semantic realism that is stressed in the ordinary understanding of language) speaking and apprehending, describing, proving are bound up with each other; that we learn these activities, as speech acts, only along with language; that there is a cultural tradition hidden within what we learn there and how we learn it; that knowledge is not a passive acceptance of distinctions antecedently given, but an active exercise of an art that is learned; that the picture we make of the world is the product of a cultural accomplishment in which language plays an important part.

Along these lines, Johann Gottfried Herder in his *Abhandlung über den Ursprung der Sprache* [91] explicitly conceives language and reason to be a unity and the condition of the possibility of all specifically human cultural accomplishments, and he adopts therefore the Aristotelian definition of man as a ζῷον λόγον ἔχον.[11] It is on the horizon of precisely this understanding of language that the formula of the world mediated by language has its place.

(2) Further, we have already urged in Chapter IV.2 that two aspects must be distinguished in speaking of a 'dominion language has over our knowledge': A culture forms its language together with its understanding of the world in the course of its encounter with its environment. There is surely no dominion of language over knowledge here, then, but rather, on the large view, a unity of language formation and the cognitive process. The individual, however, receives the languages he uses from the culture he belongs to. When he makes a picture of the world for himself, he is in every respect subject to a determinative influence. Again, however, this influence is not language as an isolated system of signs but the *whole cultural tradition*, into which language is intimately woven. Furthermore, this influence, so far as knowledge is concerned, consists not so much in a system of restrictions as in a system of contrivances placed at the individual's disposal to help him to know. Nothing hinders him from adding new devices or modifying the old. The limits he confronts in acquiring a language are not so very much restraints that are forced upon him, but lie rather in the limited number of possibilities that are offered him and – this must of course be added – in the difficulty of creating new possibilities himself.

(3) If there is talk of language determining experience, that is not to be understood as meaning that language determines what we experience. To begin with, what language places at our disposal is only the concepts, as descriptive resources for empirical observations, the predicate 'red', for example, for distinguishing between red and non-red things. Whether a specific object is red or not is then a matter of observation and is not prejudiced by language. In a way, then, language is only a net of coordi-

nates for specifying the position of a point, a net which does not yet fix the point's coordinates, but first makes it possible to specify them.

One can also say that language does settle the validity of some propositions, the analytic propositions. Even if the boundary between analytic and synthetic is not a sharp one, as we discussed that point in Chapter II.3.2, there is nevertheless a large set of unambiguously synthetic sentences, and language says nothing at all about their truth.

Furthermore, language is made for the analysis and systematization of experiences and the natural languages are such as have proved themselves equal to that task. The languages are somewhat like systems of tools that have proved useful in working some material. Thus they were not free inventions, but were tested, and to that extent experience also determines language, as the material determines the choice of tools. For example, not every conceptual system is equally suited for the formulation of simple law statements with a high degree of generality. So the introduction of fruitful concepts into the sciences signifies an important accomplishment and that accomplishment is confirmed empirically by the fact that we are successful in giving a simple formulation to a large number of lawlike connections by means of those concepts.[12]

Of course it is not only the material that determines the choice of tools, but also the purpose of working on the material. And in the same way, what has been called somewhat vaguely, but impressively 'the will of the culture [*Kulturwollen*]', in particular the cognitive intent and interest, also determines the choice of language form, and so there are even entirely different languages for working on the same 'materials of experience'.

(4) The relativity thesis is not a negative existential thesis with the content that there is no one true reality or reality *an sich*.

Every 'There is' – or 'There is no' – statement makes sense only within the boundaries of the language to which it belongs, and its meaning is defined within the whole system of that language. For every descriptive language, as a language with which we speak about something, there is an ontology, i.e. a totality of objects, properties, descriptions, and facts we use the language to speak about. Whether this ontology is viewed as independent of language within the realistic understanding of language or along pragmatic lines as mediated by language plays no role in this connection. The understanding of this language always relates to this ontology. It does not make sense, therefore, to deny the existence of the objects presupposed within the language, or to assert the existence of objects that do not belong to this ontology.

For purposes of illustration and clarification, two examples:

(a) The declarative sentence '*a* does not exist' – in symbols $\neg \bigvee x(x=a)$ – is trivially false or meaningless. For if '*a*' is a name, then there is an object *a* that it designates, and the statement is then (analytically) false; or if '*a*' is not a name, then it is meaningless.[13]

(b) In constructing a language of predicate logic, one grounds the interpretation of it in a non-empty domain of objects γ as the set of all objects one can talk about in this language. A sentence of the form 'There is an *F*' is then interpreted to mean that there is an object in γ with the property *F*. The sentences 'There are no objects in γ' and 'There is an object that is not contained in γ' are then trivially false as sentences in this language. If you are convinced that γ is empty or if you wish to speak of objects that are not contained in γ, then you must just choose a new language.[14] The only existential sentences that are informative concern the distinctions within the ontology of the language, i.e. sentences of the form 'There is an *F*', where '*F*' is a predicate defined on γ, but not one which defines γ.[15] In Wittgenstein's words: The language defines the limits of the range of objects of which we can make meaningful statements in it.

J. L. Austin's statements in [62b], Chapter 7, are aimed in the same direction. According to them, 'real' is not a predicate with which we can sketch out an ontology but serves to make descriptive distinctions that differ from case to case within the confines of an ontology. Thus we distinguish 'real' friends from pretended or untrustworthy friends, 'real' illnesses from imaginary, and so on. A use of this word in the context 'real world', 'really existing object', on the other hand, is not defined.[16]

There stands behind these arguments the simple fact that we can never make statements with the content that something has such and such a character except in a particular language, and that we are thereby presupposing in using the language an ontology that we cannot meaningfully call into question within that language. Of what lies beyond the limits of a language, what cannot be said in it, we cannot speak in it. We cannot even say in it that there is something beyond those limits. It does not follow from our understanding that for every language there are limits of what can be said in it that there is something that cannot be said in it. That can only be shown, by saying something in another language that cannot be translated into the first. That there is something that lies beyond all bounds of linguistic possibility, something that cannot be said at all, cannot be shown, then.

All that does not mean that there is for us only the 'bespoken' world, as represented in our language, but no 'real' world. 'Real' and 'bespoken' are superfluous epithets: The world in which we live and act is for us the 'real' world, if that word is supposed to have any meaning at all – there is none more real. And this is the world we talk about, for language is part of our life and action.

Again the relativity thesis reduces to a very simple statement, then: Our knowledge, in the stronger sense in which, for example, it is different in type from the experience of animals, is a matter of conceiving, grasping in language. For that reason, there is no knowledge beyond the limits of language. As far as my knowledge will reach, so far will my language reach, too; wherever there is something to be known, it is also to be grasped in language. The significance of this simple statement here again lies only in the fact that we are not permitted to distinguish the world antecedently given and language as an instrument for describing it. Instead we must always see that the world conceived, known and spoken of is always a world disclosed to us with the cognitive instruments of knowledge, and represents the outcome of a cultural process and accomplishment.

(5) The relativity thesis is no skeptical thesis. If it is said that for us 'reality' always coincides with the ontology of our language, it does not follow that we are shut up in our language as in a cage and are incapable of knowing what can not be said in it, or that 'reality in itself' is hidden from our view.

We have already insisted: Language is an open system, so far as our knowledge will reach, our language will also reach. And the statement that there is a reality we cannot comprehend in terms of language is not only just as unprovable as the old principle of skepticism 'There is no certain knowledge' (in order to prove that proposition, one would definitely have to know for certain that it is true), but downright meaningless. It was already shown why a sentence in language S: 'There are objects of which one can not speak in S' is meaningless. Wittgenstein has this to say along these lines in the *Tractatus*: 'Skepticism is *not* irrefutable, but obviously nonsensical, when it chooses to doubt where no question can be raised. For there can be doubt only where there is a question; a question, only where there is an answer; and that, only where something *can* be *said*.' 17

If there are different languages with different ontologies, what does emerge from that fact is a relativism, but no skepticism. One cannot say: There can be only one correct ontology, but which one is correct we are incapable of deciding, for all of them represent interpretations that are possible, i.e. compatible with experience. Only sentences are true or false in this sense, not conceptual systems. We must add to the conceptual systems, then, the basic assumptions that are formulated in terms of those concepts, and so look on different world views as theories. Theories formulated in quite different languages can stand all alongside each other without our being able to say that the correctness of the one excludes the other's being correct. In this sense, then, relativism does not imply any skeptical component with the content: only *one* world view can be correct, but we do not know which.

NOTES

1 See e.g. the work by Brown and Lenneberg [54] discussed in Chapter IV.2.

2 The appelation 'pragmatic theory of meaning' is of course not quite suitable especially for Humboldt's ideas, since he never identified meaning and use – for him meanings belong to an ideal mental sphere – but what decides the matter in this case is that linguistic expressions are not viewed as signs for communicating pre-existent objects, but the objects are mediated only by way of language.

3 On the following, see the discussions in Stenius [60], Chapter XI, as well as the presentation in Stegmüller [65], Chapter XI, I, 4.

4 See Wittgenstein [22], 4.12ff.

5 According to Wittgenstein the like is also true of the meanings of expressions. Thus Wittgenstein says: "The identity of meaning of two expressions is not something about which a *claim* can be made. For in order to make some claim about their meaning, I must be cognizant of [*kennen*] their meaning; and in that I am cognizant of their meaning, I know that they mean the same or different things." ([22], 6.2322). See also [22], 3.262.

6 Wittgenstein [22], 6.54.

7 See Wittgenstein [22], 4.111, 4.112 and 4.003.

8 See Wittgenstein [22], 4.111 and 4.112.

9 Wittgenstein [22], 5.6.

10 See Carnap [50].

11 See Aristotle, *Politics* A, 1253a10.

12 On this point see what Hempel has to say about the *systematic import* of concepts in [65a].

13 We have pointed out in Chapter III.2.1.2 how it is possible in a language like *L* to

speak of things that are regarded as non-existent. If a distinction is made between the set U of possible objects and the set U' of existing objects, then the sentence 'a does not exist' can be formulated either as '$\neg \bigvee x(x=a)$' in the sense of 'a is not a possible object' or as '$\neg \bigvee .x(x=a)$' in the sense of 'a is not a real object'. In either case the object a has to belong to the ontology of L, i.e. to the set U, or U'.

[14] 'Language' always means 'interpreted language' in this connection. Naturally it is also possible to interpret the expressions of a language as a syntactic system concerning a different domain of objects.

[15] On this point see R. Carnap's remarks in [50].

[16] See also Savigny [69], p. 233ff.

[17] Wittgenstein [22], 6.5.1.

BIBLIOGRAPHY

Abraham, S. and Kiefer, F. [66]: *A Theory of Structural Semantics*, The Hague 1966.

Alston, W. P. [63a]: 'Meaning and Use', *Philosophical Quarterly* 13 (1963), 107–124; reprinted in Parkinson [68].

Alston, W. P. [63b]: 'The Quest for Meanings', *Mind* 72 (1963), 79–87.

Alston, W. P. [67]: *Philosophy of Language*, in Edwards [67], Vol. IV, pp. 386–390.

Antal, L. [61]: 'Sign, Meaning, Context', *Lingua* 10 (1961), 211–219.

Arnauld, A. and Lancelot, C. [60]: *Grammaire générale et raisonnée* (The Grammar of Port Royal), Paris 1660. Edited by H. Brekle, 2 Vols., Stuttgart 1966.

Austin, J. L. [61]: *Philosophical Papers*, Oxford 1961.

Austin, J. L. [62a]: *How to Do Things with Words*, Cambridge/Mass. 1962.

Austin, J. L. [62b]: *Sense and Sensibilia* (ed. by G. J. Warnock), Oxford 1962.

Ayer, A. J. [63]: *The Concept of a Person and Other Essays*, London 1963.

Ayer, A. J. (ed.) [59]: *Logical Positivism*, New York 1959.

Bach, E. and Harms, R. T. (eds.) [68a]: *Universals in Linguistic Theory*, New York 1968.

Bach, E. [68b]: 'Nouns and Noun Phrases', in Bach [68a], pp. 91–122.

Bacon, R. [57]: *The Works of Francis Bacon*, edited by Spedding, Ellis and Heath, London 1857–1874.

Bacon, F. [69]: *Grammatica Graeca*, Oxford Manuscripts (ed. by E. Charles), 1869.

Bambrough, R. [60]: 'Universals and Family Resemblances', *Proceedings of the Aristotelian Society* 61 (1960/61), 2–22; reprinted in Pitcher [66].

Bar-Hillel, Y. [50]: 'On Syntactical Categories', *Journal of Symbolic Logic* 15 (1950), 1–16.

Bar-Hillel, Y. [53]: 'A Quasi-Arithmetical Notation for Syntactic Description', *Language* 29 (1953), 47–58.

Bar-Hillel, Y. [70]: *Aspects of Language*, Jerusalem 1970.

Bar-Hillel, Y. and Shamir, E. [60a]: 'Finite-State Languages: Formal Representation and Adequacy Problems', *The Bulletin of the Research Council of Israel*, 8F, No. 3 (1960), 155–166.

Bar-Hillel, Y., Gaifman, C., and Shamir, E. [60b]: 'On Categorical and Phrase Structure Grammars', *The Bulletin of the Research Council of Israel*, 9F, No. 3 (1960), 1–16.

Basilius, H. [52]: 'Neo-Humboldtian Ethnolinguistics', *Word* 8 (1952), 95–105.

Becker, K. F. [42]: *Ausführliche deutsche Grammatik*, Vol. I, Prague 1842.

Beckmann, G. A. [63]: 'Die Nachfolgekonstruktionen des lateinischen Instrumentalis in den romanischen Sprachen', *Beihefte zur Zeitschrift für romanische Philologie*, Tübingen 1963.

Bierwisch, M. [66]: 'Strukturalismus, Geschichte, Probleme und Methoden', *Kursbuch* 5 (1966), 77–152.

Black, M. [59]: 'Linguistic Relativity', *Philosophical Review* 68 (1959), 228–238.

Bohnert, H. G. [63]: 'Carnap's Theory of Definition and Analyticity', in Schilpp [63], pp. 407–430.

Brekle, H. E. [69a]: 'Generative Semantics vs. Deep Syntax', in Kiefer [69], pp. 80–90.
Brekle, H. E. [69b]: 'Review of N. Chomsky "Cartesian Linguistics"', *Linguistics* **49** (1969), 74–91.
Brekle, H. E. [70a]: *Generative Satzsemantik und transformationelle Syntax im System der englischen Nominalkomposition*, Munich 1970.
Brekle, H. E. [70b]: 'Generative Satzsemantik versus generative Syntax als Komponenten eines Grammatikmodells', *Linguistik und Didaktik* **1** (1970), 129–136.
Brentano, F. [30]: *Wahrheit und Evidenz* (ed. by O. Kraus), Leipzig 1930; English edition: *The True and the Evident* (transl. by Roderick M. Chisholm *et al.*), London 1966.
Brinkmann, H. [50]: 'Die Wortarten im Deutschen', *Wirkendes Wort* **1** (1950), 65–79.
Brown, R. W. and Lenneberg, H. E. [54]: 'A Study in Language and Cognition', *Journal of Abnormal and Social Psychology* **49** (1954), 454–462.
Bühler, K. [34]: *Sprachtheorie*, Stuttgart 1934, ²1965.
Carnap, R. [28]: *Der logische Aufbau der Welt*, ¹Leipzig 1928, ²Hamburg 1961. English edition: *The Logical Structure of the World* (transl. by Rolf A. George), Berkeley 1967.
Carnap, R. [32]: 'Über Protokollsätze', *Erkenntnis* **3** (1932/33), 215–228.
Carnap, R. [37]: *The Logical Syntax of Language*, London 1937.
Carnap, R. [49]: 'A Reply to L. Linsky', *Philosophy of Science* **16** (1949), 347–350.
Carnap, R. [50]: 'Empiricism, Semantics, and Ontology', *Revue Internationale de Philosophie* **11** (1950), 20–40; reprinted in Linsky [52].
Carnap, R. [52]: 'Meaning Postulates', *Philosophical Studies* **3** (1952), 65–80; reprinted in Carnap [56].
Carnap, R. [55]: 'Meaning and Synonymy in Natural Languages', *Philosophical Studies* **7** (1955), 33–47; reprinted in Carnap [56].
Carnap, R. [56]: *Meaning and Necessity*, Chicago ²1956.
Carnap, R. [63]: 'Reply to Quine', in Schilpp [63], pp. 915–922.
Chappell, V. C. (ed.) [64]: *Ordinary Language*, Englewood Cliffs/N.J. 1964.
Charlesworth, M. J. [59]: *Philosophy and Linguistic Analysis*, Pittsburgh, Louvain 1959.
Chomsky, N. [56]: 'Three Models for the Description of Language', *I.R.E. Transactions of Information Theory*, Vol. IT 2 (1956), 113–124; reprinted in Luce [65].
Chomsky, N. [57]: *Syntactic Structures*, The Hague 1957.
Chomsky, N. [59a]: 'On Certain Formal Properties of Grammars', *Information and Control* **2** (1959), 137–167; reprinted in Luce [65].
Chomsky, N. [59b]: 'Review of Skinner's "Verbal Behavior"', *Language* **35** (1959), 26–58; reprinted in Fodor [64].
Chomsky, N. [61a]: 'On the Notion "Rule of Grammar"', in Jakobson [61], pp. 6–24; reprinted in Fodor [64].
Chomsky, N. [61b]: 'Some Methodological Remarks on Generative Grammar', *Word* **17** (1961), 219–239.
Chomsky, N. [62a]: 'A Transformational Approach to Syntax', in A.A. Hill (ed.): *Proceedings of the Third Texas Conference of Linguistic Analysis in English*, Austin 1962, pp. 124–158; reprinted in Fodor [64].
Chomsky, N. [62b]: 'Explanatory Models in Linguistics', in Nagel [62], pp. 528–550.
Chomsky, N. [64]: 'Current Issues in Linguistic Theory', in Fodor [64], pp. 50–118.
Chomsky, N. [65]: *Aspects of the Theory of Syntax*, Cambridge/Mass. 1965.
Chomsky, N. [66a]: 'Topics in the Theory of Generative Grammar', in Sebeok [66], pp. 1–60.

Chomsky, N. [66b]: *Cartesian Linguistics*, New York 1966.

Chomsky, N. [67]: 'Recent Contributions to the Theory of Innate Ideas', *Synthese* **17** (1967), 2–11.

Chomsky, N. [68]: 'Quine's Empirical Assumptions', *Synthese* **19** (1968/69), 53–68.

Chomsky, N. and Miller, G. A. [59]: 'Finite State Languages', *Information and Control* **1** (1959), 91–112; reprinted in Luce [65].

Church, A. [43a]: 'Carnap's "Introduction to Semantics" ', *Philosophical Review* **52** (1943), 298–304.

Church, A. [43b]: 'Review of Quine: Notes on Existence and Necessity', *Journal of Symbolic Logic* **8** (1943), 45–47.

Church, A. [46]: 'Reviews of M. G. White and M. Black', *Journal of Symbolic Logic* **11** (1946), 132–134.

Church, A. [50]: 'On Carnap's Analysis of Statements of Assertion and Belief', *Analysis* **10** (1950), 97–99; reprinted in Macdonald [54].

Church, A. [51a]: 'The Need for Abstract Entities in Semantic Analysis', *Proceedings of the American Academy of Arts and Sciences* **80** (1951), 100–112.

Church, A. [51b]: 'A Formulation of the Logic of Sense and Denotation', in Henle [51], pp. 3–24.

Church, A. [54]: 'Intensional Isomorphism and Identity of Belief', *Philosophical Studies* **5** (1954), 65–73.

Cohen, L. J. [64]: 'Do illocutionary forces exist?', *Philosophical Quarterly* **14** (1964), 118–137.

Copi, I. M. and Beard, R. W. (eds.) [66]: *Essays on Wittgenstein's Tractatus*, London 1966.

Cordemoy, G. de [77]: 'Discours Physique de la Parole', facsimile reprint of the 1677 edition with a commentary by H. E. Brekle, Stuttgart 1970.

Cresswell, M. J. [73]: *Logics and Languages*, London 1973.

Curry, H. B. [61]: 'Some Logical Aspects of Grammatical Structure', in Jakobson [61], pp. 56–68.

Davidson, D. [63]: 'The Method of Extension and Intension', in Schilpp [63], pp. 311–349.

Davidson, D. [68]: 'On Saying That', *Synthese* **19** (1968/69), 130–146.

Davis, M. [58]: *Computability and Unsolvability*, New York 1958.

Duhem, P. [06]: *La theorie physique, son objet et sa structure*, Paris 1906; English edition: *The Aim and Structure of Physical Theory* (transl. by Philip P. Wiener), Princeton 1954.

Dummett, Michael [73]: *Frege Philosophy of Language,* Londen 1973. Bibliography includes a list of English translations of Frege's works.

Edwards, P. (ed.) [67]: *Encyclopedia of Philosophy*, 8 Vols., New York 1967.

Fearing, F. [54]: 'An Examination of the Conceptions of B. Whorf in the Light of Theories of Perception and Cognition', in Hoijer [54a], pp. 47–81.

Feigl, H. and Sellars, W. (eds.) [49]: *Readings in Philosophical Analysis*, New York 1949.

Fillmore, Ch. [68]: 'The Case for Case', in Bach [68a], pp. 1–88.

Findlay, J. N. [61]: 'Use, Usage, and Meaning', *Proceedings of the Aristotelian Society Suppl.* **35** (1961), 231–242.

Fodor, J. A. and Katz, J. J. [63]: 'The Structure of a Semantic Theory', *Language* **39** (1963), 170–210; reprinted in Fodor [64].

Fodor, J. A. and Katz, J. J. (eds.) [64]: *The Structure of Language, Readings in the Philosophy of Language*, Englewood Cliffs/N.J. 1964.

Frege, G. [79]: *Begriffsschrift. Eine der arithmetischen nachgebildete Formelsprache des reinen Denkens*, Halle 1879 [2] (ed. by I. Angelelli), Darmstadt 1964.

Frege, G. [92a]: 'Über Sinn und Bedeutung', *Zeitschrift für Philosophie und philosophische Kritik, N.F.* **100** (1892), 25–50; reprinted in Frege [67].

Frege, G. [92b]: 'Über Begriff und Gegenstand', *Vierteljahresschrift für wissenschaftliche Philosophie* **16** (1892), 192–205; reprinted in Frege [67].

Frege, G. [18]: 'Logische Untersuchungen, I: Der Gedanke', *Beiträge zur Philosophie des deutschen Idealismus* **1** (1918/19), 58–77, 'II: Die Verneinung', *ibid.*, 143–157, 'III: Gedankengefüge', *ibid.* **3** (1923/26), 36–51; reprinted in Frege [67].

Frege, G. [67]: *Kleine Schriften* (ed. by I. Angelelli), Darmstadt 1967.

Frege, G. [69]: *Nachgelassene Schriften* (ed. by H. Hermes, F. Kambartel and F. Kaulbach), Hamburg 1969.

Frege, G. [English translations]: See Bibliography in Dummett [73].

Gewirth, A. [53]: 'The Distinction Between Analytic and Synthetic Truths', *Journal of Philosophy* **50** (1953), 397–425.

Gipper, H. [69]: *Bausteine zur Sprachinhaltsforschung*, Düsseldorf [2]1969.

Goodman, N. [49]: 'On Likeness of Meaning', *Analysis* **10** (1949/50), 1–7; revised draft reprinted in Linsky [52].

Goodman, N. [51]: *The Structure of Appearance*, Cambridge/Mass. 1951, [2]Indianapolis 1966.

Goodman, N. [52]: 'On Some Differences about Meaning', *Analysis* **13** (1952/53) 90–96; reprinted in Macdonald [54].

Goodman, N. [61]: 'About', *Mind* **70** (1961), 1–24.

Goodman, N. [67]: 'The Epistemological Argument', *Synthese* **17** (1967), 23–28.

Grebe, P. (ed.) [66]: 'Grammatik der deutschen Gegenwartssprache', *Der grosse Duden*, Bd. 4, Mannheim [2]1966.

Grice, H. P. [57]: 'Meaning', *Philosophical Review* **66** (1957), 377–388.

Grice, H. P. and Strawson, P. F. [56]: 'In Defense of a Dogma', *Philosophical Review* **65** (1956), 141–158.

Griffin, J. [64]: *Wittgenstein's Logical Atomism*, Oxford 1964.

Groot, A. W. de [56]: 'Classification of the Uses of a Case Illustrated on the Genitive in Latin', *Lingua* **6** (1956/57), 8–66.

Hallet, G. [67]: *Wittgenstein's Definition of Meaning as Use*, New York 1967.

Harman, G. H. [63]: 'Generative Grammars Without Transformation Rules: a Defense of Phrase Structure', *Language* **39** (1963), 597–616.

Harman, G. H. [67]: 'Quine on Meaning and Existence', *The Review of Metaphysics* **21** (1967/68), 124–151, 343–364.

Harman, G. H. [68]: 'An Introduction to *Translation and Meaning*, chapter two of *Word and Object*', *Synthese* **19** (1968/69), 14–26.

Harman, G. H. and Davidson, D. [72]: *Semantics of Natural Language*, Dordrecht 1972.

Hartmann, H. [54]: *Das Passiv. Eine Studie zur Geistesgeschichte der Kelten, Italiker, Arier*, Heidelberg 1954.

Hartmann, P. [52]: *Einige Grundzüge des japanischen Satzbaus – gezeigt an den Ausdrücken für das Sehen*, Heidelberg 1952.

Hartmann, P. [56]: *Wortart und Aussageform*, Heidelberg 1956.

Heger, K. [63]: 'Homographie, Homonymie und Polysemie', *Zeitschrift für Romanische Philologie* **79** (1963), 471–491.

Heger, K. [69]: 'Die Semantik und die Dichotomie von Langue und Parole', *Zeitschrift für Romanische Philologie* **85** (1969), 144–215.

Hempel, C. G. [34]: 'On the Logical Positivists' Theory of Truth', *Analysis* 2 (1934/35), 49–59.

Hempel, C. G. [65]: *Aspects of Scientific Explanation and Other Essays in the Philosophy of Science*, New York 1965.

Hempel, C. G. and Oppenheim, P. [36]: *Der Typusbegriff im Lichte der neuen Logik*, Leiden 1936.

Henle, P. (ed.) [65]: *Language, Thought and Culture*, Chicago ²1965.

Henle, P., Kallen, H. M., and Langer, S. K. (eds.) [51]: *Structure, Method, and Meaning: Essays in Honor of Henry M. Sheffer*, New York 1951.

Herder, J. G. [91]: 'Abhandlung über den Ursprung der Sprache', in J. G. Herder: *Sämtliche Werke* (ed. by B. Suphan), Vol. V, Berlin 1891.

Hermes, H. [61]: *Aufzählbarkeit, Entscheidbarkeit, Berechenbarkeit*, Berlin 1961; English edition: *Enumerability, Decidability, Computability* (transl. by G. T. Herman and O. Plassmann), New-York 1965.

Hintikka, J. J. [68]: 'Behavioral Criteria of Radical Translation', *Synthese* 19 (1968/69), 69–81.

Hjelmslev, L. [43]: *Prolegomena to a Theory of Language* (from the Danish (1943), transl. by F. J. Whitefield), Bloomington/Ind. 1953.

Hörmann, H. [67]: *Psychologie der Sprache*, Berlin 1967.

Hoijer, H. (ed.) [54a]: *Language in Culture*, Chicago 1954.

Hoijer, H. [54b]: 'The Sapir-Whorf Hypothesis', in Hoijer [54a], pp. 92–105.

Holdcroft, D. [64]: 'Meaning and Illocutionary Acts', *Ratio* 6 (1964), 128–143; reprinted in Parkinson [68].

Humboldt, W. v. [03]: *Gesammelte Schriften*, Berlin Academy Edition, Berlin 1903.

Husserl, E. [00]: *Logische Untersuchungen*, Vol. 1, Halle a.S. 1900.

Jakobson, R. (ed.) [61]: 'Structure of Language and Its Mathematical Aspects', *Proceedings of the 12th Symposium in Applied Mathematics*, Providence 1961.

Kamlah, W. and Lorenzen, P. [67]: *Logische Propädeutik*, Mannheim 1967.

Katz, J. J. [64a]: 'Analyticity and Contradiction in Natural Language', in Fodor [64], pp. 519–543.

Katz, J J. [66]: *The Philosophy of Language*, New York 1966.

Katz, J. J. and Postal, P. [64b]: *An Integrated Theory of Linguistic Descriptions*, Cambridge/Mass. 1964.

Keenan, E. [72]: 'On Semantically Based Grammar', *Linguistic Inquiry III* 4 (1972).

Kemeny, J. G. [63]: 'Analyticity vs. Fuzziness', *Synthese* 15 (1963), 57–80.

Kiefer, F. (ed.) [69]: *Studies in Syntax and Semantics*, Dordrecht 1969.

Köhler, W. [37]: 'Psychological Remarks on Some Questions of Anthropology', *American Journal of Psychology* 50 (1937), 271–288.

Kripke, S. [72]: 'Naming and Necessity'; in Harman and Davidson [72], pp. 253–355.

Kutschera, F. v. [64]: *Die Antinomien der Logik*, Freiburg 1964.

Kutschera, F. v. [67]: *Elementare Logik*, Vienna 1967.

Kutschera, F. v. [72]: *Wissenschaftstheorie. Grundzüge der allgemeinen Methodologie der empirischen Wissenschaften*, Munich 1972.

Kutschera, F. v. [72a]: 'Eine logische Analyse des sprachwissenschaftlichen Feldbegriffs, *Studia Leibnitiana, Sonderheft* 3 (1973), 71–84.

Kutschera, F. v. [73]: *Einführung in die Logik der Normen, Werte und Entscheidungen*, Freiburg 1973.

Kutschera F. v. and Breitkopf, A. [71]: *Einführung in die moderne Logik*, Freiburg 1971.

Kutschera, F. v. [74]: 'Partial Interpretations', in Keenan (ed.): *Formal Semantics of Natural Language*, Cambridge 1974.

Lakoff, G. [70]: 'Linguistics and Natural Logic', Ann Arbor 1970 (mimeographed).

Lambek, J. [61]: 'On the Calculus of Syntactic Types', in Jakobson [61], pp. 166–178.

Lambert, K. (ed.) [70]: *Philosophical Problems in Logic*, Dordrecht 1970.

Langford, C. H. [42]: 'The Notion of Analysis in Moore's Philosophy', in Schilpp [42], pp. 321–342.

Lashley, K. S. [51]: 'The Problem of Serial Order in Behavior', in: Jeffress (ed.): *Hixon Symposium on Cerebral Mechanism in Behavior*, New York 1951.

Lees, R. B. [57]: 'Review of Chomsky's Syntactic Structures', *Language* 33 (1957), 375–408.

Lenk, H. [67]: 'Zu Wittgensteins Theorie der Sprachspiele', *Kant-Studien* 58 (1967), 458–480.

Lenneberg, E. H. and Roberts, J. M. [53]: 'The Denotata of Color Terms', Paper read at Linguistic Society of America, Bloomington/Ind., August 1953.

Lewis, C. I. [43]: 'The Modes of Meaning', *Philosophy and Phenomenological Research* 4 (1943/44), 236–249; reprinted in Linsky [52].

Lewis, D. [68]: 'Counterpart Theory and Quantified Modal Logic', *The Journal of Philosophy* 65 (1968), 113–126.

Lewis, D. [69]: *Convention, A Philosophical Study*, Cambridge/Mass. 1969.

Lewis, D. [70]: 'General Semantics', *Synthese* 22 (1970), 18–67.

Lewis, D. [73]: *Counterfactuals*, Oxford 1973.

Lewis, H. D. (ed.) [56]: *Contemporary British Philosophy*, London 1956.

Linsky, L. [49]: 'Some Notes on Carnap's Concept of Intensional Isomorphism and the Paradox of Analysis', *Philosophy of Science* 16 (1949), 343–347.

Linsky, L. [52]: *Semantics and the Philosophy of Language*, Urbana/Ill. 1952.

Linsky, L. [67]: *Referring*, London 1967.

Lorenz, K. [70]: *Elemente der Sprachkritik. Eine Alternative zum Dogmatismus und Skeptizismus in der analytischen Philosophie*, Frankfurt a.M. 1970.

Luce, R. D., Bush, R. R., and Galanter, E. (eds.) [65]: *Readings in Mathematical Psychology*, Vol. II, New York 1965.

Lyons, J. [69]: *Introduction to Theoretical Linguistics*, Cambridge 1969.

Lyons, J. [66]: 'Towards a 'Notional' Theory of the 'Parts of Speech' ', *Journal of Linguistics* 2 (1966), 209–236.

Macdonald, M. (ed.) [54]: *Philosophy and Analysis*, Oxford 1954.

Mace, C. A. (ed.) [66]: *British Philosophy in the Mid-Century*, A Cambridge Symposium, London ²1966.

Malcolm, N. (ed.) [58]: *Ludwig Wittgenstein – A Memoir*, London 1958.

Marchand, H. [69]: *The Categories and Types of Present-Day English Word-Formation: A Synchronic-Diachronic Approach*, ²Munich 1969.

Martin, R. M. [52]: 'On "Analytic"', *Philosophical Studies* 3 (1952), 42–47.

Martin, R. M. [59]: *The Notion of Analytic Truth*, Philadelphia 1959.

Mates, B. [50]: 'Synonymity', *University of California Publications in Philosophy* 25 (1950); reprinted in Linsky [52].

Mates, B. [51]: 'Analytic Sentences', *Philosophical Review* 60 (1951), 525–534.

Mates, B. [58]: 'On the Verification of Statements about Ordinary Language', *Inquiry* 1 (1958); reprinted in Chappell [64], pp. 64–74.

McCawley, J. D. [68]: 'The Role of Semantics in a Grammar', in Bach [68a], pp. 124–169.

Mittelstrass, J. [68]: 'Die Prädikation und die Wiederkehr des Gleichen', *Ratio* **10** (1968), 53–61.
Montague, R. [70]: 'Universal Grammar', *Theoria* **36** (1970), 373–398. German translation with a commentary by H. Schnelle, Braunschweig 1972.
Montague, R. [70a]: 'The Proper Treatment of Quantification in Ordinary English', manuscript of a lecture at Stanford 1970.
Morris, Ch. W. [38]: *Foundations of the Theory of Signs* (*International Encyclopedia of Unified Science*, Vol. 1, No. 2), Chicago 1938.
Morris, Ch. [46]: *Signs, Language and Behavior*, New York 1946, [2]1955.
Naess, A. [49]: 'Toward a Theory of Interpretation and Preciseness', *Theoria* **15** (1949), 220–241; reprinted in Linsky [52].
Naess, A. [53]: 'Interpretation and Preciseness: A Contribution to the Theory of Communication', *Skrifter Norske Videnskaps Akademi, Oslo II. Hist-Filos. Klasse* (1953), No. 1.
Nagel, E., Suppes, P., and Tarski, A. (eds.) [62]: *Logic, Methodology, and Philosophy of Science*, Stanford 1962.
Neurath, O. [32]: 'Protokollsätze', *Erkenntnis* **3** (1932/33), 204–214.
Öhmann, S. [51]: *Wortinhalt und Weltbild*, Stockholm 1951.
Pap, A. [55]: 'Belief, Synonymity and Analysis', *Philosophical Studies* **6** (1955), 11–15.
Pap, A. [57]: 'Belief and Propositions', *Philosophy of Science* **24** (1957), 123–136.
Pap, A. [58]: *Semantics and Necessary Truth*, New Haven/Conn. 1958.
Parkinson, G. H. R. (ed.) [68]: *The Theory of Meaning*, Oxford 1968.
Patzig, G. [70]: *Sprache und Logik*, Göttingen 1970.
Peach, B. [52]: 'A Nondescriptive Theory of the Analytic', *Philosophical Review* **61** (1952), 349–367.
Pitcher, G. [64]: *The Philosophy of Wittgenstein*, Englewood Cliffs/N.J. 1964.
Pitcher, G. (ed.) [66]: *Wittgenstein – The Philosophical Investigations*, New York 1966.
Postal, P. [64a]: *Constituent Structure*, Bloomington 1964.
Postal, P. [64b]: 'Limitations of Phrase Structure Grammars', in Fodor [64], pp. 137–151.
Postal, P. [64c]: 'Underlying and Superficial Linguistic Structure', *Harvard Educational Review* **34** (1964), 246–266.
Putnam, H. [54]: 'Synonymity and the Analysis of Belief Sentences', *Analysis* **14** (1953/54), 114–122.
Putnam, H. [61]: 'Some Issues in the Theory of Grammar', in Jakobson [61], pp. 25–42.
Putnam, [62a]: 'The Analytic and the Synthetic', in H. Feigl and G. Maxwell (eds.): *Minnesota Studies in the Philosophy of Science*, Vol. III, Minneapolis 1962, pp. 358–397.
Putnam, H. [62b]: 'It Ain't Necessarily So', *Journal of Philosophy* **59** (1962), 658–671.
Putnam, H. [67]: 'The 'Innateness Hypothesis' and Explanatory Models in Linguistics', *Synthese* **17** (1967), 12–22.
Quine, W. V. [48]: 'On What There Is', *The Review of Metaphysics* **2** (1948/49), 21–38; reprinted in Quine [64a].
Quine, W. V. [51a]: 'Two Dogmas of Empiricism', *The Philosophical Review* **60** (1951), 20–43; reprinted in Quine [64a].
Quine, W. V. [51b]: *Mathematical Logic*, Cambridge/Mass. [2]1951.
Quine, W. V. [56]: 'Quantifiers and Propositional Attitudes', *The Journal of Philosophy* **53** (1956), 177–187; reprinted in Quine [66].

Quine, W. V. [57]: 'The Scope and Language of Science', *The British Journal for the Philosophy of Science* **8** (1957/58), 1–17; reprinted in Quine [66].

Quine, W. V. [58]: 'Speaking of Objects', *Proceedings and Addresses of the American Philosophical Association*, Eastern Division, 1958; reprinted in Quine [69a].

Quine, W. V. [59]: *Methods of Logic*, New York ²1959.

Quine, W. V. [60]: *Word and Object*, Cambridge/Mass. 1960.

Quine, W. V. [63]: 'Carnap and Logical Truth', in Schilpp [63], pp. 385–406.

Quine, W. V. [64a]: *From a Logical Point of View*, Cambridge/Mass. ²1964.

Quine, W. V. [64b]: 'Reference and Modality', in Quine [64a], pp. 139–159.

Quine, W. V. [64c]: 'Notes on the Theory of Reference', in Quine [64a], pp. 130–138.

Quine, W. V. [66]: *The Ways of Paradox and Other Essays*, New York 1966.

Quine, W. V. [69a]: *Ontological Relativity and Other Essays*, New York 1969.

Quine, W. V. [69b]: 'Propositional Objects', in Quine [69a], pp. 139–160.

Quine, W. V. [69c]: 'Natural Kinds', in Quine [69a], pp. 114–138.

Reichenbach, H. [47]: *Elements of Symbolic Logic*, New York 1947.

Rescher, N. [68]: *Topics in Philosophical Logic*, Dordrecht 1968.

Robins, R. H. [51]: *Ancient and Medieval Grammatical Theory in Europe with Particular Reference to Modern Linguistic Doctrine*, London 1951.

Russell, B. [05]: 'On Denoting', *Mind* **14** (1905), 479–493; reprinted in Feigl [49].

Russell, B. [18]: 'The Philosophy of Logical Atomism', *The Monist* **28** (1918), 495–527; **29** (1919), 32–63, 190–222, 345–380.

Russell, B. [40]: *An Inquiry into Meaning and Truth*, London 1940.

Russell, B. [56a]: 'Logic and Knowledge', *Essays* 1901-1950 (ed. by R. C. Marsh), London 1956.

Russell, B. [56]: 'Logical Atomism', in Russell [56a], pp. 323–343.

Ryle, G. [49]: *The Concept of Mind*, London 1949.

Ryle, G. [53]: 'Ordinary Language', *The Philosophical Review* **62** (1953), 167–186; reprinted in Chappell [64].

Ryle, G. [60]: 'Use, Usage and Meaning', *Proceedings of the Aristotelian Society, Suppl.* **55** (1960), 223–230; reprinted in Parkinson [68].

Ryle, G. [66]: 'The Theory of Meaning', in Mace [66], pp. 237–264.

Sapir, E. [12]: 'Language and Environment', *American Anthropologist* **14** (1912), 226–242; reprinted in Sapir [49].

Sapir, E. [29]: 'The Status of Linguistics as a Science', *Language* **5** (1929), 207–214.

Sapir, E. [49]: *Selected Writings of Eduard Sapir* (ed. by D. G. Mandelbaum), Berkeley 1949.

Saussure, F. de [16]: *Cours de Linguistique Générale*, Paris ¹1916. German: *Grundfragen der allgemeinen Sprachwissenschaft*, ²Berlin 1967; English edition: *Course in General Linguistics* (transl. by Wade Baskin), New York 1959.

Savigny, E. v. [69]: *Die Philosophie der normalen Sprache*, Frankfurt a.M. 1969.

Savigny, E. v. [70]: *Analytische Philosophie*, Freiburg 1970.

Scheffler, J. [54]: 'An Inscriptional Approach to Indirect Quotation', *Analysis* **14** (1953/54), 83–90.

Scheffler, J. [55]: 'On Synonymy and Indirect Discourse', *Philosophy of Science* **22** (1955), 39–44.

Schilpp, P. (ed.) [42]: *The Philosophy of G. E. Moore*, Evanston/Ill. 1942.

Schilpp, P. (ed.) [63]: *The Philosophy of Rudolf Carnap*, La Salle/Ill. 1963.

Schlick, M. [36]: 'Meaning and Verification', *The Philosophical Review* **45** (1936), 339–369.

Schmidt, F. [61]: Logik der Syntax, Berlin ³1961.

Schnelle, H. [73]: *Sprachphilosophie und Linguistik*, Reinbek b. Hamburg 1973.

Schwyzer, H. R. G. [62]: 'Wittgenstein's Picture Theory of Language', *Inquiry* 5 (1962), 46–64; reprinted in Copi [66].

Searle, J. R. [58]: 'Proper Names', *Mind* 67 (1958), 166–173.

Searle, J. R. [68]: 'Austin on Locutionary and Illocutionary Acts', *The Philosophicla Review* 77 (1968), 405–424.

Searle, J. R. [69]: *Speech Acts*, Cambridge 1969.

Sebeok, T. A. (ed.) [66]: *Current Trends in Linguistics*, Vol. 3, Theoretical Foundations, The Hague 1966.

Shwayder, D. S. [60]: 'Uses of Language and Uses of Words', *Theoria* 26 (1960), 31–43; reprinted in Parkinson [68].

Shwayder, D. S. [63]: 'Critical notice on E. Stenius "Wittgenstein's Tractatus"', *Mind* 72 (1963), 275–288; shortened version under the title 'On the Picture Theory of Language' in Copi [66].

Skinner, B. F. [57]: *Verbal Behavior*, New York 1957.

Snell, B. [52]: *Der Aufbau der Sprache*, Hamburg 1952.

Stegmüller, W. [56]: 'Das Universalienproblem einst und jetzt', *Archiv für Philosophie* 6 (1956), 192–225 and 7 (1957), 45–81.

Stegmüller, W. [57]: *Das Wahrheitsproblem und die Idee der Semantik*, Vienna 1957.

Stegmüller, W. [65]: *Hauptströmungen der Gegenwartsphilosophie*, ³Stuttgart 1965. English edition: *Main Currents of Contemporary German*, British and American Philosophy (transl. by Albert E. Blumberg), Bloomington/Ind. 1970.

Stegmüller, W. [70]: *Theorie und Erfahrung*, Berlin 1970.

Stenius, E. [60]: *Wittgenstein's Tractatus, A Critical Exposition of its Main Lines of Thought*, Oxford 1960.

Stenius, E. [67]: 'Mood and Language-Game', *Synthese* 17 (1967), 254–279.

Stenzel, J. [34]: *Philosophie der Sprache*, Berlin 1934.

Stevenson, Ch. [44]: *Ethics and Language*, New Haven 1944.

Strawson, P. F. [49]: 'Truth', *Analysis* 9 (1948/49), 83–97; reprinted in Macdonald [54], pp. 260–277.

Strawson, P. F. [50]: 'Truth', *Proceedings of the Aristotelian Society*, Suppl. 24 (1950), 129–156.

Strawson, P. F. [50a]: 'On Referring', *Mind* 59 (1950), 320–344.

Strawson, P. F. [54]: 'Review of Wittgenstein's Philosophical Investigations', *Mind* 63 (1954), 70–99; reprinted in Pitcher [66].

Strawson, P. F. [64]: 'Intention and Convention in Speech Acts', *The Philosophical Review* 73 (1964), 439–460.

Tarski, A. [23]: 'O wyrazie pierwotnym logistyki', *Przeglad filozoficzny* 26 (1923), 68–89. English translation 'On the Primitive Term of Logistic', in Tarski [56].

Tarski A. [35]: 'Der Wahrheitsbegriff in den formalisierten Sprachen', *Studia Philosophica* 1 (1935/36), 261–405, English translation in Tarski [56].

Tarski, A. [44]: 'The Semantic Conception of Truth and the Foundations of Semantics', *Journal of Philosophy and Phenomenological Research* 4 (1943/44), 341–375; reprinted in Feigl [49].

Tarski, A. [56]: *Logic, Semantics, Metamathematics*, Oxford 1956.

Thiel, Ch. [65]: *Sinn und Bedeutung in der Logik Gottlob Freges*, Meisenheim a.G. 1965.

Tinbergen, N. [51]: *The Study of Instinct*, Toronto 1951.

Trier, J. [31]: *Der deutsche Wortschatz im Sinnbezirk des Verstandes – Die Geschichte eines sprachlichen Feldes*, Heidelberg 1931.

Trier, J. [32]: 'Sprachliche Felder', *Zeitschrift für deutsche Bildung* **8** (1932), 417–427.

Trier, J. [34a]: 'Deutsche Bedeutungsforschung', in: *Germanische Philologie, Ergebnisse und Aufgaben, Festschrift für Otto Behaghel* (ed. by Alfred Goetze and Wilhelm Horn), Heidelberg 1934, pp. 173–200.

Trier, J. [34b]: 'Das sprachliche Feld', *Neue Jahrbücher für Wissenschaft und Jugendbildung* **10** (1934), 428–449.

Uexküll, J. v. [21]: *Umwelt und Innenwelt der Tiere*, Berlin ²1921.

Uexküll, J. v. [28]: *Theoretische Biologie*, Berlin ²1928.

Wackernagel, J. [24]: *Vorlesungen über Syntax*, 2 Vols., Basel 1924/26.

Waismann, F. [56]: 'How I See Philosophy', in Lewis [56]; reprinted in Ayer [59].

Wang, Hao [55]: 'Notes on the Analytic-Synthetic Distinction', *Theoria* **21** (1955), 158–178.

Weinrich, H. [64]: *Tempus. Besprochene und erzählte Welt*, Stuttgart 1964.

Weisgerber, L. [58]: 'Der Mensch im Akkusativ', *Wirkendes Wort* **8** (1958), 193–205.

Weisgerber, L. [62]: *Von den Kräften der deutschen Sprache*, Vol. 1: 'Grundzüge der inhaltsbezogenen Grammatik', Düsseldorf ³1962. Vol. II: 'Die sprachliche Gestaltung der Welt', Düsseldorf ³1962. Vol. III: 'Die Muttersprache im Aufbau unserer Kultur', Düsseldorf ¹1950, ²1964. Vol. IV: 'Die geschichtliche Kraft der deutschen Sprache', Düsseldorf ²1959.

Weisgerber, L. [63a]: *Die vier Stufen in der Erforschung der Sprachen*, Düsseldorf 1963.

Weisgerber, L. [63b]: 'Die Welt im "Passiv"', in: *Die Wissenschaft von deutscher Sprache und Dichtung, Festschrift für F. Maurer* (ed. by Siegfried Gutenbrunner), Stuttgart 1963.

Wheatley, J. [63]: 'Some Aspects of Meaning and Use (abstract)', *Journal of Philosophy* **60** (1963), 643–644.

White, M. G. [50]: 'The Analytic and the Synthetic: an Untenable Dualism', in S. Hook (ed.): *John Dewey: Philosopher of Science and Freedom*, New York 1950, pp. 316–330; reprinted in Linsky [52].

Whorf, E. L. [56]: *Language, Thought and Reality* (ed. by John B. Carroll), New York 1956.

Wittgenstein, L. [61]: *Notebooks 1914–1918* (ed. by G. H. von Wright and G. E. M. Anscombe), Oxford 1961.

Wittgenstein, L. [22]: 'Tractatus logico-philosophicus', in Ostwalds *Annalen der Naturphilosophie* (1921); German-English edition, London 1922.

Wittgenstein, L. [53]: *Philosophical Investigations* (ed. by G. Anscombe and R. Rhees), Oxford 1953, ²1965, ³1967.

Wittgenstein, L. [56]: *Remarks on the Foundations of Mathematics* (ed. by G. H. v. Wright, R. Rhees, and G. E. M. Anscombe), Oxford 1956.

Wittgenstein, L. [58]: *The Blue and Brown Books*, Oxford 1958.

Woodruff, P. W. [70]: 'Logic and Truth Value Gaps', in Lambert [70], pp. 121–142.

Wright, G. H. von [55]: 'Ludwig Wittgenstein: A Biographical Sketch', *The Philosophical Review* **64** (1955); reprinted in Malcolm [58], pp. 1–22.

Xenakis, J. [54]: 'Meaning', *Methodos* **6** (1954), 299–327.

Ziff, P. [60]: *Semantic Analysis*, Ithaca/N.Y. 1960.

INDEX OF SUBJECTS

INDEX OF LOGICAL SYMBOLS

$\neg$	not
$\wedge$	and
$\vee$	or
$\supset$	implies (if – then)
$\equiv$	is equivalent to (if and only if)
$\bigwedge$	for every
$\bigvee$	there is (at least) one
$\bigvee = n$	there are precisely n
$=$	is identical with
$:=$	is by definition identical with
$\rightarrow$	entails (as a logical consequence)
$\wedge$	null set
λx	class of x such that –
$\{x_1, ..., x_n\}$	class with elements $x_1, ..., x_n$
$\in$	is a member (element) of
$\cap$	intersection
$\cup$	union
$\subset$	is a subset of
$\bigcap_i$	intersection of all classes with indices i
$\bigcup_i$	union of all classes with indices i

SYNTHESE LIBRARY

Monographs on Epistemology, Logic, Methodology,
Philosophy of Science, Sociology of Science and of Knowledge, and on the
Mathematical Methods of Social and Behavioral Sciences

Managing Editor:

JAAKKO HINTIKKA (Academy of Finland and Stanford University)

Editors:

ROBERT S. COHEN (Boston University)
DONALD DAVIDSON (The Rockefeller University and Princeton University)
GABRIËL NUCHELMANS (University of Leyden)
WESLEY C. SALMON (University of Arizona)

1. J. M. BOCHEŃSKI, *A Precis of Mathematical Logic*. 1959, X + 100 pp.
2. P. L. GUIRAUD, *Problèmes et méthodes de la statistique linguistique*. 1960, VI + 146 pp.
3. HANS FREUDENTHAL (ed.), *The Concept and the Role of the Model in Mathematics and Natural and Social Sciences, Proceedings of a Colloquium held at Utrecht, The Netherlands, January 1960*. 1961, VI + 194 pp.
4. EVERT W. BETH, *Formal Methods. An Introduction to Symbolic Logic and the Study of Effective Operations in Arithmetic and Logic*. 1962, XIV + 170 pp.
5. B. H. KAZEMIER and D. VUYSJE (eds.), *Logic and Language. Studies dedicated to Professor Rudolf Carnap on the Occasion of his Seventieth Birthday*. 1962, VI + 256 pp.
6. MARX W. WARTOFSKY (ed.), *Proceedings of the Boston Colloquium for the Philosophy of Science, 1961–1962*, Boston Studies in the Philosophy of Science (ed. by Robert S. Cohen and Marx W. Wartofsky), Volume I. 1973, VIII + 212 pp.
7. A. A. ZINOV'EV, *Philosophical Problems of Many-Valued Logic*. 1963, XIV + 155 pp.
8. GEORGES GURVITCH, *The Spectrum of Social Time*. 1964, XXVI + 152 pp.
9. PAUL LORENZEN, *Formal Logic*. 1965, VIII + 123 pp.
10. ROBERT S. COHEN and MARX W. WARTOFSKY (eds.), *In Honor of Philipp Frank*, Boston Studies in the Philosophy of Science (ed. by Robert S. Cohen and Marx W. Wartofsky), Volume II. 1965, XXXIV + 475 pp.
11. EVERT W. BETH, *Mathematical Thought. An Introduction to the Philosophy of Mathematics*. 1965, XII + 208 pp.
12. EVERT W. BETH and JEAN PIAGET, *Mathematical Epistemology and Psychology*. 1966, XII + 326 pp.
13. GUIDO KÜNG, *Ontology and the Logistic Analysis of Language. An Enquiry into the Contemporary Views on Universals*. 1967, XI + 210 pp.
14. ROBERT S. COHEN and MARX W. WARTOFSKY (eds.), *Proceedings of the Boston Colloquium for the Philosophy of Science 1964–1966, in Memory of Norwood Russell Hanson*, Boston Studies in the Philosophy of Science (ed. by Robert S. Cohen and Marx W. Wartofsky), Volume III. 1967, XLIX + 489 pp.

15. C. D. BROAD, *Induction, Probability, and Causation. Selected Papers.* 1968, XI + 296 pp.
16. GÜNTHER PATZIG, *Aristotle's Theory of the Syllogism. A Logical-Philosophical Study of Book A of the Prior Analytics.* 1968, XVII + 215 pp.
17. NICHOLAS RESCHER, *Topics in Philosophical Logic.* 1968, XIV + 347 pp.
18. ROBERT S. COHEN and MARX W. WARTOFSKY (eds.), *Proceedings of the Boston Colloquium for the Philosophy of Science 1966–1968*, Boston Studies in the Philosophy of Science (ed. by Robert S. Cohen and Marx W. Wartofsky), Volume IV. 1969, VIII + 537 pp.
19. ROBERT S. COHEN and MARX W. WARTOFSKY (eds.), *Proceedings of the Boston Colloquium for the Philosophy of Science 1966–1968*, Boston Studies in the Philosophy of Science (ed. by Robert S. Cohen and Marx W. Wartofsky), Volume V. 1969, VIII + 482 pp.
20. J. W. DAVIS, D. J. HOCKNEY, and W. K. WILSON (eds.), *Philosophical Logic.* 1969, VIII + 277 pp.
21. D. DAVIDSON and J. HINTIKKA (eds.), *Words and Objections: Essays on the Work of W. V. Quine.* 1969, VIII + 366 pp.
22. PATRICK SUPPES, *Studies in the Methodology and Foundations of Science. Selected Papers from 1911 to 1969.* 1969, XII + 473 pp.
23. JAAKKO HINTIKKA, *Models for Modalities. Selected Essays.* 1969, IX + 220 pp.
24. NICHOLAS RESCHER *et al.* (eds.). *Essay in Honor of Carl G. Hempel. A Tribute on the Occasion of his Sixty-Fifth Birthday.* 1969, VII + 272 pp.
25. P. V. TAVANEC (ed.), *Problems of the Logic of Scientific Knowledge.* 1969, XII + 429 pp.
26. MARSHALL SWAIN (ed.), *Induction, Acceptance, and Rational Belief.* 1970. VII + 232 pp.
27. ROBERT S. COHEN and RAYMOND J. SEEGER (eds.), *Ernst Mach; Physicist and Philosopher*, Boston Studies in the Philosophy of Science (ed. by Robert S. Cohen and Marx W. Wartofsky), Volume VI. 1970, VIII + 295 pp.
28. JAAKKO HINTIKKA and PATRICK SUPPES, *Information and Inference.* 1970, X + 366 pp.
29. KAREL LAMBERT, *Philosophical Problems in Logic. Some Recent Developments.* 1970, VII + 176 pp.
30. ROLF A. EBERLE, *Nominalistic Systems.* 1970, IX + 217 pp.
31. PAUL WEINGARTNER and GERHARD ZECHA (eds.), *Induction, Physics, and Ethics, Proceedings and Discussions of the 1968 Salzburg Colloquium in the Philosophy of Science.* 1970, X + 382 pp.
32. EVERT W. BETH, *Aspects of Modern Logic.* 1970, XI + 176 pp.
33. RISTO HILPINEN (ed.), *Deontic Logic: Introductory and Systematic Readings.* 1971, VII + 182 pp.
34. JEAN-LOUIS KRIVINE, *Introduction to Axiomatic Set Theory.* 1971, VII + 98 pp.
35. JOSEPH D. SNEED, *The Logical Structure of Mathematical Physics.* 1971, XV + 311 pp.
36. CARL R. KORDIG, *The Justification of Scientific Change.* 1971, XIV + 119 pp.
37. MILIČ ČAPEK, *Bergson and Modern Physics*, Boston Studies in the Philosophy of Science (ed. by Robert S. Cohen and Marx W. Wartofsky), Volume VII, 1971, XV + 414 pp.
38. NORWOOD RUSSELL HANSON, *What I do not Believe, and other Essays*, ed. by Stephen Toulmin and Harry Woolf, 1971, XII + 390 pp.

39. ROGER C. BUCK and ROBERT S. COHEN (eds.), *PSA 1970. In Memory of Rudolf Carnap*, Boston Studies in the Philosophy of Science (ed. by Robert S. Cohen and Marx W. Wartofsky), Volume VIII. 1971, LXVI + 615 pp. Also available as a paperback.
40. DONALD DAVIDSON and GILBERT HARMAN (eds.), *Semantics of Natural Language*. 1972, X + 769 pp. Also available as a paperback.
41. YEHOSUA BAR-HILLEL (ed)., *Pragmatics of Natural Languages*. 1971, VII + 231 pp.
42. SÖREN STENLUND, *Combinators, λ-Terms and Proof Theory*. 1972, 184 pp.
43. MARTIN STRAUSS, *Modern Physics and Its Philosophy. Selected Papers in the Logic, History, and Philosophy of Science*. 1972, X + 297 pp.
44. MARIO BUNGE, *Method, Model and Matter*. 1973, VII + 196 pp.
45. MARIO BUNGE, *Philosophy of Physics*. 1973, IX + 248 pp.
46. A. A. ZINOV'EV, *Foundations of the Logical Theory of Scientific Knowledge (Complex Logic)*, Boston Studies in the Philosophy of Science (ed. by Robert S. Cohen and Marx W. Wartofsky), Volume IX. Revised and enlarged English edition with an appendix, by G. A. Smirnov, E. A. Sidorenko, A. M. Fedina, and L. A. Bobrova. 1973, XXII + 301 pp. Also available as a paperback.
47. LADISLAV TONDL, *Scientific Procedures*, Boston Studies in the Philosophy of Science (ed. by Robert S. Cohen and Marx W. Wartofsky), Volume X. 1973, XII + 268 pp. Also available as a paperback.
48. NORWOOD RUSSELL HANSON, *Constellations and Conjectures*, ed. by Willard C. Humphreys, Jr. 1973, X + 282 pp.
49. K. J. J. HINTIKKA, J. M. E. MORAVCSIK, and P. SUPPES (eds.), *Approaches to Natural Language. Proceedings of the 1970 Stanford Workshop on Grammar and Semantics*. 1973, VIII + 526 pp. Also available as a paperback.
50. MARIO BUNGE (ed.), *Exact Philosophy – Problems, Tools, and Goals*. 1973, X + 214 pp.
51. RADU J. BOGDAN and ILKKA NIINILUOTO (eds.), *Logic, Language, and Probability*. A selection of papers contributed to Sections IV, VI, and XI of the Fourth International Congress for Logic, Methodology, and Philosophy of Science, Bucharest, September 1971. 1973, X + 323 pp.
52. GLENN PEARCE and PATRICK MAYNARD (eds.), *Conceptual Chance*. 1973, XII + 282 pp.
53. ILKKA NIINILUOTO and RAIMO TUOMELA, *Theoretical Concepts and Hypothetico-Inductive Inference*. 1973, VII + 264 pp.
54. ROLAND FRAÏSSÉ, *Course of Mathematical Logic – Volume I: Relation and Logical Formula*. 1973, XVI + 186 pp. Also available as a paperback.
55. ADOLF GRÜNBAUM, *Philosophical Problems of Space and Time*. Second, enlarged edition, Boston Studies in the Philosophy of Science (ed. by Robert S. Cohen and Marx W. Wartofsky), Volume XII. 1973, XXIII + 884 pp. Also available as a paperback.
56. PATRICK SUPPES (ed.), *Space, Time, and Geometry*. 1973, XI + 424 pp.
57. HANS KELSEN, *Essays in Legal and Moral Philosophy*, selected and introduced by Ota Weinberger. 1973, XXVIII + 300 pp.
58. R. J. SEEGER and ROBERT S. COHEN (eds.), *Philosophical Foundations of Science. Proceedings of an AAAS Program, 1969*. Boston Studies in the Philosophy of Science (ed. by Robert S. Cohen and Marx W. Wartofsky), Volume XI. 1974, X + 545 pp. Also available as a paperback.
59. ROBERT S. COHEN and MARX W. WARTOFSKY (eds.), *Logical and Epistemological*

Studies in Contemporary Physics, Boston Studies in the Philosophy of Science (ed. by Robert S. Cohen and Marx W. Wartofsky), Volume XIII. 1973, VIII + 462 pp. Also available as paperback.

60. ROBERT S. COHEN and MARX W. WARTOFSKY (eds.), *Methodological and Historical Essays in the Natural and Social Sciences. Proceedings of the Boston Colloquium for the Philosophy of Science, 1969–1972*, Boston Studies in the Philosophy of Science (ed. by Robert S. Cohen and Marx W. Wartofsky), Volume XIV. 1974, VIII + 405 pp. Also available as paperback.

61. ROBERT S. COHEN, J. J. STACHEL, and MARX W. WARTOFSKY (eds.), *For Dirk Struik. Scientific, Historical and Political Essays in Honor of Dirk J. Struik*, Boston Studies in the Philosophy of Science (ed. by Robert S. Cohen and Marx W. Wartofsky), Volume XV. 1974, XXVII + 652 pp. Also available as paperback.

62. KAZIMIERZ AJDUKIEWICZ, *Pragmatic Logic*, transl. from the Polish by Olgierd Wojtasiewicz. 1974, XV + 460 pp.

63. SÖREN STENLUND (ed.), *Logical Theory and Semantic Analysis. Essays Dedicated to Stig Kanger on His Fiftieth Birthday*. 1974, V + 217 pp.

64. KENNETH F. SCHAFFNER and ROBERT S. COHEN (eds.), *Proceedings of the 1972 Biennial Meeting, Philosophy of Science Association*, Boston Studies in the Philosophy of Science (ed. by Robert S. Cohen and Marx W. Wartofsky), Volume XX. 1974, IX + 444 pp. Also available as paperback.

65. HENRY E. KYBURG, JR., *The Logical Foundations of Statistical Inference*. 1974, IX + 421 pp.

66. MARJORIE GRENE, *The Understanding of Nature: Essays in the Philosophy of Biology*, Boston Studies in the Philosophy of Science (ed. by Robert S. Cohen and Marx W. Wartofsky), Volume XXIII. 1974, XII + 360 pp. Also available as paperback.

67. JAN M. BROEKMAN, *Structuralism: Moscow, Prague, Paris*. 1974, IX + 117 pp.

68. NORMAN GESCHWIND, *Selected Papers on Language and the Brain*, Boston Studies in the Philosophy of Science (ed. by Robert S. Cohen and Marx W. Wartofsky), Volume XVI. 1974, XII + 549 pp. Also available as paperback.

69. ROLAND FRAÏSSÉ. *Course of Mathematical Logic* – Volume II: *Model Theory*. 1974, XIX + 192 pp.

70. ANDRZEJ GRZEGORCZYK, *An Outline of Mathematical Logic. Fundamental Results and Notions Explained with all Details*. 1974, X + 596 pp.

75. JAAKKO HINTIKKA and UNTO REMES, *The Method of Analysis. Its Geometrical Origin and Its General Significance*. 1974. XVIII + 144 pp.

77. STEFAN AMSTERDAMSKI, *Between Experience and Metaphysics. Philosophical Problems of the Evolution of Science*, Boston Studies in the Philosophy of Science (ed. by Robert S. Cohen and Marx W. Wartofsky), Volume XXXV. 1975, XVIII + 193 pp. Also available as paperback.

SYNTHESE HISTORICAL LIBRARY

Texts and Studies

in the History of Logic and Philosophy

Editors:

N. Kretzmann (Cornell University)

G. Nuchelmans (University of Leyden)

L. M. de Rijk (University of Leyden)